THE CULTURE OF FOOD IN ENGLAND,

1200–1500

THE CULTURE
OF FOOD
IN ENGLAND
1200–1500

C. M. WOOLGAR

YALE UNIVERSITY PRESS
NEW HAVEN AND LONDON

For information about this and other Yale University Press publications, please contact:

U.S. Office: sales.press@yale.edu   www.yalebooks.com
Europe Office: sales@yaleup.co.uk   www.yalebooks.co.uk

Typeset in Minion Pro by IDSUK (DataConnection) Ltd
Printed in Great Britain by TJ International Ltd, Padstow, Cornwall

Library of Congress Control Number: 2016930746

ISBN 978-0-300-18191-3

A catalogue record for this book is available from the British Library.

10 9 8 7 6 5 4 3 2 1

CONTENTS

ILLUSTRATIONS

TABLES

WEIGHTS, MEASURES AND CURRENCY

Medieval weights and measures were standardised, but only up to a point, with many local variations and different usages for different commodities. Where the detail of these is important, the notes to the text give further information. The principal units are given below, with approximate metric equivalents for the main measure in each class.

Liquid measure
2 pints = 1 quart; 4 pints = 1 pottle; 8 pints = 1 gallon
1 pint = 0.568 litres

Dry capacity
4 pecks (pks) = 1 bushel (bus.); 8 bushels = 1 quarter (qr)
1 peck = 9.092 litres

Length
12 inches (ins) = 1 foot; 3 feet = 1 yard; 1760 yards = 1 mile
36 inches = 1 verge, a cloth-yard; 45 inches = 1 ell
1 yard = 0.914 metres

Weight
16 ounces (oz) avoirdupoids = 1 pound (lb); 14 pounds (lbs) = 1 stone;
8 stones = 1 hundredweight (cwt). For weights in weys, see the notes.
1 pound = 0.454 kilograms

Currency

12 pence (*d*) = 1 shilling (*s*); 20 shillings = 1 pound (£1 = 240*d*). The penny was divided into 2 halfpence and 4 farthings. 1 mark was worth 13*s* 4*d*, two-thirds of £1 (160*d*).

Currency as weight

The English royal household in the fourteenth century and early fifteenth century recorded the weight of plate using Tower pounds, expressed as pounds, shillings and pence, rather than Troy weight. In the Tower system 1 pennyweight (dwt) = 22½ grains of barley; 20 dwt = 1 oz. The penny-weight was the weight of an English silver penny and is taken in this book as 1.35 grams. Troy weight uses a pennyweight of 24 grains, that is, about 1.56 grams.

PREFACE

THIS BOOK HAS BEEN in mind for a long time. My interest in food first arose when I found some medieval domestic accounts in the archives of Magdalen College, Oxford, in 1979. I have gradually come to the notion that there is much more to be said about food, beyond the sustenance it provides: most medieval people, much of the time, were closely engaged in its cultivation, preparation and consumption. My ambition has been to understand the many meanings it had for people, as a part of their ways of life. To illuminate the subject, indeed, to find any evidence for some parts of the study, it has been necessary to cast the net widely and sometimes obliquely. What I have found has convinced me more and more of the importance of food for a study of medieval mentalities. I am therefore grateful to Yale University Press and to Dr Robert Baldock for the opportunity to bring my ideas to publication. They have tolerated as well my tardiness in completing the writing as I followed a new line of research, which has opened up new ways of approaching the subject but which took me time to analyse.

I have incurred many debts in preparing this book. Audiences at Bristol, Cambridge, Glastonbury, Harlaxton, Leeds, Leicester, London, Oxford, Newcastle, Southampton and Tours have commented on papers. Colleagues in the Medieval Diet Group have heard parts of this text over several years, as have some of my students. I have acknowledged others in the notes where I have drawn on things they have said, or references and advice they have proffered: there have been many kindnesses and I much appreciate the generosity of those who have helped in this way. I am also grateful to Yale University Press's reader for thoughtful remarks and additional references. The errors that remain are, of course, mine.

My research has been facilitated by major digital projects, which have brought to my study at home resources beyond compass, generously free at the point of use. I would single out two in particular for the difference they have made: the Anglo-American Legal Tradition website (aalt.law.uh.edu/) has enabled me to work through sequences of legal records from the UK's National Archives; and the digital collections of the Bavarian State Library (www.digitale-sammlungen.de/) gave me ready access to early printed materials, especially the works of the Dominican preacher John Bromyard. Beyond this, dictionaries, especially the *Middle English Dictionary*, edited by H. Kurath, S. M. Kuhn and others (Ann Arbor, 1956–2001), in hard copy and in its online version at quod.lib.umich.edu/m/med/, the second edition of the *Anglo-Norman Dictionary* at www.anglo-norman.net/ and the *Dictionary of Medieval Latin from British Sources*, edited by R. E. Latham, D. R. Howlett and others (1975–2013), have offered a great trove of material for this study as I attempted to work through all words relating to food and their usage. Scholarship depends on these works to an extraordinary extent, yet they are often unacknowledged. I am also indebted to many libraries and record offices which have allowed me to use their collections in a traditional manner. Beyond those whose permission to reproduce items in their collections I acknowledge below, for their help during longer periods of research I would like to thank Durham University Library; the East Sussex Record Office, now at Falmer, but then at Lewes; Lambeth Palace Library; and the Shakespeare Birthplace Trust Record Office, Stratford-upon-Avon. Equally the library of my home institution, the University of Southampton, and especially its Inter-Library Loan section, has done much over the years to support this project.

I have edited the *Journal of Medieval History* for more than seven years and I am grateful to Taylor & Francis, its publishers, for allowing me to draw on and develop material from two articles that appeared in the journal at an early stage in this work: 'Food and the Middle Ages', *Journal of Medieval History* 36 (2010), pp. 1–19; and 'Gifts of food in late medieval England', *Journal of Medieval History* 37 (2011), pp. 6–18.

Writing this book has spanned a major change in my working life. After some 30 years looking after the Special Collections in the Library of the University of Southampton, I transferred to History, in the Faculty of Humanities, in the same institution in February 2013. A period of leave from my duties both in the Library and the Faculty of Humanities has enabled me to do the research and some of the writing for this book. I am grateful to Dr Mark Brown, then the University Librarian, and to Professor Anne Curry, the Dean of Humanities, for their support during this transition.

No book is written without cost. Friends and colleagues, old and new, have borne a good deal, mainly cheerfully and kindly. Much of the work and the writing has been done at home, and it is here that I have the greatest debts. I am acutely conscious of Bromyard's complaint at those who use wooden tallies as a means of credit, rather than paying for their food immediately with silver coin. The spirit of this must resonate with my family – Sue, Tom, Matt and Dan – who are owed a great deal, and the first recompense I can make is to dedicate this book to them with thanks.

Acknowledgements

For permission to use images, I am grateful to the British Library Board; Glastonbury Abbey; Haddon Hall, Haddon Estate, Bakewell, Derbyshire; the Hereford Mappa Mundi Trust and the Dean and Chapter of Hereford Cathedral; the National Trust; the Dean and Chapter of Norwich Cathedral; the Society of Antiquaries of London; Southampton City Council Archaeology Collections; Southampton City Archives; and the Victoria and Albert Museum.

Christopher M. Woolgar
University of Southampton
16 July 2015

CHAPTER ONE

FOOD CULTURES

A WORD GAME, POPULAR IN the great households of late medieval England, had at its heart the creation of collective nouns. In the lists of these names, alongside the laughter of hostellers, the glossing of taverners, the promise of tapsters and the fighting of beggars, were household references – a carve of pantlers (who looked after the bread), a credence of servers ('credence' was the process of tasting or 'assaying' foods against poison), a provision of stewards of household – and a hastiness of cooks. The pressures of the medieval kitchen, the precipitate hurry and the irritation of the cooks are all captured in medieval meanings of 'hastiness'. The word embodied a further dimension, however, through word play: 'hasta' was the medieval Latin for a spit, and we see at once the heat of the fire that has aggravated the cooks, the profligate use of fuel in roasting, a busy-ness and the hard work that was necessary to produce the finest foods for table.[1] This book is about what that food and drink, from the finest to the commonplace, meant to people in the later Middle Ages and how they expressed meaning through it in their daily lives – and many of them would have been engaged in cooking, even if they were not hasty professional cooks. The premiss is that food and drink mattered for a whole host of reasons beyond simply providing the necessities of life.

Connections that come through food reveal the experience of the day-to-day: from expectations of eating, cuisine, presentation and patterns of service, to the social contexts of dining. The principal focus of this book is not diet,[2] although it does contain much about that, for it is necessary to understand a good deal about foods in order to comprehend the arrangements for their consumption. Rather, it examines the contexts of acquiring food, cooking and eating it in the principal social groups in late medieval England: in the countryside, in civic society, in the monasteries and ecclesiastical institutions, and in elite life. Beyond this it looks at institutional cultures of food, the distinctiveness of food and special food products, the cooking process, links between health and eating virtuously, and food in popular mentalities. The ways in which medieval society used food open new perspectives on daily life. Even 'ordinary' food could be distinctive in a whole range of ways, from the point of cultivation onwards, and it is well worth understanding its implications and effects across a wide range of commodities. It was not only foodstuffs, however, that were important: the manner in which foods were prepared, brought to table, the fashions of service and tableware, all have much to tell us about the aspirations of medieval people.

In order to survey this field, this book draws on a wide range of evidence. Its primary focus is on the written record: although reference is made to material culture, standing remains and archaeology, documentary sources are the foundations of this study. But there are challenges: on the face of it, the historical record is much stronger for the elite and for the production of food, particularly that resulting from agriculture and livestock husbandry on the great estates of England in the later Middle Ages, than it is for the preparation of food for consumption and the ways in which it was eaten. There are, for example, tens of thousands of financial accounts from medieval manors or estates, especially in the period 1200 to 1400; but there is very little that tells us about peasant farms and gardens, which made up a greater proportion of the land under cultivation. On the other hand, even for elite, secular households, beyond the financial records of the crown, consumption is documented in no more than 500 domestic accounts – and there is almost nothing analogous for households at lower tiers in society. Yet there are also some exceptional sequences of records that illuminate particular events, such as the long run of accounts that record the feasts of the guild of the Holy Cross at Stratford-upon-Avon for much of the fifteenth century.

This apparent unevenness in the record has meant that it has been necessary to seek information from a wide range of less obvious or tangential documentary sources – and I have deliberately sought to balance the wealth of writing we have about food in royal and great households with a broader view of food in society. For example, the book draws extensively on legal records, especially those of coroners. Records of sudden deaths enable us to see inside the peasant kitchen in unique ways – and patterns can be established, such as times of the day at which water might be drawn, or what equipment was used for domestic brewing and who was responsible for it. While this material has a fascination of its own, what is important is less the immediate circumstances of individual tragedies than the trends of activity they demonstrate in aggregate. Collections of miracles provide evidence for similar incidents, even if the outcome is usually more fortunate. Nor was medieval food preparation and cooking solely for the accident-prone. Examples of regulation, such as town ordinances, tell us about retail and wholesale arrangements for food, as well as about its consumption. Another form of regulation – monastic customaries – charts the patterns of life in these institutions, and their detail provides an account of both the normal and the exceptional experience of food: how it might be regulated, prepared and delivered to table, along with a great deal of detail about meals, their consumption and their significance. Here there are questions of etiquette, too. The fifteenth century saw a great elaboration in ceremony, particularly in elite households, and the fashions were mirrored down the social scale. The ways in which food came to table, the rituals of service, can be found set out at great length in the handful of household ordinances to survive. Some of this is evident, too, in medieval illustrations of food preparation and consumption. Illuminations in manuscripts, such as the well-studied sequence showing the preparations and service of Sir Geoffrey Luttrell's food, in the Luttrell Psalter (Plate 1), and depictions of biblical events involving food and drink such as the Last Supper (Plate 2), offer us further perspectives on food culture. Items these images portray may be found listed in inventories, sometimes in wills, and these are useful sources for the development of kitchens, their equipment and the composition of dinner services. Some of the tableware, such as elaborate drinking cups, was exceptional – and the connotations of these objects have much to tell us about practices of eating and drinking. We have further elite dining practice in cookbooks – some 4,000 recipes survive from medieval England, giving useful insight into the ways in which dishes were prepared; and we have a handful of menus, largely for special celebrations, which, despite their exceptional nature, are important evidence for the structure of meals, for ways in which food and drink came to table.

There are many other references to cooking and food: domestic life features in literary works – although some sources, particularly poetry describing the great household at feasts, are disappointing in this respect, often making little reference to foodstuffs and patterns of service. Collections of exempla – stories used by preachers to bring points to life for their audiences – offer glimpses of the place of food in domestic life and have been effective in establishing the moral contexts of eating. A further source has been language itself. Medieval vocabulary – Middle English, Anglo-Norman French and medieval Latin – contains a great many words for food and drink and the ways in which they are used are illuminating. Proverbs show the prominence of food in their references to eating, drinking and the range of commodities; vocabulary lists and specimen conversations provide further indications.

These are some of the sources on which this book draws. In fact, we have such a wealth of references to food and what it meant to medieval society that what at first sight might seem like a difficulty – the lack of, say, financial records for the peasantry – is more than compensated for by the breadth of other evidence. The challenge for the researcher is not a lack of material, but the opposite, how to make sense of very large amounts of information.

Food, in its preparation and consumption, must have dominated the lives of many. Certainly it did so from an economic point of view, and the aim of this book is to show it did so in many other ways as well. For households at the lowest level, on some occasions it must have constituted almost all expenditure as well as major elements of daily work. In the households of the great, the investment in food was less as a proportion though, while variable, in total it still might be very substantial: in 1296–7, Joan de Valence, Countess of Pembroke, spent £414 on food and drink, about 40 per cent of her income; in 1412–13, Alice de Bryene probably disbursed 65 per cent of her domestic expenditure on food, if a valuation is made of goods drawn directly from her farms – her direct cash expenditure on running her household was some £160;[3] in 1503–4, Edward Stafford, Duke of Buckingham, spent £307 on bread and ale alone, 15 per cent of his household's total expenses on food. Food was an integral part of lordship, of social impact and standing.[4] At the same time, the productive capacity of the country was overwhelmingly devoted to food, yet there is much that we do not know about it and which a close reading of the evidence can help us understand. Historians have underplayed the cultural aspects of food in contrast to examinations of its production and provision. This book aims to redress that balance, and this chapter turns to some of the fundamental questions relating to food: what was considered food; its relationship to moral and religious questions; what meals were eaten, when and where; and the relationship between men, women and children and their food.

What did medieval men think of as food? Although a very wide range of foodstuffs was consumed, there were assumptions about what in the first place should constitute food. Texts from the late fourteenth century give a glimpse of the beliefs of medieval men about the earliest foods. John Mirk's *Festial*, a sermon cycle from the late 1380s, noted that before the Flood, men had eaten no flesh and had not drunk anything other than water. The soil was fertile, and men needed no food other than what grew in the earth. But after the Flood, God gave man leave to eat the flesh of clean beasts and to drink wine.[5] According to William Langland, in *Piers Plowman*, Adam and Eve had eaten apples 'unroasted', that is, food in its natural state.[6] John Gower believed that the first cookery had been simple, that men had cooked foods without any elaboration. Later cookery, with the reshaping of foodstuffs and cooking in juices, changed the divine order of things.[7] Foods, thus, had a straightforward place in the natural world and a place in God's universe.

It was a bountiful world. Beyond corn and foods that might be gathered, meat and fish were obvious resources; but both were hedged around with ideas, closely linked to religion, about what might be eaten, and when. The dietary laws of Leviticus and Deuteronomy did not pass through to Christian Europe, or at least not without modification: instead, Christian practice led to a pattern of dietary consumption that functioned more by forbidding some foods at certain times than by excluding certain foodstuffs altogether.[8] 'Meat' typically meant the flesh-meat of quadrupeds – not always including them all: on the Continent, goats were excluded, although they were eaten in England; horses were usually excluded, although they may have been eaten in some places at some times, typically worn-out animals, in the countryside.[9] Birds were not wholly considered meat, as they had appeared on Earth on the fifth day of Creation, the same day as fish, while domestic and wild animals were created on the sixth day. Theologians therefore saw birds as different from meatstock, and in some ways as more similar to fish.[10]

Eating came with a high moral and spiritual charge. The original sin of Adam and Eve had been brought about through food. The central act of Christian worship, the Mass, centred round a re-enactment of a meal and of a miracle, the transubstantiation of bread and wine; the use of the chalice was mirrored in many secular rituals of eating and drinking. In the Lord's Prayer, supplicants asked to be given their daily bread. Other miracles of Christ, such as the changing of the water into wine at the marriage at Cana, or the Feeding of the Five Thousand (Plate 3), revolved around food and drink. Lives of saints served as models for consumption, albeit their devotional practices, sometimes living in the desert, were more extreme than many would have wished to follow. An English fifteenth-century life of St Hilarion recounts what he ate at each period of his life. From the age of 20 until 26, he lived off dried bread, water and salt; the bread was of clean barley, with ash; from the age of 26 to 30, he had each day a thin gruel ('water-pottage') and 7 oz of barley bread – and as he became older he ate less and less, after the age of 77 forsaking bread, turning to worts (vegetables like cabbage or brassicas) with milk and salt, but no more than 5 oz a day. He would only eat and drink after sunset.[11]

Christianity came to see the consumption of food, especially abstinence from some foods, as inextricably linked to virtue – St Hilarion's consumption was emblematic of holiness in its modesty, its use of penitential elements like ash, its avoidance of meat, and the times at which he ate. This had far-reaching consequences for the culture of food, which was shaped by the Church's injunction to avoid meat on certain days, for its connection with carnality (the Latin for meat is 'caro', 'carnis') and the vices that flowed from it. In England, by the thirteenth century, this meant avoidance of meat not just every Friday, but also on Wednesdays and Saturdays; throughout Lent, when abstinence would extend to eggs and dairy products; sometimes in Advent, and also on other saints' days or the immediately preceding day (the eve of the feast), particularly the great feast days commemorating the life of the Virgin Mary and the feasts of the Apostles. The pattern of abstinence varied from country to country and, potentially, from diocese to diocese, across Europe.[12] In all, however, a higher degree of abstinence was expected from the clergy, both secular and monastic, with longer periods of food avoidance at Lent and Advent. On days of abstinence those who could afford it might eat fish, although that was only one of the possibilities for abstinence. By about 1300, a secular noble household in England might abstain from meat on about half of the days of the year;[13] and a clerical one, for a further two months, or more, depending on individual conviction. The expectation was that some food and drink would be consumed on all days: abstinence – regularly spoken of in medieval sources as 'fasting' ('ieiunium', whence 'jejune') – did not mean that no food and drink were to be taken. The exception was Good Friday, and even then consumption of some food and drink was not unusual.

Mirk's *Festial*, in its sermon for the Sunday immediately before Lent, summarised the position of who was to fast and when. All were to fast for the 40 days of Lent, except those below the age of 21, pregnant women, the elderly without the strength to fast, pilgrims, the sick and the poor, as well as those whose work involved hard manual labour.[14] Individual conscience was to guide those in these groups. The evidence of personal devotion shows some with more extreme patterns, some less. The exemption of pregnant women would have provided substantial mitigation for many women; but any overall difference on the basis of gender was probably balanced by the exemption of those whose living was based on physically arduous work.

Abstinence was a defining element in medieval perception of the course of the year. Disturbances, known as 'Gladman's insurrection', in the city of Norwich in January 1443, were sparked off by a pageant of the months and seasons of the year, in which John Gladman appeared (with his horse) as the personification of Lent, dressed in the leftovers from foods of abstinence: 'clad in white with red-herring skins and his horse decked with oyster shells after him representing that sobriety and abstinence should follow and that it should be a holy time'.[15] Food might be essential for life, but preachers recognised that man might sin through the quality of the food consumed – to be considered truly penitential food, fish might not be cooked luxuriously – or because it was eaten at a season or time prohibited by the Church: eating meat in Lent was as fatal to the soul as eating poisonous food was to the body.[16] This moral or spiritual dimension to diet is therefore one of the themes that underlies all food consumption in the Middle Ages.

Of the seven deadly sins, two were closely linked to the consumption of food: lust, through the carnality inspired by the consumption of meat – and gluttony (Plate 4). The exposition of the sin of gluttony provides further insights into the ways in which people thought about food. Shortly before the Black Death, the Dominican friar John Bromyard, in his great manual for preachers, the *Summa predicantium*, described the castles the Devil would build in the soul of the impious. In the third castle, gluttony ('Gula') was the kitchener: he was a marvellous cook who intoxicated many; more died by food than by the sword.[17] *A myrour to lewde men and wymmen*, of the fifteenth century, ran through the possibilities for gluttony, drawing on the analysis that had been made by Pope Gregory the Great (590–604), who had divided the sin into five branches, all capable of infecting men and women equally. First, 'overtimely' eating, failing to wait until the proper time for a meal or drink, which came from a great, lecherous lust, like a beast without reason. It was said that men could not fast, but that was false, as some men, for the winning of worldly goods would gladly fast all day until nightfall, but for the love of God and to gain eternal goods they would not fast until noon. The second branch of gluttony was eating or drinking outrageously, without decent measure: moderation was also important for keeping the body healthy. Thirdly came eating too quickly: the more greedily a man ate, the more he sinned; he should not eat his food like a dog or another beast. The fourth area was eating 'over dainteously', spending extravagantly on foods – squandering more on dainties in a day than might supply common meat sufficient for 100 poor men. Fifth was the curiosity that sought out or ordered delicious foodstuffs and delighted in them. There were three aspects to this: the getting and preparing of the food;

secondly, the delight in eating it; and thirdly, the vainglory of recording or recounting how well they had been fed.[18] The perils of consumption thus lay in far more than over-eating: the contexts of actions and intentions were important in any full consideration of this sin.

Abstinence was a crucial component in a worthy life in this world and in preparation for the next. Bromyard laid out how the feast days of the Church should be observed. Men were to make themselves worthy to celebrate the saints by abstinence on the eve of the feast, by confession and penance, just as the saints, by these practices, had shown themselves to God to be worthy of the eternal feast. In anticipation of the good feast the following day, men were the more cheerfully to abstain on its eve, in the same way that they were the more cheerfully to abstain and work in the brief vigil of this world, in the hope of the eternal feast – just as an apple held out to a child makes him come smiling.[19] The clergy aimed to create a mentality in which abstinence, however difficult it might be, was a regular feature of life.[20] It was rooted, however, in practice and custom, and that led to a degree of variation.[21] John Mirk turned to the question of observance of fasts: he noted that there were many who fasted only at one meal in the day, but who would sit up much of the night and drink. Fasting meant the avoidance of both flesh meat and 'white meat', that is, dairy foods and eggs: 'For as St Jerome says, "Eggs and cheese are moulten flesh, and milk is with blood."'[22]

The moral consequences of fine food, or fashionable eating, were writ large from the pulpit. A by-product of saving late medieval Englishmen from perdition is a great deal of useful information about eating habits and patterns. A tract by Richard Rolle, known as the 'Judica me Deus' ('Judge me, God'), is typical in its coverage of gluttony among the seven deadly sins. This part, probably written in the late 1320s, posed a list of questions for the priest to cover at confession:

> If he has eaten before the due time and especially whether he has eaten
> at times of fasting ordained by the Church. If he has over-indulged in a
> pleasing fashion in food or drink, either by quantity or variety. If he has
> been accustomed to eat greedily, hastily or with undue ardour. If he has
> eaten excessive quantities. If he has sought delicate or overly expensive

food. If he has vomited. If he is often drunk. If through gluttony he has vomited the Eucharist. If he has encouraged others to eat or drink too much through malice or vainglory. If he has stolen food and drink as a result of his gluttony. If he has frequented taverns and taken others there. If he has forced someone to drink to excess. If he has eaten meat at times when he should not.[23]

There were also taboos and other restrictions on consumption. Was all meat from quadrupeds suitable? What if it were diseased? The nuns of Lacock Abbey in Wiltshire noted in their accounts for 1347–8 that the 85 carcasses of sheep that had died from disease that year were to be considered as the flesh of cadavers and they were not used for food. On the other hand, meat from a living creature, however worn out, might be considered edible as food, such as the ox, the flesh of which was like a cadaver – but which was nonetheless placed in the larder.[24] An English chronicler, Robert de Avesbury, reported the captain of Calais, besieged by the English, writing to the King of France in 1347. The town was running out of corn, wine and meat. The inhabitants were eating all living things, dogs, cats and horses – but not the flesh of men – for it would be far better to die honourably on the battlefield than to eat each other.[25] Cannibalism might feature in medieval mentalities, but references to it were almost certainly derived from the exemplar of the siege of Samaria in 2 Kings 6 and 7.[26]

A vegetarian diet lay at the heart of monastic food, as outlined by St Benedict of Nursia (c.480–c.550) in his Rule[27] – but by the later Middle Ages monastic foodways had modified patterns of consumption very considerably, as we shall see in Chapter 8. There are, however, references to individuals adhering to vegetarian diets. R. M. Clay, in her survey of English medieval hospitals, identified two women among the inhabitants of God's House, Southampton: Sister Elena who 'ate nothing that had suffered death' and Sister Joan 'who does not eat flesh throughout the year'.[28] While the diet of many before the Black Death may have been heavily based on cereals and with comparatively little meat, it was still exceptional to identify vegetarians in this way.[29]

There was another inspiration for constraints on the consumption of some kinds of meat, birds and fish: status. After the Norman Conquest, there were legal restrictions on the killing of some animals and birds – the beasts of the chase and warren – reserving them for the elite who had grants from the Crown of rights to hunt them.[30] Certain classes of food, such as wild birds, were also by custom reserved for the elite (Plate 5): in the Northumberland Household Book, c.1512, cranes, heronsews (young herons), mallards, woodcock and seagulls were among those birds to be consumed solely as part of the Earl of Northumberland's own meals, with other birds, such as plovers, only to be eaten by those sitting with him at his table.[31] A statute of 1363, enacted at the request of the Commons, but repealed shortly afterwards, noted that many individuals indulged in practices of consumption beyond their estate and degree. It was therefore ordered that grooms ('garsons'), both servants of lords and craftsmen, should be served with food – meat and fish – and drink once a day only; and that the remainder of their food should come from milk, cheese and butter, and other, similar foods, according to their estate.[32]

The characteristics of medieval food

One theme which runs through this book are the influences on cuisine in late medieval England, the connections between practices across society, on the one hand, and, on the other, the roles of men and women in cooking. By about 1200 – and probably at least a century earlier – there had emerged across Europe common perceptions of what might constitute an elite cuisine. This was a style of cooking characterised by thin, acidic sauces and by the use of exotic spices; and it was also transformative cooking, based on grinding and pounding ingredients to pulps of various consistencies, which might then be remoulded into new forms. This pattern of consumption was seen as highly desirable, and was emulated across society. Equally, elite cookery sometimes drew on dishes popular at other levels.[33]

Anthropologists have commonly distinguished contrasting cuisines within society: typically an elite cuisine, usually the preserve of men, of master chefs or master cooks; and a demotic cuisine, often the work of women, for whom food preparation and cooking form major elements of domestic life. The latter is seen as traditional and conservative, and in practice very closely connected to local resources. Elite cuisines may be largely distinct from this, with wider horizons in terms of ingredients, fashions and ways of cooking, but may nonetheless draw on elements of the demotic.[34] Yet how far was this true for medieval England?

Research into cuisine on the Continent has pointed to the use of 'peasant' elements in elite cookery: in fourteenth- and fifteenth-century Italy, for example, there was an elite interest in peasant dishes, and a return to simplicity in food in an intellectual consideration of it. Petrarch liked to eat 'vulgar' dishes, ones that were popular in the countryside; and an analysis of food at the papal court has shown how fifteenth-century cardinals such as Oliviero Carafa had a taste for peasant dishes.[35] An English cookbook of the mid fifteenth century, the *Liber cure cocorum* (the *Book of the business of cooks*), like most examples of the genre, focused on the highly spiced dishes of the elite. Yet it also recognised the importance of other cookery as well, making a special description of 'petty curry' ('pete cure') or 'little cookery': 'First I will show to you the points of cooking, one after the other, of pottages, spit roasts and baked meats, and I will not forget "pete cure".'[36] Petty curry was explained for the poor man, who might not have spicery – people had to recognise their means – and the author then turned to outline the herbs that were good for pottage. He followed this with a discussion of the preparation of dishes that had close associations with peasant foods, but which might still be made with elite spices, dishes with leeks, peas and cabbage.[37] Cuisine in medieval England was marked by a great many cross-connections, as we shall see throughout this book.

Meals and their structure

Just as foods and the dishes they constituted might exhibit connections across society, so too did the meals they composed, both in terms of the meals that were eaten and the structure of the meals themselves, their food grammar.[38] The principal meals were breakfast ('jantaculum'), lunch ('prandium') and supper ('cena'). Although these meals do not entirely map onto present-day occasions for eating, 'breakfast', 'lunch' and 'supper' are used as translations of these medieval terms throughout this book. What they contained, who ate them and their timing varied. Meals and mealtimes fitted into a wider social context, partly in conformity with religious practice – keeping set mealtimes was an essential part of the late medieval pattern of dietary consumption, as much as its pattern of fast and flesh days. Eating at other than the prescribed, or accepted time, was gluttony, as we have seen.

Whenever the first meal of the day was eaten, whether breakfast or lunch, food was not supposed to be taken until after the first Mass of the day had been said. In one of the fables of John Sheppey, Bishop of Rochester (d.1360), a wolf arrived hungry from the wood and found by chance a sow and her piglets. 'Good lady, I am very hungry; give me one of your piglets for breakfast.' The sow happily conceded this; but, she continued, 'It is not yet time to eat. Have you heard Mass yet?' The wolf admitted he had not. The sow advised him to do so: 'You are of age and you ought to hear something of God before you eat. I will call priests and clerks and you will hear the office, and in the meantime I will prepare your breakfast.' The wolf agreed – allowing the sow time to call all the boars and other pigs, and to chase off the wolf.[39]

Working men might eat breakfast, sometimes well after they had started the day's labour. In the Cambridgeshire village of Over, in August 1346, William Byschop had been digging red earth in a pit in the field, and was sitting eating his breakfast at the bottom, when the earth collapsed upon him, engulfing him.[40] Otherwise breakfast was an aristocratic meal, one for travellers, an occasion for politics or important business, sometimes a meal for children, and it was also eaten by some in monasteries, especially novices.[41] From the fifteenth century, when mechanical clocks came into regular use in elite households, the timing of the meal is apparent: breakfast was eaten about 8 a.m., at which point some of the household servants, especially the cooks, would have been up for about four hours.[42]

A moral or virtuous pattern of eating might emerge from eating breakfast. In 1307, the commissioners enquiring into the life and miracles of Thomas Cantilupe, who had been Bishop of Hereford (d.1282), examined the case of Nicholas, the son of John the fisherman. Seven years previously, when Nicholas was about 10 years of age, he had drowned in the River Wye and, miraculously, had revived on the intervention of the saint. Nicholas, asked when he had fallen in the river, replied that he had had breakfast, and fell in the water around the middle of the morning. His father reported that about sunrise his son had led his red cow, with a white star on its head, to a piece of pasture next to his croft and the lord's field at How Caple (a little to the north of Ross on Wye), and that he had returned home after the hour of Terce (said at the third hour after daybreak) and eaten bread and milk, and that about halfway between Terce and midday he had sent his son to his boat on the Wye to fetch a rod. An unelaborate breakfast, perhaps, but one that was not excessive or immoderate in any degree – wholly appropriate to someone who was to be miraculously revived.[43] There was a suspicion about breakfast, however, even one of dairy foods. In a miracle of St Thomas Becket, Salerna, daughter of Thomas of Ifield, in the absence of her mother, obtained the keys of the buttery, which allowed her to fetch cheese to go with bread for breakfast for herself and her sister. They were fond of good or dainty things like breakfast ('jentaculum liguriens'), that is, breakfast was classed as a luxury with all the moral connotations that entailed. On her return, the mother quickly realised that a cheese was missing, to Salerna's consternation. In fact, Salerna was so perturbed by what she had done that, after a sleepless night, wandering anxiously in and out of an orchard, she threw herself into a well – to be rescued by a vigilant shepherd, with the guidance of St Thomas.[44]

Lunch was the principal meal of the day, and it was eaten around noon, by which may be understood in the period before clocks the ninth hour after daybreak. In a great household of the later Middle Ages, the timetables that can be reconstructed from household ordinances, after the appearance of clocks, suggest the cooks may have been preparing this for about five hours: one of the first acts of the morning was 'portion control', with food struck out to match the number of those expected to be present. In the household of the fifth Earl of Northumberland, c.1512, this happened in summer at 5 a.m., in winter at 6 a.m. There may have been two sittings for lunch and possibly also for supper: many of the servants ate first, and the meal with principal guests followed. The first sitting for lunch took place at 9 or 10 a.m. It occurred later on days of abstinence, especially if it was a Friday. On Fridays, there was often no supper, and the day's fast was not broken until all the religious services for the day were over. The timing of the day's services was advanced, with Vespers taking place around the middle of the day, after which lunch was eaten.[45] In the period before the

Black Death, John Bromyard noted that on days of abstinence it was expected that people would eat at the ninth hour – noon – and that the meal would comprise somewhat more than on other days.[46]

At most levels of society, lunch was commonly followed by a period of rest, or of sleep. At Bicker, in Lincolnshire, in May 1375, Thomas Pevy had taken his son, William, with him to a salt-cote on the marsh, belonging to the Abbot of Swineshead. He was sleeping – it was the 'time of sleep after noon' – when his young son wandered off on to the sands.[47] Oliver Sutton, Bishop of Lincoln, added a codicil to his will on 28 May 1294, at his manor of Theydon Mount, with his clerks in the period of the day known as the 'relevium' (the 'getting up again') – they had just arisen after the lunchtime sleep.[48]

Supper was a lighter meal than lunch, at least in the great household. For those in the countryside working further away in the fields and unable to return at lunch, or away from home generally, an early evening meal may have been more significant. In the great household, supper might take place at 4 or 5 p.m., depending on the time of year. In winter, there was advantage in having it earlier, so that it could take place using natural light.[49] After the Black Death, the timing of the meal may have been less crucial. The plague changed the ratio of animals, especially cattle and sheep, to humans, but despite the increased availability of animal fats for lighting, traditional patterns of consumption endured in many places. Supper is described as being eaten at an evening hour, or the hour of Vespers, in the village of Market Deeping in March 1351: John on the Hill had eaten his supper and was standing in his doorway when Robert the son of Robert Wrighte the hayward came by, and they had an argument.[50]

Eating might also take place at other points in the day, although these might not be sanctioned as appropriate. A thirteenth-century treatise on Anglo-Norman vocabulary mentions that, while brewing was going on, it was the custom to eat a cake with spices known as a 'brachole'.[51] Late suppers – 'rere soperis' – were both gluttonous and generally indicative of bad character; they were, for example, among the vices of Sardapalle, the King of Assyria, in Lydgate's *Fall of princes*.[52] *A myrour to lewde men and wymmen* noted that just as one could sin by eating too much, 'right so he may sin in overlate suppers, wherefore those men and women that sup late and stay awake late into the night and waste the time in idleness and vanity, waste and fussiness, going to bed late and getting up late, they sin in many ways.'[53]

There were other points in the day when it was common practice to drink together. There was typically a mid afternoon drinking, at which there might also be bread. At Sherborne Hospital in Dorset, refounded by Bishop Neville of Salisbury in 1438, the residents of the almshouse were to have their first meal at 11 a.m., their second immediately after the evensong of St John; and at 3 p.m. in the summer they were to have a 'resonable drynkyng.'[54] The breaks that workmen might take for drinking were sometimes written into their contracts: at York Minster, in 1370, the masons swore that for their afternoon drinking, in their lodge (their works' building in the Minster Close), between Michaelmas (29 September) and Lent, they would cease work for no more time than it took to walk half a mile; and between the first Sunday in Lent and Michaelmas, their drinking time in the afternoon was not to exceed the time it took to walk a mile.[55] In great households, there might also be evening drinking for guests. A set of household regulations probably compiled in the late fifteenth century noted that 'Strangers, such as the servants of men of worship and such others who are honest people of the country, after they had dined or supped and made obeisance to the head officers of the household, the usher is commanded by one of the head officers of the household to take them to the cellar bar and there to give them wine.'[56] Evening drinking was a common element across society: in 1441, Bishop Alnwick of Lincoln had to enjoin the prioress and nuns at Ankerwick Priory to abstain from all drinking after Compline.[57] For residents in the great household, there was also a further issue of drink and bread, known as 'all night', that was made just before bed, at 8 or 9 p.m., but usually earlier in winter.[58] Commonly, as guests came to leave or to retire, there was a parting drink, or food, with wine and spices, known as a void or voidy.[59]

The structure of meals was culturally determined: it varied from country to country, and there were different expectations as well for different social groups, although the elite pattern of consumption was very influential.[60] In England, at an elite level, food was served in portions ('fercula'), which came to the table in courses ('mes'). There might be two or three courses in elite meals, each of which would consist of a number of prepared dishes and which would come to table together – the pattern of service was very different from contemporary Western meals, where dishes are brought in consecutively. The household Rules written by the great scholar Bishop of Lincoln, Robert Grosseteste, for the Countess of Lincoln, *c*.1245–53, advised that in the bishop's own household at lunch ('al manger') there were served two large and full courses ('mes') – with the intent of increasing alms – along with two intervening dishes ('entremes', literally 'between courses') for all the free household (that is, not everyone in the household had them, but only the gentle members and the upper tiers of servants); and that at supper there was a single course of lighter food, followed by one 'entremes', and then by cheese.[61]

Table 1.1 sets out a specimen menu, from John Russell's *Boke of nurture*, from the mid fifteenth century, designed to give a servant aspiring to life in a great household a glimpse of what he should expect. The diner would then be helped to food from a range of dishes in the course, as he chose – which would be served on to a trencher, a slice of bread, in front of him. Liquid dishes, pottages, would be eaten from bowls with a spoon. Otherwise the diner had simply a knife. On a meat day, it was common for the first course to contain boiled and stewed meats, the second roasted. The meats from younger animals – more tender – and from foods that might be reserved on the grounds of status, such as wild birds and game, might be saved for the second and third courses. The third course might also contain more special-ised cooking, in this case, some freshwater fish and crustacea. A fried dish might be a part of each course. The structure of the meals was designed to allow for pauses, sometimes for entertainment, at which 'entremes', or 'subtle-ties', would be brought to table. By the fifteenth century, these had become set pieces, sometimes models – and it may have been in this way that the Annunciation of the Virgin in Russell's specimen menu would have been represented. Sometimes there was acting, mumming, or other displays, often with a political or religious message – but at an earlier period, the 'entremes' were probably simply a contrasting special food. Equally entertainment might happen at the end of the meal – once a meal had been cleared away there would be space that might be used for dancing.[62] Collections of menus, such as a late fifteenth-century listing of 'royal feasts' in Plate 6, circulated at an elite level: these texts were designed to record prestigious occasions, information of great value to household stewards and clerks of the kitchen, to help them understand the nature of these events and to plan for similar ones. The same text also devoted a section to a listing of which meats and birds were in season, month by month (Plate 7). These menus, like late medieval cookbooks, were not intended for use in the kitchen, but by those who controlled the purse strings and planned the meals.

Eating and drinking were social activities. The ways in which meals were structured made links to the contexts in which they were eaten, to display and to the personnel involved in food service. These differing patterns will be investigated further as this book looks at the detail of food-ways in different social settings.

Where was food eaten?

The significance of food can be further understood by considering where it was eaten. On one level, it was portable: food was taken out to those working in the fields, or looking after animals there; and many people must have carried food with them, or enjoyed eating outside.[63] At home, in the countryside, people ate communally, in the hall of the house if possible. John Bromyard recounted a tale of avarice, of a man who had resources for a whole year except a single day. The man planned with his wife that she should consider him dead for the day. 'Put me in the hall and cover me and therefore that day eat nothing, either for yourself or the household, out of sorrow and solicitude – and we shall then have enough for the whole year.' Returning from the fields and meeting the grieving widow at the door, the household viewed things differently, however, and set to eating. When the man heard this, he rose up and protested – only to be struck dead by a servant who thought the body was possessed by the Devil.[64]

The patterns of upper-class meals were mirrored in the countryside in terms of timing, location, utensils and patterns of service down to the parish clergy and possibly some of the upper echelons of the peasantry. Inventories of households at this level show halls with trestle tables and the utensils and cloths one would expect for these meals.[65] Ecclesiastical statutes set out the goods that were to pass from a parson or vicar to his successor, which would have enabled him to live in this style at a basic level: in those for the diocese of Worcester in 1219, the goods were to include a table with two sets of trestles, and more if they were to be found; a large brass pot or cauldron ('olla') and more if they were found there; a chest, barrel and vat, along with a cart.[66] Typical were a pair of Norfolk clergy. When the rector of Heydon, William de Aylesham, made his will on 16 May 1373, he left to the rector succeeding him in the church a range of domestic goods, including in the bequest a long sanap (or 'sauvenap', a cloth to lay over a tablecloth, to protect it) and a short towel, along with a basin and ewer, indicative of the rector's dining practices.[67] Robert, the parson of Fritton, left William atte Moore of Fritton a brass pot and two brass pans, along with two tablecloths and two towels.[68] At St Mary Bourne, in Hampshire, in July 1385, the vicar's servant, John Brounrobyn (his name places him as a servant in a great household: a 'Brown Robin' was a large cauldron), was preparing the table for lunch at noon. He came into the vicar's chamber carrying bread and the cloth, along with a knife wrapped in the cloth – but unfortunately he tripped and fell, with disastrous results. His table preparations, however, setting out the bread, and presumably the slicing of trenchers, mark out the vicar's household by his actions as one that followed elite practices in dining, at least in a modest way.[69]

Dressing the table in a basic way might be expected on manors, for example, for the manorial bailiff and the 'famuli' – the manor's wage labourers. At Downton, in Wiltshire, in 1301–2, a tablecloth with a towel were bought for the bailiff's use for 2s 1¼d.[70] At Cuxham, in Oxfordshire, in 1349, the goods delivered to Hugh ate Grene, the manorial bailiff, included a tablecloth and towel, and those that had been owned by Robert Oldman, the bailiff who had died sometime earlier in the year, also included a tablecloth worth 18d and a towel worth 6d.[71] On the Norwich Cathedral Priory manor of Hindringham, c.1350, the pantry goods included a sanap: there was also a large table with two trestles, two tables dormant (with fixed legs), three forms, that is, simple benches, and a chair, along with a smaller table in the pantry. The utensils included 12 dishes and 12 saucers.[72]

What these references show as well is that eating took place in a space that was intended for many uses. Trestle tables might be cleared away, and the space reused, from the hall and great chamber of the elite household, to the peasant farmhouse. At an elite level, however, eating in hall became

Table 1.1: A specimen menu from the mid to late fifteenth century, for a meat day in an elite household

All the dishes in each course were expected to come to table together. The subtleties or 'entremes' were brought to table between the courses.

The first course

Mustard with brawn of boar
Pottage: vegetable
Beef
Mutton
Stewed pheasant
Swan chaudon (a sauce made with giblets)
Capon
Pork
Baked venison
Leche Lombard
(a sliced pudding of pork, dried fruit and egg, with a sauce of wine and almond milk)
Friture viant (a meat fritter)

A subtlety: the Annunciation of the Virgin

The second course

Two pottages, a blanc manger ('white food': ground chicken with rice and almond milk), and a jelly
Roast venison or roast rabbit
Bustard, stork, crane, peacock dressed in its feathers
Young herons, bittern, with bread
Partridge, woodcock, plover, egret, young rabbits
Other larger birds
Larks
Sea bream
Doucet (a set dish of egg, sugar and cream), pain puff (a filled pastry), with a jelly
A fritter

A subtlety: an angel singing to three shepherds on a hill

The third course

Cream of almonds and malmeny (minced poultry)
Roast curlew, snipe, quail, sparrows
Perch in jelly; crayfish; another fish dish
Baked quince
Sage fritter

A subtlety: the visit of the Three Kings to the Virgin

Fruit: blaunderels or pippins, with a caraway comfit
Wafers and hippocras

Source: MM, pp. 164–6

something for special occasions only. By the second half of the fourteenth century, there was a complaint that the elite had deserted the hall for a more comfortable life in smaller chambers and parlours (Plates 8 and 9).[73] The lord's great chamber might be used for dining – as well as sleeping and many other activities. Instructions for gentlemen ushers, who controlled the ceremonial of the great household, in an early sixteenth-century volume probably intended for the establishment of the Earl of Northumberland, pointed to the travails of multiple uses for the great chamber. The gentlemen ushers were to set up a trestle table for the lord – removing the board to allow the lord to sit down. Immediately the lord had sat down, all extraneous persons were to be removed from the chamber, and the service of food was to begin. The gentlemen ushers were not to let any man place any dish on the bed in the chamber, for fear of hurting the bed linen. 'And the said usher take good heed that no man wipe or rub their hands upon the arras [tapestry] or other hangings in the said chamber whereby the hangings where the lord is might be damaged.'[74]

Separate dining rooms in houses were a late evolution, and only become common in royal palaces from the 1510s and 1520s – when chambers might also be designated as breakfast rooms.[75] Banqueting houses, that is, places to eat a banquet, at this date the term used for just the course of sweetmeats served at the close of a meal rather than for a whole feast, may have been in evidence in the fifteenth century – and are clearly so from around 1500.[76] There may have been fixed areas for eating at an earlier date in taverns. In a contract for building in Paternoster Row, London, from 1342, seating was to be built in over two floors in a tavern.[77] There must have been tables, too, even if temporary, in some taverns, as at an alehouse at Leake, in Lincolnshire, in August 1353, where chess was being played.[78] Food was commonly sold in inns, from the wine and pears that appeared on Richard Calle's bill at the Cardinal's Hat in 1471,[79] to the more substantial entertainment provided for the mayor and corporation of Rye (who had no hall of their own) – including a bill split with the mayor of Faversham, at Swan's house in Romney, in January 1490.[80]

Monastic refectories were the most substantial of medieval buildings that were set aside primarily for eating. The features of these are discussed further in Chapter 8, but frequently included a lectern, sometimes set into the wall, for a reader during mealtimes (a feature of some pious, secular households too), as well as a raised dais for the table of the presiding monk.

To manage the service of food, to bring it to table, there was a common suite of servants. Pantlers were responsible for bread and for cheese; butlers for wine, ale and silverware generally; waiters – servants of honour in attendance, literally 'in waiting', sometimes called ushers – brought the food to table. A carver might be on hand to slice roasts and other prepared dishes. A marshal or steward of the hall oversaw the whole, and kept order. An almoner gathered the remains of food, to be given away as alms. A further usher would typically have been placed at the entrance to the dining area. The exact pattern of service varied from establishment to establishment – but these household servants will be seen in many of the contexts discussed in this book.

Gender and food

One of the paradoxes of the study of medieval food is that most is known about elite cookery, and the male cooks that worked in great households, yet the greatest part of food preparation and cooking, most of the time, took place in other environments. Much of it was in the hands of women, with foods that were 'housewifely made', or were to be sold retail by them.[81] It was not only the preparation of food that fell to women: they were also often responsible for its service outside elite environments. A 'stepmother shive' – a slice or portion – for example, was an inadequate share of food, which she had dispensed parsimoniously.[82] It has also been argued that in developing their spirituality, women chose to focus on something that was particularly their preserve, food – either in terms of fasting, or as makers of special types of food.[83] This association of women with food is one of the recurring themes of this book.

Did medieval people expect there to be differences in diet between men and women? The short answer is that they probably did not. Ecclesiastical rules about abstinence applied equally to men and women, although we have seen that there were some practical exceptions; they were also rejected by heretics on behalf of both sexes. On 18 April 1430, Richard Grace of Beccles confessed among the tenets of his heresy:

Also that no man nor woman is bound to fast in Lent, the Ember Days, Fridays, vigils of saints, nor at other times which are ordained by the Church as fasts, but it is lawful to every person on all such days and times to eat flesh and all manner of foods without distinction as he chooses.[84]

In medieval medical theory, the different humoral make-up of men and women might imply different foodstuffs or cooking processes would be necessary to match an individual's complexion, or that of their sex as a whole. Apart from a few suggestions that pregnant women should avoid some foodstuffs, however – and these are mainly slightly later, Renaissance suggestions – women's diet was not usually a specific subject of academic treatises on diet, that is, there was no medical assumption that it should be different.[85] When there are examples setting out diets destined for both men and women, as in joint hospitals or religious houses, or in corrodies – set allowances of food for particular residents in a hospital or religious house – the diets are indistinguishable except perhaps in quantity. At the Brigittine house of Syon, which had separate buildings for men and women, there were some 60 sisters and 25 brothers (13 priests, 4 deacons and 8 lay brothers).[86] In the detailed listing of what the cellaress was enjoined to supply 'for the sisters and the brothers', there was no distinction made between them in the provisions.[87]

Children and food

If the ways in which men and women experienced food were likely to have had a good deal of uniformity about them, the Church's rules about dietary consumption usually applied only from the agreed age of adulthood. It was just the most saintly of children whose dietary patterns prefigured sanctity: St Nicholas, for example, while in his cradle, was reputed to have fasted on Wednesdays and Fridays, taking suck from his mother but once on those days.[88] The period of weaning might vary. In the fifteenth-century prose *Merlin*, a child might be considered weaned at 10 months.[89] At Wharram Percy, data from the isotopes in bone suggest that children were weaned between two and three years of age.[90] In November 1297, at the proof of age of Ralph, the son and heir of Thomas Jocelyn – he was a tenant holding land directly from the Crown, and an inquisition was therefore held to establish if Ralph was under-age and would therefore become a royal ward – John Den, one of the Essex jurors, recounted that he was sure of the date of Ralph's birth because he had a daughter, Agnes, who was born almost two years before and her wet-nurse went at that time to perform the same service for Ralph.[91] The early fifteenth-century *Speculum sacerdotale* recounts the 'ablactacion' of the Virgin Mary at the age of three, marked by offerings in the Temple[92] – and it is possible that the weaning of children was marked more generally by feasting.[93] Nurses were expected gradually to introduce children to adult foods: they might chew it themselves first to soften it for the child.[94] Wet-nurses appear to have been employed across all sections of society. It was forbidden by statute in 1253 and 1271 for Jewish women to act as wet-nurses for Christians, and vice versa.[95] Nurses might require supplementary supplies of milk. In a Lincolnshire village, Donington, in January 1354, a nurse left a house in search of milk for two young girls, whom she left in their cradles.[96]

There are occasional glimpses of children and their interests in food once they were weaned, but there is comparatively little that distinguishes their patterns of consumption from that of adults. Fruit was popular. John Bromyard noted how a child would rather have an apple than money;[97] he noted, too, how if a child had once been given an apple or coin, if one tried to take it back, the child would cry.[98] Children from a young age were sent out to play taking fruit with them. In Melbourn, Cambridgeshire, in August 1341, John son of George de Baldok, who was one and a half, went out to play in the street after the hour of noon with an apple in his hand.[99] At Surfleet, to the north of Spalding in Lincolnshire in August 1379, Margaret, the daughter of John Pauk, aged one, went out with a pear in her hand.[100]

Children might always clamour for food – men who could not fast for religious purposes were like 'wanton children that will always have bread in their hands'.[101] Walter de Bibbesworth advised that if a young child stretch out his hand in the morning towards bread, he should be given a morsel of it, or a slice. For lunch ('au diner') he might be given eggs, with the shell removed – especially the yolks, avoiding to give the child an egg that had been fertilised.[102] Children of the elite may have had special access to dairy products: Dame Katherine de Norwich bought milk for the children in her household throughout Lent 1337.[103] The diet of children in schools appears to have been similar to that of adults – and in some instances it was composed of the leftovers from their meals. At Winchester College, in 1397, the 16 choristers, all described as poor, were to have the fragments and remains of the food from the tables of priests and scholars. The scholars here were to start their day with breakfast, if they were under the age of 16.[104]

Children had their own utensils – small cups and dishes – and in one instance, at Wrangle in Lincolnshire in May 1379, a child came to grief while trying to fill an eggshell with water.[105] At the other end of the social scale, the Studley bowl, a piece of fine English silverware of *c*.1400, is decorated with engraved letters of the alphabet in a form similar to that used in primers, and may have been intended for use by a child in a wealthy or upper-class household (Plate 10).[106] Children used knives like adults, although the utensils may have been smaller. At Spalding in Lincolnshire in May 1374, two boys, Robert Staner and William Wadyngton, aged 10, were together eating supper; William had in his hand a small knife and he got up to cut some bread and in play Robert knocked his arm against the knife.[107]

Although evidence for children and their relationship to food, from its acquisition, perhaps gathering foods, to preparation and consumption, is thin, we shall see more of it throughout this book. Children around the home and croft were always close to the preparation of food and drink.

To take these questions about medieval individuals and their food further, the following chapter sets out to contextualise the food culture of the peasantry – the experience of the vast majority of men and women. It looks at ideas about food in the countryside and, more practically, at who was doing the cooking, where cooking took place and how it was done. The focus then shifts to drink and drinking, and an examination of the principal foodstuffs and their supply, before turning to the role of foodways in the life of guilds and urban communities, in church institutions, and in elite households.

CHAPTER TWO

COOKING IN THE COUNTRYSIDE

FOOD WAS FAR FROM ordinary. Delight in the taste of food went far beyond elite investment in gastronomy. It was something to be savoured, and was greatly enjoyed. Expectations were shaped by the distinctiveness of foods and cuisines, the result of a whole range of variables, from locality, the character of crops and plants grown in fields, the produce of gardens and the gathering of wild foods, to techniques of preservation and storage, the creation of specialised foodstuffs, notably meat and dairy products, and other, distinctive preparations, such as sauces. The composition of peasant diet in the later Middle Ages is well known to historians, with its emphasis on cereals, particularly the poorer grains such as rye, barley and oats; a limited amount of livestock, giving both some dairy produce and small amounts of meat, especially pork; and the benefits of gardens, at least for some. While we can see a marked amelioration in diet with the changes to the economy that followed the Black Death in, for example, the provision for harvest workers, many of the time-honoured components of peasant diet remained important.[1] This chapter points to the characteristics of cuisine in the countryside that made eating much more than a question of a subsistence diet, characteristics which can be found in the special attention that was given to foods from the point of cultivation, or stock husbandry, right through to consumption.

While we should not be misled into thinking that country food was unsophisticated and perhaps spartan and unappetising, in the highly moral world of the later Middle Ages, with its condemnation of excess, softness, carnal pleasures and luxurious foods, there was virtue to be found in a simple peasant diet. A fable by Odo of Cheriton, written around 1220, tells of a house mouse and a field mouse. The house mouse asked his country friend what he ate. He replied hard beans and dried grains of wheat or barley – to which the house mouse answered: your foods are dry; it is a wonder you do not die of hunger. His own diet included fat morsels, sometimes white bread, and he therefore asked his friend to lunch, to eat of the best. The field mouse readily went with his friend. Men sitting at table dropped crumbs. The house mouse said: 'Come out of the hole, see what good things have been dropped.' The field mouse took a morsel and out jumped a cat after him, and he scarcely managed to escape back into the hole. 'See, brother, what good morsels I frequently eat,' said the house mouse. 'Stay with me for a few days.' That the food was good the field mouse readily acknowledged, 'But do you always have such company, a great cat which almost ate me?' 'Yes,' replied the house mouse: 'He killed my mother and my father, and many times I have scarcely escaped.' The field mouse replied: 'I would rather live off bread and water in safety than have all the delicacies with that companion; as the saying goes, "I would prefer to eat beans rather than have to watch perpetually against being eaten."' This parable was directed against unworthy rectors of churches, simoniacs and usurers, their souls devoured by the Devil (the cat): many preferred to eat barley bread with a good conscience than delicacies in such company.[2] There was doubtless reassurance for the rural audience that virtue was inherent in their simple country diet.

Virtue notwithstanding, there might be many pressures on life in the peasant household. There is disorder in the early thirteenth-century household of *Hali meiðhad* (*Holy maidenhood*), a tract in praise of virginity, possibly written at Wigmore Abbey, in Herefordshire. The young housewife – who might have led a life of chastity and devotion and assured the future of her soul – is overwhelmed by domesticity and the tasks that are her charge: the cat is at the bacon flitch, while the baby is screaming, the cereal cake on the bakestone is burning, the dog has hidden and the calf is suckling (taking the milk she should have already drawn for her dairy work), the pot is boiling over on the fire, and her husband is chiding her.[3] Foodstuffs and food preparation were deeply embedded in the daily round of the peasant woman, and were emblematic in popular mentality of key stages in life. There was a traditional link between bacon flitches, domesticity and a good married life – and other foodstuffs were linked to marriage as well.[4] The expression 'to win the flitch', directed to newly-weds, meant to have lived for a year and a day in marital harmony.[5] A long poem, Peter Idley's *Instructions to his son*, of c.1445–50, includes a cautionary tale in praise of marriage and against adultery, about winning the flitch of the priory of Dunmow – Chaucer's Wife of Bath also makes a passing allusion to it. Idley saw this particular flitch as a metaphor for adultery and its disasters: the adulterer's prize was 'a little bacon flitch that has long hanged and is rancid and tough', far from the desirable and well-prepared flitch, the reward found in a model domestic environment.[6]

Other references to bacon and pork had different connotations, but one informed by the ubiquity of this foodstuff in peasant households. Two proverbs from a fourteenth-century collection report that 'It is better to have an ounce of meat from a pig, than bacon from an ass': a little of something good is to be preferred to a lot that is bad; and that bacon is never to be found in the bed of a wastrel – it comes as a reward for virtue and the work involved in preparing it.[7] Others reflect the sameness of things: 'The child is the pig, and the father is the flitch', that is, like father, like son; and that the young may be best controlled, for the older have minds of their own: 'When you offer me the pig, open the sack; for when he is an old swine, you won't be able to control him.'[8] More generally, links were made between meat and status: 'Who sits as a lord, eats brawn (flesh meat)';[9] and it is possible that the expression now known as 'to rule the roost' was current as 'to rule the roast'.[10] The expression 'to speak of cold roast' seems to have meant to tell old news – which in turn suggests the less than appetising quality of leftovers.[11] These proverbial links between household, domesticity and cuisine are not accidental, and give an important indication of the cultural importance of meats as foodstuffs.

Women typically appear as responsible for cooking in peasant and urban households of modest standing. In 1429, evidence for the heresy of Margery, the wife of William Baxter of Martham in Norfolk, came from two girls of 14 and 16 respectively, in the service of a neighbour. Going into

Margery's kitchen when she was not there, one of the girls, Agnes Bethom, said she found a brass pot standing over the fire – she lifted the lid and found a piece of bacon, with oatmeal, boiling in it. As this was the first Saturday in Lent, this was strong testimony to something heretical: the Lollards, whose detection was the object of this enquiry, believed that it was lawful to eat all manner of foods on any day.[12] There is no doubt that Margery was responsible for the cooking, and that female servants were also commonly involved; the technology was basic, with a pot in a fire, but with a lid; the food itself must have been commonplace among the peasantry. In another Norfolk heresy case, John Burell reported how he saw in the buttery of the house of Thomas Mone of Loddon a quarter of a cooked piglet, stuffed and cold. He believed that the piglet had been cooked and prepared on the advice of Thomas's wife, and that it was eaten on the eve of Easter – at a point when eating meat was prohibited – by four people, including the housewife. On Easter Day, Thomas Mone's wife sent her daughter with the remains of the pork to the house of Thomas Burell (who was one of those who had partaken of the meal the previous day).[13] This is symptomatic of the references to cooking at this level in general: women are responsible for the cooking of food, for its preparation and perhaps for some special skill in that connection – in this case, for a stuffing – and often for sharing it or giving it away.[14]

Food preparation happened both within and outside the home. Many peasant households would not have produced or processed every foodstuff they needed: some essential foods, including bread and ale, would have been bought in. While much cooking happened around a hearth, possibly in a separate room or kitchen, more prosperous peasants had outbuildings that included areas for both processing and storage: bakehouses, brewhouses, larders, barns and granaries.

Hearths might be very simple affairs. If the fuel was wood, it could be set directly on a floor. This was the principal way of providing means for cooking in peasant houses. A bakestone might be set in it, or pots might be set directly in the fire, placed around the edge, or suspended over it using chains, hooks and crooks; they might be set on tripods, or they might have feet of their own, or be supported on wedges. There were exceptions, however. A raised fire basket is needed to give an up-draught for fuels other than wood, for coal, for example, and may be needed for turf as well (but does not always appear to have been). In those areas where coal was the principal fuel, in Derbyshire and in the north-east of England, there are references to a 'caminum', later anglicised as a 'chimney' – a portable piece of ironwork into which coals might be put, raised off the floor – and referred to in more recent sources as a 'chaumin dish'. Pots would rest directly on the chimney; and a house might have no specific hearth area.[15]

The chimneys varied in size and value: in the mid 1340s, when the daily wage of a skilled worker such as a tiler might be 3*d*, examples ranged in price between 4*d* and 12*d*.[16] They must have been between one and two feet high. While chimneys must have been quite sturdy and stable, they were hazardous, and overhanging pans might be dislodged. At Alvaston, south-east of Derby, in February 1346, Fresaunta, the daughter of Geoffrey de Billesdon, who was one and a half, was sitting next to the fire in her father's house. An earthenware pot was standing on the chimney, full of boiling water; it fell off and broke over her.[17]

It was not just pots that stood on top of the chimney: quite substantial dishes, such as pans ('patelle', similar to paella pans: 'patella' and 'paella' have a common derivation), were also placed there. The chimney could also be a portable cooking apparatus. Some had handles, or tangs, and they may have employed charcoal or coal in an enclosed box. One was among the bequests made by William Bowland, the rector of St Nicholas in Durham, in September 1380, where it is listed alongside a posnet (a saucepan with a handle), which could have been intended for use on it.[18]

From the second half of the fourteenth century we have references in north-east England to brandreths – a grate, or iron framework, to go on the fire, from the Old Norse 'brand-reið', a 'fire-carriage' – which provided a framework on which pots might be stood and which, in larger households, came to be linked to the development of the cooking range. Brandreths appear, for example, at the monastery of Monkwearmouth in 1360,[19] and among the bequests of cooking equipment by Nicholas de Schirburn, a chaplain of York, in 1392.[20] There is some uncertainty about their exact form, and their evolution from trivets and gridirons more generally.

Fires burned in peasant houses much of the time. People expected to cover them when they left the house and at night, using a curfew (in its original form, a 'couvre-feu', a cover for a fire) – but did not always do so effectively.[21] One reason for this was that it was easier than relighting a fire. Individuals are reported as carrying fire with them, perhaps embers in earthenware pots.[22] Straw was used as tinder or as an accelerant. At Great Doddington in Northamptonshire in September 1361, a brass pan was set on the fire, and straw was then added to the fire to help heat it.[23] In another Northamptonshire example, from 1350, the fire was being set under a pan when it spread to some of the straw around – there was always a great deal of straw on the floor in peasant houses.[24]

Gathering fuel for domestic fires was a major preoccupation of the peasantry, just as it was in the construction of the great woodpiles needed by aristocratic housholds.[25] We find turves cut in the fens, kept in piles in gardens;[26] coal pits in Derbyshire and Yorkshire; and children sent to gather branches from trees, as at Woodford in Northamptonshire in 1365, from a willow overhanging the Nene.[27] Peasants might be entitled to collect fallen branches, the dead wood in woodland, typically in return for a hen at Christmas, known as a 'woodhen'.[28]

Examining the principal implements in the peasant kitchen demonstrates expectations of the cooking process there. In a Worcestershire sample of peasant goods – of the principal goods of the tenement, not the sum of peasant chattels, but those that belonged to the property rather than to the individual – from 1380 to 1434, there were typically pots ('olle') of brass and pans, also of brass, along with vats, brandreths, table linen and chests, even among those who had less than half a virgate (about 15 acres). Those with larger holdings had bigger pots and pans – in some cases, up to 10 gallons – and more goods, as well as more in the way of table linen, basins and ewers. These references indicate that both earthenware and brass pots were in use. The brass had a larger capacity, but there was an overlap in function (Plate 11).[29] Little is known about these brass pots from physical remains, as the brass was usually recycled when these vessels broke or fell out of use; many of the pots must have been imported, as at this period there was no native source of metal for brass in Britain.[30]

Earthenware pots were used widely for storage and for fetching and carrying; but, as with brass pots, cooking was a major use. In the peasant household, we find earthenware pots used for hot water[31] and set on the fire, containing foodstuffs. At Great Cheverell in Wiltshire in February 1342, John Deles, a boy of two, was in his father's house, and an earthenware pot, full of boiling vegetables, was standing precariously over the fire. John went to the pot with the aim of spooning out vegetables, but the pot and vegetables fell on him.[32] In April 1350, at Laverstoke, near Salisbury, Anabilia, the daughter of Thomas Kedere, was sitting next to a pot in which vegetables were being cooked, and by misfortune it fell on her.[33] A brass pot worth 12*d* was being used for vegetables at Orlingbury, Northants, in July 1366, when the cooking led to the death of a young boy.[34] The following year, at Rushton (in Rothwell Hundred, Northants), a young girl sitting next to the fire pulled a ladle from a pot of vegetables, with disastrous consequences.[35]

Earthenware pots used for cooking stood either directly in the fire; or some may have been hung over the hearth, having 'ears' to aid lifting or suspending. Many cooking pots have sagging bases – they do not have flat bottoms. In order to stand in the fire, they had to be propped up on brands, or stones, or placed on trivets or stands. Some forms had feet, especially pipkins (like modern saucepans), as did some jugs, but most did not have these features.[36] Earthenware pots exhibit a very conservative range of patterns, which remain stable over a long period of time. The standard guide to medieval pottery notes over 65 different forms between the tenth to eleventh century and the sixteenth century. Strikingly, however, there were only three principal forms that were common before the mid fourteenth century – the cooking pot; the bowl, pan or dish; and the jug or pitcher. In the later Middle Ages, there was a different emphasis, possibly because of the increased use of metal for pots: there were fewer pots for cooking but, in some places, more earthenware pipkins; there were also more bowls, dripping pans and a few other forms, especially cisterns and cups.[37] Within the principal categories of vessel, there were some standard forms and sizes. Cooking pots in Sussex, from the Chichester area, in the Saxo-Norman period, for example, group in three broad sizes, with radii of 7–8 cm, 9–10 cm, and 12–13 cm. There were then storage pots of much larger size, twice that of cooking pots; and another group varying between 45 and 90 cm high.[38]

These vessels must have been used for many things – and the standard sizes suggest that these were found widely useful. Earthenware pots were employed for gathering food and for storage. Robert Gryme of Fosdyke in Algarkirk in the Parts of Holland, in February 1377, was drowned in a creek after going to recover an earthenware pot that had been left on the sands, perhaps for gathering shellfish.[39] Two examples from the household accounts of the Le Strange family of Hunstanton, Norfolk, from 1348–9, record the purchase of earthenware pots immediately after the purchase of whelks, cockles and mussels. In each case the purchase of both shellfish and pots is made by the same person. These were probably large vessels (the cheapest costing ¼d) for carrying and storing the shellfish, possibly with seawater to keep them fresh.[40] Traces of food residues in some pots show them to have been used for cooking. Fatty acids indicate use for meat stews, as well as dairy products – and a good many vessels were needed for separation in the dairying process. Some bowls show sooting suggesting they were heated, perhaps in separating cream.[41]

Changes in the forms of earthenware in the later Middle Ages indicate different possibilities for cooking. The use of legged pots, standing directly in the fire or used over small fires in rooms other than the kitchen, demonstrates cooking in a different context. Another simple, but major, innovation of the later Middle Ages was the pot lid – or at least one of earthenware. Lids allow economies in fuel, and also, if sealed, bring more intense flavours. That these were available at an earlier date can be deduced from the shape of pots, especially the brim, but the lids must have been made of another material, such as wood. Some recipes include descriptions for lids, wrapping them with paper or linen cloth, and using a batter of flour and eggs, or dough, to seal them.[42] In Sussex, lids first appear in pottery assemblages between 1250 and 1300, and it is believed their appearance coincides with developments in pottery production, at a point when it became a more significant industrial process.[43]

Some pots were very much larger and the volume cooked was as well. In July 1353 in an accident, a brass pot full of boiling pottage was standing over the fire, at Knapwell in Cambridgeshire, and the pot was appraised at 14d.[44] An example from a suicide's goods at South Kelsey in Lincolnshire in June 1350 was valued at 2s 6d. The goods show the man, who was married, to have had three cows, three draught animals, two calves and a colt, a quarter of malt, two piglets and 5 acres of corn, beans and peas, as well as a cart worth 2s – valued in total £1 2s 10d. This was an environment in which the scale of the pot reflected a larger family group, perhaps with other workers too.[45] A pot stolen from Weston in Cambridgeshire in 1335 was valued at 3s,[46] and an example, among a felon's goods at Stuchbury in Northamptonshire in 1347, was also valued at 3s.[47]

As with the pots, there were both earthenware and brass pans. They were used firstly for boiling water: at Kirton in Holland in January 1379 Robert son of William son of William Conayn of Kirton tripped over a spade that was leaning against a wall of the house and fell into an earthenware pan full of hot water.[48] There was also a widespread association between earthenware pans and the processing of dairy foods, principally milk. In 1353–4, at Asgarby in Lincolnshire, Richard the son of William Coke was playing in his father's house when he knocked into a pan full of hot milk. The pan was appraised at no more than ½d, as it was earthenware.[49] At Bulkington, near Devizes in Wiltshire, in August 1383, a young boy aged one and a half went past an earthenware pan and knocked it, and the hot milk scalded him.[50] Some of the smaller brass pans were also used for milk. At Sibsey in Lincolnshire in 1356, a two year old girl fell into a pan full of milk – the pan was valued at 3d.[51] In 1380, there was a further accident with a brass pan full of hot milk, recorded at Kingsley, east of Alton in Hampshire, but a larger pan this time, worth 6d.[52]

The brass pans were probably mainly vessels of a concave shape – in some instances they are simply called 'concavus', as at Elsworth in Cambridgeshire in 1354.[53] Many of the brass pans were found with water, or with liquids that were part of the brewing process, although there were occasional mentions of other uses. In May 1355, at Ringstead near Raunds in Northamptonshire, Elizabeth, the daughter of John de Thynden of Ringstead, was sat next to a pan boiling vegetables, which fell upon her. The pan was appraised at 2d.[54] At Moulton in Spelhoe Hundred in Northamptonshire in March 1361, peas were being cooked in a pan, valued at 6d.[55]

Brewing was a key rural industry. The brewsters who dominate the historical literature and who were licensed through the manorial courts were in the main brewing for sale.[56] Much brewing in the countryside, however, was on a smaller scale, using the pans in the household. These pans were positioned over the domestic fire, propped up on tripods. The combination of brewing as a domestic activity and children, especially children at play, was lethal. At Caldecote in Cambridgeshire in June 1347, a young boy, not much more than a year old, was sat in the house of Simon the carpenter of Caldecote next to a pan on a tripod, full of 'cooked' ale. The pan and the tripod were valued at 6d.[57] At Lolworth, in May 1353, the two year old Thomas, son of William Kech, was playing in his father's house, and there was there a pan standing full of boiling new ale, which fell on him.[58] These vessels were at a low level, just above the fire.[59] At Rushden Northamptonshire in 1356, Agnes the daughter of John le Snayth, aged three, was standing next to a pan full of wort ('granomellum') when her foot slipped and she fell into it.[60] At Walgrave in 1360, a girl of six and a half years fell into a brass pan full of hot grout,[61] and at Welford in Northamptonshire in August 1363, John the son of Maud Mandevill, aged one and a half, in play ran up to the brass pan, which was full of boiling water for brewing, and took a dish full of the water and put it on his head.[62] Just occasionally the capacity of the vessel was stated by a coroner's jury – and the quantities were small. In 1381, Agnes, aged six, went into the house of Richard Betfolde in Basingstoke and fell into a brass pan of hot wort, containing 2½ gallons and valued at 8d.[63] Values of Cambridgeshire and Northamptonshire pans from the 1340s and 1350s show the scale of this work was very modest: the Lolworth case, with a pan and ale worth together 2d, suggests the pan contained little more than half a gallon, that is, the size of a modern casserole pot.[64] These pans were used for this purpose across England, from Hampshire to Yorkshire.[65]

While brass pans were employed for brewing in a domestic environment, brass pots do not seem to have been used for this purpose, although use might be made of a smallish cauldron: one, with a tripod, was valued at 12d at Teffont (*Uptefante*) in Wiltshire in February 1345.[66] Brewing leads – open vessels originally made of the metal (much as the later 'coppers' were first vessels for boiling made of this metal) – were also in use. These came in different sizes, and they were used for comparatively small quantities, for domestic work, through to larger vessels for commercial production. At a domestic level, leads were stood on tripods, over the fire, as at Great Cheverell in Wiltshire in September 1343.[67] At Wigtoft in Lincolnshire in March 1361, a lead of 12 gallons was being filled with wort by Cecily, the wife of John Hardik, when she tripped and fell into it. The lead was appraised at 12*d*.[68] A lead worth 12*d* was also in use in Scarborough, in June 1341, when Alice, formerly the wife of Nicholas de Wessenby, a tanner, fell into the hot grout that it contained.[69] In 1340, another Scarborough lead was appraised at 6*s* 8*d*, and was housed in a separate building – and this must have been a substantial container, employed in an industrial process.[70]

The brewing process was a lengthy one: even in a domestic environment, it might be carried on overnight. At Peakirk in Northamptonshire in March 1366, Joan Levesham had set a fire under a lead and she was looking after it when she fell asleep – perhaps because this was a long process – and the fire burned down the house.[71] At Leicester, in a house in Dod Lane in August 1364 Alice, the wife of Thomas Unwyn, a servant of John de Braybroke, got up in the night, and in the darkness could not see a pan full of boiling water, into which she fell. Presumably this was part of the brewing process, even though we are not told that the liquid was other than water; it was a domestic hazard, but the fire must have been shielded, as there was no light.[72]

Vessels known as kimelins (or kimnels) were also to be found full of ale or hot wort. They were smaller tubs, with an open top.[73] At Baumber in Lincolnshire in November 1354, a two year old fell into a kimelin full of ale – the kimelin was worth 3*d*.[74] Another, in Uffington, Lincolnshire, was worth 2*d*, in 1358.[75] In June 1353, John, the son of Alice de Geddeney, aged four years, was at Fleet near Holbeach in Lincolnshire, in the house of William de Harcroft, who was a common brewer. He sat down in the house next to a kimelin with boiling wort. He knocked his head against it, but in getting up he grabbed the kimelin with his hands and it fell over, scalding him with the wort. The kimelin was valued at 3*d*.[76] Many of the kimelins were appraised at around this price.[77] A larger one, valued at 12*d*, was described as a 'lead kimelin' at Moulton in Holland in September 1380, which suggests that some of the vessels described as leads may equally have been known as kimelins.[78] Other containers with wort are simply described as 'vessels' ('vase') or stoops ('stoppe').[79]

Another vessel, a 'bowl' ('bolle'), can be linked to brewing. One worth 1*d* at Folkingham in Lincolnshire in March 1350 was described as a 'bolle scapo' ('a bowl-shaped bowl') and was full of hot water, into which a two year old fell while playing.[80] At Wyberton, Lincolnshire, in 1352, there was an angry dispute between John Bally of Boston and his servant, Joan of Lincoln, over a bowl of wort.[81] In Lincoln itself, in the dean's house, a servant was carrying a bowl full of wort when he tripped into a vat of boiling grout, in April 1366.[82]

The tripod was an essential piece of kitchen hardware for those who did not have access to chains or similar equipment for suspending pots over the fire. A decrepit example, valued at 1*d*, was in use at Great Cheverell in Wiltshire in February 1342 for an earthenware pot.[83] Larger tripods, with values from 2*d*, as at Stuchbury in Northamptonshire in 1347,[84] to 3*d* at Over Lyveden,[85] were used to hold more substantial vessels over the fire. At Great Cheverell in September 1343, a tripod with a defective leg failed to keep up a lead full of hot water.[86] Tripods provided support for pans, as at Cottenham in Cambridgeshire, in 1351.[87]

Cauldrons were vessels that were placed in the fire, or were surrounded by fire. They had metal feet of their own. At Stone in Buckinghamshire in a coroner's case from May 1363, there was a brass pot on the fire, full of boiling water; one of the pot's feet – perhaps broken – was resting on a stone, from which it slipped. The pot was appraised at the substantial sum of 2*s*, a level of valuation that indicates this was a cauldron of some kind.[88] The iron wedges that frequently appear in inventories may also have had a role in propping up pots that had no feet.[89] Fewer cauldrons were to be found in peasant households than in larger establishments. The goods of the vicar of Guilsborough in Northamptonshire in June 1356 were those of a substantial farm and included among the kitchen goods a cauldron, lead, brass pots and pans and other utensils, together worth £1 18*s* 6*d*.[90] But occasionally they were found in smaller households, sometimes used in brewing, as at Teffont in Wiltshire, in 1345, when a tripod and cauldron (which had been full of boiling ale) were together valued at 12*d*;[91] and an example from Southwick (in Willbrook Hundred) in Northamptonshire, which had been full of hot water, was valued at just 3*d*.[92]

There was also a group of vessels known as yetlings – a pot especially for boiling, often made of a cast metal, particularly brass.[93] Vessels with this name were to be found in the north of England from the 1350s and some were very substantial.[94] In 1378–9, one was made for the kitchen of the Prior of Durham for 12s, using 30 lbs of brass.[95] This type of vessel may have been free-standing and was different from the kettle – at its most basic, a container, usually of metal, for boiling liquids over a fire. John Brompton, a wealthy merchant of Beverley, included in his will of 1444 a brass kettle with handles ('klpe'), which probably weighed 28 lbs.[96] The kitchen of Elizabeth, the widow of William Sywardby of Sywardby in 1468, had two kettles.[97]

There was a class of standalone boilers, although it is sometimes hard to distinguish them from ovens generally, or malt ovens, as the same word ('furnus' or 'fornacus') may be used. On 23 December 1364, Alice, the daughter of Walter Ferrour of Leicester, was sitting in front of the boiler to keep herself warm, when Isabel, Walter's servant, came with a vessel to take boiling water from it.[98] At Longtoft, in Lincolnshire, a young boy, William Bate, was sitting next to a boiler full of hot water when the boiler broke, scalding him. The boiler was valued at 2s.[99] The boilers were open-topped vats. Isabel Hachard, at Southwick in Hampshire in 1379, came for boiling water, and tripped and fell into one.[100] In some instances the vessels were of wood – presumably separated from direct exposure to the fire by inter-vening material. A wooden vat full of boiling water was in use in a house in Cottenham in Cambridgeshire in April 1351.[101] These vessels were all in the possession of individual households.

Ovens were much less common, and probably not often in the posses-sion of individual peasants – at least, not until brick chimneys were built in houses, with the potential for small ovens as part of the structure (Plate 12). Where they were in operation over a period of time – as at Norwich Cathedral Priory – they required continuing structural attention. The oven at Norwich (later referred to as 'our oven', in the bakehouse) was built for 6s 11½d in 1278–9,[102] and then required purchases of clay – either for repairing it, or for stopping it up for baking – in accounts running into the mid 1310s.[103] Ovens were heated with rapidly burning fuel, such as straw, to produce a fierce heat, then cleared out; the foodstuffs were then put into the oven and it was sealed up. The bean straw that is sometimes found stacked in peasant houses would have been especially useful for this purpose.[104] At Stanley, just west of Chippenham, in 1338, John de Salisbury was cleaning out the wisps of straw from the oven when his broom broke and he fell into the oven and was killed by the heat.[105] Ovens and bakehouses were notable as places where people congregated, to keep warm and to sleep. At Kirton in Lincolnshire in 1370, a madwoman aged 25, by the name of Agnes, was sleeping in the bakehouse when the building was consumed by fire.[106] At Bescote, near Walsall, about the hour of curfew on a summer's evening in 1375, John de Stretton, the baker and servant of Sir Roger Hilary, and Gromyl, a Frenchman from Picardy, were sat together in the bakehouse when a fight broke out.[107]

By the end of the Middle Ages, kitchen goods had become much more plentiful. Listings show pothooks and other equipment for suspending pots over the fire – as well as many more pots – in quite modest households, and they were sufficiently important to feature in wills. Thomas de Malton, a chaplain, who may have been an architect as well as a clerk in holy orders, left, in 1400, a rackan-crook – a vertical bar, with holes for pot hooks – for suspending pots over a fire.[108] Isabella, the wife of Alan Hamerton, a citizen of York, made a will on 15 May 1432 bequeathing to a York spicer a pair of forks for hanging pots in the racks and crooks, which probably had a similar function.[109] In 1479, Agnes Rynglon of Northampton made a special bequest of a vessel called the 'Sonday pott' – and one can imagine that she had spent many Sundays working with it. In 1480, Margaret Hancok, a widow of Northampton, made bequests of brass pots holding 2, 3 and 4 gallons. She also bequeathed a brass pan holding 18 gallons.[110] In 1505 John Cobbe of Northampton left to his daughter Margaret a pot and pan that had been her mother's, a bequest which shows how the female interest and connection to cooking equipment might be sustained.[111] These references speak of the new and widespread importance of cooking utensils in households at this level.

This equipment focused on boiling and stewing. There is little evidence for frying in the countryside, at least before the Black Death: frying implies the availability of fat or oil – while the peasantry had limited numbers of animals, their main source of fats would have been from pork, or from dairy foods. After the plague, when there was proportionately more livestock, the appearance of greater numbers of frying pans points to increased use of fats.[112] There is also much more evidence for roasting in the period after the Black Death: the appearance of dripping pans for fat in the archaeological record (often sooted only on the one side, that facing the fire) and a range of spits listed in inventories show this had become an increasingly popular way of preparing food. Very few spits are found in peasant contexts until the later fourteenth and fifteenth centuries. One, worth 6*d*, was the murder weapon in a fight following a theft of capons near Wollaston in Northamptonshire, in December 1360.[113]

Cooking at the end of the Middle Ages offered more possibilities for the peasantry and the urban lower classes than the challenges faced by the young wife in *Hali Meiðhad* in the first quarter of the thirteenth century. The young wife had little in the way of equipment for preparing food: a bakestone and a pot on the fire – and we know nothing of the equipment that she would have used to serve it. In 1475, William Harysson, a fuller of Northampton, left to his kinsman Thomas Harysson as cooking equipment his best brass pot and best brass cauldron, along with another brass pot and brass pan holding 4 gallons; a pan holding a half gallon; a chafer, for keeping food warm, or for warming the room, with two ears (for lifting it); two iron spits; a pair of cob-irons, on which the spits would rest; two eel-spits of iron; a skimmer and a fleshhook. His mother, Agnes, was to have, inter alia, a skillet – like a frying pan – with a handle; his kinswoman Katherine a spit of iron, a further two cob-irons, and an iron eel-spit; and John Batman was to have a brass pan holding a half gallon. In addition to the cooking equipment, there were vessels for serving food, or for eating: among the bequests, Agnes, William's mother, was to have a large dish ('parapsis'), two dishes of pewter, and three silver spoons; Thomas Harysson was to have a charger – a large serving dish – of pewter, four large dishes, four dishes, eight saucers, a salt cellar, a chafing dish of laten and a pewter pot; a sauce pot ('salsarium') of pewter with a cover, and two pewter saucers were left to Walter Mayndow; and Katherine, the testator's kinswoman, had another container for sauce with a cover, and two pewter pots.[114]

William Harysson could readily have boiled food in his pots and cauldron; his roasts of meat and fish were prepared on spits; and he had a skillet for frying, now comparatively commonplace as a cooking method. He also had a taste for sharp sauces, with sauce containers that would have come to table. There he also used separate dishes for sauce – saucers – as well as a salt cellar and serving dishes, and he had ways of keeping food warm at table. His tastes mark him as typical of late medieval England: its passion for sharp, acidic and thin sauces, well known from aristocratic tables, was a feature of the cuisine of many of lesser status. There were categories of vessel that did not appear here that would have been standard kitchen or eating equipment, made of leather, of pottery, or of wood. Culinary possibilities were substantially greater for those of William's rank than 250 years previously. But there were still things he could not do: there is no reference to an oven, or to the equipment that went with it; despite his taste for sauces, he had no mills or querns for preparing his own. He may have made use of the large pan for brewing, but he had no vats for this purpose. Therefore, he would have had to purchase baked foods, from bread to pies and more elaborate preparations – or pay for them to be baked for him; his sauces he would have bought; and he would have had to buy ale and other drinks.

The peasant experience of food was far from immutable. Dietary change, especially from the mid fourteenth century, when meats and fats became more widely available, produced new possibilities for cookery in the countryside. While there may have been a long period of conservatism in peasant food, in terms of equipment and commodities, the second half of the fourteenth century and the fifteenth century saw a greater investment in kitchen equipment at all levels. This raises questions about technology and food. Most peasant cooking from around 1200 was boiling or stewing, and there was limited access to baking and roasting – and this may have had an important effect in terms of vitamin intake.[115] Patterns of cooking changed from the middle of the fourteenth century and possibly earlier. The development of new techniques, of the availability of cooking equipment even at the lowest levels that allowed those in the countryside to roast or fry food, to move beyond the pot standing over the fire, speak of very great changes in the character of food, cuisine and the routines for eating that went with them. Dishes for service at table point to connections across class.

These changes are best understood by looking at individual commodities and the customs and practices associated with them. The range of differences is nowhere more apparent than in drink and drinking. We can see as well distinctive elements in the preparation of beverages that might create commodities that were especially attractive to consumers. Here brewers, many of them women, might make their mark.

CHAPTER THREE

THE CULTURE OF DRINK AND DRINKING

I T IS HARD TO underestimate the importance of drinks and drinking to late medieval society. Preparing beverages was both a domestic routine and a major industry, and one that touched almost all households, even if they did not prepare drink for resale. Drink was a key element in conviviality, as well as in ritual. There are many references to cups that were special – and the drink that went in them was clearly distinctive as well. Variety was about much more than noteworthy drinks, however; it was an expectation of ordinary consumption. Drink was one of the areas where contemporaries expected to find the greatest variation in products and flavourings, resulting from brewing and distillation practices, given the multitude of producers and the connotations drink and drinking were to have.

At one end of the scale was water. To drink water was an indication of poverty, for example, in rural nunneries,[1] but it might also reflect other concerns: when Langland reported that Lecherye, on a Saturday, was to 'Drink but with the duck and dine but once' – given in one variant form as to drink 'with the goose' – it was proffered as a penance;[2] and, to the same end, rations of bread and water were used as a disciplinary regime in monastic houses.[3] A diet of bread and water was also seen as virtuous. As we have seen, Odo of Cheriton, *c.*1220, in contrasting the life of the town mouse with his country cousin, rejected the delights (and snares) of good things in favour of a hard diet, essentially of bread and water – the message was that although this diet might have been common in the countryside, its virtues were significant.[4] This suggests that drinking water, and drinking straight from streams and ponds, was probably much more common than historians have allowed. At the end of his Vision, Piers Plowman awakes and meets Need, who takes him for a beggar and points out that poor men may do three things without asking, the third of which is to lap water from the ditch.[5]

A sample of coroners' rolls tells us about normal practices of obtaining and drinking water. Children were regularly sent to wells with pots to fill for the household. At Barrington in Cambridgeshire, in July 1346, the 12-year-old John, the son of Warin ate Lane, went first thing in the morning out into the courtyard with two pots to fill them with water from the well: this was often a task for the start of the day;[6] and in May 1349, at Comberton, just west of Cambridge, John, aged seven, the son of Mariota le Deye, was sent to fetch water with an earthen pot from a nearby pond.[7] In November 1363, at Werrington, near Peterborough, Agnes Couhirde, who was possibly old and infirm, went to a well with a vessel described as a water pot ('idria').[8] Water in these cases was almost certainly to be brought back to the house to be used for cooking there or other processes. In other examples, water for drinking was taken direct from streams and wells, by hand, or with smaller containers. When, in late July 1338, Agnes, the two-year-old daughter of Simon Darnel of Saxton in Ditton Camoys in Cambridgeshire, went to a common well, known as Bakhouspot, between her father's house and the highway, she was intending, so the coroner's jury believed, to drink water from her hand.[9] For children, going just outside to get a drink on a hot summer's day may have been a common occurrence. At Caldecote in Cambridgeshire, in mid June 1341, Henry the son of Nicholas de Brunne, aged three, did something similar: he took with him to the ditch just opposite his father's house a dish to scoop up the water;[10] and the three-year-old son of Thomas Gille, at Bassingbourn in Cambridgeshire in August 1344, took a dish with him to a ditch that was across the street from his father's house in order to drink water.[11] When dishes feature in accidents around water sources, an intention to drink there and then was often mentioned by inquest juries.

Water was kept in households in pots and barrels. Pots for water (and other liquids) are referred to as 'stenes', large earthenware vessels, and they are likely to have been used to store water rather than to transport it, given the weight involved.[12] Larger quantities filled cisterns in bigger establishments,[13] or for those which needed large quantities for industrial processes, especially brewing. Even with the wells and conduits found in some towns, or institutions, such as that which drew water direct from the River Wear to Durham Cathedral Priory in 1466–7[14] – and especially without them – water had to be carried to meet this demand. It was taken piecemeal, by water-carriers, or bitters, using bittes and bouges (leather water-bags and bottles), as Lydgate put it, 'Carried by horses, bouges are brought from rivers and wells to brewers for good ale.'[15] 'Cans' – vessels for liquids, but without any implication at this date of shape or, indeed, of material – were used for carrying water. In 'The hermit and the outlaw', a ballad probably in origin dating from the late fourteenth century, the outlaw, whose penance that day is not to drink water, meets a young woman bearing a water can on her head – which must have been a common sight (Plate 13). 'On her head she bore a can; / Over the brim ran the water, / which seemed to him fair and clear. / "Maid," he said, "I am very thirsty. / If you are carrying water, / set down your pot right here!" / "Sir," she said, "at your will / Here may you drink your fill!" '[16] When, in August 1353, Baldwin of Bruges wanted fresh water while his ship was moored at Boston, Lincolnshire, he started to clamber ashore along a rope with a pot in his hand for the water.[17] If water was needed in bulk, it might come by water cart. Also in August 1353, Alice, the maidservant of Walter Taverner of Boston, had gone with a mare cart to fetch water for brewing, when it overturned at nearby Toft.[18] At Friskney, about 12 miles north-east of Boston, in late September 1355, Ranulph Redy went out of his house to meet Thomas Flaynne's cart, which was full of water. Ranulph asked for water from the cart, and the carter got down to give it to him, but the horses that were in the cart started to move and caused the cart to run him over.[19]

Water might be provided for men working, particularly those performing some of the customary labour services in the countryside. At Banstead in Surrey, in 1325, the provision was distinguished by the name of the service: 'alebedrepes' were those labour services at which the lord gave ale, offset by his provision only of water at other services, 'waterbedrepes'.[20] The third of the harvest labour services due – probably in the thirteenth century – from

St Denys Priory's tenants in Portswood, to the north-east of Southampton, was similarly a 'water bedrip': there was food for the tenant and his man that day, but only water to drink.[21] That water should be the only drink made available for the tenants on these occasions clearly reflected a balance of interest, beyond the performance of the service, in favour of the lord.

Drinking water directly from streams might be hazardous. At Lamport in Orlingbury Hundred, Northamptonshire, in August 1358, Nicholas Bernard was found dead by his wife: he had been mowing the meadow and the heat had made him so thirsty that he drank from a brook – the jury ascribed his death to drinking the water.[22] The physician John of Gaddesden, in his *Rosa Anglica medicine*, probably *c.*1313, advised travellers not to drink water at all on a journey.[23] Distinctions were made between water that was 'sweet' – fresh water – and brackish or salt water. Bartholomew the Englishman drew on Aristotle to demonstrate that salt water was 'more heavy' than fresh, as an egg would sink in fresh water, but float in salt water, because it was more earthy and thick and held up the weight of the egg.[24] In some instances in elite households, it was the practice to boil water before it was drunk. The saintly Edmund of Abingdon, who died in 1240 as Archbishop of Canterbury and who normally did not drink at all before the main meal of the day, did, however, in the heat and thirst of summer drink boiled water – known as 'cisona'.[25] Adam, the Queen's goldsmith, made anew at Bordeaux in March 1287 a silver pot that was used for boiling water for King Edward I.[26] Water was used for diluting other drinks:[27] Bartholomew the Englishman advised it particularly for full-bodied red wine, as it 'is most strong and much grieves the head and smites the wit'.[28]

Ale was a key drink in medieval England. It was made from an infusion of malt – principally barley malt, but also of malted wheat, oats and mixed grains, depending on the quality that was required. The heating and fermen-tation process generally ensured that it would have been a much safer drink than water. It did not, however, keep long – a maximum of two weeks – and in England it was not until the fifteenth century, with the addition of hops to the process of producing a beer, that its keeping qualities were improved.[29] Contemporaries were keenly interested in the qualities that came from its brewing, from the domestic hearth upwards. Like many food-processing activities, this work was largely in the hands of women – at least in small-scale trade.[30] The potential variety of the drink can be glimpsed from occasional descriptions of the constituents of ale. A recipe by Sibill Boys was copied out by William Paston, probably around 1430: 'For a wholesome drink of ale, take sage, avens, rosemary and thyme, chopped small, and put it in a bag with a new-laid hen's egg and place it in the barrel; also, cloves, mace and spikenard, placed in a bag and put in the barrel. The hen's egg will stop the ale going sour.'[31] Herbs, spices 'and nutmeg to put in ale' were abundant in the forest through which Chaucer's Sir Thopas rode.[32]

Ales had their own reputations. Welsh ale may have been particularly praised: John Bromyard pointed out a little before the middle of the four-teenth century that there were many delightful things in this life that were simply not appreciated. The Italians did not think much of ale because, unlike the Welsh, who considered it the joy of heaven, they did not have this drink.[33] The inhabitants of Norfolk – the butt of many medieval jokes for their alleged slow-wittedness – were said to drink an ale called 'buskys' in vast quantities and get very drunk, but as it was in practice water and dregs, it was not known how this could really have been the case.[34] In a tale told by Friar Nicholas Bozon, a father believed the quality of his ale would encourage his son to visit, but in practice it merely served to provide excuses for his son to put off an irksome duty. The son replied that the ale would be too new for his father and would be bad for his nose; asked a second time, he answered that the ale would be too strong and would hurt his head; and on the third occasion, he held that the ale would have aged too much and gone off.[35]

There might be great variation in ale, and regulation of its quality was important. Manorial and municipal ale tasters oversaw this, on the one hand;[36] on the other, in institutions, producing their own brew without this supervision, there was also a close interest. In the 1330s or 1340s, the sub-cellarer of St Augustine's, Canterbury, was expected to ensure that the convent's ale was well made, of a good colour, clear, made from good malt and to have a good flavour – and if it was not, and the convent did not care for it, the prior and senior monks were to make enquiry, to establish whether the fault was that of the monk or the servant, and they might expect punish-ment.[37] The convent's refectorer was also expected to taste all drink, to make sure that it was fit, before it was brought to the refectory.[38]

The practice of adding flavourings to ale suggests the way in which hopped ale – beer – came about. This was imported from the Low Countries, from the 1370s;[39] but beer-brewing had become an established, if still exceptional, trade in East Anglia and the capital by the mid fifteenth century. On 1 February 1459, the mayor and assembly of Norwich agreed that a quay, which they had recently purchased from the Abbot of Wendling, should be repaired with all possible speed, and that buildings should be erected there with the advice of the city's chamberlains so that it might serve for a man brewing beer. It was further agreed that no stranger or anyone else of whatever condition should brew and sell beer, except the man who was to live on this quay, although any citizen might brew beer for his own use and that of his household. The assembly further agreed that beer barrels were to be measured according to the agreed system of measures for the barrel, overseen by the mayor.[40] In May 1464, the beer brewers of London laid a petition before the city's corporation seeking a formal regulation of their trade, as there were no ordinances governing it, 'for as much as the common people for lack of experience cannot know the perfectness of beer as well as that of ale' – to which the city was pleased to agree.[41]

Ale-making was well established, and there were associated trades, such as maltmaking, with maltmakers and maltmongers identified by surnames indicating their occupations from the late twelfth century onwards.[42] The making of the wort, the unfermented or partly fermented ale, was a practice familiar to all, and preachers in their tales depicted the environment in which this happened. Odo of Cheriton, c.1220 – and John Sheppey, over a century later – recounted the tale of a cat that chanced upon a mouse squeaking that he could not escape from the froth of the ale that was fermenting. The cat asked the mouse what he would give him if he rescued him, to which the mouse replied 'whatever you ask'; so the cat proposed that the mouse should come to him when he called, and the mouse firmly promised he would. But the next time the cat passed the mousehole and called for the mouse, he refused to come, despite having sworn to do so – 'I was drunk when I undertook this,' the mouse retorted. Odo pointed to the broader complaint, that many who were sick, in gaol or otherwise in peril promised to mend their ways, to fast and so forth, but once they had escaped danger did not fulfil their vow, claiming they made it *in extremis* and should therefore not be bound by it. The common expression 'to be as drunk as a mouse' suggests that the brewhouse was indeed a frequent resort of mice.[43] The investment in brewhouses could be a constant element in the expenditure of an institution. At Norwich Cathedral Priory, the Master of the Cellar in 1263–4 paid more than £1 for labour for a new lead roof for the brewhouse and bakehouse; the materials cost a further £2; and the oven there was new-made for 15s 11d. The two buildings shared a chimney that was painted in colours, and had its own weathercock.[44] In 1307–8 two new leads were made for the brewhouse, at a cost of 5s.[45]

Ale-houses were not necessarily special premises: at one end of the scale they were the houses of individuals who had brewed and who were selling ale – they had brewed marginally more than those peasants who did so for their own use. The house might be simply marked with a sign, typically a broom (Plate 4). At Belton, in Manley Wapentake in the West Riding of Lincolnshire in June 1371, the village watchman, Ralph Dulle, fled to a tavern at the house of William Turner at dawn, after he had been assaulted with a knife by a suspect he and his colleagues had attempted to arrest.[46] Even in towns taverns may have been semi-domestic environments. In April 1396, the tithing of Netherpavement in Nottingham reported to the town's court two tipplers – tavern-keepers – who were selling ale within their houses in dishes and cups against the assize, that is, the measures had not been checked and sealed.[47] While drinking took place on the tavern's premises, ale might also be bought there to be taken away. In April 1377, at Holbeach in Lincolnshire, Joan del More went to the tavern of John Fysscher and was returning, drunk, with the ale she had bought in an earthen pot when she tripped and fell into the common water next to the house in which she lived.[48] Almost anyone might carry about pots of ale. At Kennett, to the north-east of Newmarket in Cambridgeshire, in July 1338, Peter, the son of William Fraunkeleyn, was carrying a pot containing ale when he had an altercation with a dog.[49] Margery, the wife of William Wryght of Boston, was coming from that town on 8 January 1369 with a pot of ale when she fell into a common ditch ('graftum') called 'Dippehole'.[50]

Taverns were divided between those that sold wine and those that sold ale alone. Piers Plowman's Vision pictured taverners, crying out their wares:

'White wine of Osey [Portugal] and red wine of Gascony, / Of the Rhine and of La Rochelle to help digest the roast!'[51] John Gower described a tavern that must have been similar to a contemporary wine bar, to which the ladies of the city trotted along in the morning – rather than going to the monastery or the market – only to be hoodwinked by the taverner. He offered them an array of wines, but Gower had seen 10 varieties all drawn from the same barrel. And the taverner would say to them, 'O my dearest ladies, make good cheer, drink everything at your pleasure, for we have plenty of opportunity.'[52] The retail trade in wine increasingly became concentrated in the hands of vintners, especially those in London: they were granted a monopoly of the retail sale of Gascon wine in 1364.[53]

Taverns speak of drinking as a social activity. This can also be seen in the drinking parties – the 'bede-ales', 'bede-wynes' (parties to which the public were invited, sometimes for a religious purpose, perhaps for fund-raising) and other entertainments – that competed with the proper duties of Sunday;[54] and bede ales were sufficiently troubling to the town and liberty of Newport on the Isle of Wight for them to be banned in October 1462.[55] Drink was widely available for sale, not just from taverns: representatives of the corporation of Rye, going to a brother guild, a meeting of the leading men of the Cinque Ports, on this occasion held at Romney after Easter 1483, paid for a pennyworth of beer at the ferry at Saltcote near Rye;[56] and in September 1483, on a similar journey, they paid for the expenses of the town's common clerk going to Romney and for drinking at the ferry for the whole party on the way home.[57] On the Tuesday after Twelfth Night, in January 1490, the Rye party bought Rumney wine at a tavern for their supper; they then paid further for malmsey wine at supper 'and to bedward'. On their way back, they paid a penny to the hermit at Camber (*Cambirston*) for a drink – whether this was a profitable sideline at the hermitage, or a more charitable arrangement, is unclear.[58]

Something of experience of drinking survives in toasts that were drunk: 'wassail', 'be in good health', has its origins in the Old English 'was hál' and Old Norse 'ves heill', but does not seem to have been associated with drinking until the end of the Anglo-Saxon period.[59] Its use with drink was recorded by Geoffrey of Monmouth and by Wace in his *Roman de Brut*: 'The custom is, sire, in their country, when a friend drinks with other friends, that the first drinker says "Wesheil", while the one who receives the toast says "Drincheheil".[60] Related drinking games are recorded. 'Passilodion' was explained in the fifteenth-century romance 'King Edward and the shepherd':

> When you see the cup, unless you say 'passilodion' you will not drink this day. Silly Adam shall sit in a noble fashion, and answer with 'bera-frynde'...'Passilodion' means this: who drinks first [shall say] 'Wassail is the mare's tail.' 'Berafrynde' also, I believe, is said when the cup is drained. And fill it full often.[61]

From a toast, wassail came to refer to the practice of drinking in revelry, for example, in payments made by the sacrist of Bury St Edmund's Abbey in 1369–70 and 1401–2, for wassail at Christmas;[62] and to the drink itself.[63] Wassail, however, was only one special drink among many. Bragot, made from ale and honey, was recorded by John Russell in his *Boke of nurture* as suitable for serving at the end of a franklin's feast, alongside mead, with spiced cakes and wafers;[64] burgerastre was a spiced drink made with honey;[65] there was a range of drinks involving spices and wine, such as caudle, sometimes heated too (caudle *ferré* was warmed by having a hot iron placed in it).[66] Beyond this were spiced drinks, such as piment;[67] 'bitter-sweet', a drink combining both tastes;[68] and drinks made with pepper.[69] There were also waters – such as barley water.[70] Stronger alcoholic drinks were available in the form of spirits – 'burning water' or 'ewe ardant' – used occasionally in cooking. A recipe for 'little castles' ('chastletes'), pastry castles, filled with a mixture of pork and fruits, envisaged them coming to table with the spirit as a flambé.[71]

Mead and other drinks made from honey, such as metheglin, were less common in the later Middle Ages than they had been earlier. They still had a special place, however, and mead continued to be brewed in ecclesiastical institutions. It featured at Westminster Abbey in the customs of *c.*1266 as a pittance, one of the additional dishes and drinks that had been given to the abbey out of charity, but even then it was unusual and the pittancer was allowed to substitute wine or ale.[72] The composition of metheglin is not well described, but it was distinct from mead. In *A talking of the love of God*, from the fourteenth century, as the author speaks of Christ, it appears in a list of 'sweet' things as 'meth': 'You are sweeter than honey or milk in the mouth, mead, meth, or piment made with sweet spices, or any similar liquor that may be found anywhere.'[73] One of the few descriptions of it being made associates the process with women. At the visitation of Fotheringhay College in June 1442, it was alleged that one of the fellows, John Palmere, made metheglin and on account of this had sometimes four, five or six women with him in his chamber – and, on occasion, just one, from which suspicion resulted – which Palmere in turn denied.[74] 'Medemaker' is recorded as an occupational surname, but it occurs but rarely in comparison with surnames associated with brewing ale or the wine trade.[75]

Cider was a regional speciality. Unlike ale, cider can only be made in a short period of the year, as the apples are harvested. It then needs to be stored while it ferments. A good deal was made in Kent and other southern counties, through the Welsh marches, particularly Herefordshire and Worcestershire. The tomb of a cider maker, Andrew Jones, d.1497, and his wife, in Hereford Cathedral, depicts a barrel of cider at their feet, along with apples (Plate 14). On the manors of the Bishop of Winchester, spread across southern England, most of the cider was to be found in Hampshire. At Marwell, 21 tuns of cider were in store at the start of the accounting year 1210–11, two of which were sent to the bishop's palace at Wolvesey, and the remaining 19 to the buttery of the palace at Marwell; the manor of Bishopstoke sent one tun to the palace at Bishop's Waltham, one to Marwell, and seven to Wolvesey; at Bishop's Waltham, 12 tuns of cider were produced by the garden, of which 10 were passed to the bishop's butler for the bishop's use, and two were given away; the tithes of East Meon produced seven tuns, all of which were consumed by the bishop, at Meon, Waltham, Lovington (Itchen Stoke) and Hambledon.[76] Langland's reference to pomade – 'May no piment, pomade nor precious drinks quench my thirst completely' – suggests that there may have been other apple-based drinks, but for consumption in elite circles. The '-ade' suffix was commonly applied to fruit preserves, particularly those made with sugar as we shall see, and other references to pomade, for example, to two pots in the household accounts of the Duke of Clarence in 1418–21, are to an expensive preserve rather than a drink.[77] Perry appears occasionally, as in a poem of c.1330, which mingles praise of the Virgin and Christ with praise of women generally:

'Piment, clary, no liquor, / Milk, perry, no mead; / And who so loves them with honour, / shall die no shameful death / through guilt!'[78]

Milk may be referenced in this poem, but it was unusual as a drink in an elite household, except for children.[79] It may have been no more common in the countryside, but that depended on the scale of animal husbandry and on cultural patterns of dairying. After the Black Death, there is evidence for a stronger pastoral economy, and the increased consumption of veal in the later Middle Ages is indicative of a dairy industry. How much of the milk was for drinking, as opposed to other dairy products, is less clear. English proverbs have much to say about things being milk-white, or being bountiful, like the biblical land of milk and honey, but there is little or nothing about milk as a drink.[80] A Robert Drinckemilke appears in a subsidy roll for Framlington in Northumberland in 1296, but one cannot tell how he acquired his surname, whether it reflected an unusual personal predilection or an ironic sobriquet.[81] Milk came to table in monasteries, however. At Norwich Cathedral Priory, in a series of entries added to the priory's customary, around 1379, arrangements for collecting up the spoons were noted 'when the convent has milk in the refectory out of custom, as in Lent from the refectorer, and in summer from the cellarer'.[82] Whey may have been of importance in the countryside: Piers Plowman, facing hunger, pointed to his well and a small group of dairy products, two green cheeses, a potful of whey and boiled curds.[83] Possets – a hot drink, made from curdled milk with ale, or occasionally wine – may have been a rural drink at one point, but recipes for it in cookery books show that it was enjoyed as well in an elite environment, and that it was heated over a fire.[84] Other methods of heating drink included the use of hot iron, as in the caudle *ferré* noted above, and also the use of stones: a medical recipe for a respiratory complaint gave an additional treatment at its conclusion – the patient was to have goat's milk each day in which three heated stones taken from the river had been quenched.[85] In 1300, four goats were bought for Edward I so that he might have milk in summer: the reasoning behind the purchase is not clear, however, whether for some medicinal purpose or whether it was a personal preference.[86]

Of all drinks, wine was the most prestigious and the most expensive. It made up only a small fraction of the nation's beverages as a whole, but its association with religious practice, particularly in the wine accompanying the bread at Mass, its links to elite culture and its availability largely only as an import, guaranteed it a significance far beyond the volume consumed. Its prestige made wine a peculiarly acceptable gift. Where did this wine come from? There were vineyards in England from the eleventh century into the fifteenth, but their produce was modest and not necessarily of a high quality. On some estates, grapes were a source of verjuice – used as a mordant for sauces – as well as wine.[87] In March 1290, Bishop Swinfield of Hereford, staying at Ledbury, in Herefordshire, drew seven tuns of white wine from his vineyard there and almost another one of verjuice, of the previous autumn's vintage, allowing £8 to the bailiff of the manor.[88] In 1431–2, the household of John de Vere, twelfth Earl of Oxford, consumed 2,705 gallons of wine, not including waste and gifts. This was overwhelmingly red wine: 16 pipes of it, to one of white. In addition, the Earl, various visitors and gentlemen had some 50 gallons delivered to them in 'bottles' ('in botellis'). The Earl's vine-yard at Wivenhoe produced 34 gallons of wine that year, made by two of the Earl's servants, and filling two barrels.[89] A little was therefore known about viticulture. John Bromyard, shortly before the Black Death, noted that the more difficult the work, the more meritorious it was, just as the better wine came from high and stony places.[90] It was natural, too, that he should caution against drunkenness and its consequences: as the proverb had it, he said, wine and the confessional revealed everything; there was no secret where drunkenness reigned.[91]

Assuring a good supply of wine was essential to one's standing, but was not necessarily straightforward. The pattern of imports – and the wines – changed considerably over the period 1200–1500, in part depending on political and military positions on the Continent. The white wines of northern France, frequently imported in the early thirteenth century, were replaced by light red wines from the south-west of the country, especially in the fourteenth century, with the connections to Bordeaux and Gascony. Sweet white wines came from the Mediterranean; and further white wines came from the Rhine and Moselle areas.[92]

The English royal household was the largest consumer of wine in the kingdom. William Paston III wrote apprehensively to John Paston III in March 1487: Henry VII was expected in East Anglia, and to be at Norwich for Palm Sunday – 'Wherefore you had better warn William Gogyne and his fellows to purchase sufficient wine, for everyone is saying that the town will be drunk as dry as York when the King was there.'[93] Despite the variety of wines that Piers Plowman saw in his Vision, and that implied by Gower's taverner, there had been very little variety in the bulk of wine bought for the royal household in the 1330s and 1340s. When, in 1338–9, the King's butler made purchases for the royal household, he acquired some 1,553 tuns of Gascon wines, but less than 7 tuns of other varieties. This was a greater stock than usual, as the King was preparing to go overseas: four additional cellars had to be hired in London to house the wine in anticipation.[94] The most highly prized wines at this point were sweet wines, such as Cretan wine (malmsey) from the eastern Mediterranean (it did not necessarily come from Crete), and vernage, from Italy. These wines appeared only in small quantities in the royal accounts of the period.[95] The King made the most of his wines in other ways: as prestigious gifts. There was, for example, a small group of religious houses that each received from him, as a tradition, a tun of wine for celebrating Mass: Westminster Abbey, the Augustinian priory of St Denys near Southampton, and three Cistercian monasteries – Beaulieu, Netley and Waverley. Three of these institutions – Beaulieu, Netley and St Denys – were located close to Southampton, where many of the wines arrived from Gascony; and two of these, Beaulieu and St Denys, were in origin royal foundations.[96]

Beyond the use of wine for the Eucharist, in a monastic context it often had a celebratory or commemorative function. At Westminster Abbey, wine was assigned as a pittance for some of the most important feasts of the year. In 1266, it was noted that wine had recently become the drink that was to be served as part of the pittance at Christmas Eve, the feast of Edward the Confessor, a special saint for the abbey (5 January), Easter, Whitsun, Trinity, the Assumption of the Virgin (15 August), the translation of the Confessor (13 October), and at All Saints (1 November). There were a further 25 feast days on which wine might be served – by permission. Other local religious, such as the nuns of Kilburn, were to be given wine whenever it was served at Westminster.[97]

There were significant variations in the supplies of wine large institutions were able to purchase. In 1263–4, Norwich Cathedral Priory bought its wines – 10 tuns – at Lynn, for £10, a much lower price than it was to record at any point in the next 60 years.[98] In 1315–16, one tun came from the Prior of Yarmouth, but generally the place of purchase was not recorded.[99] In 1279–80, the Cathedral Priory purchased 11 tuns at three points in the year, but the purchase price and getting them to Norwich amounted to some £22.[100] In 1283–4, the expenses on wine came to £25 18s 6d.[101] In 1291–2, there were 16 tuns, purchased through the year – it is not possible to date all the purchases, but there seems to have been some bought in Lent for many years.[102] This was the peak point of provision: the annual variation presumably reflects what was available in the market. As few as 5 tuns were bought in 1310–11, of which one was sent to the priory's manor of Hindringham.[103] As well as these bulk provisions, there were occasional much smaller purchases in the city of Norwich itself, probably from taverns – we have already seen in the case of Rye how wine might be bought piecemeal by customers.[104]

Drinking vessels and commemoration

Drinking was a communal and public act of consumption that had an important place in medieval society. That the equipment that went with it, particularly cups, had especial connotations is clear from literary sources.[105] Drinking from a shared cup created bonds between lord and man, bonds of service, of a common culture and tradition, much as the chalice at the Eucharist created a common bond through the central commemorative act of Christianity. Some cups made special links to family and lineage, and some were among the most significant items of plate there could be in a household. Many must have featured too in the arrangements for displaying plate on tiered cupboards (literally, boards with cups on them) in the household, exhibiting the connections that came with plate, whether by gift or otherwise.[106]

The cups of Queen Philippa in 1331–2 demonstrate the pattern of use in the royal household. The basic stock of silver cups for routine drinking in the Queen's household consisted of two groups of 14 and 21 silver cups (Table 9.1). There were then groups of much more important items: two silver gilt cup and ewer sets, that were given away by the Queen to her visitors from Guelderland during the year, and a pounced silver gilt cup, enamelled in part with the arms of England and Hainault, a silver gilt cup and ewer set without arms, and a further set, of silver gilt but with the foot and cover enamelled with birds.[107] The Queen acquired a series of prestigious cups during the year. The most important of these was her New Year's gift from the King at the start of 1332: a silver gilt cup, pounced, with leaves, enamelled at the bottom with a tree with images in seven circles garnished with precious stones and pearls, with butterflies and parrots ('papeiaiis'), with a matching cover and tripod.[108] Then there were gifts from the Earl of Warenne, the Bishop of Chichester, the Abbot of St Albans, the Prior of St John of Jerusalem and others. But gifts might not always be kept – further connections might be created by giving cups away; there was no guarantee that recognition of an association might endure. Sometimes even the gifts of close family were recycled: Queen Philippa gave away to her own mother the gold cup that she had received as a New Year's gift in 1332 from her mother-in-law.[109] The royal family, however, had many items like this and its prestige was in no way diminished by passing on these donations.

Cups came in different forms: hanaps were drinking bowls, broad and shallow. While they were commonly of silver, some were made of maple and were known as mazers, often fashioned with elaborate mounts.[110] Other forms of drinking vessel included bowls, usually a semi-spherical shape with a foot ring, and often quite a large item (cups were deeper and narrower).[111] Despite the implication of size in modern usage, bowls were used for drinking: in 1382–3, Thomas Lexham, a canon of Hereford, bequeathed to Roger, the rector of Wilton, the bowl and mazer from which he was accustomed to drink.[112] A canon of Exeter, Roger Vaggescombe, made a bequest of a silver cup called a 'trussyngbolle', one into which other cups might be placed.[113] Another group of cups were known as 'bells' from their shape. Sir Nicholas de Loveyn, in his will proved in 1375, left William of Wykeham, the Bishop of Winchester, a silver gilt cup, with a cover, made 'in the manner of a bell'.[114] Beakers were large vessels, with a wide mouth. As a form in aristocratic circles, they came to prominence in the fourteenth century. In 1368, Robert de Ufford, Earl of Suffolk, bequeathed to William his elder son the sword that the king gave them with the earldom, a little horn, and the gilt beaker that Robert's mother had bequeathed to him.[115] There were beakers of glass by the 1380s,[116] but most often these items were covered silver cups, with tapering, straight sides. Nuts – a coconut shell mounted in the form of a cup – were equally prestigious. One, identified as 'the cup called "note"' in the will of Robert Vaggescombe was bequeathed by him to his sister in 1381.[117] Another exotic variety, a griffin's egg, may have been based on an ostrich egg – an example was bequeathed by John Hill of Spaxton in Somerset to his son and heir in 1434.[118] Goblets – cups which were bowl-shaped and usually without handles, sometimes without feet – also feature: one, a gilt cup called 'gobelett' with a cover, was left by John Talbot of New Romney to his daughter Joan in 1403.[119] Godets, some- times derived from the containers used to import treacle, also appear among significant bequests.[120]

Commemoration is apparent in the use of many of these vessels. In 1426 Sir John Bigod left a cup (probably a drinking bowl, a 'crater') to his daughter Katherine Crathorn, inscribed with the words 'Sovenez de moy' ('Remember me').[121] The use of named cups to create memorials was a strategy employed by testators when they lacked male heirs, or heirs at all. William, Lord Latimer, a Garter knight, who had a prominent military career in the service of Edward III, but was accused of corruption in the Good Parliament of 1376, had no male heir – his landed property went to his daughter Elizabeth Willoughby. In July 1380 he left to the prior and convent of Guisborough, where he was to be buried, the great gilt hanap called St George, the mazers and the almsdish he had in his wardrobe in London, to be kept in the frater (refectory) of the priory so that they might serve the prior and convent there in perpetuity.[122] Commemoration formed a part of the round associated with these vessels in monasteries: the 'cup of St Aethelwold' at Winchester Cathedral Priory in the fourteenth century evoked the memory of the great Anglo-Saxon reforming Bishop of Winchester.[123] That cups that were given were intended to have a memorial connotation was at least implicit in other cases. Some gave instructions for their cups to be turned into chalices: in 1425, Roger Rye left to the church of Charing his cup (a bowl) to become a chalice, well and sufficiently decorated with a shield of his arms.[124]

Among the different classes of vessel, one group that might make partic- ular connections were the mazers. Lineage was one bond pointed out in this way. The goods of the English royal wardrobe at the Tower of London, for which John de Flete was responsible in 1324–38, included a green coffer holding mazers, among them a great mazer with a silver foot called 'Edward'.[125]

This may already have been of some antiquity, given the way in which goods passed to the Tower for storage – but it was clearly an item of great significance, and of enormous size. The same object can be traced through the household of Edward III to his son Thomas of Woodstock, and then in the goods of Richard II – it held some 3 gallons, and its cover was decorated with the royal helm.[126] More modestly, John de Berney, in his will of 1374, ensured that his wife Katherine was to have the mazer that she brought with her at their marriage.[127]

Mazers were also popular in ecclesiastical circles. Individuals and clerks left these cups to institutions, and we can trace the giving – and re-giving – of these vessels. John de Bleoburi, a clerk, made gifts to Wilton Abbey in his will of 1368. In particular he gave a nun there, Margaret de Calston, his greater mazer with a cover, and 10 marks to pray and distribute for his soul.[128] In 1371, Adam, the rector of Cawston, north-west of Norwich, bequeathed to Campsey Priory and the prioress there his black mazer, which Alesia, once the prioress there, had given to him.[129] In 1438, John Lovelich gave his sister – the Prioress of Markyate – his new gilt mazer, with a gilt foot, for the term of her life, and then to his kinswoman Margaret, also a nun there, for the term of her life, with a remainder to the house of Markyate where it was to be used to serve the prioress at her table to recall in prayer the testator's soul and those of his benefactors.[130]

When Cardinal Ottobuono, the papal legate, made his reforming canons of 1268, with regard to monastic refectories, he noted how monks and other religious, thinking themselves better than others and wishing to demonstrate it, had striven to use more precious vessels. He therefore ordered that no monk, nun or regular canon was to use a silver cup or something more precious in refectory or in other places, as if it were a personal possession, for all were equal.[131] How far this was followed is, however, an open question. It may have been an expectation that new members of the community would bring vessels like this with them. Expenses at the veiling of Joan, the daughter of Nicholas Sambourne, at Lacock in 1395–6, included the costs of a mazer and a silver spoon, along with clothing and bedding.[132]

The evidence from the cathedral priories at Canterbury and Norwich suggests that these cups had complex sets of associations. Drinking vessels in the refectories at these institutions had their own pedigrees, connected to

individual monks and benefactors, and this brought a special connection to
the act of drinking there. At Norwich, two inventories made in 1393–4 and
1410–11 give an overview of the refectory's goods.[133] In 1393–4, there was a
great silver gilt cup, weighing 1.563 kg (£4 16s 6d). There may have been a
second, of slightly lesser weight. Beyond that there were at least 18 silver
cups, along with two formed like a chalice, two great mazers, two nuts and
a mazer beaker. Another series of mazers followed, the first two described
as formerly 'heavenale and runnale', connected perhaps to a special brew, or
to part of a drinking ceremony.[134] There was a strong association between
wine and silver vessels;[135] mazers, on the other hand, were used for ale, but
possibly for other drinks too. In a further inventory of 1425 these were
described as 'beautiful mazers'.[136] The first inventory records who had given
the other mazers or whose they had previously been – and in some cases
whose they now were. For example, Richard de Middilton had the mazer
that had been that of the former prior, Simon Bozon (whose priorate ended
in 1353). There were further mazers in the prior's chamber.

The mazers at Canterbury Cathedral Priory, inventoried in 1328, offer a
parallel to those at Norwich.[137] There were prominent commemorative
links between the mazers and members of the Canterbury community. The
numbers of mazers at Norwich were fewer, and we can see less of the
connections to earlier monks than at Canterbury, but the brethren clearly
recalled who had held some of these objects and also the silver cups: they
may well have known the individuals concerned. Sometimes the connection was explicit. Alexander Tottington, Bishop of Norwich, who died in
1413 and who had been prior of Norwich Cathedral Priory before he
became bishop, bequeathed to the refectory at Norwich a silver gilt cup,
with a cover of cedar, decorated with silver and ebony, with the words
'Siphus Alexandri' ('Alexander's cup') inscribed on it.[138] Monastic refectories were focuses of commemoration: food and drink, in pittances, recalled
earlier benefactors; routines and rituals, like the maundy – commemorating
Christ's washing of the feet of the disciples at the Last Supper – or the presence at table of food for the deceased monk in the period immediately after
his death, emphasised these traditions.

To drink using these cups, therefore, was to evoke memories and connections. On the one hand, there were associations of family; on the other,

there were communal links. Food and drink were routinely blessed and sacralised in many household and institutional contexts. It was no accident that the vessels that were to hold these liquids were given such importance. The Eucharist made a formal and miraculous connection through drink with the blood of Christ – and created an exemplar which cannot have been far from the minds of those partaking of drink in a social context.

But drink did not only have these connections: aside from being one of life's essentials, it was widely enjoyed by medieval people. We can see the special attention they gave to preparing drinks, and the delight they must have inspired, a delight that some moralists dearly regretted. This range of associations and motives can be found with many other foodstuffs: on one level, commodities that might simply be essential could equally, with care and attention, acquire characteristics that might have far-reaching connections and consequences in medieval mentalities. Beyond drink, nowhere was this more true than with bread. Access to other commodities, such as meat and dairy foods, might be less certain, at least for some people some of the time, yet they too might attract investment and thought in preparation, as well as in wider associations. And it is to these commodities that the next chapter turns.

CHAPTER FOUR

BREAD, MEAT AND DAIRY FOODS

MOST PEOPLE IN THE later Middle Ages obtained most of their energy from cereals, all of them processed in some way, either ground as flour and then baked or added to pottage, malted for ale and beer, or as whole grains boiled, again, for pottage or other dishes. Bread was one of the most significant ways in which corn might be consumed, and it cannot but have featured prominently in the medieval mind. The daily bread of the Lord's Prayer was ever present in the liturgy, and the Eucharist itself, the body of Christ, was a transubstantiation of bread. Audiences for sermons were familiar with miracles centred on bread, from the five loaves and two fishes that fed the five thousand, to many later examples, like that recounted by Gregory the Great, about bread providentially supplied by St Laurence to feed the workmen rebuilding a church dedicated to him.[1] A fragment of bread from the Last Supper was obtained as a relic by Westminster Abbey in the early 1260s. William de Radnor, Bishop of Llandaff, having seen the relic for himself, offered a release from 40 days of penance for those who went to see it in the spirit of contrition – a release that was itself issued in 1262, on Maundy Thursday (the day on which the Church commemorated the Last Supper).[2] Westminster also made prominent reference to the miracle of the Feeding of the Five Thousand: it was among the miracles in the tapestries of the Life of Christ which the abbey was given for the choir area in 1246 by Abbot Richard of Berkyng, and it was depicted as well on the retable of the convent's high altar, with Christ and St Peter playing a central role, probably complete by 1269.[3] If bread was a staple food, however, it was also one where we can see a very great deal of variation, from methods of preparation to patterns of consumption.[4]

At one level, making bread or cereal-based cakes could happen around the domestic hearth, made, for example, on a bakestone by the distracted wife in *Hali meiðhad* early in the thirteenth century.[5] In practice, however, much baking appears to have been at least in part a commercial activity: many people expected to buy bread, or to take dough they had prepared to be baked elsewhere. At Great Shelford, in Cambridgeshire, in November 1342, Juliana Turling had left her house to buy bread, closing the door behind her; a chicken which remained in the house had scattered straw on the fire, which then set light to the building – and, disaster aside, she would have been typical of many.[6] If individuals prepared their own dough, they would have expected to pay to have access to ovens.[7] Ovens were expensive of fuel, and it made sense for them to be run at a capacity that would have far surpassed the requirements of most households except those of institutions and the elite (Plate 12): economics dictated that ovens were to be loaded as full as they could be, a practice referred to obliquely in the expression 'baken bred in cheke', that is, to stuff one's mouth full.[8]

In the preparation of dough there was likely to have been a good deal of skill and individual attention, and resulting differences in the finished product. What went into dough? One of the biggest sources of difference were the flours from which bread might be made – the different grains, the fineness of the flour, plus any additions. Bread of different qualities might be made from any of the grains, or mixtures of them (apart from deliberate mixtures, the maslins and dredges, medieval crops were far less homogeneous than present-day ones), as well as from beans and peas in times of dearth. All these breads might have different names, different destinations and different purposes; they might also have different baking procedures, such as hotter ovens, or multiple bakings. Wheat bread, at its finest, wastel loaves, pain-demaine and simnels, represented the highest quality. In the *Alphabet of Tales*, in its retelling of the story of Piers Toller and the beggars who wagered whether they could get anything from him, it was bread from a basket of rye loaves that Piers seized to throw at the beggar.[9] Loaves of barley, which produced a poorer and denser bread, were more commonly eaten by the peasantry before the Black Death.[10] Barley loaves were also often given in alms, baked for the purpose by institutions as special alms-loaves in a deliberate echo of the Feeding of the Five Thousand, where it was barley loaves that had been distributed (Plate 3).[11]

A further difference came from whether bread was leavened or not, and what form of leaven was employed. Two choices of leaven were available: sourdough and yeast from barm, a by-product of the brewing process. Sourdoughs, which resulted from yeasts found in the air acting on dough left exposed, with a portion of dough kept as a 'starter' to add to the next batch, were probably common in peasant homes, but we are not always clear about the process. In an injunction to avoid the fellowship of the wicked, as it would affect one's reputation, the *Ayenbite of Inwyt, c.*1340, made the analogy of yeast souring the dough and affecting its taste.[12] Bartholomew the Englishman noted that 'Sourdough is called *fermentum*, for it makes the paste ferment and causes it also to rise.' It had the the natural capacity 'to change and alter the taste thereof'.[13] 'Meal is ground at the mill and sifted with a sieve, and mixed with hot water and with sourdough to have the better taste, and is kneaded and moulded to the shape of loaves, and is then baked.'[14] Yeast from barm, occurring in the froth from the brewing process, must have been readily available, given the scale of brewing in late medieval England.[15]

The fifteenth-century translation of the *Book of the Knight of La Tour-Landry* gives a glimpse of bread-making. After an absence, a knight visited his two nieces, one of whom went to array herself before coming to see him – and took so long about it that he rode off; the other came straight to him just as she was – 'Notwithstanding this woman a little before, for her pleasure, took upon her to make levain for wheat bread, and with her hands as they were all floury, covered with the yeasty paste she had handled, came out just as she was with great joy and embraced him pleasantly in her arms' and made him welcome.[16] Note, too, the pleasure in making bread that is expressed here.

Walter de Bibbesworth describes some of the bread-making process, although he does not tell us how the dough was prepared. After the winnowing and milling of the grain, and the bolting of the meal, warm water was mixed with the flour, and the dough was kneaded. The oven was heated – using ferns if no straw was available, or pea-straw – and the dough placed inside using a peel, an implement like a long-handled spade.[17]

The contents of bakehouses – often located with brewhouses – record a common suite of equipment: kneading troughs, mould or moulding boards on which the dough would be worked and shaped, and bolting tuns for sifting the flour. There might be other tubs and containers, and querns as well, suggesting that far from all corn was milled outside the household. All these were present in the inventory of the bakehouse and brewhouse that belonged to Thomas Morton, a canon residentiary of York, in 1449, including two quern stones in a wooden case.[18] These implements in their domestic setting may have been associated with women, or they may have felt a strong practical interest in them. Stephen Motte of Linsted, in Kent, in October 1464, left a series of properties to his wife, Alice, for her life, but others to his son Piers. He added an important rider: 'Also I will that my wife shall not in any way take out of my property the quern or kneading trough.'[19] Pastry boards, where dough or 'paste' was worked, were found in larger households or institutions: in the household of Thomas Morton, the pastry board was in the kitchen;[20] at Norwich Cathedral Priory, at Michaelmas 1436, the 'pist-rilla', the small bakehouse (which also included brewing equipment) had two pairs of querns, a series of troughs and a vat to mix things in, a small pastry board and a moulding board.[21] 'Paste' might be other things besides dough: it might be no more than a mixture of flour and water, used for making cases or containers for food that was to be preserved, such as fresh-water fish or meat, which might then be transported; or mixtures that were to be cooked and then brought to table, like flans.[22] It might also signify special products, 'pastries', and there were specialist bakers, 'pastellers', for this work. Among the bakers hired for the annual feast of the guild of the Holy Cross at Stratford-upon-Avon in 1442–3 was a 'pastillator', a servant of Robert Palmer, one of the bakers that year, who was paid 6d for his labour.[23]

Much of what we know about the bread that was commercially available comes from municipal regulations and accounts of their infringement. The sale of bread was regulated in the first place by statute, the assize of bread, which provided a sliding scale which reduced the weight of a loaf as the price of corn rose. The size of the loaf was therefore expected to vary, but the expectation was also that if one had a penny, a penny loaf could always be bought, even if its size varied.[24] The proviso, however, was echoed in a fourteenth-century proverb: if a 'muid [measure] of wheat costs a penny, woe to he who doesn't have a penny'.[25] Beyond that, individual municipalities regulated the conduct of business, inspecting bread in their markets, weighing it and checking that it was sealed with the baker's mark that was required by statute.[26] Bread was also brought into towns by bakers from outside – and it seems likely by the start of the fifteenth century that in villages and small towns many bakers did come from outside. If capital investment was needed for ovens, it was essential to recoup it by ensuring effective distribution for sale – and bread was readily transportable. At Southampton, the civic ordinances of c.1300 required anyone who brought bread into the town by cart to sell it himself, by his own hand;[27] and at Norwich in 1454 the mayor declared before the civic assembly the scandal that the loaves of the country bakers were heavier than those baked in the city.[28] Despite municipal regulation, we should expect to see considerable variation among breads, in terms of size and shape, especially in those not made for sale but within households and institutions: some of these loaves are discussed in later chapters.

Bread, as a key foodstuff, had a special place in medieval mentalities. In what was presumably a wry observation on the Sermon on the Mount, a fourteenth-century proverb tells us that 'The meek will have their bread in another oven.'[29] A further proverb notes that 'Good service will receive paindemaine', the household loaf in the great household, often given as a reward.[30] The importance of not wasting this commodity is reflected in a saying about the preparation of loaves, of the process of removing the crust, which acted in the same way as modern packaging: 'The more crust, the less crumb' (the crumb was the soft interior of the loaf). The asperity of the diet of the peasantry is neatly summed up in the expression 'Hot vegetables make hard crusts soft.'[31] Another proverb made a link between hard bread and digestion – 'A crokyd cake makyth a stronge wombe': tough bread makes a tough stomach, that is, a tough lesson makes you strong.[32] The daily bread was, therefore, never far from the consciousness of medieval people.

Meat and its preservation

In manorial custumals, foods provided by the lord that might be eaten with bread at labour services undertaken by peasants were given the general term 'companagium'. Literally 'food that goes with bread', often loosely (and obscurely) translated as 'relish', it suggested an indeterminate accompaniment, and one that may have varied, perhaps sometimes meat, or dairy foods like cheese.[33] In practice, however, the consumption of meat was closely linked to status: eating fresh meat, and meat from young animals, or meat that came from hunting, was regarded as prestigious. But eating any meat at all was also at some points a mark of status, especially in England from the end of the thirteenth century to the middle of the fourteenth century – the Black Death marks a transition from a society in which meat was highly esteemed, yet little was available to most people, to an economy in which increasing amounts of meat, to the point of excess, might be available, at least some of the time.

There was a distinction between the meat of quadrupeds – which was typically dealt with commercially by butchers – and poultry, the province of poulterers. It was a distinction that might be obscured on the street, especially when foods were for sale already cooked, for example, in the cries of cooks and their assistants, 'Hot pies, hot! Good geese and piglets! Go we dine, go we!'[34] Different economic patterns lay behind these two trades, as well as the theological ones outlined in Chapter 1. If the livestock trade might be in the hands of butcher-graziers, or large-scale pastoral farmers, poultry production was typically the province of the peasantry, and it was unusual to find flocks of hens larger than those from the barnyard.[35] When the guild of the Holy Cross at Stratford-upon-Avon wanted to assemble poultry for its annual feast, its officers had to trawl the country round about: in 1468–9, the young geese were bought from no fewer than 20 individuals, in quantities ranging from four up to 20.[36]

The care given to livestock destined for meat shows the interest of medieval people in the quality of their food. As a fifteenth-century text, *A myrour to lewde men and wymmen*, noted, 'The ox that men will keep will be fed hard food and put under the yoke, but the ox that is destined for the larder will be fed the best food and feel no labour.'[37] Pigs were only ever kept for meatstock and were usually fattened up in the autumn, shortly before slaughter: on the Battle Abbey manor of Barnhorne, in Sussex, in 1342–3, 2*s* 4*d* was spent on acorns for fattening the pigs, although at other times the abbey bought pigs directly for the larder rather then raising them on its own estates.[38] Some animals that were killed were destined for immediate consumption. Sir Robert Plumpton, writing to his wife, Agnes, on 9 September 1502, asked for eight sheep and one head of cattle to be killed ready for supper the following Tuesday, 13 September.[39] But in many cases, the intention must have been to preserve the meat for consumption at a later date – there would simply have been too much meat to eat fresh from the carcasses of cattle, unless there was a large gathering to feed – and, in addition, there was a pragmatic calculation, whether to feed an animal through the winter before killing it or whether to kill it and preserve the flesh. Killing for immediate consumption was therefore often not an attractive option. The process of fattening animals for slaughter, butchery, the preservation of the carcass for meat and the use of as much of the animal as possible either for food or for other purposes, such as leather, created a range of distinctive practices.

Who were the butchers? Outside the major towns, at least before the Black Death, there were few professional butchers. There might be individuals on estates who butchered animals, but this was only one of their tasks. At Bleadon, Somerset, a manor of Winchester Cathedral Priory, early in the fourteenth century, the keeper of the cattle ('pastor') – if the lord was proposing to kill animals in his custody to stock the seigneurial larder – was to have from each animal slaughtered a series of customary perquisites: the neck, the blood, two pieces of meat (the 'hasting-sticche' – a piece for roasting – and another piece known as the 'revelsticche'), five parts of the small intestine, the large intestine and various other entrails, possibly also a loaf, or a loaf served with entrails (the 'pane bachþerm', to be as long as the distance from the elbow to the hand). Although the keeper of the cattle was not described as the butcher, that he received perquisites like this from each animal suggests he had a close involvement with the butchery.[40] Indeed, it seems that before the Black Death there may well have been peripatetic butchers in the countryside. In a fable told by Odo of Cheriton, c 1220, the farmer's ass was disenchanted that the pig had better food than him, while doing no work; the ass played sick and received better food, but repented rapidly when the farmer brought a butcher with his axe and knife to despatch the pig.[41] Larger institutions had butchers on their staff, or paid a retainer to them.[42] At Durham Cathedral Priory, approximately £115 worth of cattle were purchased by the cellarer in 1438–9, and Thomas and John

Proudlok were paid 26s 8d together as butchers.[43] In 1443–4, the transition had been made almost to a 'butcher-grazier': Durham's caterer, its principal purchasing officer, was also a butcher, and doubtless managed the supply of livestock.[44] In the fifteenth century, both Norwich Cathedral Priory and Durham Cathedral Priory had their own slaughterhouses.[45]

To have one's own butcher may have been more than convenience: John Gower in the *Mirour de l'omme* expressed his outrage at the charges made by butchers, at least twice what they should have been.[46] Lydgate's description of 'vulgar butchers, all sprayed with blood' tells us further of the experience of preparing meat.[47] The butcher was reputedly accompanied by his dog. The early fifteenth-century *Master of Game* talks about the great butchers' dogs, necessary for rounding up escaped cattle. These animals had a reputation for ferocity, and images conjuring up their bloody mouths confirm, like hounds, they were fed in part on the entrails from the animals their masters butchered.[48] Town councils demanded they be tethered at night.[49] In the words of *The pilgrimage of the lyf of the manhode*, 'You never saw in your life mastiff or bitch in a butcher's shop that would so gladly eat raw flesh as I eat it.'[50]

There was extensive municipal regulation of butchery. At Norwich, in February 1441, the city's butchers were forbidden from selling meat except at the accustomed place in the market, that is, the marketplace by St Peter Mancroft, except for those who came from outside the city, who were only allowed to make sales on Saturday. As with many regulations to do with the retail trade in food and drink, the butchers were not allowed to forestall the market by buying meat from outsiders before it could be brought to sale.[51] In 1458, complaints about the dearness of meat were made against Norwich's butchers, that they sold 'a sheep's head and meat that might be cooked or roasted' for 1½d and 2d respectively, to the great harm of poor. Summoned before the mayor and aldermen they were ordered to make amends.[52]

A major contrast between the English experience of shopping for meat and that in southern Europe was that in England meat was sold by the piece, by the joint, and by estimate, rather than by weight – until 1529, when the system was changed.[53] The archival record tells us increasingly about the patterns of butchery and the sale of joints of meat. There are comparatively few references to named joints in the first half of the fourteenth century, perhaps reflecting the fact that those whose accounts we have principally had their own livestock butchered for them, rather than buying in the market. Large animals such as oxen were first quartered, and then each quarter might be cut into four again – a tild (probably from the Anglo-Norman French 'tille', an axe or hatchet) – which might then be divided into four strokes.[54] When we have accounts recording purchases in the market, or piecemeal, for example, for the corporation of Rye in the fifteenth century, we can see a range of joints. In 1455, entertaining the lieutenant of the Cinque Ports, the corporation bought ribs of beef and a leg of veal; a similar entertainment in 1456 included two quarters of mutton, a forequarter of mutton and three quarters of lamb; and for 1459, a butcher supplied an ox's dewlap.[55] Cuts of meat were available in small quantities in inns. In 1480, returning from the brother guild at Romney, members of Rye's corporation had a homecoming supper which included a breast of veal, a side of lamb and a rack and a breast (of lamb) in a stew.[56] Cookbooks and accounts give us references to pestles, loins and fillets ('the loin of pork is from the hip bone to the head ... the fillets are those that are taken out of the pestles'), hocks and sirloins, shoulders of mutton, and marrowbones.[57] These references are indicative of the development of butchery in the second half of the fourteenth and fifteenth centuries, and of the commercial availability of small quantities of meat.

Beyond flesh meat itself, as much of the carcass as possible was used. The Le Strange household at Hunstanton, in Norfolk, bought beef from Alan Grey in the week of 22 January 1346, with a further purchase of a cow's belly and four cow's feet; a similar purchase was made in the week of 10 February 1348.[58] Lesser cuts and offal all had a purpose – the cow's feet would have produced gelatine – and there were further products derived from offal. If butchers were male, those working with offal were often women, and they had a reputation for the quality of the special preparations they made. At St Augustine's Abbey, Canterbury, in the mid thirteenth century, women were employed when the larder was made, that is, animals were slaughtered and the meat was preserved. The women were there to clean the entrails of the pigs and the cattle, and to make the puddings (like black pudding, 'boudin') from them.[59] This was women's work par excellence. Robert de Graystanes provides a vignette from around 1280 of women squabbling at the stream while washing the intestines of animals, intestines or 'manifolds' destined to become chitterlings.[60] At Durham Cathedral Priory, in the mid-fifteenth century, a succession of women were entrusted with the responsibility for the entrails of the animals that had been slaughtered – and they were probably engaged in working with this offal for sale. They also had family connections with those purchasing food, especially livestock, for the priory. In 1438–9, it was Thomas Bawde who accounted for the sale of entrails (worth 73s 4d); but in 1440–1, it was Alice Bawde, probably Thomas's widow.[61] In 1443, the wife of Robert Tyddeswell, the priory's butcher, received a fee of 1s 8d (for half a year) for the sale of the fees of the kitchen, the perquisites from the meats.[62] She received the fee for the full year in 1444–5;[63] and she accounted for the fees of the kitchen range that had been sold along with the entrails in 1445–6 and for the next three accounting years.[64] Yvette Broun was responsible for the sales in 1455–6;[65] and then, from 1459–60 to 1462–3, Isabella Levechild accounted for the sales and Margaret Levechild received the priory's fee for this work.[66] In 1465–6 the business had passed to Elizabeth Dixon, who continued to conduct it until at least 1479–80. There may also have been a family connection here: Nicholas Dixon is recorded as the priory's purchaser of victuals, the caterer, in 1475–6 and 1478–9.[67] That these products might be popular across the board is well illustrated by a present from Mistress Davys to Queen Elizabeth, the wife of Henry VII, of puddings and chines of pork.[68]

Meat dishes based on filled entrails were commercially available: the entrails were not simply kept and prepared by cooks within the household for consumption.[69] Cookshops were an important element in food provision in medieval towns and cities, although their reputations were varied. They sold a wide range of prepared foods, from pies and puddings to elite foodstuffs, such as roast bitterns (Plate 5).[70] A remark by Wyclif, discussing the failings of prelates, noted the sale of papal pardons, with the excuse that the charge was for the sealing, not for the pardon itself – and in his outrage he made a comparison to a popular dish of goose, stuffed with garlic, retailed at one of these shops: 'They sell a fat goose for little or nought, but the garlic costs many shillings.'[71]

Offal-based dishes were widely consumed. Haggis had a distribution across England in the Middle Ages, and, indeed, was a popular English dish into the eighteenth century. One treatise on vocabulary, from the middle of the thirteenth century, instructed the cook on how to use a fleshhook to take the haggis out of the posnet (in which it had been boiling).[72] The haggis might also be found in a gentry or upper-class environment: on the Sunday after the feast of St Valentine, 1348, one was bought for 2*d* for the household of John de Multon of Frampton in Lincolnshire – and it appeared in recipe books in the first part of the fifteenth century, where it was made in part from sheep's entrails.[73] Some of these dishes were demotic foods, travelling up the social scale. Other entrails were used for popular dishes, such as 'umbles' or 'noumbles' of deer, based on the organ meat[74] – or might be eaten by themselves as part of popular refreshment. The churchwardens of St Mary's, Sandwich, in Kent, paid at Easter 1449 for a refreshment for the choir after High Mass of a calf's head, a calf's gather – that is, the pluck (heart, liver and lungs) – along with bread and ale.[75]

How was meat preserved? Preparing the larder divided up the meat that was for long-term preservation from those elements that would be handled separately, such as offal, and other parts that would probably be eaten within a short compass of time. Crucial here were the salting of meat, its preservation in various salt-based liquors, and the drying and smoking of meat. At Norwich Cathedral Priory, in 1436, the larder overseen by the sacrist had a trough with lead at the bottom and a cover of timber, three vats for salting flesh, and a little tub 'pro le sous' – for preparing a salt liquor (Plate 15).[76] A supply of salt was critical for the preservation of meat and fish, and large quantities were consumed to this end. In 1443–4, the cellarer of Durham spent 25*s* 10*d* at Newcastle on 5 qrs 3 pks of coarse salt, along with carriage;[77] in 1447–8, 4*d* on a sieve for coarse salt;[78] and by 1465–6 the priory had a salt-house for storage of this commodity and possibly also for foodstuffs that were in the process of being salted.[79]

Salt was produced at many locations round the English coast as well as inland, at salt pits and mines.[80] At Bicker, on the Lincolnshire coast, in August 1356, Thomas de Wigan of Bicker was driving a horse and cart, in which there was a saltpan – for evaporating brine, to leave behind the salt crystals – when the cart overturned in a ditch. The saltpan was appraised at 6*s*, the same value as the cart.[81] Saltpans could be very productive. The Bishop of Winchester's manor of Bitterne, in Hampshire, with marshy land close to the mouth of the River Itchen, where salt production was an important industry, had, in 1210–11, 240 sesters (quarters) of salt in hand at the start of the accounting year; nearby Bishop's Waltham had just over 300 sesters, of which 152 had come as rent from Burslerdon, on the River Hamble. Thirty-three sesters at the palace at Bishop's Waltham were then used for the larder and more than four more on salting venison; 91 sesters were sent to the bishop's palace at Wolvesey.[82]

The primary function of salt was to absorb the moisture in the meat, creating an environment in which bacteria and fungi could not function due to lack of water; it also had an impact on the speed of oxidisation, slowing down the rate at which meat might become rancid. The *Proverbs of Alfred*, a Middle English work of c.1150–65, probably from Sussex, describing the effects of over-indulgence in drink, turned to the process of salting: 'Sorrow soaks through him as does salt into meat, it is sucked through his body as the leech sucks blood, and his morning's sleep will be long-lasting, whoever in the evening has drunk to excess.'[83] Salt from different places had different qualities: finer salts ('white' or 'minute' salt) absorbed the moisture faster than coarse salt, which was often known as 'Bay salt': some came from the Bay of Bourgneuf, but the term was probably applied to salt from coastal saltpans more generally. Fine salts were more expensive: the household of John de Vere, twelfth Earl of Oxford, in 1431–2, used 7 qrs 5 bus. of coarse salt and 3 qrs of fine salt.[84] The nuances of the process would have had an impact on taste and flavour, and medieval salters are known to have used a combination of different salts to achieve their effect. Different concentrations had different consequences for preservation. A set of instructions from c.1381 for preserving venison – butchered in the field – recommended covering it as soon as possible with bracken, to keep the air off it; then bringing it home as soon as possible, taking it to a cellar to dismember it so that sun and wind were excluded. There it was to be left in clean water for half a day and placed on hurdles to dry. It was then to be salted as required, including boiling it in a brine – as salty as water of the sea and much more. The expectation was that it would rest in this solution for three days and nights, after which it was taken out, salted with dry salt in a barrel – and the barrel was then to be sealed lest the sun and the wind get to the meat.[85] A lighter salting, sometimes described as 'powdering', was all that was necessary for meats (and fish) that were only to be preserved in the short term.[86]

One recipe collection advised 'powdering' for keeping goose meat over-night, almost as a marinade: 'Powder it with salt for the night and, in the morning, wash off the salt.'[87]

Much of this salting aimed to produce what was essentially a dry cure. It might be combined with smoking, particularly in the preservation of flitches of bacon, hung up in peasant houses. In the debate poem *Wynnere and Wastoure*, probably from between 1352 and 1370, Wastoure, who eats and drinks extravagantly, presents an impressive image of plenty, 'The beams bending at the roof, such bacon there hangs'.[88] Wet cures were used with some pork butchery, as a way of preserving parts of the pig other than the sides that were destined to become hams and bacon. A series of allegations made at the visitation of Fotheringhay College, Northamptonshire, in September 1438 refers to piglets preserved in pickle ('in salsamento'). John Redburne, the college's steward, was said to have consumed the common food of the college in his own house. Richard Assheby, one of the fellows, believed that he had recently seen the heads of three piglets, in pickle, which he thought had come from the college. Master William Appeltone, another fellow, reported that eight days previously a servant woman had secretly taken from the college to Redburne's house a breast of mutton and three piglets' heads, of which one had been lost on the way. Margaret, the wife of John Wengrave of Fotheringhay, aged 29, recounted how Ellen, Redburne's 18-year-old servant, had brought in her lap a piglet's head, which she declared had fallen from the lap ('a gremio') of little Joan, Redburne's daughter, and they ate it together – little Joan had been carrying three pigs' heads and a breast of mutton from the cook of the college. Further, John Toune, a fellow of the college, had encountered a servant carrying the head and hind quarter of a sucking pig to Redburne's house.[89] Aside from the information this incident provides us with about means of preserving pork, it is striking that it is the women of Redburne's household who are involved in this incident at each point.

At the Benedictine nunnery of Barking, in the mid fifteenth century, the nuns were entitled to special liveries from the 'sowsse' at what must have been the making of the larder, or at least pork butchery, at Martinmas (11 November). From the Abbess's kitchen, every nun was to have the cheek, the ear and the foot; or the snout and two feet; a whole hog was to serve three nuns. The nuns were to have further liveries from the 'sows' (the parts preserved in brine) of the pigs killed for the convent's cellaress: the Abbess's kitchen had at least 13 pigs, possibly 14, and the cellaress was to have another 9 or 10 pigs killed at this time.[90]

Some animals, or parts of animals, were associated with consumption at particular times, or for special celebrations. Boar's heads were used at prominent feasts: the household of Dame Katherine de Norwich, for example, in 1336 had one at the feast of her name saint, Katherine (25 November), one on the first Sunday in Advent (1 December) and was given one for the great feast she held to mark the obit – the commemoration of the dead on the anniversary of their decease – of her second husband on 20 January 1337.[91] The household of John de Multon of Frampton had a boar's head and half a boar on the Sunday after Christmas in 1343.[92] Bishops, such as Richard Mitford of Salisbury, in 1407, might have lamb served on Easter Day.[93] Although this might reflect the new availability of the meat (and the ability to eat it after Lent), it also echoed a wider tradition in Western Christendom, marking the risen Christ, the Lamb of God: in the ninth century, popes had distributed roast lamb at this time, but by the thirteenth century this had been replaced by a wax lamb, with the pope's name impressed into it.[94] The period of abstinence occasioned by Lent shaped consumption in particular ways. If Shrove Tuesday, the day before the start of Lent, was the last day of the consumption of eggs and dairy food, Collop Monday, the preceding day, was marked for the eating of slices (collops) of meat – usually ham or bacon. The combination of egg and bacon was a typical peasant dish.[95] The dish was so popular that at Nettleham, just outside Lincoln, the rector provided and blessed boiled eggs and collops before Mass on Easter Day – breaking the convention that food was not to be taken until after the first Mass of the day had been said.[96]

There was a strong element of seasonality to the butchery of meat, fattening up and culling animals that would not be kept through the winter. The autumn slaughter, often linked to the feast of St Martin (Martinmas: 11 November), matched peaks in the trade of livestock in the fourteenth and fifteenth centuries, even if individual markets may have had different rhythms or specialisms.[97] The period from the end of September to November was also a peak time for the rustling of animals fattened in pasture, ready for sale. In 1345, William Purlok of Clopton – who turned 'approver', or informer, confessing to a series of crimes implicating others, too, in the hope of leniency – recounted how, just before Michaelmas 1341, he and four others stole 19 cattle in Northamptonshire and drove them to be sold at the Michaelmas fair at Stortford (he had done something similar the previous year with 31 young cattle); also in 1341, just before Martinmas, along with two others, he stole 67 sheep belonging to the Abbot of Warden and drove them to St Neots, where they were sold to a butcher, who knew them to be stolen.[98] It was not surprising, then, that precautions were taken. The cellarer of Durham paid 4s 4d for watching the animals for fear of robbers in nearby pastures between Michaelmas and Martinmas 1443.[99] 'Meat of St Martin' had other uses beyond food: it was employed in medical recipes, for example, as part of a preparation that was to be laid on dead flesh to destroy it (salt mutton was another possibility), and one imagines that it was the action of the salt that was particularly sought after.[100]

Suet and fat, reserved as part of the butchery process, were used both as a cooking medium, to enhance dishes, and as a major element in them. In the latter case, it was especially significant in monastic diet: historically, it was the first food derived from quadrupeds that Benedictine monks had been permitted to consume.[101] At Norwich Cathedral Priory, the daily food accounts for 1284–5 and 1326–7 show fat – lard or suet ('seym' and 'adeps') – eaten some weeks on every flesh day, and in substantial quantity. On Sunday 1 October 1284, 1s of the day's expenditure of 19s 6½d went on fat; the following day it was 2s out of 25s 3d; on Tuesday it was 1s out of 18s 5¼d; and on Thursday 1s out of 16s 7d.[102] At the visitation of Elstow Abbey in January 1443, one of the nuns, Rose Asteby, reported that on the days when they ate in the refectory they ate larded food ('commedunt adipata') in the mornings and for supper they had meat – capons and other two-legged creatures; this was the reverse of what might have been expected, although the arrangements for eating poultry were more flexible than those for the meat and products of quadrupeds.[103] We know little of how these fats were processed, but some were salted.[104] One recipe, from the mid-fifteenth century, describes taking thin slices of lard of venison and laying them on a dough, almost like a checker board, before putting on top of it a stuffing of chicken, pork, eggs, salt and cheese – to be followed by other stuffings for each of the four quarters, and by a layer of meat.[105] In August 1505, the treasurer of Henry VII's chamber paid a reward of 3s 4d to a woman who clarified deer suet for the king – a further example of the association of women with the handling of offal and also of the special skills they had in food preparation.[106]

Dairying

White meat – dairy produce – was highly sought after and much enjoyed in the later Middle Ages. As a source of protein, the contribution of dairy foods to diet might be significant, but in the century and a half before the Black Death the evidence is that they were of modest importance. Monastic diets, such as that at Beaulieu Abbey in 1269–70, encompassed a daily allowance of just over 63 grams (2¼ oz) of cheese and just under 14 grams (½ oz) of butter per monk/lay brother in the periods when dairy foods were eaten.[107] These figures speak of the lack of livestock compared to the size of the human population: within this, the proportion of livestock that might devoted to dairying was not large. The Black Death changed this ratio: 40 to 50 per cent of the human population died while the numbers of livestock were relatively unchanged, at least at first. It is difficult, however, to establish the exact position of dairying in the economy, as it is not usually described in our main sources, the records of lords' estates – because lords increasingly found it more profitable to lease their dairying herds than to market the produce themselves. Nonetheless, it looks as if it remained significant. While cheese might be a premium product, it was more difficult for individuals – as opposed to great estates – to market their foods over distance: the great Norman abbeys had cheese carried from their English estates back across the Channel.[108] Buttermen and buttermongers, both male and female, retailed their products in neighbouring towns. 'Buttershops' in Chester served for the retail of dairy foods, an area identified from 1270 on, but in later centuries also served for the sale of other goods.[109] As part of the marketing process, butter may have been marked (just as loaves carried a mark to indicate who had made them), or there was equipment to mark it as it was portioned out – a 'buttir marke' is listed in the late fifteenth-century English-Latin wordbook known as the

Catholicon Anglicum.[110] Cheese might also be marked: Thomas Billop writing to Sir William Plumpton in August 1469 noted that six of the cheeses he was sending had two marks, which he thought indicated they were the best of them.[111]

Dairy goods might still travel long distances. Queen Isabella, the wife of Edward II, sent cheese from Brie from Westminster to Yorkshire as a gift to Lady Isabella de Vesci: it was wrapped in canvas and packed in baskets before being taken on horseback.[112] In November 1439, however, a statute of Richard II that had made Calais the staple, or point through which cheese, butter and honey for export should be traded, was repealed, on the grounds that cheese and butter did not keep well awaiting sale.[113] It was to Calais, however, in 1480 that John Cely sent a cheese to George Cely in a wool ship, as a gift for George's host, John Parker.[114]

Milk might be consumed directly in modest quantities, as noted in Chapter 3, but much dairy work was about separating off the cream and making butter and cheese, saving it for consumption at a later date – and working with the by-products of this process, whey and butter-milk. Milk came from cows, sheep and goats, although there were many fewer of the last (Plate 13).[115] Milking was carried out by both men and women: the construction of byres, with stalls, would have facilitated this, and these were in use at manorial level, even if peasant buildings were less likely to have them.[116] In July 1361, in Alvingham in Lincolnshire, John, the son of Richard Souter of Alvingham, came across a woman milking a cow in what was probably a garden, called Staggarth – he struck the cow with his hand and it gored him.[117] The *Husbandry*, a text possibly assembled *c.*1300 for the auditors on the estates of Ramsey Abbey, expected the dairy to function all the year round, but with a reduced yield outside the period from the beginning of May to the end of September – noting that it was better to sell the milk in the period after Christmas, as it would fetch a higher price than milk sold at other times. The dairymaids were expected to produce cheese and butter in a ratio of 7:1. Implicit in this calculation was the skimming of the cream from the milk so that it could be used for butter before the remainder (the butter-milk) was turned into cheese.[118] Walter of Henley's *Husbandry* of *c.*1275–90 expected a larger proportion of butter, with implications for the type of cheese that could be made.[119]

There was a long association between women and dairying. The manorial dairy maid, the *daie*, was frequently the only woman among the directly employed manorial servants. Homiletic references link her to sexual misconduct,[120] and auditors clearly had difficulty in keeping track of dairy work, although it may have been male dairy servants as much as female who committed frauds. A treatise on manorial accounting in a manuscript of about 1260 demonstrated how an ambitious and deceitful dairy servant might make cheese for himself or herself, as well as for the lord, by reserving a part of the milk each day.[121] Walter of Henley warned against servants, reeves and dairymaids, who denied the levels of dairy production that he believed were possible.[122] Perhaps it was not incredible to the auditors to imagine the witch and her slop, the magic bag that suckled the milk of men's cows out in the pasture morning and evening, recounted in Robert of Brunne's *Handlyng synne* at the start of the fourteenth century.[123] On the other hand, the poor widow in the Nun's Priest's Tale is marked as virtuous by her diet, among which dairy foods were prominent – she was almost like a dairywoman.

> Her board was provisioned mostly with white and black –
> Milk and brown bread, in which she found no lack,
> Smoked bacon, and sometimes an egg or two,
> For she was, as it were, a dairymaid on a manor.[124]

This involvement of women can be seen, for example, in the fifteenth-century records of the guild of the Holy Cross at Stratford-upon-Avon. For its annual feast it regularly bought dairy foods, especially milk and cream. In 1495–6, milk, cream (at least 8½ gallons) and curds were purchased from five individuals, four of whom were women.[125]

Inventories of dairies show the equipment of dairymaids and a little of the processes in which they were engaged. Here can be found an abundance of bowls; cheese 'vats', open-topped containers for straining and shaping curds (of wickerwork or cloth – cheese-cloth), with the curd sometimes pressed down with stones; and storage arrangements, such as racks for cheeses, and in places sometimes separate buildings designated as cheese-houses.[126] A miracle of Thomas Becket centred round a lost cheese – that had been placed by a child in a very old butter-churn.[127] As we saw in Chapter 2, these activities might go on in ordinary peasant households too. Large earthenware pans, full of heated milk, were a hazard from Lincolnshire to Wiltshire.[128] The separation of cream, the churning of butter, the pressing of curds, the preparation of whey, were all part of these processes. Medical texts saw the operation of rennet – cheeselip – on milk as analogous to the way embryos were created in the human body: 'Just as rennet and milk make a cheese, so both the sperm of man and woman create an embryo.'[129] The etymology of 'cheeselip' suggests that rennet had its origin in a herb, perhaps ladies' bedstraw, although animal-derived rennet was doubtless in use too.[130] Some salt was also important as a preservative for many butters and cheeses. 'Foul salt is good enough for foul butter' ran one mid fifteenth-century proverb.[131]

Special store was set by the product of different times of the year. May butter was held to be sweet – it was probably not salted, but produced in sufficient abundance for some to be intended for immediate consumption, and was sought out particularly for sweet dishes[132] and for medical preparations, especially as ointments and creams. A mid fifteenth-century collection of medical recipes specifies, for preparations for curing wounds, 'Take May butter, made of raw cream, and ewe's milk with dew water, and if you cannot get butter of ewe's milk, take butter of cow's milk'; and for stickiness of the eyes, a cream or ointment was prepared based on 'raw cream of ewe's milk in May' or, if that was not available, then May butter from ewe's milk.[133] A further recipe from the same collection uses 'marsh' butter ('March' butter is another possibility, but perhaps less likely) as part of an ointment for the stomach area.[134]

Parts of the country rich in marshes were famed for dairy products. Walter of Henley's *Husbandry* expected up to 50 per cent more in dairy products from cattle and sheep pastured on salt marsh than elsewhere.[135] When the household of Robert de Vere, Earl of Oxford, was in Essex in the August and September of 1273, there was dairy produce in abundance. On the feast of the Assumption of the Virgin Mary (15 August) there were two cheeses bought for the pantry and the kitchen; a further one was used in some form of sport, weighing Janekim, probably one of the younger members of the household – as it was accounted as expended, eating the cheese was an element in the activity. Two further cheeses were taken with the Earl to Canfield.[136] In *Piers Plowman*, when Envy asks for penance, and to be shriven – he is ashamed. 'I would be gladder, by God, that Gybbe had misfortune, than if I had this week won a wey of Essex cheese.'[137] In the fifteenth century, the county's most prominent nunnery, Barking, required special provisions of butter to be made for the celebration of Easter, Whitsun and the feast of St Ethelburga (11 October).[138] The nuns' marshland alongside the Thames was held to be especially valuable. Butter from the cows that grazed on Hackney Marshes was famed: John Russell's *Boke of nurture* recommended sweet butter of 'Claynos' (Clayness) or Hackney as an accompaniment for salt fish, stockfish, whiting and mackerel.[139]

Those responsible for making butter and cheese probably changed little in the later Middle Ages. In the 1430s, Rilley, a manor of the cellarer of Durham Cathedral Priory, was not leased out, but was assigned for the production of butter and cheese for the house.[140] The serjeant of the manor, John Wynȝard, and his wife were paid 20s for making butter and cheese in 1443–4.[141]

What did cheese look like? Fables, recycled from Aesop through the thirteenth and fourteenth centuries by Odo of Cheriton, Nicholas Bozon and John Sheppey, Bishop of Rochester, repeated the story of the crow, with a cheese in its beak, and the fox, that flattered the crow to show off its beautiful song – and to drop its cheese. These tell us about the size of some cheeses as well as vanity. Even if this was an ancient story, it was one that was still plausible to its medieval audiences.[142] The tale of Nicholas Bozon of the fox that tricked a sheep into believing that there was a large cheese in a well – the reflection of the moon – and that it was good and flavoursome, indicates a common shape and colour for cheese, and offers the proverb 'For it was never my way to find cheese in a well' – perhaps meaning to look for something in the wrong place, but more probably meaning not to be easily deceived.[143] These may have been small cheeses that were made from sheep's milk, but the reflection in the well may also have looked like green cheese, an unripe cheese. The burlesque known as the Feast of Tottenham, of fifteenth-century date, talks of cheese rind in charlet, 'as red as any scarlet' – the colour may refer to the spicing of the charlet, but it may possibly also be the colour of the rind.[144]

Cheese had different characteristics at different times of the year. Its age was significant for those consuming it. In his encyclopaedia, which circulated widely in late medieval Europe, Bartholomew the Englishman discussed dairy products in general and those of each milk-producing animal (from camels to pigs). His information was based largely on the *Etymologies* of Isidore of Seville (d.636) and the dietaries of Isaac Israëli (d.*c*.932), and underlying his statements was the notion that all things were composed, in differing proportions, of the four humours, and that a correct diet was needed to balance what one consumed with the humoral make-up of one's body – the composition of which was individual and hence variable from person to person. Bartholomew concluded that old cheese was 'sharp and dry'; milky cheese moistened the stomach; new – green – cheese was least strong in taste and easiest to digest. Cheese without salt was the most nourishing.[145] The instructions contained in John Russell's *Boke of nurture* made a series of distinctions about the qualities of these foods: cream, from cows and goats, was not to be eaten in the evening; but hard cheese was an aperient and was a good conclusion to a meal, especially eaten with white bread. Likewise hard cheese was to be eaten after milk, cream, curds, junket and posset, all of which closed a man's stomach.[146] Dairy foods were often used as ingredients in other recipes: from the sweet creams popular in elite cookery books, combining cream with, for example, egg yolks, sugar and saffron,[147] through to the flans which had a prominent position in ecclesiastical food.[148]

Works of courtesy also tell us how dairy foods were to be eaten. A Latin poem from the late twelfth century advised that old cheese be cut thin, but fresh cheese thick. One was to eat it with bread, not by itself, unless he were the lord. It was bad manners to press either cheese or butter into the bread with one's thumb; rather, it should be spread either with a knife or with a crust of bread if it were soft. The bread and cheese should be held with a cloth, so that once the crust had been taken from the bread, the cheese might be placed inside the crumb.[149]

There can be no doubt that dairy foods were enjoyed by all, but the food-stuffs were associated first with the countryside, and secondly especially with women and with the clergy. The household of Anne Stafford, dowager Duchess of Buckingham, bought cream by itself in June 1465;[150] between 1 June and 14 July milk and cream were bought for junket for the Duchess;[151] and towards the end of August an account was settled for 14*d* worth of butter, milk, cream and fresh cheese for 'pastis', perhaps 'pastries'.[152] Cheese was one of the most common provisions at entertainments, appearing at occasions like boon feasts for harvest workers,[153] and at municipal celebrations for benefactors.[154] The portability of cheese made it very suitable for eating outdoors, or taking on journeys: along with beer and bread, cheese was in the picnics provided at Rye for the boats going out to accompany the launch of Henry VII's new warship, the *Regent*, in August 1488.[155] Special associations, now obscure, led to dairy-related personal names, such as John Buttermouth,[156] Geoffrey Cheese and Bread,[157] and William Cheesecrumb.[158]

Dairy foods were not to be eaten in Lent, although they might be eaten on other days of abstinence. There were comparatively few formal dispensations from this, but this may be because there was already a good deal of latitude in terms of abstinence. In 1464 and 1466, two widowed noblewomen, daughters of Richard Beauchamp, Earl of Warwick – Eleanor, the widow of the Duke of Somerset, and Margaret, Countess of Shrewsbury – obtained papal dispensations to eat meat, eggs and dairy produce in Lent and on other days of abstinence on account of the frailty of their condition.[159] In distinction to this orthodox position, while followers of the Lollard heresy believed that all God's creatures might be eaten at any time of year, some chose to blur their position by eating dairy foods on days of abstinence, rather than betraying it by eating meat.[160]

These usages of dairy foods are reminders of the imperatives underlying diet: morality and religious belief were important determinants. Yet it is equally clear that there was enjoyment to be had in all foodstuffs, from breads to meat in all its forms, and a wide range of dairy foods. The next chapter looks at a group of foodstuffs that posed a particular problem from a moral perspective – sauces and spices, along with sugars and preserves. However necessary they were for the long-term preservation of food, inherent in many forms of these was sensory stimulation, and it was the temptations that they brought which particularly excited religious commentators.

CHAPTER FIVE

SAUCES AND SPICES, SUGARS AND PRESERVES

O NE OF THE GREAT practical problems in the Middle Ages was the
preservation of foods, to ensure that the corn harvest and foods that
had been gathered from the wild, as well as fish, meat and dairy products,
might be available in the longer term and in forms that might survive
distribution as well as storage. Using salt, or a pickling solution based on
salt, was a principal method of preservation, and it had important consequences for consumption and created distinctive characteristics for medieval food. Salt solutions almost certainly contained other elements as well:
this was a subtle way of shaping flavours, and came to constitute an important separate element in the food culture of the Middle Ages: 'sauce'.

The origins of sauce are to be found in two similar Latin words with
essentially the same meaning: 'salsa' and 'salsamenta' – salted things. Medieval
dietary theory held that, without salt, nearly all foods were without taste,
perhaps in itself a reflection of the amount of salted food that there was.[1] It
is difficult to establish when sauce might have come to be a separate element
in culinary preparations in the Middle Ages. Its use was closely intertwined
with other preservative liquors, such as vinegar and verjuice, and with the
use of spices and locally grown flavourings. The late fourteenth-century
English translation of Bartholomew the Englishman's encyclopaedia of
around 1250 noted that the liquid in which meat was left to soak sometimes
had spices mixed with it: 'Spices are sometimes placed in the water in which
flesh is soaked, and various sauces are made from it, which keep and preserve

the flesh well, and improve both its flavour and its taste ...'[2] Together with sharp, acidic liquors, these sauces and spices were hallmarks of European cuisine in the later Middle Ages – and may have been for some while before that.[3]

At all levels of society, there was a passion for acidic sauces and spices, or for flavourings that might emulate them more cheaply, derived from the produce of gardens or gathered locally. It was an expected part of the meal. The language of devotion frequently made reference to these sauces. A sermon of Odo of Cheriton, from the early thirteenth century, discussed the case of a Cistercian monk who struggled with the harshness of the food he was served. He confided in another monk, who then offered him the coarsest of loaves – the monk could not eat it, but the other told him to dip it in the very best sauce, and showed him five wounds, and dipped it in one. The monk realised that he was in the presence of Christ his saviour, and returned, most devout, to the cloister.[4] The fifteenth-century *Myrour to lewde men and wymmen* understood the place of sauce well in its reflection:

> For all kind of meat that is food to man is food to those that are good, and especially to him who will use it with skill and measure, and eat it with the sauce of the dread of God; for men should always dread God so that he should not use what God has sent but in a measured way, without outrage, and love God and thank him for his son.[5]

Sauce and spices were seen as stimulating appetite; further, spices continued to operate after food had been consumed, heating food and assisting with digestion.[6] By the year 1000, the first consignments of spices had arrived in southern Europe, their places of origin half a world away. They were highly desirable and expensive, and those cooks who could work with them best were eagerly sought after. The chronology of spice use shows two trends: a limited range of spices, at first in southern Europe, but gradually traded northwards, at very great price; secondly, a wider range, and diminishing price, especially from the thirteenth century, so that some of the things that had been valued extremely highly, such as pepper and cloves, came as peppercorns and individual cloves to stand for a nugatory value.[7] The earliest household account to survive from medieval England, for an unidentified household in London in the late twelfth century, includes purchases of spices – pepper, cumin and saffron, as well as sugar (possibly intended as a medicine); beyond this for flavouring, there were mustard, garlic and onions.[8] Elite households like that of a London churchman in the 1230s provide evidence for liquorice; in 1265, Eleanor de Montfort, wife of Simon de Montfort, leader of the barons who had rebelled against her brother, Henry III, was using ginger, cinnamon, pepper and almonds.[9] In England, there was a major change from the 1270s: the range and quantity of spices reaching the country, and the number of spicers and pepperers based in London, became much greater. Galleys arrived direct from the Mediterranean carrying spices as a high value cargo – and one that took up little space – on vessels involved in the the bulk transport of alum to the cloth-producing centres of northern Europe.[10] The fourteenth and fifteenth centuries provide an even broader range of spices, now encompassing anise, capers, caraway, cassia bark, cloves, cubebs, fenugreek, galantine, galingale, mace, nutmeg and sanders.[11] At the same time, some spices, such as pepper, had become so widely used that they were of less significance in elite consumption: other, more precious, flavourings were to be preferred.[12]

In the thirteenth century, great households and large institutions made their bulk purchases of spices at the kingdom's great fairs, usually annual or bi-annual events, at which they might be bought alongside wine, cloth and wax. For these purchases, the Countess of Lincoln was advised, c.1245–53, to use the fairs at Boston, Winchester, Bristol and St Ives, depending on where her household was staying.[13] In 1273–4, Norwich Cathedral Priory spent £5 10s 6d at the fair at Boston on spices – principally on almonds, mustard, sugar, ginger, galingale, cinnamon, cloves and cubebs, along with electuaries (sugary palliative medicines);[14] and in 1278–9, expenditure on spices at the same fair came to £7 13s 4d.[15] Consumers increasingly might also go to the largest towns and especially the capital for this variety. The pepperers were the earliest of the London trading guilds, recorded from 1180.[16] Spicers, on the other hand, were more likely to be engaged in a retail trade, and were often associated with pharmacy and provision of spices for medicines.[17] There was a major focus of the spice trade at Winchester in the thirteenth century, with a Spicers' Row in the High Street, and merchandise for visitors to St Giles' Fair – the royal household and households of great churchmen shopped here.[18] But spicers' shops were principally to be found in London, the only market sufficiently large to support a year-round spice trade, especially from its connection to purchasing for the royal household – there was a cluster of these premises in Soper's Lane.[19] A visit to a spicer's shop was an enduring experience: its sweet smell and the variety of its spices were called to mind by John Mirk in the late 1380s in his *Festial*, but it could not compare with the sweetness of the Virgin Mary.[20] The shopper would have found here a wide range of individual spices, distilled waters and infused oils, as well as powders. The corporation of Rye, in the 1450s, 1460s and 1470s, bought its spices from a prominent London grocer, John Young (grocers were those who sold these goods in bulk, in gross).[21] Entertaining the lieutenant of the Cinque Ports in 1456, he supplied the men of Rye with powdered cinnamon, pepper, cloves, mace, saffron and currants for 3s 6d;[22] the following year, again for entertaining the lieutenant, at Dover and Rye, he supplied a similar range of spices, with the addition of sugar, amounting to 5s.[23] Longer shop inventories were not common in the provinces in some cases until the sixteenth century: a listing of an apothecary's premises in Southampton in 1571 enumerated no fewer than 346 different types of waters, oils, powders, pills and spices.[24]

Preparing spices for sale required, first, the removal of waste material, a process known as 'garbelling'. The grocers in London had an official, known as the 'garbelatour', whose job it was to oversee this – in 1393 it was expected for pepper, ginger and cinnamon, as well as other goods.[25] While spices might be used whole, grinding released their flavour. Individual spices could be sold by weight, or they might be ground by the spicerer and sold as a powder. It was possible to buy ready-mixed spice powders (much like curry powder today), for example, white or blanch powder, powder douce and powder fort, powder marchant and powder Lombard – recipes for these combinations are found in cookbooks.[26] These shops also sold other special preparations, such as treacle, at this point a confection – allegedly from Genoa – with medical benefits.[27] Sauces and other preparations, such as mustard, were readily available in markets, and many in the lower ranks of society must have made their purchases there or prepared them from ingredients found in their own gardens. John Paston III, writing to his brother in May 1469 about the attempts of the family bailiff, Richard Calle, to secure the brothers' approval for Calle's marriage to their sister, was adamant that 'he should never have my good will if my sister should have to sell candles and mustard in Framlingham.'[28] Mustard, or mustard-like preparations, must have been available in several qualities for it was worthwhile, in the early fourteenth century, to make a counterfeit mustard, using radish seed, and to try to pass it off as 'gentle mustard'.[29] The clerks of the Earl of Northumberland, in the early years of the sixteenth century, noted a change in provisioning arrangements: 'Whereas mustard has been bought from the saucemaker, now it is to be made in my lord's house and there is to be a groom of the scullery employed to make it' – that is, this was a fairly common preparation that many might make.[30]

Two things, the value of spices and their power to transfer their flavour, were to ensure that they were to be kept separately. On the one hand, there was careful control over their issue, as at St Augustine's Abbey, Canterbury, where the senior of the abbot's chaplains looked after the spices of the chamber; on the other, there were separate locations and containers for their use. References to Isaiah 39:2 – where Hezekiah shows the storeroom or 'cell' with his aromatic spices, silver, gold, perfumes and ointments to the Babylonian messengers – encouraged anchoresses, female recluses who had taken religious vows and who were then enclosed for life, in the 1230s to think of their cells in sensory terms in this way.[31] In 1488, Durham Cathedral Priory had a 'spice house' attached to the cellarer's office.[32]

Customers often paid for packets, or for paper, at the same time as they bought spices and some, at least, was required to wrap the spices.[33] Other containers were sometimes bought at this time: the Master of the Cellar at Norwich Cathedral Priory in 1291–2 bought a basket, along with two ells of canvas and a little sack for the spices he had acquired at Boston.[34] Some spices and dried fruits, however, may have been shipped from the Mediterranean already packaged, such as the frails (baskets) of figs, or bales of dates on the branch, or larger quantities of other spices.[35] Sugared confections, such as citrinade (made from citrons, the precursor of the lemon) and green ginger, were typically imported in pots and boxes – possibly like modern 'Turkish delight'.[36] The inventory of the goods of John de Sandall, Bishop of Winchester, found at his manor of Sandall (near Doncaster) on his death in 1319, shows how a major spice purchase would have been transported. There were two

80-gallon barrels, full of sugar, white powder and other spices, along with 50 lbs of cinnamon. Beyond this, there were six bales of almonds, and a bundle, trussed for carriage, which contained 36 lbs of saffron, 68 lbs of ginger, 40 lbs of galingale, 30 lbs of cloves, 30 lbs of mace, 12 lbs of cubebs, 30 lbs of pepper, 12 lbs of cinnamon, 6 lbs of sanders and 30 lbs of currants. No valuation was given of the sugar, white powder and other spices in the two barrels, but the rest of this astonishing haul came to £41 0s 11d.[37]

Beyond these containers were the pots that might be bought from sauce-makers, to carry home their sauces, mustard and verjuice.[38] These containers all served for transport and for bulk storage. Boxes of preserves may have come to table, but there is no firm evidence for this beyond the provision of dedicated forks. As well as use in the kitchen, in the preparation of food, some spices, especially in powdered form, may have been brought to table. Special boxes for powder were intended to be seen. In September 1443, Sir Hugh Willoughby of Wollaton bequeathed two each of these silver boxes to two of his sons.[39] A silver powder box, bearing the legend 'Strew on powder', was among the goods of Thomas Morton, a canon of York, inventoried in June 1449.[40] The goods of Edward III and Richard II both included spoons for blanch powder, suggesting that it may also have been strewn in this way, at table.[41] But there was an association with excess: in the words of a fifteenth-century translation of Petrarch's *De remediis*, 'Saints could eat well enough though the powder box blew not on their saucer.'[42] Further silver spice boxes were available as prestigious containers for the storage of small quantities of these precious substances.[43]

Making sauces

It was the work of cooks and saucemakers to turn these spices and other preparations into delights for the table. The greatest of the households had separate departments for making sauces (the saucery) and for looking after spices (the spicery). Occupational surnames identify saucers (that is, sauce-makers) and mustarders or mustardmen.[44] The grinding of spices was an essential part of the work of the spicer and saucemaker in the elite house-hold, a distinctive mark of its status. This was delicate work: special fine ('subtilis') weights were available at St Augustine's Abbey, Canterbury, for spicers grinding spices, to ensure the right proportions.[45] In 1310, the executors of Bishop Bitton of Exeter handed to his successor in the see a hand-mill for sauces, along with associated equipment, listed among the goods of the bishop's wardrobe.[46] Pepper-mills or pepper-querns are found in inventories, as are mustard-querns.[47] In 1488, the kitchen of Durham Cathedral Priory was equipped with a brass mortar with two iron pestles for grinding spices.[48] There may also have been special cooking arrangements associated with some spices: Nicholas de Schirburn, a chaplain of York, in his will of 1392, left a 'pepperpan' to Margaret the wife of John Goldbeter.[49]

For making sauce, a liquid was essential, especially an acidic one. Vinegar and verjuice were commonly used, vinegar, for example, with mustard. By 'verjuice' is to be understood not only the sour juice of unripe grapes, but also that from crab apples.[50] The goods of William Coltman, a York brewer, who died in 1481, included a brake, a wooden mill for crushing crab apples, and one imagines that he was selling the juice for sauce.[51] The liquor from crab apples was mixed with the prioress's wine to make 'the sauce known as verjuice' at St Radegund's in Cambridge in 1450–1.[52] In 1467–8, the cellarer at Durham bought 11 bushels of crab apples for making verjuice, and a similar amount was spent on verjuice in 1474–5 and 1475–6.[53] Vinegar and verjuice were stored in barrels – they were in some instances sufficiently distinctive, perhaps in shape, or through some marking, to be identified as for verjuice even when they were empty.[54]

Eating sauces and spices

Sauces came to the table in elite establishments at any of the principal courses of the meal. To eat fine – and costly – sauce was a mark of status. When Edward III produced sumptuary legislation in 1336–7 seeking to curb expenditure on food (so that the funds might be available for him through taxation to support the war against France), the elite were allowed to serve sauce with each course of food, provided it was not an expensive preparation.[55] Sauces, spices and other condiments had special equipment at table. While some elements of this, such as salts, are well known, others have been less extensively discussed. Sauces were served at table in dishes known as saucers ('salsarii') – different in purpose from today's saucers, but not dissimilar in size. Smaller than platters and dishes, they came in a range of designs – there are some striking examples that are deep, but have broad rims, among the pewter vessels from the *Mary Rose*, Henry VIII's great warship which sank in 1545.[56] Saucers were to be found at all social levels – and this tells us about a common aspiration in dining. In 1309–10, the Master of the Cellar of Norwich Cathedral Priory, in preparation for a feast at Newton, bought more than 260 platters, 225 dishes and 200 saucers, as well as 100 cups, all for 14s 10d. The scale of this purchase may suggest the equipment was of wood or pottery (the saucers were 10 a penny). Usefully it also gives us a ratio of dishes per diner: if each person had one cup, he or she may have had access to at least two saucers during the feast, perhaps accompanying different courses.[57] Saucers had a place in the most modest households likely to have practised dining in elite style, those of clergymen in the countryside. When William de Aylesham, the rector of Heydon, died between Easter and July 1373, he left a bequest of pewter vessels to his successor (provided he did not pursue the executors for dilap-idations) – which included half a dozen each of dishes, platters and saucers.[58] Robert, the parson of Fritton, who died in August 1375, left William atte Moore six each of platters, dishes and saucers of pewter.[59] They were found, too, among the possessions of the leading inhabitants of towns. An early example of a pewter saucer, from c.1290 (Plate 16), came from a stone-lined cesspit associated with an early thirteenth-century stone house – the largest house of this period known in the country – in Cuckoo Lane, Southampton, immediately on the quayside, and partly built into the town wall in the fourteenth century. This find presents a striking collocation of the consump-tion of sauce within yards of where high-value spices were landed. The saucer is made of a high quality alloy, differentiating it from the pewter patens that were buried with priests, and thus indicating that it was intended for use as a saucer. It is strikingly heavy: at 0.113 kg it is in the same weight range as the silver saucers from Queen Philippa's household listed in Table 9.1; and it has a diameter of 12.7 cm. It has the letter 'P' punched in the rim, probably to indicate ownership – a practice we shall see referred to else-where.[60] Richard de Dalton, a barber of York, who made his will in October 1392, was also to leave half a dozen each of dishes, platters and saucers, as well as a salt of pewter, that is, a container for salt at table. Some of these in great households, made of precious metals, were impressive table pieces in their own right (Plate 29).[61]

Spice plates formed a standard part of the equipment for elite meals, for handing round spices at its conclusion, or for separate occasions when spices and wine were consumed together, sometimes at the end of the day.[62] In 1310–11 the Master of the Cellar of Norwich Cathedral Priory had made two pieces of silver gilt plate for spices, for 7s.[63] Pieces like this were found in many households, from the gentry upwards. When Robert de Ufford, Earl of Suffolk, made his will in 1368, among the domestic plate he left his eldest son, William, was one of the better spice plates that had been made at Paris; and Thomas de Vere, Earl of Oxford, who made his will in 1371, left Maud, his wife, as part of the domestic plate, two spice plates of silver, enamelled at the base, along with a silver gilt spoon – spoons for handing out the spices were separately identified in the greater households, and sometimes they were of gold.[64]

What were the sauces, and how did they link to cooking? Works like John Russell's *Boke of nurture* offered ready advice for the aspirant servant in the great household: 'Also to know your sauces fitting for meat: it provokes a fine appetite if there is sauce ready for your meat, so to please your lord make sure you have ready such sauce as he likes, to make him glad and merry.'[65] Russell then went on to set out the sauce for each meat – for example, garlic, vinegar and pepper went with roast beef and goose – and for wild birds and fish.[66] Cookbooks provide us with a much more extensive listing, as well as further indications of which sauce to serve with which dish – important because menus and reports of feasts do not always tell us which sauces were served with the long lists of meats and fishes they contain (Plates 6 and 7).[67] The sauces are revealing of taste and the style of medieval eating. Egredouce, for example, was a sweet and sour sauce, found in the *Forme of cury*, the great cookbook made for Richard II's household, with different recipes for its service with meat and fish;[68] cameline sauce had a cinnamon base, including in its English forms currants, walnuts, bread as a thickener and vinegar;[69] and peverade speaks of its peppery foundation.[70] Other sauces, such as 'verte sauce' (green sauce, often used with fish), 'sauce noir' (black) and 'sauce Sarazin' (red), were noted for the colours they imparted to food.[71] 'Sobre sauce', made with ground raisins, bread, wine, spice powders and salt, appeared on days of abstinence, accompanying roasted and fried fish.[72] One category of sauce, made with bread, was especially thick – sauce sage, for example, was like a stiff bread sauce, with hard-boiled egg yolks, and its association with pork (for example, 'pigs in sauce sage', now conflated as 'sausage') anticipates contemporary meat products.[73] Stuffings were similarly constituted, sometimes used in a present-day manner, sometimes as an accompaniment, sometimes like a sausage-meat mix, cooked in a separate piece of canvas in the cauldron with boiling meat, then roasted with a basting of a batter of eggs, flour and spices.[74] All these examples bring to the fore a use of spice and strong flavourings that was a defining element of late medieval English cuisine.

Oils

Oils were both a medium for cooking and a condiment. For cooking, however, the use of oil was restricted by its expense. Unlike cooking in southern Europe, in England animal fats were generally used rather than oils; but the ability to use fat at all depended on its availability and, as we have seen with the discussion of dairy products, only modest amounts of butter may have been used in many circumstances.[75] Which oils were used, and for what purpose? Olive oil was certainly present, although the fifteenth-century expression 'as brown as oil' may suggest that the quality of the oil brought to England was not of the finest – and many of the oils found in England were used as fuel for lamps.[76] A few recipes in cookbooks make reference to oil, mainly as a medium for frying; only a handful refer directly to olive oil, perhaps no more than three or four in total (on two occasions in recipes for 'appulmos', a dish of apple purée, in its fish-day version made with olive oil and spices; and once for fried fish).[77] But olive oil can be found in household accounts: on 31 October 1336 (the eve of All Saints), Dame Katherine de Norwich spent 7d on olive oil, and the household of John de Multon of Frampton spent 4d on it, probably as part of the provision of spices close to Christmas 1343.[78] The timing of these purchases suggests that it may have been consumed as part of a celebratory food. Another use – for unspecified oil – was for salads: John Paston II sent his brother two pots of oil for this purpose at the end of April 1472.[79] There was more oil, almost certainly olive oil, imported from the mid fifteenth century onwards by English merchants, especially from Portugal and Spain, and that it was within the reach of the purchasing power of the upper reaches of the gentry – the Pastons – has much to tell us about its diffusion in England.[80]

Beyond olive oil, essential oils of many herbs, nuts and other foods were used in medicine.[81] Cooks may have employed other vegetable oils, such as rapeseed oil, which was produced in England as well as imported – and these oils were presumably worked with by the various oilmakers, oilmen and oilers, whose surnames record these occupations from the 1220s onwards.[82] Bartholomew the Englishman tells us, however, that rapeseed oil (and radish seed oil) was used for lamps.[83] 'Mete-oil' may have been another vegetable oil, also used for cooking – a dispute that came to court before the Lord Mayor of London in 1414 alleged an annual payment of half a gallon of 'metoyle' was due, along with a bushel of green peas, while the defendant lived in Sir Robert Denny's tenement in Bread Street;[84] and sweet 'mete-oil' was probably olive oil.[85]

Not all oils employed were of vegetable origin. In the north-east of England oil, or blubber, from seals (seal-smear) and possibly from cetaceans (train-oil) or from fish was imported. While these items may have been employed as foods or a medium for cooking, it is harder to pin down their exact use.[86]

Honey, sugars and preserves

Sweet things had an important place in medieval mentalities and were commonplace in expressions of endearment and religious devotion, defining as well the character of language, both excellent speech and the words of hypocrites. Absolon, parish clerk and expectant lover in Chaucer's 'Miller's tale', had chewed the spice known as grain along with liquorice in anticipation of his assignation, so that he might smell sweet, calling to Alison, 'What are you doing, honey-comb, sweet Alison, / My fair bird, my sweet cinnamon?'[87] The devout monk to whom the Virgin appeared in a fifteenth-century account of her miracles 'loved Our Lady always, his life was sweeter than honey from the comb'.[88] Chaucer's translation of Boethius pointed to the things anointed with the honeyed sweetness of Rhetoric and Music.[89] In the words of *Cursor mundi, c.*1300, hypocrisy was inherent in Pilate's name: 'By "Pilate" we understand a fiend of hell, for his judgement book is a honey mouth.'[90]

Honey was the most accessible sweetener in medieval England, and there was a long tradition of bee-keeping in both countryside and in gardens across the country, beyond collecting it from wild sources. Taxation records from 1225, when the Crown required individuals to pay a fifteenth of their movable wealth, show hives and large quantities of honey. At Broadchalke, in Wiltshire, of the 55 individuals assessed for taxation, no fewer than 12 had hives, and some had more than one, like Thomas Wil who had six, assessed at 2*s*.[91] At Kirby Sigston, near Northallerton, in the North Riding of Yorkshire, the goods of Thomas Birdale, the rector, inventoried on 22 November 1446, contained two beehives, worth 2*s*; the goods of William Capes of Northallerton itself, in November 1497, also contained two hives worth 2*s* 8*d*;[92] and in his will of 20 May 1500, William Wright of Bishopthorpe left his parish church an old stock of bees with a swarm, probably a hive, the curate was to have another swarm, as were each of three others.[93]

The productivity of hives depends on the plants in the neighbourhood and their pollination cycles, weather and much else besides, and the bulk of honey production may be concentrated in a few weeks in late spring and early summer: an average modern hive produces some 25 lbs of surplus honey per annum.[94] Knowledge of medieval production comes largely from the information about food renders, and about purchases by large institutions or for feasts – usually given in liquid measure. At Norwich Cathedral Priory in the late thirteenth century and early fourteenth century, the purchases of honey by the Master of the Cellar were modest – 2 gallons in 1290–2, 5 gallons in 1303–4 and 8 gallons in 1314–15[95] – but the purchase of two pots for keeping honey in 1297–8 and 6*d* spent on beehives in 1303–4 indicate that the priory produced its own honey too.[96] In 1438–9, the cellarer of Durham Cathedral Priory bought 35½ gallons of honey from six individuals, in quantities ranging from 2 to 11 gallons. This suggests peasant production: purchasing from numbers of small producers[97] – although in 1488 Durham had three hives of its own in the cellarer's West

Orchard, these were a recent gift.[98] The cellarer's goods in this last year included a wooden gallon measure for honey.[99]

Honey must have been commonly available in the marketplace too: when the prior and kitchener of Maxstoke Priory in Warwickshire wanted honey in 1475–6, it was bought at Coventry.[100] Besides its use in complex culinary preparations in elite cookery – and for drinks, as discussed above – a recipe for 'pokerounce' had its origin simply in bread, or toast, and honey, and this must have been a common dish.[101] A recipe for pain ragoun looked for honey, sugar, pine nuts and ginger; when set, it was sliced – it looked like slices of bread – and was served as an accompaniment to meat and fish.[102] This last recipe referred to the viscosity of the liquid that had been boiled: 'Take up a drop thereof with your finger and cook it in a little water, and see if it thickens' – and the expression 'as thick as honey' was found in other recipes too.[103]

Around 1200, sugar was scarcely known in northern Europe, even among the elite. It was initially important for its medicinal uses, particularly as a component in electuaries, syrups and cordials.[104] From this, it made a transition to a highly desirable flavouring, and then to a preservative, for fruits and spiced confections. It partly displaced honey and fruits as a sweetener, as larger quantities became available in England in the latter part of the fourteenth century and through the fifteenth, notably in elite circles. It made a transition from a market that saw it as a 'spice' to wider use: while it was still essentially a luxury commodity, it was sufficiently a part of diet of the elite by the end of the fourteenth century for the criticism of the love of sweet things by English prelates to have a special resonance in terms of the regular presence of sugar in their diet.[105] At the end of the first millennium, the principal centres of production had been Syria and Egypt – but that production spread west through the islands of the Mediterranean (especially Cyprus and Crete, the latter formerly known as Candia, from the Persian and Arabic 'kand', sugar) to Spain, to the Kingdom of Granada. During the first half of the thirteenth century, the oriental product came to northern Europe overland from the Mediterranean, but from the second half of the thirteenth century the Genoese established a sea route, with their galleys, which carried sugar, along with other high value spices, and dried fruits from the production centres at the western end of the Mediterranean to the countries bordering the North Sea.[106]

The oriental and Mediterranean origins of sugar are apparent from the names by which it appears in late medieval accounts: sugar of Babylon, Cyprus, Marroc and of Alexandria.[107] These links continued to be made in dishes flavoured with sugar: for example, in a recipe for 'vyaund de cyprys bastarde', a dish made with ground chicken, wine and spices, sugar was the second item listed in the ingredients.[108] Other references tell of quality, that is, to what stage it had been refined: 'blaunk' or white, for the highest quality, 'Caffatin', white sugar of a lesser quality, 'black', that is brown sugar (a recipe for furmenty recommended sugar candy for service in a great lord's house, but black sugar for lesser men), and 'pot' sugar, for a low quality product ('cooking' sherry would be a good analogy).[109] Another reference was to the number of times it had been 'cooked' ('cuit') in the refining process. John Paston III, writing to his mother in late October 1471, reported on the price of sugar of three 'kwte' ('cookings'), that is, it had been refined three times, and was selling at 10*d* a pound.[110] Sugar was also distinguished by its form: sugar loaf, 'rock' sugar, plate or tablet sugar – a flat piece, sometimes made with flowers and flavoured with rose water – and powdered, or grain, sugar, to be strewn like other spices, or with them, for example, with ginger as blanch powder.[111]

The purchases of Norwich Cathedral Priory between 1267–8 and 1318–19 demonstrate how one major ecclesiastical institution acquired sugar (Table 5.1). It was bought by the Master of the Cellar in many of the years for which we have his accounts, at the fairs at Boston and St Ives, and once at London. The gaps in purchasing, as well as occasions when there are several purchases in the year, suggest that sugar was not available in the quantities Norwich would have liked: even the Prior of Norwich could not guarantee that this flavouring would be available. In some years, honey was bought as well, as in 1314–15, when 8 gallons were purchased; but in 1315–16 neither sugar nor honey featured in the purchases – although honey would have been available without purchase, the weather conditions in these disastrous years of famine cannot have been conducive to its production.[112] The level of purchase almost always exceeded 50 lbs per annum, and in three instances exceeded 100 lbs. At this point, Norwich had about 60 monks,[113] so setting aside its use as a medicine (which may have taken a significant element, in addition to the electuaries that were purchased), this represents an average weekly consumption of about 1 lb

Table 5.1: Electuaries, cordials and sugar at Norwich Cathedral Priory, 1267–8 to 1318–19

In 1273–4, 1278–9, 1282–3, 1283–4 and 1290–2, the purchases were made at Boston fair; in 1279–80 and 1284–5, the purchases were made at St Ives.

	1267–8	1273–4	1278–9
Sugar	8 lbs (5s 3d)	–	? (Part of spices, £7 13s 4d)
Sugar of Alexandria	–	54 lbs (27s)	–
Sugar 'Marroc'	–	–	–
Sugar: rose	–	–	–
Electuaries	–	2 lbs (6s)	–

	1279–80	1282–3	1283–4
Sugar	5s 1½d at St Ives 31¼ lbs (15s 7½d)	76 lbs (34s 10d)	35 lbs (35s)
Sugar of Alexandria	–	–	–
Sugar 'Marroc'	–	–	–
Sugar: rose	–	–	–
Electuaries	–	–	–

	1284–5	1290–2	1302–3
Sugar	–	119 lbs (60s)	–
Sugar of Alexandria	40 lbs (29s 4d)	–	–
Sugar 'Marroc'	20 lbs (7s 6d)	–	–
Sugar: rose	–	–	¼ lb (6d) [medicine]
Electuaries	–	–	–

	1303–4	1308–9	1309–10 (22 Henry de Lakenham)
Sugar	27 lbs (22s 6d)	41 lbs (58s)	60 lbs (77s 6d)
Sugar of Alexandria	–	–	–
Sugar 'Marroc'	6 lbs (1s 2d)	–	–
Sugar: rose	–	–	–
Electuaries	–	6s 2d	5s 6d

Table 5.1: (*continued*)

	1309–10 (1 Robert de Langele)	1310–11	1313–14
Sugar	9½ lbs (12s 9d) 34½ lbs (37s 2½d) 10¾ lbs (13s 8d) 1 lb (10d)	16 lbs (21s 2d) 13s 4d (London) 16 lbs (21s 6d)	104 lbs (£4 11s)
Sugar of Alexandria	–	–	–
Sugar 'Marroc'	–	–	–
Sugar: rose	–	–	–
Electuaries	–	–	–

	1314–15	1318–19
Sugar	129 lbs (75s 6d)	79 lbs (55s 11½d)
Sugar of Alexandria	–	–
Sugar 'Marroc'	–	–
Sugar: rose	–	–
Electuaries	–	–

Sources: Norfolk RO, Norwich Cathedral Priory, accounts of the Master of the Cellar, DCN 1/1/9 [poss. 1267–8]; DCN 1/1/3, mem. 2d (1273–4); DCN 1/1/4, mem. 1r (1278–9); DCN 1/1/5, mem. 2r (1279–80); DCN 1/1/6, mem. 2r (1282–3); DCN 1/1/7, mem. 2d (1283–4); DCN 1/1/8, mem. 2r (1284–5); DCN 1/1/10, mem. 3r (1290–2); DCN 1/1/15, mem. 1r (1302–3); DCN 1/1/16, mem. 1r (1303–4); DCN 1/1/19, mem. 1r (1308–9); DCN 1/1/21, mem. 1r (1309–10, 22 Henry de Lakenham); DCN 1/1/21, mem. 2–3r (1309–10, 1 Robert de Langele); DCN 1/1/22, mem. 1r (1310–11); DCN 1/1/23, mem. 1r (1313–14); DCN 1/1/24, mem. 2r (1314–15); and DCN 1/1/27, mem. 1r (1318–19).

for the whole community, although consumption may have been concentrated rather than spread through the year. Sugar formed a modest element in the flavourings – but, given that the palate of the monk would not have been overwhelmed by sweetness, a little sugar used as a flavouring would have made a noticeable difference to foods. This usage was probably not that different from that of the papal court – a much larger institution – under Clement VI (1343–50), where the annual amounts bought ranged from 215 to 367 lbs.[114] The household of Elizabeth de Burgh, Lady of Clare, consumed 346¼ lbs of sugar in 1339–40 and purchased a much greater amount, 669 lbs, in 1344–5.[115]

In addition to sugar itself in its different forms, there were also sweet confections and preserves. A group of these – signalled by the suffix -*ade* –

originated from the Mediterranean and arrived in England already in boxes and pots. Among them were pinionade (a confection made with pine nuts), festucade (made with pistachio nuts), citrinade, 'gingerbrade', that is, ginger-bread (made with green ginger and white ginger), pomade (made with apples) and succade – simply a confection made with sugar. Dame Katherine de Norwich acquired boxes of pinionade, festucade and gingerbrade in 1336–7.[116] Citrinade appears towards the end of the fourteenth century, at a great price: 2 lbs bought for Henry, Earl of Derby, cost 56s;[117] and it also appears along with pomade, succade and coinade, a quince preserve, bought for the household of Thomas of Lancaster, Duke of Clarence, in 1418–21.[118] By the mid fifteenth century, citrinade was used as a cosmetic as well, as a sweet-scented powder, possibly also for the colour it gave. This transition in use was also to be made by pomade.[119]

Preserves were made in England, as well as imported, by the mid fifteenth century. In the first instance the confections were prepared using honey, which was more abundant than sugar: 'char de quince', preserved quince flesh, sometimes mixed with that of warden pears, was made in this way.[120] Comfits, prepared sweetmeats (although sometimes simply a sweet sauce), and compotes were never common, but they began to establish themselves in ways that suggest they had a distinctive place in food culture. On the one hand these might appear, like electuaries, as palliative medicines, but they also featured in dining, among the foods that might come with spice plates at the conclusion to a meal, or for distribution on special occasions, such as funerals. John Grandisson, Bishop of Exeter, in his will of 1368, instructed that there should not be a drinking with spices around his body in the choir, but allowed that this might happen in the chapter house or elsewhere.[121] When the body of the Duke of Clarence was brought back to England for burial in 1421, his household spent £1 3s 3d in London on confections for the day of his burial.[122]

Spices, sugars and preserves were of great importance for the food culture of medieval England. They connected individuals to commodities that had travelled halfway round the globe, commodities that were fabulous in their reputation and price; they fuelled the literary imagination and the vocabulary of sensory devotion; and they brought exotic tastes – and a passion for them – to the country. It is perhaps no wonder that moralists saw them as symbolic of exaggerated expenditure, as a harbinger of perdi-tion; but they also saw in them heavenly qualities, qualities that inspired religious imagination. Their rarity contrasted them in many ways with the foods that could be found readily to hand, that could be grown in domestic gardens, gathered in the wild, or hunted. Yet even here, with obvious native food resources, not all was straightforward. It is to the connotations of these native foodstuffs that we now turn.

CHAPTER SIX

GARDENS, WILD FOODS, FISH AND HUNTING

Gardens, fruit and wild plant foods

MEDIEVAL SOCIETY THOUGHT A good deal about plants and their products. Gardens, like fields, were crucial to the supply of food, and passing on a knowledge of plants and their potential as food products was essential. It was also in gardens that much took place that would have had an impact on the qualities of foodstuffs: the care of the gardener, the knowledge of the housewife, the range of plants cultivated or gathered, all had an important influence on what food meant to individuals. On the one hand, a good deal of plant lore organised for the learned could be found in herbals, particularly that attributed to Macer.[1] On the other, parishioners would have heard in English from the Wycliffite Bible such texts as Proverbs 24:31, 'I passed by the field of a slow man, and by the vineyard of a foolish man; and, lo! Nettles had filled all, thorns had covered the greater part thereof, and the wall of stones without mortar was destroyed' – and learned the moral importance of cultivating their gardens.[2] Preachers, like John Bromyard, knew that bad gardeners were those who did not dig up the roots of nettles or other noxious weeds.[3] Encyclopaedists, including Bartholomew the Englishman, summarised the characteristics of plants, for example, noting two different kinds of nettle, but that both were better for medicine than for food.[4] Medieval authors also knew about the etymological associations of 'garden' or 'orchard' with 'Paradise'[5] – and of the connections to the

Fall of Man. It was the sin of gluttony that had taken hold of Eve.[6] Like much else to do with food, therefore, gardens and their produce came with a potent moral charge.

Gardens were part of the culture of both peasant life and of large institutions. A copy from the mid fifteenth century of a text probably a century earlier, ascribed to Master John Gardener and believed to be associated with English royal gardens,[7] tells us a little about the sowing and setting of vegetables, 'Worts we must have, both for master and for servant', and goes on to describe a planting regime, with four separate sowings, to ensure that there are 'young vegetables at all times of the year'.[8] Beyond this it focuses on trees, vines, the setting and sowing of garlic, leeks and onions, and the cultivation of green plants ('herbs' from a medieval standpoint), including lettuce and all the salad herbs listed in the *Forme of cury*, some soft fruits such as strawberries, as well as flowers and saffron. Herbs are identified as important ingredients of sauces and for pottage.[9] The importance of horticulture varied from region to region, and was linked to the size of the peasant holding: gardens formed a more significant element in areas where smallholdings predominated.[10] Large institutions, or great lords, might distinguish between kitchen gardens, gardens focused on plants with medicinal uses, particularly infirmary gardens, orchards and pleasure gardens.[11] These elements are likely to have been present in peasant gardens as well, even if we can now see no formal distinctions in their plots.

Gardens were enclosed areas: from the peasant croft to the lord's garden, it was important to exclude animals and birds that might cause damage, as well as to protect against theft. In Lydgate's 'The churl and the bird', the churl (the countryman) has made a beautiful garden, with turved benches on which to sit and water features; the garden is laid out with paths strewn with sand, and sweet herbs, and protected by a hedge and ditch.[12] In a specimen conversation prepared as part of a manual for teaching Anglo-Norman, *c*.1396, the keeper of a garden and a labourer discuss their pay and work, outlining more of the resources of gardens. The labourer has had no more than 12*d* and his expenses for a week's work digging the land and making ditches. The keeper of the garden has been pruning the trees in his garden, and the best are already beginning to shoot again; he has dug another garden and planted cabbage, leek, parsley, sage and other virtuous herbs; he has dug out stinking nettles and other bad weeds; and he has sown much good seed. He also has many beautiful trees in his garden: apples, pears, plums, cherries and nuts, and they are well dressed. He has earned only 3*d* that week and also the previous week, but he is happy. The two men go off to the inn to eat together – and are served with good country food, cabbage larded with fat and butter together, milk, and hard-boiled eggs. Although the text has something of the character of a vocabulary list, it shows a clear awareness of the potential and rewards of gardens.[13]

There would have been a wider range of activities that went on these in gardens – these were often small farmyards as well, even if idealised descriptions place less emphasis on these aspects. Robert, the five-year-old son of Adam Coke of Helpringham west of Boston in Lincolnshire in April 1352, went across his mother's garden to fetch the geese that were around the well, but fell into it.[14] At Oakington Cambridgeshire in June 1365, Robert Dam went into the garden of Robert Custe and found a boar and pigs rooting in the ground there – and went to drive the animals from the garden.[15] And at Markby in Lincolnshire in the summer of 1365, Sarah de Redisdale went into the garden of Roger de Staynow, where she found a cow calving – the coroner's jury believed she should have left well alone, and put the misfortune of her upsetting the cow, which gored her, down to her stupidity.[16]

The fifteenth-century cellarers' accounts of Durham Cathedral Priory allow a glance at a garden in a larger institution. In 1443, Richard Collom, one of the priory's cooks, was paid 18*d* for his work with the green plants (herbs) in the cellarer's garden.[17] There were regular payments for the purchase of seed: in 1467–8, the cellarer's garden was sown with 1½ lbs of onion seed for 1*s* 3*d* – enough for more than an eighth of an acre; a further 1*s* 5*d* was spent on labour and other seeds.[18] In 1471–2, slightly less onion seed was purchased, 1 lb, along with other herbs and seeds, for 2*s*;[19] and purchases continued at this level over the next decade, for example, in 1474–5, 1 lb of onion seed and other herbs and seeds were bought for 1*s* 8*d*.[20] The cellarer's garden was also where livestock and poultry were kept: in 1445–6, there was work on the pigsties there, along with the preparation of a dresser – a board or table at which meat was made ready – perhaps in readiness for slaughtering the animals.[21] In 1459–60, the slaughterman's house was located in the priory's West Orchard; the 'pig garden', the Swynegarth, was cleaned during the year and fenced; and there were fishponds to be cleaned.[22] A coneygarth – a rabbit warren – was made in the West Orchard in 1461–2, and in that year a stone wall was built in the plant nursery ('le impegarth') and the orchard.[23] In 1465–6, there was an area with a dovecot in the West Orchard;[24] and in 1474–5, a goose-house, laid with flagstones.[25]

Gardening may have been especially the preserve of women: Walter de Bibbesworth's *Treatise* from the 1230s exhorts them to be good gardeners ('devendra bone curteller'), but does not tell us much about the crops that were sown, beyond linseed and hemp.[26] Paid workers were often men, however, but occasionally female workers are found, such as the woman who looked after the garden at Durham Priory's dependent cell of Monkwearmouth in 1360;[27] and Alice Payntour, 'garthwoman', paid a stipend of 6s 8d, along with two further 'garthwomen' who each received 5s, from the household of Lady Margaret and Sir William Cromwell at Tattershall in Lincolnshire in 1417–18.[28] Many women would have worked the gardens of their houses and crofts.

Herb gardens were designed to provide pot herbs and flavourings, and herbs for medicinal use. The word 'herbarium', however, was also applied to a variety of gardens and garden features, from a grassed area to an arbour, and it is not therefore always clear what type of garden, or part of it, was at issue. At the Norwich Cathedral Priory manor of Eaton, in 1291–2, a labourer was paid for making a 'herbarium'. The manor was also to produce crops of garlic, leeks, beans and hemp, and it had apple and quince trees.[29] Vegetable or wort gardens might be attached to manorial gardens,[30] and they were commonly worked by peasants in the countryside. It was here that Piers Plowman's parsley, leeks and cabbages ('plant koules'), shallots, onions, chervil and cherries had grown.[31] In Malory's *Morte d'Arthur*, Sir Gawain and Sir Hector 'saw a poor house, and beside the chapel a little curtilage where Nacien the hermit gathered worts for his food'.[32]

Fruit trees were often to be found in these gardens: it would have been unusual for peasant crofts to have had more than half a dozen, but they were considered especially valuable, and their profits were well understood.[33] A draft of an agreement between Cristine Battescomb and Robert Battescomb, probably from the 1470s, leased to him all her land in Vere's Wootton in Symondsbury near Bridport in Dorset, reserving to her the little orchard and six apple trees in the great orchard.[34] Almost anyone might be involved in collecting the fruit – to judge by the records of accidents. At North Carlton in Lawress Wapentake in Lincolnshire, in September 1373, Agnes the daughter of Simon Miln climbed up an apple tree to collect the apples and fell from the tree.[35] At Wheaton Aston in Staffordshire in August 1390, Agnes Cowherde had climbed a pear tree, to collect the pears, when a branch broke.[36] At Oakington Cambridgeshire in June 1347, a boy fell into a well trying to collect plums hanging over it;[37] and in July 1359, in another Cambridgeshire village, Graveley, a three-year-old girl was drowned falling from a tree over a well while climbing after plums.[38] These examples pinpoint the ripeness of fruit in the summer months – as one might expect – and there were measures to protect the crop from depredation by birds in the lead-up to this period. On 30 June 1498, Henry VII paid 20*d* to the man who kept the birds from the cherry trees in the King's garden (probably at Greenwich);[39] and in May to August 1505, payments were made to the man watching for crows, in one instance at Richmond.[40]

In Walter de Bibbesworth's orchard there grew fruit trees, their boughs laden with apples, pears, cherries and plums, along with other trees and shrubs more wild than cultivated – hawthorns, blackthorns (bearing sloes, a wild plum), dog-roses, bullace (a larger type of wild plum) and a service tree ('alier'). There was also a barren quince tree.[41] And it was to fruit, to apples, that John Bromyard turned as a way of explaining the transubstantiation of the Eucharist, noting particularly their smell. After its conversion, the wafer retained the taste and colour of bread, just as a hand which has held an apple will retain the odour of the fruit.[42] As we have already seen, children were often found with fruit: in September 1319, Ellen, the two-year-old daughter of Richard Noger of Whitstone in Somerset, dropped the apple she was carrying in a spring, and tried to retrieve it.[43]

Fruit was popular with all, however, not just the young. Odo of Cheriton included in a sermon a tale of a bishop who was prepared to commit the cure of more than 100 souls to a young nephew, but was not prepared to let him have charge of a fine pear tree.[44] When Queen Philippa, the wife of Edward III, was staying in houses belonging to Peter de Montefort, in the summer of 1331, she recompensed his gardener, Henry, 10*s* for the losses her household had caused him in apples, pears and other fruit.[45] The food cravings of pregnancy might also focus on fruit – pears, dates, even oranges, an exotic import only present in England in small quantities in the fifteenth century.[46] There was an element of courtesy in serving these foods: fruit was among the gifts that any man might give,[47] and to find them offered as hospitality was to make a similarly appropriate mark. In the life of St Thomas Becket in the South English Legendary of c.1300, Becket had fled overseas and was attempting to survive incognito, but he was recognised in one house: the housewife began to serve dainties, bringing him apples, pears and nuts.[48]

Different varieties of fruits are in evidence – apples known as blaunderels (a prized variety), costards (probably with pronounced 'ribs'), pippins, queenings, red stars, Ricardons;[49] pears Jonette, pearmains and wardens (possibly a cooking variety);[50] and there was a variety of white plum.[51] There is some evidence about the different times at which they were ready to eat: a pannier full of pippins, for example, was presented to Queen Margaret when she came to stay in Coventry on 15 June 1457.[52] Pears Jonette had their name as they were expected to ripen around the feast of the Nativity of St John the Baptist (24 June) – an early variety, as Langland noted, along with peasecods (peas in the pod, especially young ones, eaten whole), plums and cherries, 'What ripens earliest, rots first.'[53] The blessing of apples at the feast of St James (25 July) marked another element in this; apples were to be blessed on this day at Norwich Cathedral Priory at the conclusion of Mass.[54] In the arrangements set down around 1266, the gardeners at Westminster Abbey were expected to provide fruit, particularly for Mondays, Wednesdays and Fridays, and in Advent and Lent. There were always to be apples at the feast of St James, and cherries at that time; and plums, pears, nuts and medlars, if they had them in the garden, for the feast of St Laurence (10 August), and especially on all days of abstinence, not just Wednesdays and Fridays, for as long as the crop lasted. The fruit was to be provided for the monks and for guests; to individual monks dining in the area known as the misericord; and on Septuagesima Sunday (the third Sunday before Ash Wednesday and the start of Lent), the gardeners were required to find apples, whether they had apples in the garden or not.[55] From this evidence, it is clear that medieval men were keen observers of fruit, its varieties and the timescales in which it might become available.

What parts of these fruits were eaten? We have references to chopping apples,[56] to the peeling and coring of apples and pears as part of culinary preparations,[57] and the expression 'to spare neither the apple nor the core', meaning 'to do all one can', suggests that while it was normal practice not to eat the core of apples, in exceptional circumstances the whole fruit would be used.[58] Apples might be stored for much of the year – perhaps in hay or bracken, sometimes in barrels[59] – and sometimes in a dedicated building, if the quantities were sufficient, an apple-house.[60] Care was essential, however: John Bromyard noted how it was important for the skin of the apple to be intact if it was to be preserved, lest air get in and corrupt the flesh, just as when one was inattentive, what passed through the eyes and ears might corrupt the person.[61] Most fruit appears to have been stored without further processing, although plums may have been stored dried, as prunes: their use in recipes alongside other dried fruit – dates and currants – makes it clear that 'prune' is more than just a synonym for 'plum'.[62] We have seen, too, that a limited number of fruits were stored as sweet confections.

Fruit was grown more extensively in some regions of England than others. Cider production, as discussed in Chapter 3, indicates some of the more important apple-producing areas.[63] Clusters of place-names, probably of considerable antiquity before they were recorded in the twelfth and thirteenth centuries, are suggestive of naturally occurring fruits, such as pears in Surrey, at Pirbright and Pyrford, and in Oxfordshire, Waterperry and Woodperry;[64] and sloes were also marked in this way in Sussex and Wiltshire.[65]

Nuts were among those foods that might both be gathered in the wild and be cultivated. Obligations for peasants to gather nuts were widespread across central and Midland England. In the customs recorded on the manors of the abbey of Bec, before 1248, at Atherstone in Warwickshire the virgaters and half-virgaters – that is, those holding farms of around 30 and 15 acres, respectively – were required to send a man for one day (who would not receive food for the service) to collect nuts if the woods bore them; and at Quarley near Andover in Hampshire, the virgaters were required to gather a basinful of nuts as often as they were summoned to do it.[66] At Banstead, Surrey, in 1325, the obligation of the customary tenants to collect nuts and apples had been commuted, payments in lieu ranging from half a farthing to 1*d* – and for those for whom it had not been commuted, the work was to be done without food.[67]

What nuts were involved? Aside from almonds, which were imported from southern Europe and were available alongside spices and dried fruits such as figs and dates,[68] nuts were a local resource. Collecting nuts was an autumn and winter activity – some were known simply as 'winter-nuts'.[69] Walnuts were available in abundance: the bursar of Durham Cathedral Priory bought 2,000 for 2*s* 6*d* in 1368–9.[70] While walnuts might be eaten straight from the shell, they were also used by the fifteenth century in prepared dishes. A recipe for 'colde bakyn mete' described how to apply gold foil to walnuts, which were then used to decorate the dish.[71] Hazelnuts – also known as avelanes, or filberts – grew wild, 'without gardeners' craft'.[72] It was possible to cook with a hazelnut milk, just as it was with almond milk, the ground nuts mixed with water or a broth – a practice used particularly on days of abstinence as, although called 'milk', no dairy products were involved.[73] Chestnuts were gathered in autumn and early winter.[74] Pine nuts (albeit not a true nut), although used in cookery, seem to have been imported rather than being local products, and were to be found alongside the purchases of spices and in a sweet confection.[75] In 1335–6, Durham Cathedral Priory bought 1½ lbs of pine nuts, along with 2 lbs of grain (a red colourant), ½ lb of mace and ½ lb of sanders (a sandalwood producing another red colourant).[76] The domestic trade in fruit and nuts was largely a small-scale, local affair, except in connection with supplying the capital and large establishments such as the royal household. Fruiterers, however, along with spicers, were linked to the import of the dried fruits and nuts, like dates, raisins, currants and almonds, that were a feature of elite cookery during periods of abstinence.[77]

Arrangements for consumption linked nuts to other fruits, and they were clearly intended to be eaten as far through the year as resources would stretch, some treated as cultivated locally, others bought in. At St Augustine's Abbey, *c*.1330–40, it was the custom for the convent to eat apples, pears, plums, cherries, nuts or greens on Wednesdays and Fridays in Lent, and the remains were to be collected by the almoner before the refectorer collected up the spoons.[78] It was also enjoined that no monk was to crack open nuts noisily with his teeth if there was a reading during the meal, but rather to use his knife to open them. However, if all had nuts, then they could be opened as they chose.[79]

Wild foods undoubtedly played an important role in medieval food culture, particularly, while not exclusively, in terms of a demotic cuisine – but they present us with difficulties when it comes to understanding what exactly they were and what they were used for. Most of the references to this material come from elite establishments, and these plants and berries were probably widely used elsewhere. Terminology is problematic: in understanding what plants were used, there is uncertainty over the names of many and how they may map on to modern species – the standard guide to plant names in medieval England lists some 1,800 examples, believed to represent about 600 species.[80] Difficulty also arises from a transformation, which may or may not mirror the transition between demotic cuisine and elite food culture: at what point did a wild plant become a cultivated one, either in elite gardens, or make a move through the hedge or fence from woodland to garden? There is some oblique evidence in the case of strawberries. We can see from accounts when strawberries were eaten – a typical Trinity Sunday dish – and the earlier in the year they occur, the more likely it is that they were cultivated and forced towards earlier fruiting. The rewards given by King Henry VII for gifts of strawberries show that his own gardener at Greenwich managed to produce them around 21 or 22 May 1506, at least 10 days before the King received gifts of the fruit from others. The King clearly enjoyed this fruit and the Prioress of Dartford sent it to him on three occasions between 31 May and 19 June that year.[81] And it was a taste that was clearly more widespread among the aristocracy: Anne Stafford, dowager Duchess of Buckingham, consumed a good deal of summer fruit, for example, with purchases of berries in June, July and August 1465.[82]

The food potential of the countryside is apparent in the narrator's dream in the early fifteenth-century *Mum and the Sothsegger*, evoking its bounteous state, and the wild foods that there might be – flowers, fish and fry, briars with their berries bent over the path, chestnuts and cherries that children desire, hawthorn, and pears, plums and peasecods, which ladies delight in.[83] These were typical of the benefits of the countryside in good times; in times of dearth, when nothing else was available, the countryside might supply haws, hips, sloes and crab apples.[84] The countryside might also support the more extreme strictures of abstinence, as in the case of hermits, like St Godric, who lived off pastilles of vegetation.[85] Mary Magdalen was reputed to have lived off roots and dew.[86] A diet of raw greens and fruit, along with bread and water, on Wednesdays and Fridays, was one of the degrees of punishment for monks who had offended at Westminster Abbey, set out in the customs of 1266.[87] It required exceptional conditions for ordinary people to eat some of these foods, in the face of famine and hunger – as we can see in the case of root crops.

Gardeners grew root crops, although it is hard to identify when some of these foods passed into cultivation. Walter de Bibbesworth listed flowers, known for their sweet smells, and herbs that were useful for medicine. Here, for example, turnips could be found in abundance – but what was at issue was almost certainly the use of their seed for medicinal purposes. This was true of a great many plants that we may now consider primarily as foodstuffs, from the wild carrot – the dauke – to lettuce and its leaves.[88] Turnips, however, might be penitential fare: the mid fifteenth-century South English Legendary, in its life of St Hilarion, noted how, in the wilderness, 'This good man had given all his life to penance: he ate 15 turnips each day and again at night.'[89] It is perhaps not surprising, therefore, to find them cited as famine food during Henry V's siege of Rouen: 'And then supplies of wheat and meal failed, and also all other grains from which they might make any bread, except bran and leftover vegetables, and turnip-roots and leeks, which were to them food of great value . . .'[90] That they should be cited along with leeks, however, is interesting, as the latter appear more frequently in household accounts, and the implication may be that root crops were more common in gardens than records suggest. Walter de Bibbesworth advocated the planting of cabbage in place of amaroke (mayweed, maithe) and possibly beets ('gletouner').[91] That did not mean that worts were popular foods, at least not for the aspirational: the day-labourers described in Piers Plowman no longer deigned, in the conditions of the later fourteenth century, to eat day-old worts, but wanted fresh meat and fried fish.[92] But the worts grown in the garden remained of great importance to peasant diet. When, in December 1367, Alice, the daughter of Richard Bocherd of Great Lyveden in Northamptonshire was found dead, it was discovered that she had fallen into a pan full of hot 'leek worts'.[93] One can only imagine the frustration felt by peasants at the depredations of hares – which they were not supposed to hunt. A poem of *c*.1300 lists 77 terms of abuse for the hare, including the 'wort-cropper', evocative of the depredation of the vegetable patch.[94]

Although a translation, the *Alphabet of tales*, in its fifteenth-century English form, presented what was doubtless a plausible scenario, talking of a holy maiden in a monastery, going into her garden and desiring greatly to eat the lettuce that was there – but she omitted to bless it, and was taken over by a fiend. Faced with a holy man conjuring the fiend to leave, it complained: 'Alas, what have I done? I sat upon the lettuce, and she came and took me up and ate me.'[95] Salads attracted suspicion: John Russell's *Boke of nurture* cautioned 'Beware of salads, green foods and raw fruit, for they lead many a man to have a sensitive stomach.'[96] They still were sufficiently unusual among the elite for the late fourteenth-century *Forme of cury* to contain a recipe for a green salad: sage, green garlic, spring onions, onions, leek, borage, mint, fennel, cress, rue, rosemary and parsley. They were to be washed and torn into small pieces by hand, and mixed well with raw oil, vinegar and salt.[97] The question here is whether salad was in fact a common, country food, a demotic food, transformed in the context of upper-class cuisine, with an elite dressing.

People also gathered herbs and plants growing in the wild. At Weston by Welland, in Northamptonshire, in October 1354, Alice Bray had been collecting water plants when she was struck by the falling sickness and drowned.[98] Watercress was used in medical recipes from the start of the fourteenth century, but was also treated as poor man's food: in the words of Repentance, in *Piers Plowman*, 'It were better for me, by Our Lord, to live entirely from "welle-cresses" [watercress], than to derive my food and support from the gains of false men.'[99] The *Liber cure cocorum*, from the middle of the fifteenth century, in its discussion of 'petty curry' registers watercress ('cresses þat growene in flode') among its ingredients, a listing that includes flowers (primroses and violets), berries ('the crop of the red briar'), nuts ('avans', hazelnuts) and herbs that might be gathered as well as grown in the garden – parsley, worts and others.[100]

Some wild foods may have been less used. There are very few references to mushrooms, although there is one recipe using them in the *Forme of cury*.[101] Shortly before the Black Death, John Bromyard, describing flowers, connected their beauty and smell to the reputation of a life lived well. Yet he chose to point out that where we see flowers, we hope to see fruit; but some flowers led to none, and were no better than the harmful weeds that grew among the wheat.[102] He may not have anticipated, however, that one of the distinctive features of English medieval elite cookery was to be its use of flowers, as colouring and for flavouring.[103] A cookbook from *c*.1430–40 contains a series of recipes for making a dish with almond milk or cow's milk, rice, sugar and honey, each coloured with a flower – violets, red roses, primroses and hawthorn – that had been boiled and pounded.[104] Sambocade was a cheese and egg tart, with sugar, elder blossom and rose water: a recipe for it appears in the *Forme of cury*.[105] Rose hips – possibly from the wild rose, the sweet briar – were used to make a dish known as 'heppee', with a broth of fresh beef or capon, salt and sugar;[106] and the red hips were one of the ingredients, along with other red colourants, alkanet and pomegranate, and red wine, that were used in 'sauce Saracen'.[107] The 'primrol' – probably originally intended to designate the cowslip or daisy, but later to encompass the primula, primrose and comfrey – was one of the ingredients named for 'petty curry' by the *Liber cure cocorum*.[108] The relationship between these flowers, demotic cuisine and the elite demonstrates that foodstuffs from the countryside might be consumed as readily by the upper classes, or, like fruit, be welcome as gifts.

Fish

Like the flowers and fruits of the countryside, fish may appear to be a readily available natural resource; but people have not always eaten fish. Only small quantities were eaten in England between the end of the Mesolithic and the Roman period, when it was only the Roman elite who ate them. In Anglo-Saxon England, consumption remained modest. Fish as a penitential food had not yet taken the place it was to have in the later Middle Ages – and fasting in most cases meant eating foods other than meat and fish; but patterns of fish-eating were to change markedly in the years around 1000–1100.[109] There were a number of late medieval answers to the question 'why eat fish?' As a food that was suitable for consumption in periods of abstinence, fish had a special place in medieval food culture. Fish, both preserved and fresh, was an important component in urban and upper-class diet, as well as in the monasteries – adding an important element of protein. It was also a foodstuff that was independent of the agricultural cycle, even if it was dependent on other patterns to ensure it came to market; and it preserved well. Beyond this, there were links between fish and health, although the ways in which this food was believed to have an impact were very different from modern perspectives; and, perhaps, in the countryside and round the coasts, there was a notion that fish was a food that was there for the taking, but that it was not necessarily a free good: the rights of lords meant that licences might be required to fish.

As a consequence of the pattern of abstinence that the Church enjoined, 'fish days' were prominent in the calendar and there were other Christian resonances as well. The first disciples had been the fishermen Peter and Andrew, shortly followed by two more, James and John.[110] Their summons to become fishers of men was part of the liturgy – at Norwich Cathedral Priory for the Octave of the feast of St Andrew.[111] At Westminster Abbey, the miraculous hallowing of the church by St Peter and the equally miraculous draught of fish caught by a local fisherman following his advice was a staple of histories and sermons throughout the Middle Ages.[112] In commemoration of this, Thames fishermen traditionally made an offering of salmon to St Peter at the abbey – on which occasion they dined in the monastic refectory and the refectorer was exceptionally to seat them more favourably than other lay guests, with the monks who had been bled. (Bleeding – the 'seyney' – was a routine therapy for both healthy and sick monks, to counter imbalances in the humours.)[113] Following the text of the miracle of the Feeding of the Five Thousand literally, barley bread and fish were typical of alms provision for the poor. In the early fourteenth century, the Prior of Norwich had herring specially bought for distribution to the poor – the costs including arrangements for preserving the fish in brine and carriage.[114]

While fish might be penitential fare, that did not mean that it might not be a luxury commodity.[115] Bromyard, using word play so that his tale might be recalled by preachers the more easily, chastised those prelates who ran more readily to the kitchen than to Mass, who looked more to roasted fish than to the suffering Christ ('plus respiciunt piscem asium quam Christum passum') and who studied salmon more than the books of Solomon ('plus student in salmone quam in Salomane').[116] An elite recipe of *c.*1325 tells of the preparation for 'gentle salmon', that is, a noble dish, filleted, ground in a mortar, flavoured with cinnamon, pepper and cloves, and coloured with saffron, and then served to the lord.[117] Dishes such as 'chisanne' – a word possibly related to Middle English 'chis', 'choosy' – contained chopped roach, tench and plaice (or even, in the later Middle Ages, carp), fried in oil with raisins and red wine; 'gin-gaudre', a fish stew, was made with fish-heads and entrails, spiced with 'good powders' and coloured green; and eels 'in sore', that is, a red sauce, were cooked with wine and minced onions, ginger and cinnamon, and coloured red with sanders. These dishes are typical of the ways in which elite households might present fish, with prominence given both to spiced flavours and to colours.[118]

The recipes were also characterised by elite fish: freshwater fish were especially valued, and to consume fresh fish of any sort was also a marker of status. For most people, consumption of fish was likely to have centred around preserved marine fish, especially cod and other white-fleshed fish, and herring. This common experience is reflected in proverbs about fishing and about individual fish. In this group can be found references to fish of various kinds – hake, red herring (that is, smoked herring, as opposed to white herring, preserved in brine), herring tails and oysters – in expressions used for reference to things of little value.[119] Fish appeared as a simile for good health.[120] In some cases, freshwater fish were specified: trout, which was quite unusual and expensive as a foodstuff, for example, in the expression 'to be as hale as a trout';[121] pike and pickerel both appeared in this way.[122] That did not reflect on their consumption, however: there was a sentiment that while it was better to eat the meat of young animals, mature fish were to be preferred to the young. In Chaucer's 'Merchant's tale', the worthy knight wants a young wife: ' "I would rather have old fish and young flesh. It is better", he said, "to have a pike than a pickerel, and tender veal is better than old beef".'[123]

The sentiment could not, of course, apply to preserved fish. There are useful insights into the arrangements for storing them, for example, in a reference to herrings in barrels, 'When you lie bound as a herring does in the mease'.[124] Christ comments to Margery Kempe incidentally about stockfish (dried and salted cod), when describing what she is to expect from others for her devotion: 'You will be eaten and gnawed by the people of the world as any rat gnaws the stockfish', and his further remark to her, 'Daughter, for you are so obedient to my will and stick as fervently to me as the skin of stockfish sticks to a man's hands when it is boiled'.[125] The detritus from stockfish was also observed by Lydgate: 'All is not gold that shines out, a stockfish bone in darkness gives off light', presumably from the phosphorus content of the bone.[126] Riddles and puzzles refer to stockfish, featherbeds and women as things that might be beaten – soaking and beating the preserved fish with 'stockfish hammers' was a major part of its preparation.[127]

Fishing was a major industry in late medieval England. The trade in preserved fish – especially herring, caught in the Baltic and the North Sea through the summer months, as well as round the coasts of Ireland and parts of western Britain, and the white-fleshed cod and codlike fish caught principally in the North Atlantic also in the summer months – was critical to a society that needed fish as food at times when fishing as an activity was much less than desirable, in the winter months and through Lent.[128] References to cod and herring, especially in their preserved forms, dominate the records, as they must have dominated the fish content of the diet of many. Variety, however, came from regional diversity: conger eel, caught and preserved in the Channel Islands, or around the rocky coasts of the West Country; hake, another West Country fish; or great flatfish, like turbot, or rays.[129] And it also came from freshwater fish.

Freshwater fisheries were of two types: those in rivers, streams, fens and natural ponds on the one hand, and the stews (or ponds) constructed solely for fish-farming on the other. The first were widely accessible, although in some cases access to them required a licence; the latter were commercial investments, providing varieties that were highly prized. Something of the importance of prestigious river fish can be seen in the supply of lampreys to Queen Eleanor in the winter of 1280–1, from the weir on the Severn at Gloucester for which the constable of the castle there was responsible. John the lampreyman and his groom made at least 14 trips between Gloucester, where John caught the fish, and Marlborough and Amesbury where the Queen was residing. The lampreys were mainly transported alive, in barrels of water – the barrels were secured with chains and locks as the fish were so valuable. On 17 December the constable was given a receipt for seven fish worth 16s each; as spring advanced, however, the price fell, perhaps for smaller fish, to as little as 3d each, receipted on 27 April. On one occasion a lamprey was baked in pastry with spices and then transported.[130] Recipes using lampreys expected that some would have been salted – 'Take a powdered lamprey and strike away the salt with your hand' – which would then need to be soaked for a day and night.[131] Another recipe, from the second half of the fifteenth century, envisaged scalding lampreys and then roasting them on a grill, grinding saffron and pepper over them, and then serving them in hall.[132]

Rivers might be fished with hook and line, fish traps, nets and other equipment – an activity for professional fishermen and for boys. In late October 1368, Thomas Couper of Burnham in Buckinghamshire was using a hook and an 'instrument', probably a rod, which he wanted to set up on the bank of the Thames for catching fish.[133] At Shepreth in Cambridgeshire, in July 1348, two boys, one 13, the other seven, were clambering along a dam to find worms for baiting hooks for catching fish, when they fell into the water.[134] Catching fish with bait was a well-understood technique. According to the biblical paraphrase *Cursor mundi*, John and James were baiting their lines when Christ came upon them.[135] Offal might be used as bait: a satire on the people of Kildare, possibly from the mid fourteenth century, refers to the 'hokesters' by the lake, with tripe, the hooves of cattle and sheeps' heads, along with what was possibly liver.[136] Others might fish with nets, such as John, the son of John at Melton Mowbray, who went into the River Wreak with other boys on the evening of 7 July 1367.[137] At South Kelsey in Lincolnshire in April 1353, William the son of Alan Fouler of South Kelsey, a fisherman, was in Redburndike with a pan searching for fish when he became involved in an altercation with William de Balne, who shot him in the leg with an arrow.[138]

Eels were of great importance in the countryside and were commonly taken in streams and rivers. In July 1352 John, the son of Alice Haverman of Benington in Lincolnshire, had gone to a spot where animals were commonly watered in order to collect eels, but fell into a deep part.[139] Elias Jonyson of Aubourn was fishing with an elgar – an eel spear, here worth 3d – in a water-course at Swineshead near Boston in May 1357 when he misjudged the depth of the water.[140] Eels were enjoyed at all levels, attested by the range of preparations in cookbooks – roasted, baked possibly in pastry, in broth with pine nuts, in ale and in wine.[141] There was a trade in eels between the Low Countries and England, suggesting an organised market and strong demand, at least in London.[142] Eels were distinguished by their size and colour – great eels, grey, black, 'red' or 'kemp' (a coarse eel), 'roasting' eels and other, smaller varieties, shaft eels, stick eels and pimpernols.[143] Some – tolling eels – may have been intended as bait.[144] Richard Rolle, writing about 'Our daily work', in Yorkshire before the Black Death, noted the slipperiness of eels: '[The riches of the world] are fickle and not lasting, aye, and slippery as an eel, which when men think they have him fast, as a phantom glides away from them and is lost to them.'[145] In the early fifteenth century, the translator Stephen Scrope noted 'an evil-kept tongue glides as an eel'; in a simile for liveliness, the author of the Towneley Plays hoped that one might be as fresh as an eel.[146] Eels and their characteristics were well known.

Fishponds – effectively fish-farming – were an important commercial resource, a symbol of status and a convenient way of providing for those, such as monks and the elite, who were major consumers of freshwater fish. John de Kevermount of Pinchbeck in Lincolnshire, late in the day on Christmas Eve 1352, was standing next to the pond in his garden with a spade in his hand, in order to break the ice for his pike and other fish, so that the air might get to them, and probably so that he might take them for consumption at this time. In the Christmas season this year, 26 December was a Wednesday, and John's fish would have been much in demand.[147] Fishing the larger ponds was a well-organised activity, with professional fishermen and nets. At Tamworth, Staffordshire, in 1381–2, three men – including one Richard Fisscher, probably a professional fisherman – were paid for four days' work fishing in the pond there, along with the hire of two carts, one for taking the fish to Salwarpe, between Worcester and Droitwich, and the household of the Earl of Warwick there, and the other for carrying to Warwick the small boat which they had used for their work.[148] The Duke of Suffolk's visit to Hellesdon, near Norwich, where he dined on the Wednesday of Whitsun week in 1478, is described in a letter to John Paston II almost like a hunting expedition: there he 'drew a stew and took great plenty of fish'. He left Paston a pike or two for when he came, which was a great comfort to Paston's friends and discomfort to his enemies – food gifts, particularly those from hunting and fishing expeditions, were a mark of especial favour.[149] Monastic institutions were often well endowed with fish-ponds. Durham Cathedral Priory had some close at hand, in its West Orchard, restocked with 15 pike in 1469–70.[150]

It was agreed that the best time for catching fish was either at dawn or dusk, or even at night. 'The biting time' according to a mid fifteenth-century treatise on fishing – of considerable sophistication – was between 4 and 8 a.m. and at the same times in the afternoon and early evening between May and September, and on a dark day in winter, although some fish, such as trout, might be best caught in the middle of the day.[151] It was at night in November 1346 that Simon, the son of William at Welhull, drowned at Abingdon (in Spellhoe Hundred, in Northamptonshire), placing basket-work fish traps in the floodgates of the watermill there.[152] A fox demon-strated the stupidity of wolves in one of the fables of Odo of Cheriton, c.1220, tricking one into believing that fish would bite on his tail if it were left dangling into a pond – the wolf's tail was frozen in overnight and it was caught and beaten in the morning by men.[153] Methods of catching fish were well known: although a night-time activity, the wolf's was not one of them.

The seashore provided access to shallow-water marine and estuarine fish, and also to shellfish. Nets might be set up on the sands in anticipation of the return of the tide and its fish. Robert Snel of Holbeach in Lincolnshire was attending to his nets on the seashore at dawn in March 1358 when he was overwhelmed by the strength of the water.[154] At Sutton St James in Lincolnshire, John Tharston had gone with his colleagues to Sutton Sands in the afternoon of 23 June 1374 to collect the fish from his nets set on the sands, but stayed behind and was trapped by the tide.[155] Some shellfish, such as oysters, were eaten all year round; but others, such as mussels, whelks, razorfish and cockles, even limpets, had a more restricted period of consumption, and were often only eaten in Lent.[156] These might be the food of the very poor.[157] Thomas, the son of William, the son of Nicholas Bally of Spalding in Lincolnshire, a 12-year-old, was gathering cockles on the sands at Weston near Moulton when the tide caught him on 5 March 1357 – that is, in the middle of Lent.[158] The following day, in nearby Boston, a small boat laden with oysters and mussels fouled a cable and capsized.[159]

Shellfish were far from food solely for the poor, however: oysters were very common fare across society. John Russell expected to see at the table of a franklin, a freeman holding land below the level of the gentry, oysters in an onion sauce ('in cevy') and 'in gravey', usually an almond sauce, 'your health to renew'. There was also 'musclade', a broth with mussels which might appear with vegetables or with almonds.[160] Musclade might also appear on elite tables, and Russell mentioned it among the dishes of the first course of a specimen menu for a fish day.[161] Scallops appeared much less often: Bishop Hales of Coventry and Lichfield had 20 for his household on Friday 11 September 1461 and 14 on Saturday 26 September 1461 – the small numbers suggest that this was an exceptional item of consumption.[162] The association of scallops with St James and pilgrimage, however, saw shells used as an emblem of the pilgrimage to the shrine of St James at Santiago de Compostela, in north-western Spain, and also as a design for special plate, possibly made with a commemorative function. At Durham Cathedral Priory, among the goods held by the feretrar (the keeper of the shrine of St Cuthbert) in 1401, there was a silver gilt scallop and boat, the gift of a pilgrim; and in 1408 the sacrist had among his goods a further silver scallop for holding salt that was to be blessed.[163]

Hunting and wildfowling

Hunting and wildfowling brought further wild foods to the table. Many of these foods had sumptuary characteristics: there were legal restrictions on taking beasts of the chase and game generally; and there was customary practice that restricted access to some of these foods, for example, by the late fifteenth and early sixteenth centuries, to many wild birds.[164] Venison – literally 'the product of hunting' – was highly prized, and commonly reserved for the Crown; but others had access to it: it was sold on, given away, stolen and poached – and the same can be said for many of the foodstuffs in this category. Consumption was shaped to achieve maximum effect.[165] Bishop Mitford of Salisbury, in 1406–7, husbanded his venison, saving it for special occasions when its presence might be noted. There was a great investment in deer parks, in farming deer – for hunting took place in a closely controlled environment.[166]

Much of the hunting was done by professionals: they could ensure a supply of venison from distant estates, harvesting the deer when they were at their best. The meat might then be salted and barrelled, and shipped to the household for consumption.[167] We can see distinctive patterns of butchery in deer bones retrieved from excavation on elite sites. Specific 'unmaking' rituals were employed by huntsmen when excoriating deer, an innovation that almost certainly came with the Norman Conquest but which may have a southern European origin, possibly from Sicily.[168] The late fourteenth-century poem *Sir Gawain and the Green Knight* describes several hunting scenes, including the butchery of slaughtered deer, with the hunters receiving their fees from the carcass, that is, the reward due for their work.[169] The venison that reached aristocratic households was typically meat from the sides, haunches and hindquarters generally; meat from the forequarters was mainly distributed in a different way, often to those taking part in the hunt or to others who might expect perquisites. At a late medieval hunting lodge in Donington Park Leicestershire for example, most of the deer bones came from the left forelimb, the shoulder, almost certainly a regular gift to the official charged with custody of the park, the parker.[170]

Other wild resources might be leased out, such as rights to wildfowling on the seashore, if the lord was not able to exploit it effectively in another way. In the late fourteenth and early fifteenth centuries, for example, the rights to catch wildfowl and fish on the beach at Eastbourne in Sussex were rented for 5s 6d a year.[171] If huntsmen turned to other game, so did poachers, for this was profitable quarry. In 1334, a Cambridgeshire felon confessed to the theft of eight swans, which had then been sold on to poulterers in Cambridge, who were well aware that the birds were stolen and that the vendor was a thief.[172] In November 1379, three men went at night near Calbourne on the Isle of Wight armed with bows and arrows and nets to catch rabbits. The keepers of the warren realised what was happening and managed to shoot one of the poachers with an arrow.[173]

Even if poaching and redistribution of the quarry gave more people access to these foods, hunting was seen as an elite activity. That medieval illuminated manuscripts, such as the Taymouth Hours of *c*.1331, probably made for Eleanor of Woodstock, the sister of Edward III, in anticipation of her marriage, feature hunting and hawking so prominently reflects on the milieu in which these books were read (Plates 18 and 19) – although the Taymouth Hours do so in a way that is probably intended to be humorous. These were activities in which both noblemen and noblewomen might participate, but it is highly improbable that women would have participated in the unmaking of deer in the way shown in Plate 18: butchery of deer was hardly the work of elite women, and the manuscript may be inverting normal practice as a form of jest.[174] John Bromyard, describing spiritual war, drew a comparison between the hunting dogs of the nobility, which sprang to activity at the sound of the hunter's horn, as opposed to the fat and lethargic village dog, lounging on a local dungheap. Christ was the spiritual hunter, calling all secular men to him to the hunt, to destroy the beasts of sin.[175]

Gifts of food for special occasions frequently featured game and attracted rewards. Jurors giving evidence to prove the age of the heir of a tenant-in-chief of the Crown turned to these memorable occasions, recording, for example, how on the birth of Edmund Holand, the brother of the Earl of Kent, in 1382 or 1383, partridges, deer, swans, a wild boar, capons and hens had been brought to mark the occasion.[176] These gifts were part of a social currency – prestigious foods were always welcome, marking status and bestowing honour on both the donor and the recipient. The Paston correspondence recorded gifts of swans and cranes, and, on one occasion, c.1503, of storks.[177] Servants bringing the game were well tipped. The cellarer of Durham gave rewards to the man of Sir William Bowes who brought game in 1465–6, and a further payment was made to one Robert Thomson who brought rabbits.[178] These connotations were long-lasting, and we shall see more of them as we look at the food cultures of the elite, lay, ecclesiastical and in the towns.

Wild foods, fish and the products of hunting and wildfowling all played important roles in late medieval food culture. They included some of the most humble and some of the most prestigious of foods. They were carefully nurtured and tended, and contemporaries were very conscious of the connections and meanings that came with them. They were also overwhelmingly seasonal products. One of the key questions, therefore, was how to preserve them, how to store them and to bring them to market, or to give them, ready for consumption at an appropriate moment. Late medieval

England was a highly commercialised society, and it was in the towns that food was most often traded – but the ways in which food and drink were used in an urban environment were also effective demonstrations of their power to create connection and community. The next chapter examines the place of foods in town life, particularly as used by civic authorities and by guilds.

CHAPTER SEVEN

CIVIC FOOD CULTURE AND THE GUILDS

POPULATION CENTRES NEEDED FEEDING, and there was a constant traffic into towns of foodstuffs from the countryside round about. Municipal regulations tell us not only about sales in the town itself, but also how unscrupulous urban traders might intervene in legitimate trading activities for their own profit rather than the common good, for example, by intercepting those from outside bringing in goods for sale (forestalling the market), buying them up before they could be offered for sale and then reselling them at a higher price (regrating). Regulations abound about the quality of foods, the timing of markets, and their inspection and supervision (Plate 17). Street cries – 'Hot food for the hungry' – proffered fast food and other eating arrangements.[1] Beyond the retail trades, food was also processed in an urban setting, and the experience of food in towns, from the poor to the elite, had its own distinctive features. Some of these aspects of food in municipalities are examined elsewhere in this book.[2] This chapter focuses on a special aspect of food culture: the use of food and drink for civic occasions and particularly in the life of the guilds that formed such an important component of the urban community. To address these, it looks at a number of towns, and particularly at Stratford-upon-Avon and the ways in which its guild feast was used in the fifteenth century, the character of the occasion and the types and qualities of the food and celebratory meal.

Food and drink in civic life

Food and drink created community, adding important elements to urban gatherings, offering opportunities for entertainment, commemoration and gift-giving to further the civic cause.[3] The dignity of these occasions was employed to add to civic grandeur: among the participants might be found the leading members of a community. These activities were widespread across urban society, and giving food on many of these occasions was a customary practice and expectation.

To this end, food had an important role at municipal meetings: drinking and, on many occasions, eating together added conviviality, common purpose and an individual character to each event. A group of Southampton examples demonstrates some of the possibilities. At the town meeting at the ancient assembly place called the Cutthorn, on Southampton Common, on 6 May 1439 the civic steward provided 10*d* worth of bread, 2*s* worth of wine, 12*d* worth of squabs (young pigeons), and 14*d* worth of beef and bacon.[4] It was not unusual for towns to mark with food and drink the audit of the main municipal accounts, often coinciding with an annual change of town officials.[5] At Southampton the audit sometimes lasted over a week, as in August 1442, and food was a constant accompaniment.[6] There might be comestibles to support and celebrate almost any civic event of importance. In 1441–2, Southampton gave a breakfast for 100 men bringing timber for a key element in its water supply, its conduit house.[7]

In the fifteenth century, the celebration of obits was a prominent feature in urban life. These must have been some of the more significant occasions, too, for the feeding of the urban poor – or at least those who merited civic confidence. In 1441–2, alms given formally by the town of Southampton were restricted to a small group of deserving poor, with weekly support for three men and one woman. More expansive donations were made at celebrations with which the town was entrusted, such as the 'mind' or obit of William Malmesyll, which included in 1441–2 a gift of 2*s* 6*d* in cash to the poor, three dozen loaves and two dozen portions of ale, three cheeses and 1 gallon of wine, the food and drink amounting to 7*s* 8*d*; the mind of Thomas Smale encompassed bread, ale, cheese and 1 gallon of wine, in total 4*s* 9*d* worth of food.[8] The number and character of these celebrations was differently calibrated over time. In 1449–50, for the mind of William Malmesyll, the cash given to the poor had reduced to 2s, but nonetheless 6s was spent on bread and ale, along with 1s 1d on wine and 1s on cheese; that year Thomas Smale's commemoration saw 1s spent on bread, 5d on cheese, 1s 6d on ale, a pot of wine for the mayor and the chanter of the *Dirige*, the Office of the Dead, at 4d, and 2d for the labour of a woman to serve on this occasion.[9]

Many guilds in towns also gathered for the occasion of obits of members, either those who had long-standing connections and whose obit might be celebrated year after year; or simply on the occasion of the death of a member – and it was not uncommon for food to appear on these commemorative occasions. In 1442–3, the guild of the Holy Cross at Stratford-upon-Avon made arrangements to celebrate in chapel for Thomas Chasteleyn, parker of Fulbrook, with 8d worth of bread, cheese and ale – and the food was given out in the guild's chapel. There was 2½d worth of bread and ale to mark the obit of the rector of Whitchurch, William Smith. And in the case of one Matilda, as well as receiving support from the guild as she lay dying, the guild gave 4d worth of bread and ale for her funeral, and a further 1d worth of ale after her burial.[10] In 1533, the Trinity Guild at Coventry celebrated an obit for Nicholas Burwey and Elizabeth his wife, which centred around cakes and ale, wine, cheese and comfits.[11] These commemorations were sometimes of long standing, a way of remembering benefactors and their work over generations. On 6 May 1533, the Trinity Guild at Coventry marked the obit of Richard Spicer, who had represented the city in Parliament in 1415, with a commemoration that included a dozen cakes, 4 gallons of ale, 1 gallon of Gascon wine and 1 gallon of sack.[12]

Urban corporations might have buildings with their own halls, or guilds might have their own guildhalls where eating and drinking might take place; but not all did so. The corporation of Rye, in Sussex, one of the Cinque Ports, had no civic hall or guildhall of its own and much of the entertainment offered by the men of Rye took place in private houses or inns. When King Henry VII came to Rye in late August 1488 for the launch of one of his ships, the *Regent*, built at nearby Reading on Romney Marsh, purchasing took place around the town for fish, including a great turbot, and for capons, chickens, wine and spices. Bread was baked. Four and a half gallons of wine were drunk at the mayor's house by gentlemen of the royal household, the mayor, his brethren and commoners; at Harry Swan's house, there was further expenditure on bread and wine for many commoners; meat was roasted at the baker's house, and it was dressed for service by John Andrew's wife at the mayor's house; one of the municipal waits (watchmen) was paid for turning two spits, and further bread and beer were bought elsewhere in the town.[13] Typically the mayor took the lead in municipal entertainment. Quite unusually for a medieval town, his wife was given an allowance each quarter of 6s 8d in recognition of expenses at her house.[14]

Beyond direct entertainment, gifts of food created bonds and might form an accompaniment to negotiations, in the short or the long term. At Leicester, the food given by the municipality to successive Earls and Dukes of Lancaster was essential to the town's welfare.[15] After Easter 1452, the men of Rye gave Richard Witherton, the lieutenant of the Cinque Ports, a fine portion of fish in order that he might be a 'good man for us' in a legal matter relating to Tenterden.[16] Southampton entertained important people passing through the town, en route to Normandy, with a gift of 2 gallons of wine for Sir John Peppard on 4 December 1441;[17] and the wine and ale bought for Lord Powis at the Angel in Southampton in October 1449.[18] The visits of the king's judges were marked by entertainment, for example, at the trial and execution of Thomas Garard at Southampton in January 1442.[19]

Guild feasts and food culture

Feasts are one of the best-known elements of guild activity. Often falling at the focal point of the guild's year, they provided a prominent occasion for the guild to come together in religious celebration and socially. Some feasts were large-scale events, attended by hundreds of guild members and others. The detail of these occasions which would illuminate the nuances of feasting and consumption, as well as guild practice, is frequently lacking. Indeed, one can read the accounts of many guilds and find no reference to feasting: this does not mean that it did not happen, rather that it was unusual for it to pass through the main financial records of the guild. Those rendering the accounts, the guild's keepers, masters or proctors, were not primarily responsible for the feasts – these events appear to have been financed largely by guild members themselves and it is only in those instances where their contributions to the feast were paid into a central fund that there was a record of it. In these cases, the scale of the event may have meant that more formal organisation was necessary, or the guild may have intended the feast for activities other than feeding the brethren and sisters, such as entertainment for prominent guests.

At guild meetings throughout the year, occasions that are described as 'speakings together' ('interlocutiones'), morrow or 'morgen' speech, it was not unusual for drink to be consumed and in many cases food was eaten as well. In the returns made to the Crown in 1389 setting out the purposes and practices of individual guilds across England, the Shipman's Guild at Lynn recorded that the first of the three 'morwespeches' in the year was to take place after a drinking, and further that anyone who was rebellious or disobedient to the alderman 'at the drinking or inappropriately at the morrow speech' was to give 4 lbs of wax to the guild's light.[20] A drinking ('potacio') appears in various ways connected with guilds, and it may have taken on something of the character of a church ale. Ordinances for the guild of the Holy Cross at Stratford, probably from the earlier part of the fourteenth century, mention a drinking in Easter week. To this every sister of the guild, and every brother, was to bring a great cup ('magnum ciphum'); all the cups were to be filled with ale and it was to be given to the poor. There were to be prayers to the Cross before the drink was distributed to the poor, and those who omitted to bring their cups were to be fined a halfpenny.[21] At many places, this communal connection to alms of food and drink made an important link in terms of the charitable purposes of the guild.

As well as drinkings, there was usually a main guild feast, or, indeed, several of these occasions in the year, often associated with the guild's saint's day. In the ordinances for the guild of St George in Norwich, from after 1418, provision was made for an elaborate feast. The alderman and the masters of the guild were to assign a day for assembly before the feast of St George (23 April), on which day 24 or the greater part of them were to chose their George, a man to bear his sword and to be his carver before him, along with a man to bear the banner of St George, and two men to carry the wax – to burn as lights on an altar or before an image. On the feast of St George itself, or a day used as the alternative, all the brothers of the guild were to be in livery on horseback. They were to go to Mass, and when Mass was done, 'all the brothers and sisters shall honestly go to their food to the place assigned by the alderman and the masters, and every brother and sister is to pay for eating together 10*d* for their food, wax [for the lights for the altar] and minstrels. And any brother or sister who is absent from the meal and the Mass, if they are within 12 miles of Norwich, they are to forfeit 2 lbs of wax.'[22] These occasions made patent the civic hierarchy as well.

The frequency with which these events took place varied from guild to guild. The guild's main feast may have been only one of a number of cele-bratory occasions with food. The fraternity of St John the Baptist at Winchester, for example, held its main feast for the brethren and sisters on the feast of the nativity of St John the Baptist (24 June). It held a lesser celebration on the feast of Corpus Christi (the Thursday after Trinity Sunday): in 1411, 20*d* was spent on bread, ale and cheese that day.[23] The feast was the culmination of the year for the guild of the Holy Cross at Stratford: it was held on the Sunday immediately before the translation of St Thomas the Martyr (7 July) and, from 1410–11, the guild's accounting year even ran from this point.[24] There is evidence too that guilds might change the date on which their principal feast took place, perhaps several times through the later Middle Ages; and we cannot take the evidence of one feast alone as establishing a pattern.

Guild feasts might take place at any of the three principal meals, break-fast, lunch and supper. At Reading, in the early fifteenth century, new members paid fines for a breakfast for the guild, perhaps a relic of what used to be the custom – and indeed, may still have been the custom – but the guild accounts, while noting the receipt of these sums, do not cover expenditure on these entry breakfasts.[25] At Stratford, in 1414–15, the allow-ance that was made for the costs of the proctors at the feast describes it as lunch.[26] Here there may have been a continuation of the feasting, at least for a smaller and possibly elite group, into the evening, as the accounts for 1426–7 have a section for expenses in hall after the feast, and they include further food expenses for a more select group of foodstuffs, including woodcocks and rabbits, which never appear in the purchases for the main feast.[27] At Winchester, the fraternity of St John the Baptist – which included the leading members of the town among its members – in 1537–8 had a supper on the feast of the nativity of St John the Baptist.[28]

It was the expectation that the brotherhood of the guild – the brothers and sisters – would be present at the feast, and consequently guild meals could be very substantial affairs. Inventories of guilds show that some had sufficient place settings in store for large numbers of diners: the Trinity Guild at Coventry, the goods of which were listed on 15 December 1441, had 20 dozen garnishes (or sets of platters, dishes and saucers) of pewter vessels, along with a further 22 dozen platters and 22 dozen dishes – if a dozen contained 12 (there is some variability in medieval accounting documentation), then there were in the region of 500 settings for table.[29] And there were similar amounts of table linen: 80¾ yards of diapered 'mete cloth', 325 yards of plain 'mete cloth', and 23 yards of sanap, the cloth that would overlie the meat cloth to protect it for those at the top table.[30]

Guild members would usually pay for themselves, or at least something towards their costs, if not for the entire feast. Around 1389, the guild of St James, Garlickhithe, London, ordered that 'the brothers and sisters of the brotherhood of one accord wearing the guild's livery ... shall come every year and hold together a feast to nurture better understanding and love, the feast to be held on the Sunday after St James the Apostle (25 July). And each person is to pay 20d towards this.'[31] Twenty pence was a considerable sum – four or five days' wages for a skilled worker – and was on top of the other payments members made to the guild. Ordinary members of the guild of the Holy Cross at Stratford in the early fifteenth century usually paid 6d. Although there was a presumption that all guild members would attend the annual feast, it was equally clear that they did not. At Stratford in the 25 years between 1405 and 1430 there were as many as 182 individuals paying 6d in 1414–15,[32] and as few as 108 in 1410–11 – in this last year 245 guild members paid another due to the guild, the contribution to its lights.[33] This discrepancy appears to have been common: although the guild feast was a communal occasion and all members were enjoined to attend – indeed, as at the Norwich St George guild, absence without due cause was usually a finable offence in the guild statutes – this does not seem to have happened in practice. At the same time, there were others present who did not pay the contribution or who had remission from it for some reason. At Stratford, in

1412–13, 160 individuals paid to attend, and there were allowances for another 15 people: the guild chaplains, proctors, servants and one or two others.[34] In 1427–8, beyond the £3 1s 10d from the brethren, suggesting that there were perhaps 120 to 125 of them at the feast, there were allowances for six chaplains, 15 brothers of the guild who acted as servants or officials at the feast, and others, guests.[35] In 1415–16 allowance was made for two people who had worked assiduously about the feast.[36] The chaplains of the guild at Stratford were exempted from payment by their contracts. Other classes of exemption tell us about the pattern of the celebration. In 1416–17, allowance was made for the food of John Clifford and Hugh Salford, of whom one was the 'sewyer', a waiter, and the other the steward in the hall; John Chambour was allowed his food because he was butler and Thomas Grene because he was helping at the dresser, where the food was prepared for service. Thomas Crope also had a food allowance because he was butler ('promptuarius'), probably in charge of ale rather than wine.[37] In the late fifteenth century, it was usual for the Stratford feast to employ an usher to keep the door during the feast,[38] and in 1498–9 a further individual was employed to collect up the spoons after the feast, much as a butler might look after silverware.[39] These officers are familiar from the great households of medieval England – there was a similar pattern of service at guild and other public feasts. Service was an honourable activity, and the dignity of these positions will have enhanced the standing of these individuals in their communities.

The pattern of officials at these feasts was in place from at least the thirteenth century. Events in the mid 1260s were recounted by Emma Proudfoot in a suit before the ecclesiastical courts to confirm that Robert Norman was her husband. She gave a report of the making of the marriage contract, in the cellar of Sir John Fitz John of Hanslope, in Buckinghamshire. Robert, however, claimed that he could not have entered into the contract as he was not there. He produced seven witnesses that he was steward at a drinking called a 'gylde' in the house of Simon le Got, from the hour of Nones (the ninth hour after daybreak) until dusk. The testimony of other witnesses indicates that this was a parish guild, that the occasion was a Sunday, and that this drinking took place annually close to the feast of St Edmund the Martyr – and that it lasted from the middle of the day until it was dark.[40]

As the Stratford feasts show, these occasions were not exclusively for guild members. At some guilds, members brought guests, perhaps friends, relations and companions;[41] and there may also have been provision for others that the guild wished to entertain. The pattern of purchasing and consumption also suggests that there was a hierarchy present at these feasts that went beyond members and the officers of the guild. One indication of this is in the level of expenditure on feasts. At Stratford in 1407–8, £3 10s 6d was received from contributions from the brethren and sisters; in addition, the accountant had receipts from a few minor sources, such as the sale of skins of animals slaughtered for the feast, or from unused food; but the costs of the feast were very much more substantial, at least £8 14s.[42] In 1414–15, there was a similar difference: £3 18s was received from the guild brethren and sisters, along with an allowance of 4s 6d for the chaplains and others, yet the costs of the feast came to £8 12s 9½d.[43] The difference in funds was drawn from the master of the guild, as, for example, in 1427–8, when the proctors were given an additional £15 4s 11½d for assorted expenses, including those of the guild feast.[44]

On what was the difference spent? While the Stratford feasts were civic events of major significance for the town, the guild itself had strong regional connections. Between 1420 and the start of the sixteenth century, the majority of the guild's members came from the town's hinterland, and there were important groups of members from Coventry, Bristol and London – and maintaining a wider connection was of primary concern for the guild.[45] The accounts for the feast give passing hints of the guests: in 1426–7, wine was bought for gentlemen – that is, guests of significance who are not otherwise mentioned in the record, and it was probably the reason why the guild spent so much more than it received on these feasts.[46] In 1434–5, wine was bought for Sir Thomas Burdet and William Bisshopusden, along with other gentlemen, on the day following the guild feast.[47] At most of the Stratford feasts, there was a payment for men carrying game to the feast – not for the game itself, which was almost certainly the gift of the Bishop of Worcester, the manorial lord of Stratford – food for important guests.[48] In 1414–15, 6 verges of linen cloth for a sanap were bought for the top table ('alta mensa'), indicative of distinction in terms of the seating arrangements.[49]

The location and setting of the Stratford feast

We can define further the overall environment of the main Stratford guild feast in the fifteenth century. The guild buildings at Stratford (Plate 20), especially its hall, were used for civic entertainment generally.[50] The annual feast was often held in the guildhall, but, when numbers were large, it may also have required a hall of temporary construction, possibly in the garden of the guildhall. In 1416–17, tables, trestles and forms were carried from the town to the hall and back again, along with hurdles and 'rasters' – a wooden framework, for making the hall, for which 1d worth of board-nails was acquired. The same year there was a payment for watching over 'the hall in the garden' ('le hale in gardino') for one night.[51] Payments for cleaning the hall, parlour and chambers in 1422–3 suggest that the ordinary space of the guildhall was also involved in that year.[52] Rushes were purchased for the hall floor in most years, even in 1416–17, and we may in this account perhaps see a distinction between things that were bought 'pro aula', that is, the guildhall, and those 'pro le hale' which may refer to a temporary building.[53] The year 1416–17 was one when the number of diners reached its highest levels, with 172 paying for the feast.[54] In 1442–3, rushes were bought against the feast for the upper hall ('aula superior') and for the counting house: this last may have been a formal setting for the audit of the accounts which took place the day after the feast.[55]

There were substantial building works to the guildhall complex around 1407. A stone dais ('scannum') was made in the hall, and a hearth in the kitchen. There were new windows for the hall; there was a porch and entrance way to the hall, and a tresance (a covered passage) in the garden, possibly linked to the kitchen. Work was also carried out on the larder; 1,000 tiles were used to cover the holes in the guildhall roof; the kitchen walls were daubed and pargetted. The guildhall at Stratford was equipped with tables dormant – that is, tables with fixed legs – made around 1407, and these tables were set up in this space all the time. The carpentry included work on their supports, the table tops, as well as accompanying forms, and boards bought for them, and for a dresser in the kitchen, a shelf in the buttery, and work on racks in the kitchen.[56] It is probable that, beyond the tables dormant, there were also trestle tables in the hall, at least from time to time, as payment was made in 1450–1 for repairing a trestle there.[57] In 1471–2, three painted cloths were bought to hang in the hall; there is no evidence for hangings there before this date.[58] Table presentation was also important. There are references to the hemming of tablecloths; to the washing of napery – table linen – both before and after feasts, a charge that occurs in almost every year; and to the purchase of sanaps.[59] Five sanaps were bought for the tables dormant in the hall in 1407–9, suggesting that there may indeed have been five of these tables.[60] In 1455–6, the washing included cloths ('mappe') and towels ('tuelle'), important for the routines that accompanied dining.[61]

There was further work on the guild's kitchen in the period 1411–17, which included partitioning it, and possibly paving the floor of a section. It was at this period that work was undertaken to create a 'herbarium' in the garden. This was a substantial investment, needing 33 cartloads of stone from Drayton, near Banbury, which with 8s for the work of the labourers on the herbarium came to a total cost of £1 8s 1d – and one imagines that the plants grown there contributed both to the feast and to the general well-being of those in the almshouses attached to the guildhall.[62] There was a privy within the guildhall, and a new catch was made for its door in 1445–6.[63] Other buildings in the complex included a clock house, constructed in 1421–2;[64] and a storehouse and a bakehouse; there was a counting house, a pantry, and an 'over-hall' or room over part of the main guildhall.[65] The guildhall had its own well.[66] The guild's resident chaplains had, by the mid fifteenth century, another place where they might eat, within the guild chapel,[67] along with their own kitchen and cook.[68] In 1407–9, wooden platters, saucers and bowls had been bought for the resident almsmen.[69]

The guild's inventory of 1454 provides a long list of utensils, which gives a good indication of the fraternity's capacity for preparing food.[70] In terms of cooking equipment, beyond the comparatively small-scale resources that were intended to provide for the priests, there were 13 brass pots, and a series of large pans: four containing 20 gallons, and a series of smaller ones ranging downwards from 10 gallons to 1½ gallons and beyond; and nine spits. The pantry and buttery had a single, silver covered cup, a great mazer called the 'pardon mazer', bound with silver and gilt, along with two lesser mazers. There was a substantial holding of pewter tableware: no fewer than

381 vessels, including 110 platters, 162 pottingers (vessels for pottage or liquid) and 91 saucers – which might all have been employed at the main guild feast. Other items look as if they were for use by a select few – such as the 21 silver spoons. Nicholas Leek had given napery for the high table. Despite these holdings of equipment, the guild, at least earlier in the fifteenth century, had had to hire utensils for the feast. In 1405–6, the proctors were charged 4d for a pewter dish which had been hired that was lost at the event.[71] And it was necessary from time to time to make repairs or to add new items. In 1440–1, three tankards and two bowls were repaired;[72] in 1468–9, 50 cups were bought, along with six drinking vessels known as godards, the latter worth 4d;[73] in 1471–2, 2s 1d was spent on new cups, and 15s on making two and a half dozen spoons for the use of the guild.[74]

The commodities of the Stratford feast

Putting on a feast on the scale of the main Stratford guild celebration was a major logistical exercise and it was a prominent feature of the work of the guild's two proctors. Preparations started some time in advance and the two men divided the labour of collecting the foodstuffs between them, some-times with assistance from the guild's master. The purchases provide some information about the way food was prepared, the dishes that were presented at the feast, and the style of dining. Unlike establishments which maintained their own stocks of food, almost everything consumed at the Stratford feast had to be purchased for the occasion: this provides useful insights into the composition of the meal that might not appear in records of other bodies. Even though the guild had its own garden, there were still significant purchases of garden produce. We therefore get an exceptionally good view of the commodities and flavourings that were used.

Every Stratford feast in the fifteenth century took place on a Sunday in early July, that is, a flesh day. A very few individuals chose to eat fish, and their pattern of abstinence would have marked them out as distinctive: in 1414–15, 11½d was spent on fish for those fasting, and in 1425–6, 7d.[75] Other guilds, such as the fraternity of St John the Baptist at Winchester, kept their feast on the same date each year – in this instance the nativity of St John – and that meant it sometimes fell on a day of abstinence.[76]

The first major purchase for the Stratford feast was wheat: for bread for the feast, sometimes in excess of 3 qrs – in 1426–7, 1427–8 and 1447–8, no less than 5½ qrs; there were more than 5 qrs also in 1442–3.[77] Gifts of 1 qr of wheat were received on several occasions, in 1416–17 from the lord of Wolverton.[78] We do not know how many loaves were baked per quarter of wheat. Fourteenth-century calculations might suggest a figure in the region of 235 loaves, but this may be misleading in that there was a tradition of baking loaves of different shapes and sizes for celebratory occasions. The loaves at peasant boon feasts were frequently much larger than those used in great households, and the indication from the numbers attending the feast – if every diner had a single loaf – is that larger loaves were used at the Stratford feast. Flour was also purchased, for bakemeats, the pastry casings for food;[79] and for pies and tarts.[80] By the second half of the fifteenth century, local bakers were being paid for baking bread – in 1471–2, four men, Philip Baker, Roger Palmar, William Tewman and John Baker, were paid to this end.[81] Earlier, however, baking may have taken place at the guild's bakehouse. In a year early in the fifteenth century, possibly 1408–9, payment was made for carrying wheat to the mill and back.[82]

Malt for brewing ale was also purchased: in 1427–8, 7 qrs were purchased, along with 36 gallons of ale ready for consumption.[83] The yield of ale varied according to the strength of the brew: in the early sixteenth century the brewery at Westminster Abbey produced between 45 and 50 gallons of best ale from every quarter of barley malt, so in the region of 350 gallons of a similar ale could have been brewed in anticipation of the Stratford feast.[84] But even that was not necessarily enough: in 1445–6, 5 qrs of malt had been bought for brewing for 12s 8d, but the ale ran out and it was necessary afterwards to spend a further 8s 0½d in the town on ale.[85]

Wheat and malt were also provided for fattening geese and pullets, marking out a distinctive culinary element of these feasts. Geese and pullets were a key component and were present in substantial numbers. Gathering the poultry was time-consuming: poultry-rearing was almost all in the hands of peasant farmers rather than manorial demesnes – and this close interest may have been a guarantee of the quality of the product. In 1427–8, the two proctors claimed 4s as an allowance for their horses and their own expenses riding for five days for gathering the 165 geese and 163 pullets needed that year.[86] The poultry were kept together alive for about a week before the feast, during which time they were fattened up. In 1407–8, 5 qrs of malt were acquired for brewing ale, but a slightly larger amount (along with more than 3 bus. of wheat) was given to the geese: 2 qrs 2 bus. of dried malt, and 3 qrs 2 bus. of undried; 12d was spent on the costs of looking after the poultry.[87] In 1408–9 a poultry-keeper was paid 4d for a week to look after the birds.[88] In 1447–8, laths and nails were needed for the windows of the schoolhouse where the pullets were kept before the feast.[89] In many years, geese and pullets were purchased in sufficient quantity for almost everyone at the feast to have had one of each. In 1407–8, 141 brethren and sisters paid for the feast, and there were 129 geese and 154 pullets;[90] and in 1445–6, 129 geese and 114 pullets, and the brethren and sisters paid £2 7s 3d (there were probably 126 brethren paying a smaller sum than usual, 4½d each – rather than 94 or slightly more at 6d each).[91] The geese were green geese, that is, they were young, between three and four months old. In 1431–2, 182 geese were bought at prices between 1½d and 2¼d a head – at the end of the four-teenth century, mature geese, usually sold around Michaelmas, retailed at about 3d each.[92] Despite this interest in poultry, there was some variation in the composition of the feast: these birds do not seem to have featured at all in 1410–11;[93] there were no geese in 1414–15,[94] and only two in 1416–17.[95] On the other hand, the practice developed of purchasing small numbers of capons, perhaps special birds, for the top table: there were seven in 1412–13; 12 in 1414–15, and nine in 1415–16. In 1416–17, the dozen capons cost just over 3¼d each.[96] But in 1447–8, when the brethren paid £3 16s 1d, the emphasis had changed and instead of geese there were 65 capons, perhaps half a capon per person, along with the 15 hens and 224 pullets; in this year, the six geese were reserved for gentlemen.[97] Geese and pullets were also fattened with peas[98] and barley.[99]

Beyond poultry, there was meat at every feast, and there was always veal, mutton and piglets. The year 1412–13 was typical of the feasts in the first half of the fifteenth century, with beef, pork, six calves, seven carcasses of mutton, 15 piglets, two knuckles of veal, and 15d worth of fat.[100] The butchers of Stratford and Shipston supplied veal, pork, marrowbones and suet in 1445–6;[101] in 1447–8, meat came from butchers in Stratford and Warwick.[102] The meat was sometimes acquired jointed, with butts, legs and other joints of pork and veal, pestles of pork, and crops of beef.[103] Payments for 'dighting' meat, the butchers' preparation of the carcass, were increasingly common in the fifteenth century, along with the purchase of jointed meat.[104] This butchery was no longer done as part of the feast preparations at the guild: it is indicative of the way the meat trade had developed, and what was available locally. As well as joints and marrowbones, there were entrails and offal.[105] There was also a cost to assembling the meatstock: in 1408–9, at least 15*d* was spent on costs in the country round about ('in patria') for that year's calves. Kids were purchased – probably as a delicacy – and they, too, had to be sought out. Ten were bought at Shrewsbury in 1410–11 for 5*s* 10*d*, and a further 1*s* 8*d* was spent on a man and a horse to fetch them.[106] On another occasion, in 1427–8, goats came from Worcester.[107] In 1495–6, the goats also came from Worcester, and a payment was made for the butchers' work in preparing them for consumption.[108] These meats were in addition to the game that was donated in many years, sometimes as much as three deer carcasses, as in 1442–3.[109] The guild itself made use of game from time to time, for example, in acquiring 8*d* worth of rabbits for the gentlemen at the audit dinner in 1456–7; but for the feast it came overwhelmingly as gifts.[110]

Although the fare at these meals was substantial, it was pitched at a level which was on the whole less elaborate than that served in great households or ecclesiastical institutions. At the same time, the guild feast might copy elite dining, and include elements of it for smaller groups, especially for visiting dignitaries. This can be seen, too, in its more reserved use of dairy foods and eggs (even though consumption of these latter might seem large by present-day standards). In 1477–8, there were 2 gallons of cream.[111] There was possibly more cream and dairy produce at the feast at the end of the fifteenth century: the 1495–6 feast saw 2½ gallons of milk, and at least 8½ gallons of cream, along with curds. For approximately 200 people, this averaged out at about a third of a pint of cream per person, but dairy produce like this was unlikely to have been distributed evenly.[112] Cheese, however, was much more unusual; it appeared in 1410–11 and 1412–13;[113] it was present at meals for carpenters employed by the guild in 1431, but did not feature as a significant element in the main guild celebrations.[114] Eggs ranged in quantity from 250 in 1422–3, 500 in 1434–5 and 800 in 1471–2, to 1,800 in 1425–6.[115] These indicate some of the variation there must have been from year to year in, for example, the quantities of tarts and flans.

Given the significance of spices and sauces for medieval food in general, it is useful to see the changes in the spices and flavourings at Stratford over the course of the fifteenth century (Table 7.1). Spices were purchased in London in at least some of the years in the later 1420s.[116] They show a common pattern in the first three decades of the fifteenth century: typically about 2 lbs of pepper, about 2 oz of saffron, figs in quantities between 4 and 20 lbs; raisins (3 lbs or more), currants (raisins of Corinth, 3 lbs) and great raisins (as much as 20 lbs), between 3 and 10 lbs of almonds, and then 2 oz of mace, between ¼ and ½ lb of ginger; sometimes 1 lb of cinnamon, and between ¼ and ½ lb each of sanders and cloves. Two prominent colourants were present in saffron (yellow) and sanders (red). By the end of the fifteenth century, the pattern had changed: there was more pepper, and seeds, such as turnsole, fennel and aniseed, were now present. The increase in the quantity of sugar was notable. The traditional and most widely available sweetener had been honey, along-side fruits. Honey appeared at almost every feast, in quantities that varied across the century but without any ostensible pattern. At its greatest, as in 1442–3, 4 gallons might be required, but the quantity could be as little as a pint to a quart, as in an early fifteenth-century account and in 1473–4.[117] Some flavourings, for example, mustard, are notable by their absence from the lists of purchases for the feast. Although it appeared in the guild accounts for the meals of building workers, or at the audit, mustard was rarely a flavouring at the main guild feast.[118] This suggests that it may have been more typical of the flavourings that went with peasant and artisan food, that it was not sufficiently distinguished for the celebratory meals of the guild.

Beyond spices, flavourings and vegetables were potentially drawn direct from the guild's garden. They were also bought in. Garlic appears regularly,[119] but onions appear at the feast in fewer years, for example in 1414–15, 1431–2 and 1442–3, although again they might form a part of the food supplied at other times to workmen.[120] Salt was bought in most years, both as a flavouring and probably to help with cleaning, the scouring of pots after the feast.[121] Wine was bought in much smaller quantities than ale – most people at the feast would not have drunk it. It was used in the kitchen, and some smaller amounts were drunk by the elite at the feast – in

Table 7.1: Spices used at the feast of the guild of the Holy Cross, Stratford-upon-Avon, 1407–8 to 1427–8, and 1490–1

	1407–8	1408–9	1410–11	1412–13
Pepper	2 lbs	2 lbs	1½ lbs	1¾ lbs
Saffron	⅛ lb	1 oz	⅛ lb	3 oz
Figs	4 lbs	9 lbs	12 lbs	20 lbs
Raisins	4 lbs	3 lbs	–	–
Mace	⅛ lb	⅛ lb	–	–
Ginger	½ lb	–	¼ lb	½ lb?
Cinnamon	1 lb	–	–	–
Sanders	¼ lb	⅛ lb	½ lb	2s
Raisins of Corinth	3 lbs	7d	3 lbs (12d)	3 lbs
Great raisins	–	–	–	20 lbs
Cloves	½ lb	–	¼ lb	–
Almonds	11d	3 lbs (9d)	6 lbs (18d)	10 lbs
Rice	2 lbs	2 lbs	4 lbs	2 lbs (flour)
Grains	–	8d	–	–
Sugar	–	–	–	½ lb
Dates	–	–	–	–
Turnsole	–	–	–	–
Fennel seed	–	–	–	–
Aniseed	–	–	–	–

	1414–15	1415–16	1416–17	1422–3
Pepper	1¼+ lbs	1 lb	3s 6d+	–
Saffron	3 oz+	2½ oz	2s+	6d
Figs	–	–	–	–
Raisins	–	–	–	–
Mace	–	2 oz	¼ lb	2d
Ginger	1 lb	¼ lb	½ lb	6d
Cinnamon	¼ lb	2 oz	12d	–
Sanders	¼ lb	–	⅛ lb	–
Raisins of Corinth	2¼ lbs	–	3 lbs	7d
Great raisins	–	–	–	–
Cloves	¼ lb	3 oz	¼ lb	6d
Almonds	2 lbs	3 lbs	–	–
Rice	–	3 lbs	–	–
Grains	–	–	–	–
Sugar	½ lb	–	–	–
Dates	–	–	2 lbs; 8d	–
Turnsole	–	–	–	–
Fennel seed	–	–	–	–
Aniseed	–	–	–	–

Table 7.1: (*continued*)

	1425–6	1426–7	1427–8	1490–1
Pepper	1¼ lbs	2 lbs	1½ lbs	4 lbs (+ part of 2s 5d)
Saffron	⅛ lb	⅛ lb	¼ lb	3 oz
Figs	–	–	–	–
Raisins	–	–	–	–
Mace	½ lb	¼ lb	¾ lb	(part of) 3s 8d +
Ginger	½ lb	1 lb	¼ lb	(part of) 14d + 1 qr
Cinnamon	½ lb	½ lb	¼ lb	(part of) 14d + 1 qr
Sanders	1 lb	1 lb	⅛ lb	½ lb + 1½ qr
Raisins of Corinth	2 lbs	3 lbs	2½ lbs	–
Great raisins	3 lbs	4 lbs	12 lbs	17 lbs
Small raisins	–	–	–	11 lbs
Cloves	½ lb	⅜ lb	¼ lb	(part of) 3s 8d + 1 qr +
Almonds	2 lbs	7 lbs ('jardin')	2 lbs	1 lb
Rice	–	3 lbs	–	–
Grains	–	–	–	–
Sugar	–	14d	½ lb	7 lbs (8d)
Dates	–	–	–	–
Turnsole	–	–	–	4d + ½ qr
Fennel seed	–	–	–	½ qr
Aniseed	–	–	–	1d

Sources: SBTRO, BRT 1/3/22–3, 25, 27–30, 34, 36–7, 39, 100.

1410–11 the purchases included 2 gallons of red wine and 1 gallon of Osey, a sweet white wine from Portugal.[122] In the kitchen it would have contributed to the thin, acidic sauces characteristic of some elements of medieval cookery, just like the vinegar, of which several gallons were usually acquired, and, occasionally, verjuice – there was 1d worth in 1422–3,[123] and no more than 3 quarts in 1431–2.[124]

Cooking and cuisine

If the accounts for the feast give some evidence for cooking practices, there is less evidence of individual dishes. The purchases of fat speak of frying, or enriching foods, as does the presence of marrowbones.[125] Beyond the roasted geese, capons and pullets of the feast, venison was baked in pasties on other guild occasions, for example, on the Monday after the main guild feast, at the audit dinner in 1449. In September the same year, when Thomas Middelton and others came to the guild to eat venison, the pasties were flavoured with pepper, cloves, mace and saffron.[126] Diners the day after the main feast, at the audit in 1442–3, were offered a traditional dish of bacon with peas, alongside geese, lamb, piglets, beef, mutton and chicken;[127] and in 1447–8 the same meal included peas freshly gathered from the fields.[128] Peas and peasecods were a food that all enjoyed at this time of year. Other suggestions about foodstuffs come from the equipment bought for the feast. In 1412–13, for example, a bolter for sifting meal or flour was purchased along with two strainers, and 2 ells of linen for keeping foodstuffs in the buttery ('promptuarium') – perhaps to cover some of the jellies and creams that had been made in advance of the feast and were being kept cool there.[129] A further two yards of linen 'for food' ('pro cibo') were bought in 1414–15.[130] Many late medieval recipes focused on working food, especially meats, to a pulp, and then reshaping it into other forms, so it is unsurprising to find an emphasis on chopping and grinding in medieval guild accounts. In 1425–6, a great stone mortar was brought from the priests' college to the guildhall for the feast at a cost of 2s, and a pestle of wood was bought for the kitchen.[131]

The supplies for the main guild feast suggest a pattern to the meal similar to that of the elite – and, indeed, like members of the upper ranks of the peasantry and beyond, guild members would probably have reckoned this a familiar style at least for celebratory dining. Typically meals at an elite level would have two or three courses, as we have seen in Chapter 1, which would contain a range of meats: a first course starting with pottages and boiled meats, and a second course with roasted meats. Other dishes, such as creams, custards and tarts, would come as part of the same service. The courses might conclude, or be interspersed, with subtleties or 'entremes'. Dishes of this nature appeared at Stratford, as in 1442–3 when 3d worth of alkanet was bought for the subtleties.[132] The opportunity would also be taken between courses to engage in other activities, especially drinking: the circulation of a cup was a common feature at guild gatherings. The guild of the Holy Cross at Stratford had a great cup and, as we have seen, by 1454, a 'pardon mazer' (like the York Corpus Christi Guild), which could have been employed in this way, much as other guilds had special cups and drinking horns.[133]

The guild of the Holy Cross was reliant on professionals for the cuisine. At the start of the fifteenth century, the guild hired a master cook for each feast, as in 1407–8, when he was paid 3s 4d, along with a second cook for 2s and assistants.[134] From the mid 1410s, however, there was a change in arrangements and the guild retained its own master cook. John Dreton and his wife were admitted to the guild between 1411 and 1417 at a special level of entry fine under an arrangement that he should be the guild's cook at the feast each year for the term of his life.[135] In 1427–8, the guild's master cook, Richard Overton, had nothing, as he had a gown from the guild. John Pope was engaged as a cook for 2s; Brown Richard received 8d; there were at least three chefs to supervise the spits, along with 12 turnspits; there was a baker and a pastry chef; and there were a further 14 servants in the kitchen and the hall.[136] Additional cooks might be hired from households round about. In 1431–2, the cook of Lady Joan de Rodebroke was paid 2s for his labour among the cooks at the feast.[137]

Some of these individuals were hired year after year, and we can see something of their careers. Ralph of Pershore first appears in the accounts for 1445–6, where he is described as a 'pastoler', and was paid 1s 8d. He continued to be employed at the feasts until at least 1472–3: he is referred to in the 1460s and 1470s as Ralph Cook of Pershore, and in 1468–9 he was paid 8s for his work; in 1471–2, 6s 8d. Overall, this looks like the rise of an individual in his profession, from pastry chef to a more senior role, with continuing business.[138] Other cooks were rehired for many years but without any ostensible progression: Richard Oxton, for example, appears from 1453–4 to 1477–8, usually paid about 10d, and was often second or third in the list of named cooks.[139]

Besides cash, and the livery of the guild's master cook, most of the cooks and kitchen servants were given a perquisite, a linen apron.[140] The amount of linen in the apron varied by rank: in 1427–8, the aprons were priced at amounts between 3d and 4½d each. Two butlers had aprons for 6d, and the two proctors of the guild had them too, for 7d, which suggests that they may have had a role in service, presiding at the feast, as guild officers.[141] In

1434–5, Richard Compton had an apron worth 5*d* as surveyor (or overseer) of the feast.[142]

Some idea of the magnitude of the work involved is evident from time-scales: in 1431–2, rushes were bought for the cooks' beds, and their food was paid for in advance of the feast: one cook for three days, and three for one day.[143] In 1416–17, the turnspits were at work over at least two days: roasted food may therefore have come to the table cold.[144] We can see in addition others helping out in the kitchen and preparing food and drink. Women were frequently employed as dish-washers,[145] or in the buttery, looking after the ale. Two women drawing ale in the buttery were each given aprons worth 3*d* in 1434–5.[146] Alice Heyne and Agnes Careles worked in the buttery in 1468–9, and that year Margery Byngham and Alice Warde worked in the kitchen.[147] Women sometimes worked in the kitchen in company with their husbands. John Beyneham was working with his wife and another in 1442–3, for which they received 18*d*; he also worked there with his wife at the feast in 1447–8.[148]

The costs of fuel for the Stratford feasts tell us more about the cooking and food preparation that was carried out. Fuel was bought for general work, probably for roasting and boiling, as well as for brewing;[149] there were 'kids' (bundles of brushwood), that would burn quickly, for heating the oven for baking;[150] and charcoal, sometimes as much as 8 qrs or in 1471–2 a cartload,[151] which could be used both for keeping food warm and also for more delicate work.

Food waste and alms

A vast amount of food was procured for these feasts: was it all eaten? The accounts suggest that most of it was, or that there was very little left. Unusually, there are records of what was left over, because it was sold off after the feast and the cash applied to the total overall charge of the occasion. In 1416–17, for example, there was 12*d* from bread left over, 6*d* from the eggs, as well as sales of skins and fat.[152] In 1422–3, bread, ale and fuel worth 3*s* were sold after the feast, along with 2*s* worth of geese.[153] In 1426–7 seven calf's feet were sold for 2*s* 10*d*, probably left over from the jelly making.[154]

We know less about the question of food alms at the Stratford feasts – we shall see more in general about these alms in Chapter 11. If what had preceded the feast was a religious ceremony, we should not see the consumption of food itself as devoid of a similar significance. Guild members broke bread together, shared it with their guests, and gave food and drink in alms as part of the day's events; formal drinking cups circulated, some at least charged with wine. The connections to the solemnity of the ritual meal of the Mass will not have been lost on participants.[155] The proctors of the Holy Cross guild gave food alms on Good Friday, in 1388–9, 2s worth of bread distributed to the poor for the soul of John de Peyto.[156] In 1438–9, ale was given to the poor men and women of the guild's almshouses at the audit of the proctors' accounts, and bread on the day of the election of the master, aldermen and proctors.[157] This transaction probably happened on many other occasions, and the broken meats from the guild feast would also have been available to the inhabitants of the guild's almshouses, but the accounts do not state this.

The Stratford feast in context

We can conclude that at Stratford the annual guild feast was one of middle rank in terms of the food served, even if its pattern was clearly modelled on that of the elite. But it was far from the only occasion for entertainment and celebration in the guild's calendar: others with a regular place were the annual audit of the guild's accounts and the election of guild officers,[158] breakfasts on the feast of the dedication of the church,[159] meetings of the guild, for which ale was provided,[160] and there were breakfasts on the reception of new guild members.[161]

The meal and the range of foods might vary according to the occasion. In 1431–2, a breakfast was given in a negotiation in which it was necessary to show the guild's deeds of title;[162] and one was given in 1448–9, when Sir William Byrmyngeham came to measure the lands of the borough.[163] When the guild entertained the Bishop of Worcester in 1427–8, probably over a period of two days, the master ensured that the foods included those redolent of high status, rarely seen at the annual feast: capons, a swan, a doe, heronsews, rabbits and squabs, along with game from Grove Park. On this occasion, the bishop's own cooks prepared the meal. The master cook of the bishop's household was paid 1s 8d, and there were two further cooks from his household. These three were given the customary aprons worth together a further 15d.[164] Two dressers were bought, probably for the same occasion.[165] In the same year, the proctors paid for food for meetings and dinners with the Bishop of Worcester's officials. Sometimes these were meetings in houses and inns, but on occasion they took place in the guildhall. Thus on the Wednesday after the feast of St George the costs of a meal that included the receiver – the chief financial officer – of the Bishop of Worcester, various other worthies and the alderman came to some £1 16s.[166] Another entertainment, in 1425–6, 'for gentlemen' in the hall included flour for 'French bread' and bakemeats, six capons, veal and pork, spices, cream and cheese, seven marrowbones, and 2d worth of peasecods. There were fresh rushes for the hall on this occasion as well, the total for which came to £1 1s 6d.[167]

The guild's officers sometimes entertained elsewhere than the guild buildings, in inns or private houses – calibrating what was appropriate with the practicalities of the occasion. In 1406–7, a breakfast was given in the house of John Brasyer, and wine was bought in the house of John Mayel on occasions for the master and aldermen.[168] In 1450–1, wine was given to the Countess of Warwick in the house of Agnes Chacombe, and there was wine given for the reception of the brethren and sisters when John Marchall was married. Conscious of its regional dimension, the guild's expenses also extended to receptions for its brethren and sisters at Shipston-on-Stour, Chipping Campden and Evesham.[169] In 1453–4, wine was given when Sir William Catesby was married, when the Abbots of Keynsham and Tewkesbury were received into the fraternity, and to the Earl of Warwick when he rode by the town on his way to Wales[170] – in September 1453, the Earl of Warwick had given the guild venison to be enjoyed by the brethren and sisters, part of the pattern of courteous gift exchange.[171] In 1459–60, expenses made 'for the profit of the guild' included gifts of wine to the Countess of Pembroke, Lord Scales and the Queen's receiver,[172] much as we have seen Leicester honour the Earls and Dukes of Lancaster.

These feasts delineate the expectations and experience of guild members. The feast was only a part of the guild's celebrations that day: the religious ceremonies, the processions and entertainment were an integral part of the occasion. Minstrels are in evidence in the accounts and may have been present at the feast itself. In 1408–9, for example, one was paid 4d;[173] in 1471–2, 2s 2d was paid to minstrels of Warwick;[174] and in 1495–6 there were minstrels from both Stratford and Warwick.[175] The meals can be placed within the rituals of elite dining: the same principal officers, patterns of service and some at least of the dishes. The foodstuffs on the table were as close as many would have come to elite food – and the foods of the top table were even then not generally accessible to all. It is striking that it was overwhelmingly male cooks who were employed to produce this food – just as in the great households of the land – not the female cooks who would have prepared much of day-to-day urban and rural cuisine. The accounts provide good evidence for the make-up of popular, celebratory meals: the goose dinners of Stratford can be paralleled by those of the guild of Corpus Christi and St Nicholas of Coventry, also in the fifteenth century held in July; or those at the same time of year at Maidstone.[176] For others, such as the St John's guild at Winchester, the feasts detail an aspirational range of fish consumption. At the feast of St John the Baptist in 1411, fresh and salt fish, mullet, bass, ray and fresh conger, alongside eels, with beans and peasecods, a range of spices and onions, and cheese were consumed. They were events at which people could meet in company, with friends and neighbours, to whom they were bound in mutual support. At Winchester at the 1411 feast, there was entertainment from minstrels and dancing.[177] Patron saints appeared in person, like St George at Norwich.

The investment in the guild feast, however, was not a constant. There was variation in the character of the occasion, sometimes from year to year, but also over the longer term. Much of the ambience of the feast must have come from the inspiration of the individuals who had to organise and enthuse their peers. The Stratford feasts point to a lessening of the significance of the occasion after the 1430s, but with a renewed interest in the closing decades of the century; the Winchester St John's guild confined its celebrations to a supper, rather than a major dinner, in the early sixteenth century; and elsewhere, as at Coventry, the number of occasions for feasting was scaled back at this period. The rhythm of celebration and commemoration depended to a great extent on the vitality of the particular guild – the guild returns of 1389 show that many had comparatively short periods of existence and small-scale resources, while others obtained resilience through combination with other guilds and links to the urban patriciate. At their most important, however, these feasts were events that were crucial to the fraternities of late medieval England, attended by large numbers, prominent in the social and religious calendar of the locality, and a major part of urban culture. The connection to religious culture is one that merits further investigation. We have already seen how the Church's calendar shaped the pattern of consumption across society. The next chapter looks at the foodways of ecclesiastical institutions, especially the monasteries, to demonstrate how these questions were addressed there.

CHAPTER EIGHT

FOODWAYS AND MONASTIC INSTITUTIONS

IN A CULTURE THAT made close connections between food and sin, the relationship between the clergy, both secular and cloistered, and food was bound to attract scrutiny. The households of the greatest prelates had patterns of consumption that were similar to those of the elite more generally. All who could in society, at least as far down as the parish priest and his assistant in the countryside, sought to emulate this experience – but emulation of secular practice was a source of great tension in clerical life, especially in the monasteries. Many monks and some nuns were closely linked to the elite, and the dietary connections they made were to the foods and foodways that they had known in family life and may have continued to experience on visits to the outside world. Food was an important element in monastic life, not only for the significance of blessed daily bread in the sustenance of God's servants, and as an instrument of charity, but also because of an impressive interest in institutional dining. This chapter looks at the food of monks and nuns; it considers the ways in which routines developed around practices of preparation and eating in these institutions, and what they can tell us about the food culture of the Middle Ages more generally.

One of the fables of Odo of Cheriton, from around 1220, tells of an abbot who gave his monks three courses ('fercula') of food. The monks said: he has given us too little, we will beseech God that he might die; and from one cause or another, he did. His replacement provided only two courses, and the monks, both cross and saddened, because they had lost one of the courses, agreed that they must again pray that God might take away the life of the new abbot. And he died. His replacement took away a further dish, leaving just the one. The monks considered him the worst of the lot, as they were now dying of hunger. The gossips among them asked that they pray again that the abbot might die. But one spoke against the others: 'It seems to me that the first was bad, the second worse, and this one the very worst. I am afraid lest a worse one still succeed him and we die of starvation.' Aside from the moral – things rarely get better – this is a direct statement of the importance of food in the monastic mentality.[1] The temptations of food were there, especially for those in positions of power: in 1215, the Abbot of Beaulieu was alleged to have had with him at table three earls and 40 knights, behaving far from decorously, drinking just like adolescents[2] – and the abbot was not alone in these practices. The stereotypical image of the ample monk had some underlying truth to it: monastic diets may have led to obesity, at least in those genetically predisposed to it. In the later Middle Ages, the diet at Westminster Abbey has been shown to have been high in protein and very substantial in terms of calories, and the daily regimen of many monks will have involved only restricted amounts of exercise.[3] Osteological evidence from Merton Priory, Bermondsey Abbey and the Abbey of St Mary Graces in London indicates similar consequences from diet and lifestyle for the religious there.[4]

Monastic diet had not always been like this. It had evolved from the fundamentals set out by St Benedict of Nursia (c.480–c.550) in his Rule, which underpinned monastic practice in the West for much of the Middle Ages. In it, Benedict outlined what was essentially a Mediterranean diet of abstinence. He envisaged that at the main meal (and, indeed, the only meal outside the period from Easter to mid September and for some days in this period) there would be two cooked dishes, known as 'pulmentaria' – typically cereals and vegetables, but perhaps with eggs and fish from time to time – and a third dish of fresh fruit or vegetables in season, along with a loaf of bread and drink. The dishes that he had described, known as 'generals', had originally been intended as alternatives but, by c.1200 and probably well before, they were both served. There were other modifications by the end of the twelfth century. Principal among these was the addition of extra dishes and pittances, that is, dishes and drinks that were given and allowed to the monks out of charity, which gradually in practice enabled monks to replicate secular fare. These included meaty dishes, of offal, but not the tissue of flesh meat.[5] Pittances quickly became an important feature of monastic life and their appearance at table was often linked to important occasions in the liturgical calendar. If the diet of society in general was shaped by the Church, with its days of abstinence and celebration, diet in the monasteries was even more finely attuned to a pattern of feast days and commemoration, often linked to the individual house – and therefore varying to a certain extent between institutions. By the mid twelfth century the monks of Bury St Edmunds had an impressive list of some 35 occasions on which pittances were expected at table.[6] The income from Westminster Abbey's manor of Benfleet in Essex was assigned for pittances in the early twelfth century.[7] Westminster's customary of 1266 set out the contents of the Benfleet pittance: it was to contain one and a half 'fercula' made up of two soles; or six salt eels, lamperns, small lampreys, gudgeon or fresh eels; or four whiting, and with further variations for other fish and shellfish.[8]

More generally, modifications to monastic diet were further agreed by popes, and also by chapters general of the different monastic orders. Through a process of negotiation, the meat of quadrupeds, which Benedict of Nursia had prohibited to all except the sick who were weak, was added to diet. A compromise was reached in 1336, when Pope Benedict XII gave dispensation for the eating of meat, but with provisos: that it be eaten in an agreed place, often known as the 'misericord'; and that on those days when meat was eaten at least half the monks should eat 'regular' food in the refectory, regular in the sense of according with the Rule ('regula' in Latin). The compromise was more a reflection of a trend that had been in place for some time than a new departure.[9] Monastic records point to other foodstuffs as customary relief from the diet of the Rule, or as elaborations of foods that were regularly consumed – such as forms of loaf, cheese and fruit, along with other dishes for special occasions. Some of these were extraordinarily popular and perhaps featured immoderately in the life of the cloister.

Monastic loaves themselves were of considerable importance. Just as there were nuances in secular food, distinctions between the loaves indicate the standing and quality of the individuals allowed to consume them. There were different loaves at different monasteries. At Norwich, there was a typical arrangement, with three principal loaves: the monks' loaf ('panis monach-orum'), a loaf of lesser weight but made of the same dough as the monks' loaf ('panis ponderis minoris'), and the knights' loaf, the loaf of poorest quality. Through an etymological misunderstanding, a 'knihta hlaf' was translated into Latin as 'panis militum', 'knights' loaf', at Norwich and much more widely, rather than as 'servants' loaf'. Unlike loaves for sale commercially, whose weight depended on the arrangements set out in the assize of bread, the weights of the different monastic loaves were usually constant.[10] At Bury St Edmunds, the customs of c.1234 noted excommunication as the penalty for anyone who dared to interfere with the quantity or the quality of the bread ration.[11] These distinctions were keenly maintained with other classes of foodstuff as well, and two examples, dairy foods and fruit, illustrate some of the passions that food might evoke.

A dispute over the cheese ration at Abingdon Abbey, at a point after 1114, required the intervention of the Bishop of Salisbury, the Archbishop of Canterbury and then King Henry I. Abbot Faritius noted that the numbers of monks had increased, and that there were something like twice as many as when Abbot Aethelwold had endowed the ration in the mid-tenth century. The compromise agreement, marked by the abbot's gener-osity, was that the ration should now be given for a five-day period rather than a 10-day one, for the cowled monks in the refectory, the infirmary and the portion for three poor. Excluded from these arrangements were the abbot's table, the guests and brethren he invited there. This was agreed and Faritius noted that he had provided 46 weys of cheese a year for the abbot's table, for his successors (effectively one wey a week outside Lent – but possibly consumption was more concentrated): this was an impressive amount. There is a little difficulty in establishing the size of a wey, but some 44 lbs (19.98 kg) of cheese a day may have been supplied, and this suggests a custom at Abingdon that was very different from monastic experience elsewhere.[12] In 1185, on the death of Abbot Roger of Abingdon, Thomas of Hurstbourne was sent to take charge of the abbey – and the cheese ration again came to the fore. Making his report to the justiciar, Ranulf Glanville, Thomas was clearly exasperated by the monks' lifestyle: truly, he said, the whole of Berkshire would not suffice to find the monks' cheese and milk, nor their lands oats for their horses. The Abingdon monks were sufficiently shrewd to contest this at the Exchequer, pointing out that Aethelwold had made provision for dairy farms to this end, and had anathematised all who might in future attempt to disrupt this arrangement. They also tartly noted that he who had wheat could always have oats. The threat of anathema was sufficient for the justiciar to confirm the cheese arrangements.[13] Episodes like this underscore the importance of these foodstuffs in monastic life, and elements of customary practice associated with them. The Abingdon cheese, for example, was to be divided in the larder, and the monk who cut it was to have a crumb of cheese on every cut; the refectioner was allowed to miss the morning Mass and Terce in order to cut and set out the cheese.[14]

Equally insistent was the fourteenth-century customary of St Swithun's, Winchester. The prior was to provide the bread, ale, wine and salt. He was also to provide the cheese each week – in this case a cheese of 32 lbs (14.53 kg). For the feast of the deposition of St Swithun (2 July), he was to find a further cheese, as provision also had to be made for nearby Hyde Abbey; for the feast of the translation of St Swithun (15 July), he had to provide two additional cheeses, as he had to make provision for the monks and for others, religious and secular. The cheese had to be good: if it was bad, it was sent back to the prior's exchequer to be exchanged for a good one.[15] Similar attention was devoted to cheese at Norwich Cathedral Priory. The inventories of the refectory in 1393–4 and 1410–11 record short towels or cloth wraps for carrying the cheese.[16]

Fruit, as we have seen, was a food that was the subject of particular care and this was no less true in a monastic context. At Abingdon the gardener was to supply 30 apples at every distribution of apples in the refectory, and in return the refectorer was to give him ale.[17] At St Swithun's, the gardener was to provide apples in Advent and Lent, on Mondays, Wednesdays and Fridays, unless there was another feast. The subprior, third prior, and fourth prior, should there be one, were each to have 10 apples, as was the refectorer; the obedientiaries – those monks holding administrative offices within the monastery – were generally to have the same; the prior was to have 15 apples. The gardener was to have a monks' (or 'conventual') loaf the first and last day of both Advent and Lent, from the allowance of the curtarian (the monk in charge of the garden); and at the feast of St James (25 July), at the blessing of the apples, the apples were to be passed out round the tables as in Advent and Lent. Gardening, here looking after the fruit trees, was well rewarded: the curtarian was allocated a loaf for 'dowel' – for 'doing well'.[18] This notion of giving additional rations for jobs well done, or for particular, often more specialised, tasks is frequently met with in monastic customaries and regularly in secular great households, where loaves were commonly given at the 'reward', part of the lord's own table.

These details give us insights into the quality of monastic dining, and the care and attention it required. More evidence for this, for cuisine and for those responsible for it comes from other groups of customaries. Among the most notable are those of St Augustine's Abbey, Canterbury.

Food at St Augustine's Abbey, Canterbury

The customaries of the Benedictine abbey of St Augustine, Canterbury, are a rich source for information about foodways between the mid thirteenth and mid fourteenth centuries. Beyond these sources, there is also a set of injunctions of December 1274 by Abbot Nicholas Thorn, reforming the arrangements for service in the abbot's household.[19] Sited just outside the walls of Canterbury, St Augustine's was one of the oldest monastic houses in England, tracing its roots back to the mission to convert the English that arrived in Kent in 597.[20] In the second half of the thirteenth century the abbey was at the height of its prestige. In the late thirteenth and early fourteenth centuries, no fewer than three separate kitchens can be identified in the texts: for the abbot and his household, eating in his chamber, much like the great chambers of secular lords, and with very similar rituals of service, but on occasion eating in the refectory; for the monks, eating in the refectory; and for the free servants of the abbey, eating in their hall. There was a major campaign of building in the second half of the thirteenth century, works including a new refectory in the 1260s, as well as a great kitchen constructed in 1287–91 at a cost of some £414 (Plate 21).[21] This work was typical of the investment that the greatest monastic institutions were to make in their kitchens, as at Glastonbury (Plates 22 and 23), the work of the 1330s and 1340s, and at Durham, in 1366–74 (Plate 24). Some monastic institutions also had separate kitchens for the infirmary, but one is not so described at St Augustine's. A customary of the abbey's subcellarer from the mid to late thirteenth century details arrangements for food in the abbot's household, as well as those for the monastery as a whole. The customary and two later counterparts were concerned, first, to define the allowances that staff were to receive for their work, in terms of bread, ale, wine and food; and, secondly, to identify additional allowances which were necessary in food preparation. Together these give an overall picture of food in the monastery, from the preparation of an elite cuisine to the more modest entitlements of visiting manorial workers.[22]

As we have seen, bread was of special interest in the monasteries. At St Augustine's, at least eight different types of bread, of different weights and qualities, besides newels and wafers, were mentioned in the subcellarer's earliest customary (Table 8.1). These were a monks' loaf, possibly synonymous with the 'miche' loaves that are mentioned later; esquires' loaves, which also went by other names, perhaps with slightly different compositions – 'stendu' or 'stend' (perhaps meaning it had been stretched), 'churn', 'smalpeys' (or 'small weight'); knights' loaves and dogs' bread; an 'abbot's loaf' and an

Table 8.1: St Augustine's Abbey, Canterbury: loaves and their weights, mid to late thirteenth century

Monks' loaf ('panis monarchorum', 'miche')	1.13 kg (£3 10s)
Esquires' loaves ('panis armigerorum')	
Stend	0.83 kg (£2 11s 4d)
Churn	0.83 kg (£2 11s 4d)
Smalpeys ('small weight')	0.83 kg (£2 11s 4d)
Knights' loaves and dogs' bread ('panis canum')	0.83 kg (£2 11s 4d)
Abbot's loaf	0.86 kg (£2 13s 4d)
Alms loaf	0.86 kg (£2 13s 4d)
Travers	0.65 kg (£2)
Repeys	0.58 kg (£1 16s)
Abbot's wastel bread[a]	1.46 kg. (£4 10s 4d)
Prior's wastel and wastels for those that had been bled[b]	1.30 kg (£4 0s 2d)
Turta	1.62 kg (£5)

[a] The abbot's wastel bread is the weight of the stend and travers loaves combined.
[b] Two wastels are said to be the weight of the monks' loaf, smalpeys and travers combined, but these three in fact weigh 12d more.
A pennyweight has been taken as 1.35 grams, the weight of a silver penny.
Source: LPL, MS 1213, p. 309.

alms loaf; and two further loaves known as 'travers', and 'repeys'. Beyond this, the abbot had wastel bread, made with fine flour; and there were slightly smaller wastels for the prior and those who had been bled. There was another loaf, largely for servants, a 'turta', which was more substantial.[23] This last may be synonymous with the 'treat' loaf, which generally under the Assize of Bread and Ale of *c*.1256 was the lowest quality of wheat bread.[24] According to the St Augustine's customary of 1310×40, however, wheat was to be used for all the loaves except for the 'turte' of the servants, which were to be of barley; and there may have been more variation earlier. These loaves formed a key part of the daily allowances.[25] There were further types of loaf, with distinctive names, that seem to have been specific perquisites rather than loaves that were commonly made. The bolter, for example, whenever wastel loaves were made, was to have from the same dough a loaf called 'mertes', in English 'shepe' – the meaning of both these terms is now obscure – which weighed about the same as the repeys loaf.[26]

How did this bread come to table? The allowance for the abbot's chamber, when he ate there, illustrates the top end of the bread range, with the finest loaves and further specialities, newels and wafers, for supper at the main feasts. At lunch, there was to be one wastel loaf, two of the abbot's loaves and two churn loaves, and at supper one abbot's loaf and two miche loaves. On days of abstinence, those eating there were to have a bread ration of one abbot's loaf and one miche between two; on other days, the ration was to be less, one abbot's loaf and a stend loaf. The abbot's loaf in this context clearly meant the best of the loaves – aside from the abbot's wastel, the finest bread – that were to be served in his chamber. For trenchers, the slices of bread on to which food was to be served, there were to be two stend loaves, and either four or six smalpeys loaves as need be. At the principal feasts, the abbot was to have newels and wafers at supper, the portion of seven monks, just like the president (that is, the presiding monk) at supper in the refectory. Anyone eating in the chamber at these suppers was to have three newels and two wafers. The scale of the food of both the abbot and the president implies that some at least was to be given away, and the courteous distribution of food from the abbot's own portion would have been an expectation of dining at this level.[27] This variety in bread is very striking and typical of monastic institutions.

Abbot Thorn's injunctions exhibit all the hallmarks of the preparation of elite cuisine. The abbot's cook had a personal responsibility for his master's food: he was to prepare with his own hands whatever the abbot desired, both food and sauces – and he was never to be without good sauces. He was to receive instructions from the abbot the day before the meal, so that he could make preparations for sauced food to be ready in due time. The cook was engaged in purchasing, going with the cellarer's purchasers into the town, to buy better things for the abbot and his guests. He was to do his work in a timely way so that if the abbot were at home he might go to lunch after the gospel reading at High Mass. The abbot's cook had to ensure cleanliness, overseeing and checking on the work of others – there should be no dirt on any of the kitchen utensils; everything was to be absolutely decent. Other injunctions looked to prevent waste, for example, of ginger, and controlled the issue and return of the kitchen's silver vessels – that is, those in which the abbot's food would have been served – also making sure that the kitchen door into the courtyard was kept locked once deliveries had been received. Nor was the cook permitted to take out of the abbey gates the perquisites allowed to him until the cellarer or master chaplain or their attorneys had scrutinised them.[28]

Special culinary practices, from sauce-making to preparing shellfish, the larder and other foods, are identified in the customaries. In the mid to late thirteenth century, when the abbot's cook made sauce of white ginger, galentine or green sauce, he was allocated either one or two wastel loaves as he needed, or two monks' loaves or miche loaves. These were for the cooking process, and it needed a refined loaf for grating to thicken the sauce.[29] Those who cleaned whelks were to have a knights' loaf each, but it is possible that the purpose of the bread here was that it was to be fed to the shellfish to purge them of grit.[30] Beyond the whelks, provision was made for other shellfish. For the oysters, six monks' loaves, more or less as need be, were to be available. There were loaves and ale for making green sauce, pepper sauce ('peveree', possibly just a spiced sauce) and cumin sauce; for galentine there were two monks' loaves. The cooks in each of the three kitchens were expected to make their own sauces.[31]

While Abbot Thorn's injunctions refer to a single abbot's cook, the customary of the mid to late thirteenth century identifies two master cooks in the abbot's kitchen. They were to have additional rations when they prepared the larder, working with the slaughtered meat and salting it – a significant event, requiring the assistance of a range of servants. When they turned the bacon, the master cooks were to have for their own food meat instead of fish; when they took the fat out of carcasses, hung the bacon or turned it, they were to have a measure of the monks' ale. Those who washed and cleaned 'le souz' – probably pork that was to be preserved, soused in brine – were to have rations for two people; and the person who collected the pigs' blood was to have one knights' loaf and one portion of food. Additional rations were also given to others at the point when the larder was made: to all the kitchen servants, one from the bakehouse, one from the brewhouse, two gardeners and the woodhewer – and one imagines they too must have been involved in some way in the preparations of the day.[32] The practice of additional food is evident, too, in the bakehouse, where the man who made the wafers and newels against the principal feasts was to have a stend loaf, a smalpeys loaf, 2 gallons of ale, and two portions of food every day while he was engaged on this task.[33]

Just as making the larder required a special investment of labour, so too did the making of flans. Flans had a special place in ecclesiastical foodways: they were often prepared for consumption on the Rogation Days, the three days immediately before the Ascension. Their use at St Augustine's, however, extended over a longer period. The convent expected to have these from Easter until the octave of St Augustine (2 June). Like many monasteries, at St Augustine's a daily ration of food came to table commemorating any monk who died during the year – and flans were to be included in this, as well as in the further three portions of monks' food that were put aside each day as the maundy or provision for the poor. The ration allocated to the prior when he ate in the refectory suggests that the flans may not have been a daily occurrence, but were to be present at Easter, on the three Rogation Days, up to the octave of St Augustine, and on that day.[34] All hands were turned to the making of flans, including the gardeners and the woodhewer: that they were given rations for breakfast suggests that flan-making was a very full day's work.[35] The customary of 1310×40 included instructions for the amounts of eggs and cheese to go into the flans: the flan case itself to have 0.32 kg (240d weight) of paste. To make 72 flans, there were to be

10 lbs (4.54 kg) of cheese (unless the cheese was freshly made, in which case 11 lbs (5 kg) was to be allowed), 2¼ oz (63 grams) per flan, along with 350 eggs, that is, just under five per flan.[36]

The 1310×40 customary follows the diet of the monks through the year and shows other special foods. On the feasts of 12 lessons – the major feasts – and festive anniversaries, they were to have a portion of dairy foods, but in Lent at these feasts they were to have pancakes ('crispis').[37] At all the principal liturgical feasts, there was to be salmon or sturgeon, and in addition the convent was to have this on their own special feast, of St Augustine (26 May).[38] There were special drinks too. There was to be mead all Saturdays at the maundy; at feasts, when the monks attended service in albs, the linen ankle-length vestments worn by all who served at the altar, at lunch there was to be simnel and mead; on the eve of double feasts, there was to be mead at Collation. The combination of simnel and mead appears throughout the year, at major celebrations.[39] The mead was made by the cellarer's servant (he was also responsible for drawing the ale and delivering it to the refectory).[40] There was a special, spiced wine for the feast of St Augustine: the clary ('claratum') was to be made to a house recipe with wine and skimmed honey (clear honey), with spices including measured amounts of ginger, cinnamon, pepper, galingale, spikenard, green fennel (possibly fenugreek) and cardamom.[41]

Fried food was notable for its appearance at major festivities. Throughout the year, on feast days there was to be a portion of fried food, and a pittance at supper. In Advent and at Septuagesima the foods were to be fried with butter, but at other times of the year lard ('sagimen') was used. Lard was put into dishes of peas and 'pulmentum' at all times of the year except those of abstinence, Advent, Septuagesima, Lent, vigils of the main feasts, the Ember Days, Rogation, and every Friday between Easter and Whitsun.[42]

Beyond the associations of food with the liturgical round, there was also an important connection between food and work: it was one of the major benefits of serving the abbey. The rations of some servants were so large that they must have been expected to share them with others, their juniors or servants, or possibly even to offer some form of hospitality. The janitor of the courtyard, for example, was to have daily two smalpeys loaves, a knights' loaf, 4 gallons of spense ale (the ordinary ale), three portions of fish on fish days and two portions of meat three times a week and a course of fish – far too much for a single individual.[43] Other monastery servants had different entitlements. The gardeners ('hortolani', probably working a market garden) were to have two 'turte', a portion of food, 6 gallons from every brewing of ale, and meat in place of fish five times a year. Another gardener ('gardiner') had similar rations, but a smalpeys loaf and 1 gallon of lesser ale whenever he caught a live mole.[44] There were also food allowances for those bringing food to Canterbury from the monastery's estates, carefully calibrated to match the extent of what they brought with them. For example, the 'aver-manni' from Minster, so called probably because of the draught animals ('averia') with which they were required to do carrying services,[45] were to have five knights' loaves and knights' ale when they brought corn by water, and each of them a knights' loaf when by land. For every 1,000 eggs they brought, they were allowed two smalpeys loaves, two portions of fish and the better ale; and when they brought the cheese rents, for every wey of cheese, two smalpeys loaves, two knights' loaves, two portions of food and four measures of mixed ale.[46]

Dining at St Augustine's

Abbot Thorn's injunctions indicate the usual scale of dining – and here institutional traditions led to some elements of difference from lay house-holds. In the abbot's chamber, including his own food, there were normally to be nine people who were to receive meals of four courses; the allowance for his free household, with three guests eating in the hall, was for 16 people, each with meals of three courses. These groups would have had portions of the best cuisine. The more routine foodstuffs would then have formed the meals of others. There was provision for 16 grooms and others, who might receive two courses. Beyond this, each day 89 others ate a single course in their offices (their places of work) in the abbey and outside the gates. These allocations of food across the abbey show a complexity that probably had its origin in customary rights to food that had grown up over a considerable period of time – some of the servants in fact inherited their positions and allowances.[47] In addition, food was made available as alms – from the loaves specially baked for this purpose (Table 8.1), the commemorative rations from table in the monastic refectory, and the broken meats left at table in all the dining areas. Secular households rarely had this depth of tradition.[48]

The pattern of meals is apparent from service in hall. Out of Lent, supper was to be served there to the free household and guests, except on Fridays throughout the year and on Wednesdays in Advent, and on other solemn feasts. However, those who wanted could eat supper between Christmas and the Purification (2 February). All guests, whether clerics or not, were to eat there unless specially called to the abbot's chamber, or unless they arrived too late or outside the hour of lunch, and it was not possible to eat in hall.[49]

The preparation and service of food was intended to underpin status and honour. When the abbot wished to dine in hall, preparations were made by the steward of the hall, who was to oversee the service there – Abbot Thorn's injunctions take us through the pattern of service of a late thirteenth-century meal.[50] The marshal of the hall, whenever the abbot, prior or other great person ate there, was to administer water for washing both before and after lunch: the public ritual of handwashing, with water poured from a ewer into a bowl, was common to many elite households. In the monastery, however, monks would have washed their hands in the lavatorium in the cloister outside the refectory (Plate 25). Once the abbot had started to sit down, the steward was to summon those deputed to serve, and service was to begin immediately the reading had begun. Reading from scriptural or devotional works at mealtimes was a common expectation in a monastic house, and was also practised in devout secular households. To this end, monastic refectories were equipped with lecterns, often built into the physical structure of the walls (Plate 26). Other than the reading and audible signals, such as the use of a bell to indicate the point at which food should be removed, the meal in the monastic refectory would have taken place in silence; it probably proceeded in a similar fashion, but perhaps with some conversation between the abbot and his guests, when the abbot dined in hall.[51] The first course followed straight after the pottage, and likewise the other courses. Guests were to be looked after and careful thought was given to the seating arrangements.[52] In the hall where secular guests and servants ate, the marshal was responsible for the general order of the room, preventing pilfering of food, noisy or rowdy behaviour, and the boorishness of those who threw bones, broth or ale on to the ground. He was to take care that no one was to get up from the meal until the tablecloth had been taken away from before him.[53] If trestle tables were in use, tables might not even be set up until diners had sat down and the process of laying the table therefore followed, rather than preceded, the arrival of diners. The process happened in reverse at the end of the meal.[54]

The abbot's principal servants waited on him at the meal. His carver was to have a clean hand towel on his arms and at least two good knives. The carver was not to begin to serve until the reading had started. If the abbot was eating in chamber, the carver was to put his bread before him, and he was to serve his cup at lunch and at the blessing.[55] There was a separate servant for the abbot's hand towel[56] – and the abbot also had his own pantler.[57] Some servants had dual roles. The abbot's messenger was expected to double as a servant bringing food from the kitchen, and collecting up the silver vessels, along with the almoner's servant; and the abbot's palfreyman, who looked after the abbot's riding horses or palfreys, served as a doorkeeper.[58]

In its customary of 1330–40, the abbey had a vade mecum for the work of monastic officials generally, and it was the cellarer, working with the subcellarer, who were especially charged with the provision of food. The customary presented a vision of the task that was closely linked to the Rule, and the commentary on it by the Benedictine monk Smaragdus (d.c.840). Here we see that the office of the cellarer was to acquire all kinds of food the monks would need, and to provide all the cooking vessels. According to the Rule he was the father of the whole congregation – and he was to supervise the food provision and service of the convent.[59] A similar commitment to the quality of food was at the heart of the instructions for the subcellarer, as were principles of courtesy and hospitality. He was also to provide the convent with pittances that were good, delicate, and well and courteously prepared; and, if they were fried, boiled ('elixa') or roasted, according to what was needed, sauces which were fitting to the pittance and other food served to the convent were to be well prepared by the servant employed by the cellarer for this purpose.[60] The cellarer was to instruct his servants doing the cooking that the convent's food should be well and properly prepared before the arrival of the monks in the refectory, lest there be a delay in the service – for it was better that the cooks have to wait to serve, than the servants of God have to sit waiting without food.[61] The subcellarer was to find sufficient bread and drink for guests, and the cellarer the 'pulmentum'.[62] Monks eating either in the refectory or in their cells, or anywhere else, were enjoined to show humanity, honour and largesse, especially to strangers.[63]

This case study of St Augustine's underscores themes that resonate widely in the study of medieval food, and the example allows us to see the detail and thought that went into everything connected with its preparation and consumption. We can see the importance of certain foodstuffs, such as bread, with the use of different loaves for different purposes and individuals; and the use of special foods and drinks, and links to commemoration and sharing food, or giving it as alms. Sauces had a prominent role and here, as at many other monasteries, special attention was given to spices as a part of anniversary commemorations.[64] It was common practice for an abbot or for obedientiaries to be responsible for the supply of spices for consumption at particular feasts or points in the liturgical calendar, such as the series of days drawing Advent to its climax, known by their antiphons, the 'O's – after the initial word of each text (for example, 'O Emmanuel') – between 16 and 23 December. The celebrations were frequently marked by the consumption of spices, possibly with wine.[65] Although monks were held not to have property of their own, in fact they did have small quantities of goods that might be considered in this way, and some of these were closely connected to food. In dividing up the goods of a dead monk at St Augustine's, spices that were not ground, such as ginger, zedoary, galingale and cinnamon, were to pass to the prior, but spices that had been ground, electuaries and medicines were to be received by the infirmarer. Gold, silver, gems, rings and brooches were to pass to the abbot, but silver cups, mazers and silver spoons were to pass to the refectory and were to be entered in its inventory – and we have seen examples of these in Chapter 3.[66] In the 1330s, the novices coming to table in the refectory at St Augustine's brought their own knives with them, but the spoons were set out on the table and collected up at the end of the meal – that is, these belonged to the institution.[67] Some further idea of the special status that could accompany diners and their utensils comes from Westminster Abbey. The refectorer – every day except

Good Friday – was reverently to set before each brother a spoon, and the monk was to bow slightly to him in return. He was to collect up all the spoons at the end of lunch, at the accustomed moment, as indicated by the monk presiding at the meal. If the abbot was among those dining, the refectorer was to keep his spoon separate from the others he collected up, holding it apart with the middle finger of his right hand. He was also to set out the spoons at supper in the same way, just as he was to set out the silver cups.[68] These were valuable goods and great care was taken over them.

Cuisine and religious women

Monastic cuisine, especially that at the table of the head of the house, was as elaborate as that of many elite establishments. But that did not mean that noble cuisine was its only inspiration. In the early fifteenth century, the Abbess of Barking had a copy of the *Forme of cury*, the great cookbook probably prepared in the household of Richard II. The same volume includes a table setting out the food allowances at the nunnery. From this it is apparent that the abbess had a yeoman cook and a groom cook – two male cooks who would have produced elite cuisine for her table – and beyond this she also had her own pudding wife, who would have worked with offal to produce sausages and puddings.[69] Here there was an important link both to demotic cuisine and to the role of women in its preparation. In the nunnery at Campsey, at the start of the fourteenth century, women were employed in the kitchen as well as the male cooks, and were engaged in brewing as well.[70] Historians have argued that in developing their spirituality, religious women chose to focus on something that was particularly their preserve, food – either through fasting, or as makers of special types of food – and it is therefore worth looking more closely at the provision of food in female houses.[71]

Cardinal Ottobuono's canons for the reform of the Church in England of April 1268 reiterated that the intention was that nuns, once cloistered, should follow a carefully regulated life; the gates of the senses were to be locked lest any malevolent spirit gain entry; and the nun's space was arranged so that she might keep her innocence of heart and body for the Lord. A nun might go to the oratory to pray; she might go to chapter, where any fault might be punished. She might enter the dormitory and the refectory at set times, by which her body might be sustained, but in a temperate way, lest her flesh rebel through a superfluity of food. But at other times she was to remain in the cloister in which she and the senses of her body were enclosed, thinking and looking at God alone with the eyes of the mind, so that she might by contemplation have a foretaste of the sweetness of eternal life.[72] Ottobuono here was guarding against the stimulation of food, working from a spiritual perspective. Yet his approach did not recognise other dimensions that nuns may have considered significant: commensality, celebration, and the power and influence of the house were expressed through food.

The tensions in this contrast are also apparent in a comparison between diet in male and female houses. Langland's comments, in *Piers Plowman*, in the persona of Wrath, outline interesting differences between the two:

> I have an aunt who is a nun and an abbess, she would rather swoon or faint than suffer any pain. I was cook in her kitchen and served the convent for many months, and also with monks. I was the pottager of the prioress and other ladies, and made them broth ('joutes') of gossip ... And of wicked words I made their vegetables ('wortes').[73]

This suggests elements of vernacular cuisine, or, indeed, a cuisine that was close to that of the peasantry. The joutes were broths of pottage or herbs; sometimes in elite cuisine, they were made with the addition of meat or fish, or using almond milk, but that was not mentioned here; and it is notable too that Wrath chose to remark on their vegetables. His service in a house of monks had also left him no appetite to tarry there: 'For I have no wish to stay with their cauldrons, I ate there unending fish and weak ale. At other times when wine came, and I drank well in the evening, I had a nasty taste in my mouth for the next five days.'[74] There had been what looks like a regular diet, with ample fish, but it had hardly been pleasing, a pattern that looks very different from the food at St Augustine's. If food in the monasteries was a reflection of upper-class diet, Wrath's experience had been disappointing, but it was still different in quality from the nunnery.

Female religious formed a very small segment of society, yet their cultural practices made them far more significant than their numbers suggest. Around 1400, there were some 1,000 religious houses in England; fewer than 150 had female communities. Estimates suggest that at this point there were around 2,300 nuns and canonesses; and 9,500 monks, canons and friars.[75] At the Dissolution, there were only two houses of nuns that were significantly wealthy, Shaftesbury and Syon, the latter with an income of nearly £2,000 p.a. Two-thirds of nunneries had less than £100 a year. There were 50 Benedictine nunneries and 93 monasteries at the Dissolution; of these, four nunneries had an income more than £400 p.a., but half the male houses did, and six exceeded £2,000 p.a.[76]

In 1323, the Bishop of Worcester heard a familiar litany of complaints against the Prioress of Wroxall:

> That in her time the carpets, linen, goblets, salt-cellars, and other vessels and utensils long ago intended for hospitable uses have been sold or destroyed; that the buildings of the house both inside and outside the walls are in a ruinous condition; that the proper and customary hospitality and almsgiving have almost entirely ceased, nor has due care been taken of the nuns when they are sick; that they have been robbed of their customary portion of ale, meat and fish, four nuns receiving scarcely a pint of very weak ale each day, and meat and fish and other necessaries being given in such small portions as to be scarcely enough to live on . . .[77]

Diet in many female monastic institutions like this was not on a par with the aristocracy, or with many male houses, but on a lower level – a critical indication coming from the lower level of wealth of these establishments. It was not only the quality of food that was at issue at Wroxall, however, but also the practices associated with it: hospitality, almsgiving and a style of living.

In terms of food consumption, organisationally, in theory, nuns followed the dietary regimen prescribed in the Rule of St Benedict, taking account of the mitigations that had been commonly accepted by the later Middle Ages. They ate together in a refectory, using a misericord as a separate dining area

for eating meat – following the pattern of male houses, and the dispensation for meat-eating given by Benedict XII. Thus, at the Cistercian nunnery
of Nun Coton (or Nun Cotham), in Lincolnshire, at the visitation of 1440,
there was a two-storey frater (refectory), and the intention was that the
nuns ate in the upper room when they had fish or dairy products, and in
the lower room when they consumed meat. Here, the subprioress did
not want them to eat elsewhere, to use the prioress's hall, where the nuns
might encounter seculars.[78] At the Benedictine nunnery of Littlemore, in
Oxfordshire, in 1445, against a report that meat was eaten in the frater every
day when the community ate there, the bishop charged them with eating in
the frater on Wednesdays, Fridays and Saturdays, and on fasting days, and
that on those days 'there shall be fish or white meat [dairy foods] or similar
as there used to be'.[79] At De La Pre Abbey, Northampton, in 1432–3, it had
been the custom to use the frater on Sunday, Wednesday and Friday: a
fourth day, Monday, was added at the bishop's injunction at visitation – that
is, this was to be a further day when a proportion of the house had to eat
regular food, rather than meat.[80]

In practice the notion of communal living had broken down among
Benedictine nuns and probably to some extent among other orders,
including the Cistercians, by the end of the fourteenth century. In the latter
part of the Middle Ages many nunneries were grouped into 'familie' or
households, groups of three, four or five nuns, who ate together, and
although the cellaress of the house supplied some common provisions,
typically bread and ale, control over food beyond this was organised household by household. This system is exposed in visitation injunctions from
the fifteenth century, where bishops tried to reverse the process and return
the nuns to communal living. At Catesby Priory, Northamptonshire, in July
1442, Sister Margaret Wavere reported that there were four households of
nuns within the cloister, and that there were four nuns in her household.
The nuns were ordered to eat and drink in one house, to sleep there, use
one oratory, and to disband these individual households.[81] At Elstow,
Bedfordshire, another Benedictine nunnery visited in January 1443, there
were five households, with between three and six nuns in them. At that
point, each nun had from the house at the start of the week seven conventual loaves and 6 gallons of ale.[82] Earlier visitations provide further infor-

mation about diet at Elstow. In 1390, Archbishop Courtenay had ordered that every Monday, Wednesday and Saturday a dish of meat or fish was to be supplied to every nun, out of the common funds and worth at least a penny. This was to take the place of eggs, which had been the usual food on these days – eggs were cheap food, consumed in nunneries in large quantities, at little cost. This change was a sign that Elstow was now a more wealthy house and that dietary improvement was possible. On other days, the nuns were to be supplied with food from the monastery's resources, as the custom had it.[83] In 1421–2, the supply ordered for each nun had been a portion of meat or fish every Monday, Wednesday and Saturday, according to the pattern, worth a penny; each nun was to have five measures [gallons] of the better ale each week, and there was to be no distinction between the abbess's bread and that of the nuns – every loaf was to weigh 0.97 kg (720d).[84] This was 0.16 kg (120d) lighter than the monks' loaves at St Augustine's, Canterbury – and the injunction that the abbess should not have a loaf that was distinguished from the others is also remarkable, given the range of loaves that could be found in male houses.

The close links between nuns and their own genealogical families and friends had an impact on diet. At Nun Coton in 1440, Dame Alice Aunselle argued that all nuns should live in common; no one was to have anything of their own, such as capons – this is probably a reference to foods sent in from outside the house – goods like this were to be held in common, by a common servant. Equally, nuns were not to have gardens or rooms set aside for them as individuals, a reference which speaks of the skill of women in growing food in a domestic setting.[85] In 1440 at Legbourne Priory, Lincolnshire, a house of Cistercian nuns, Dame Joan Fraunceys reported that each nun had one loaf and ½ gallon of ale a day; one pig a year, 1s 6d over the year for beef; in the fasting seasons of Advent and Lent, two herrings a day; with a small quantity of butter in summer, and 2 stones of cheese a year.[86] At Stixwould, another Cistercian house in the same county, the allowance that year was more substantial. Every nun received one pig, one sheep, a quarter of beef, 2 stones of butter, 3 stones of cheese; in Advent and Lent, three herrings a day, besides six salt fish and 12 stock-fish a year.[87] In 1440, at the nunnery of St Michael outside Stamford, also in Lincolnshire, at this time regarded as a Benedictine house, the subprioress reported that each nun had bread and ale from the house, with 13s 4d a year for fish, flesh and other things.[88]

The impression given by this evidence is that, by the fifteenth century, the diet of nuns in many houses would have been similar to that of the wealthier peasantry and yeomanry. There were differences between nunneries, with wealthier institutions providing more, and more variety. There was a contrast, too, with male houses: the older and larger male houses had a greater range of food traditions and customs, which they were able to maintain; and their rations were more generous.[89] There was some mitigation for the nuns, however. The grouping of nuns into households had allowed for additions to the regime, however much jealousy they provoked. These then were typical of the arrangements for the majority of female houses. A very few nunneries, such as Barking, had much more generous provision, similar to the greater Benedictine male houses.

Barking was an old foundation, established by Bishop Erkenwald of London, probably in the 660s or 670s, dedicated to the Virgin, who was to share the honour with its first abbess, St Ethelburga or Alburgh, who was Erkenwald's sister. It was one of the largest houses of nuns, and had the largest monastic church of any nunnery in England; it had approximately £725 p.a. income at the time of Dissolution. At various points in their history, monastic houses attempted to plan consumption, and there is a mid fifteenth-century budget for Barking setting out the levels of provision to which the cellaress of the house should aspire.[90] At the time of this document, there were 37 nuns, plus the abbess, prioress, two cellaresses and the kitchener. The budget readily demonstrates that the richer the house, the more substantial the allowances. The numbers of herrings, for example, match and exceed the best allowances noted previously. There were substantial quantities of meat, and there was a whole range of supplements, with custom increasing the quantities and range of food that came to table through pittances. On Maundy Thursday, 12 stub eels and 60 shaft eels were baked for the convent; the same day, there was ½ gallon of wine of Tyre for the abbess and 2 gallons of red wine for the convent. The convent had an additional 3 gallons of good ale every week in Lent, and 1 gallon of red wine at Easter. There were payments for rissoles (a popular dish of ground meat, shaped, spiced and fried): ½d, 16 times a year, but now paid only twice, at

Michaelmas and Easter, to each nun, with double for the four conventual officers; and 2*d* to each nun and officer at Shrovetide 'for ther crispis and crumkakes' – special breads, that is, pancakes of some sort, and an unleavened bread.[91]

The provision for nuns at the Wiltshire houses of Wilton, Amesbury and Lacock may also have been more closely aligned to elite consumption. At Lacock Abbey in the mid fourteenth century, the annual totals of foods consumed reflected this, with large quantities of beef, mutton and pork; with lesser amounts, but still significant, of the highly regarded flesh of young animals, with veal and piglets; along with sufficient poultry and doves for major occasions, and a generous provision of wheat (Table 8.2). These houses offered scope for religious contemplation, but they were also places of retirement from the secular world for women of powerful families. It was here that queens and princesses might live out their days, among women of the nobility – and diet here reflected the patterns of the secular elite.[92]

Table 8.2: Annual consumption at Lacock Abbey

	1340–1 or 1341–2	1347–8
Wheat	307 qrs 4 bus.	293 qrs
Malt	510 qrs	490 qrs
Oats[a]	–	24 qrs
Beef cattle	45¾ + half a quarter	45
Calves	–	24
Mutton carcases	569	521
Lambs	3	7
Pigs	172	187
Piglets	69	118
Geese	275	315
Capons	110+	97
Cocks and chickens	250	295
Doves	2,348	1,861
Eggs	7,368	7,080
Cheese[?]	–	3,727½ lbs
Butter	–	254 lbs
Milk	100½ gals	60½ gals
Herrings	20,554	20,018

[a] For pottage of the convent and servants.

Sources: BL, Add. MS 88973, f. 91v (1340–1 or 1341–2); Add. MS 88974, ff. 144v–146v (1347–8).

The diet of nuns, therefore, provides contrasts. The principal foodstuffs and the pattern of their consumption were scarcely different from that of monasteries, or, indeed, of the laity at a modest level. Differences in the wealth of individual houses led to distinctions in the amounts of food, and probably in types of cuisine available. For a very few institutions, the diet was similar to that of the aristocracy; for most, it was more modest, and in some cases, was very poor indeed. Individuals might mitigate that regime through gifts of food, or skill in gardening or food preparation – and the special dishes prepared at institutions such as Barking argue the case for the nuns' particular interest in food. Food was closely associated with commemorative practices, as we shall see again in the case of food alms and monasteries and nunneries (Table 11.1). There was little here, however, that might appear distinctive from the point of view of gender, other than female skill in food preparation. But there was a distinction to be made with the diets of ascetics – extremes of dietary restriction were not to be found in these institutional settings.

Although ecclesiastical diets were regulated, especially in a monastic environment, the links to elite cuisine and secular foodways are apparent. In their aspirations, the monks of the greatest houses might emulate the diet of their relations in the richest households. There was a great and sustained interest in food, and distinctive specialities in the monasteries and households of clerics. St Augustine's, Canterbury, was typical of the older Benedictine houses, with its complex and distinctive food customs. Its abbot expected the best sauces and had master cooks to prepare them, and a household that was to demonstrate the latest fashions in household service. Providing these foods and an honourable environment in which to consume them was of major importance to the standing of the house. Links to an elite secular life were doubtless significant in Lacock's patterns of consumption. Yet there was also doubt whether it was appropriate for the clergy, monks and nuns to live in this way – Cardinal Ottobuono would not have been alone in pointing to the temptations food brought to the cloistered nun.

It is now time to turn to the elite to complete the survey of the principal groups of society and their foodways. It was here that the inspiration lay for many of the fashions and tastes of the food culture of the later Middle Ages more generally; yet it was also a question of resource and style, as it was for monastic institutions. An examination of the material culture of dining among the greatest in the land – a style of living copied in the countryside as far down at least as the ranks of the parish clergy and the more wealthy of the peasantry, as we have seen – adds a further dimension to our understanding of the meanings that were associated with medieval food and drink.

CHAPTER NINE

THE ELITE TABLE

THE FIRST CHAPTER OF this book included a discussion of elite food, menus and dietary practices, and argued that this pattern of dining was one that had an impact across society. Those that could – even down to the upper levels of the peasantry and typically the parish clergy – chose to eat their food in a fashion that owed much to the ways in which the elite dined. The formal meal at an elite level was closely choreographed, for the honour and profit of the lord, as well as for the experience of food. The evidence for the detail of how meals proceeded is weighted towards the end of the period covered by this book, and fifteenth-century descriptions of meals are imbued with the greater interest in hierarchy and ceremony that came at that point. The Harleian household regulations, from the second half of the fifteenth century, devoted no fewer than 11 densely written pages to the instructions for serving lunch in a nobleman's house – and the scale and formality of the preparations was such that it was not until the seventh page that the lord sat down to food.[1] That said, the late medieval elaboration of elite dining practice was based around elements that had long had a place in food culture.[2] This chapter turns to one aspect of elite consumption, the material culture of dining, which was just as influential across society as the food-stuffs on elite tables.

We need an oblique approach to study the material culture of the meal at an elite level, as much was made of precious metal, and very little of it has survived. There are, however, two groups of documentary sources that are of assistance: illuminations in medieval manuscripts, and accounts for, and inventories of, plate. Together these show us how food was presented at table, and patterns of association in terms of dining equipment.

Manuscript illuminations of meals in progress rarely portray secular feasts except in works of romance, and even then there is often little on the table that can help us understand what was at issue. Religious manuscripts, on the other hand, offer many depictions of food and eating, particularly in the events of the life of Christ, from miracles, like that at Cana and the Feeding of the Five Thousand (Plate 3), to meals like that in the house of Simon (Plate 27) and the Last Supper (Plate 2). The last, the archetype for the Eucharist, the consumption of bread and wine in memory of Christ, was of special significance.[3]

Two depictions of meals from Holy Week – the last week of Lent, imme- diately before Easter – from the Taymouth Hours of c.1330, thought to have been prepared for Eleanor of Woodstock, the sister of Edward III, show the character of many illuminations of this class. The supper in the house of Simon in Bethany, with Mary Magdalen anointing Christ's feet as he eats (Matt. 26:6–13; Mark 14:3–9; John 12:2–8), was a Passover meal, with unleavened bread. In the illumination (Plate 27), the setting has been trans- formed from biblical time into a contemporary scene. Christ has penitential food on the table, as was appropriate for this period in Lent: there is a dish of fish by his left hand. Also on the table are slices of bread for trenchers and a covered cup. The contents of the other dishes are less clear. The linen tablecloth, with its swags hanging down in front, is typical of the ways in which table dressings are portrayed in manuscript illuminations: this ample cloth is covered for protection by a sanap, which lies flat along the table. The illustration of Mary Magdalen follows the text of John's Gospel, where she anoints Christ's feet with a precious spiced ointment – rather than those of Matthew and Mark, where the vessel with the ointment is broken over Christ's head. We are told by John that the odour of ointment – an indica- tion of Christ's holiness and foreshadowing the expectation that his body would be anointed after death – fills the house. The spices, for all their worldly cost and significance as sensory stimulants, were a marker of sanc- tity.[4] Mary Magdalen's actions as illustrated here also prefigure the Maundy, the washing of the feet at the Last Supper, later in Holy Week.

The Last Supper image (Plate 2), like many other images of its class, shows on the table only a restricted range of objects. The table is covered with a white cloth, gathered in swags at the front, and that cloth is again covered in turn by a sanap. We can see both gold (or silver gilt) and silver vessels: although their contents are far from clear, the gold dish at the extreme right may hold a fish – again, penitential food for Lent. There is a covered cup on the table just behind the kneeling figure of Judas Iscariot. There are slices of bread on the table, for trenchers, set out alongside the dishes. Two of the disciples, one immediately to Christ's left and the next but one, each hold a knife in their left hand. The disciples all have clothing of a similar colour and design, perhaps reflecting the livery of a household or fraternity, underscoring the unity of the body as it dined – on the eve of its betrayal. And Christ is depicted giving the sop of bread, after he has dipped it in sauce, to Judas Iscariot to mark the one who will betray him.[5] For a lord to give food from his plate to a fellow diner was one of the greatest marks of favour that one might receive – the household Rules of Robert Grosseteste, prepared for the Countess of Lincoln, c.1245–53, make plain the importance of this action.[6] The caption below the image refers to Christ washing the feet of the disciples: 'Here Our Lord performed the maundy' ('Cy fait nostre seignur sa maunde').

The maundy was one of the key elements of commemoration, not only in meals on Maundy Thursday, but also in monastic institutions through the year. John Bromyard, discussing the Eucharist, reported that in every good household it was the practice to be called to wash before eating at table, just as Christ had washed the feet of his disciples before they ate at the Last Supper.[7] The expectation was that hands would be washed before and after the meal – and the basins and ewers that were employed for this purpose abound in wills and inventories of plate. Magnificent 'cup and ewer' sets were prestigious gifts among the elite, items that were displayed and used at key moments in the meal.[8] This use of plate often had a commemorative function, recalling individuals to mind as items they had given were used. In 1372, doubtless to this end, Richard de Flosford of Ipswich bequeathed to the prior and convent of the Holy Trinity of the same town his best basin and ewer for use in their hall.[9] So, beyond the table equipment, the illuminations underscore the importance of the actions accompanying dining.

Another prelude to eating was the saying of prayers and the blessing of food. John Mirk instructed the audience of his sermon for the Sunday at the start of Lent that they should say a paternoster and an Ave Maria – and further prayers if that was the custom of their devotion – and that they should make the sign of the cross over their food. God was also to be thanked at the conclusion of the meal with a further paternoster and Ave.[10] This spiritual preparation was expected before consuming any food, even snacks, and, as we shall see in Chapter 11, changed the nature of the food. Illustrations of secular meals might also recreate them as occasions of spiritual significance: few meals would have been seen as entirely secular occasions, as the blessing of food and the saying of prayers immediately endowed eating with sacral importance. It has been argued by Michael Camille that the image in the Luttrell Psalter, c.1325–35, of Sir Geoffrey Luttrell dining with his family (Plate 1) echoes features of the Mass, for example, in the way the cupbearer or butler with his tippet has presented drink to Sir Geoffrey. Further, the appearance of this illumination in a psalter, part way through the text of Psalm 115, may have a significance of its own, reflecting unfortunate events in Luttrell's personal circumstances.[11] The case for these allusions is well made, although the identification of the occasion as an Epiphany feast is less certain – beyond its occurrence outside a season of abstinence, in the impressively decorated surroundings of the family's hall, the feast may have solely a generic significance.[12] There is more, however, about elite foodways that can be drawn from the illumination.

The meal comes as the culmination of four illuminations depicting cooking and food preparation.[13] Sir Geoffrey is seated with his wife on his right, with two Dominican friars, and, to his left, two sons and daughter-in-law.[14] This is a family group, seated at the top table: it is not the entire great household. Behind them is a hanging, a cloth decorated with a pattern derived from Geoffrey's coat of arms, of silver martlets on a blue background.[15] The table has been set up on trestles: the family is eating in a space that can be used for many activities. On the table we see loaves of bread, as well as bread that has been sliced for trenchers. Four of the diners – Geoffrey, his wife and his two sons – have trenchers of metal in front of them. These trenchers are flat and rectangular (there were other shapes in use), possibly hinged in the centre, like an open book. While they might have been prepared to receive food with slices of bread, that does not appear to have been the case here. In many illuminations from the fourteenth century, however, diners do not have a trencher in front of them, and it may be that trenchers of bread were placed directly on the cloth. It was for this reason that further cloths – sanaps – were laid over the tablecloth, to save it: the Luttrells seem to have a single cloth, without an overlaying sanap. Trenchers are identified but rarely in inventories of plate of elite households, which suggests that many were not in fact of precious metal, and were perhaps either of base metal, or wood, or that nothing was used beyond slices of bread. The few of silver gilt that appear in the plate of Richard II, inventoried at the end of his reign, were brought from France for use in the pantry of the young Queen Isabelle, that is, they were not for use as part of the ordinary equipment of diners, but were the preserve of the pantler for slicing up bread.[16] A pewterer of London in 1425 had among his equipment a mould for a trencher[17] and many others, used at lower social levels, would have been of wood.[18] In 1490–1, the master of the guild of the Holy Cross at Stratford-upon-Avon bought four dozen trenchers – at a cost of 5d, almost certainly of wood.[19]

Sir Geoffrey and his wife share a dish between them, and it is from this vessel that food is taken to go on their trenchers. His wife and his two sons are using their fingers to eat: the only utensils are the knives and spoons. While his wife slices into a chicken leg, one of the sons uses a spoon to take liquid, probably a sauce, from a bowl. The dishes being prepared in the kitchen include two meats – fowl and piglet – and are brought to table with sauce.[20] The two friars may have had a different diet: they have no trenchers. There is a dish of what may be eggs in front of them, with a further, empty dish between the friar and Geoffrey's wife. Geoffrey's daughter-in-law may also have had a different diet: she has no trencher in front of her. It was not unusual to encounter different groups within the household following different dietary regimes, for medical or penitential purposes.[21]

The butler or cupbearer, with an elaborately decorated towel or tippet over his shoulder and who kneels before the table, has presumably brought in and honourably served Sir Geoffrey's drink – and it is worth pointing to the importance of drink in this scene. Sir Geoffrey and his daughter-in-law are drinking from similar vessels; the two friars are probably also drinking, but their vessels are different. The two vessels on the table immediately above the cupbearer's arm may both be for drinking: the covered one with a band and knop is a mazer. The friar at the end of the table is also holding what may be a mazer – its band is clearly visible; and the friar next to him may also be picking up another mazer. The other, covered vessel, next to the butler is of silver: dishes for food were not usually covered in this way, so it is likely that this one is for drink, perhaps a bigger drinking bowl. The circular object with the cross pattern next to it, at the front of the table, is probably the cover of a cup, perhaps for the one from which Sir Geoffrey is drinking, which has been ceremoniously uncovered before him. Beyond the religious connections, therefore, the Luttrell Psalter's illumination gives an unparalleled vignette of a secular meal in progress, with different cups (possibly with different beverages, as discussed in Chapter 3), a fine array of foods, with their sauces, and possibly different dietary patterns.

Elite consumption at a knightly level and the style of living that went with it would have made a considerable impression: what was on the tables of the great found its mirror well down the social scale, but that did not mean it was accepted without reservation. Bromyard recounted a conversation at a prelate's table about which part of the body was the most 'sumptuous', that is, lavishly wasteful. All replied that it was the belly, as it was wiser than the others; but he replied that it was the eye, because nobles and the powerful of this age were frequently 'sumptuous' in six ways: in the extravagance ('curiositas') of their clothes, the beauty of their horses and the elegance of their houses, in the sumptuousness of their silver and gold vessels, the number of their servants, and the variety of their foods.[22] Silver and gold vessels for dining were a prominent feature of the tables of the great, and might represent a substantial investment – albeit one that could be readily converted into specie. At his death in 1313, the silver vessels of Robert Winchelsey, Archbishop of Canterbury, were valued at £357 13s 9d, about 8 per cent of his estate; and those of another Archbishop of Canterbury, John Stratford, at his death in 1348, at £684 1s 9d, some 10.5 per cent of his estate.[23] Special precautions were taken to prevent these goods being stolen, with careful inventorying and other controls, including searches at the gate of the household and as some plate was given away out of custom at major events, such as weddings, there was potential for misunderstanding here.[24]

Losses had to be made good. The saucerer of Queen Philippa, Master John Fleming, was reimbursed for the funds he had had to pay the King's exchequer for three silver saucers he had lost, which had been lent from the King's household for the service of the Queen at the time of her lying-in at Woodstock in June 1330; and the Queen's goldsmith, Simon de Berkyng, was given £5 in August 1332 to cover the damage and loss in silver vessels and other things at his house in Cheap at the time of a tournament, caused by the Queen's arrival.[25] Bromyard expressed outrage at the deceit that accompanied the systems of finance. The elite made this investment in silver goods rather than in paying for their expenses: 'so that they may eat from silver vessels, they pay for food with tallies' (tallies were notched pieces of wood, given as receipts, which vendors then had to redeem, usually at a discount and some time later). The old manner of eating, from wooden vessels, was better, paying for food in cash, rather than the present system. It was far better for the soul of the purchaser and more useful for the vendor to have 6d paid immediately than a tally for 5s that would never be paid.[26] A political song of the 1330s made a similar point: it was a sign of vice to pay for foodstuffs with 'wood', i.e. tallies.[27]

Domestic accounts and inventories of the elite provide the detail of dinner services: implicit in the idea of 'service' is the notion that plate was intended to be used together at table, and we can see this in practice, especially where new plate for dining was obtained on a single occasion. The listings of these vessels are of importance for showing how meals might be composed. In August 1297, when Elizabeth, Countess of Holland, was to be married, as she set out for her journey she was given plate for dining by her father, Edward I. Here there were 12 gold pitchers for wine and water, and 46 silver cups; six great dishes for 'interfercula' – the 'entremes' or elaborate preparations that came between the courses; 98 silver dishes and 96 saucers, along with 60 spoons of one sort and 48 of another. Other pieces of plate that formed part of the dinner service included a great alms dish (weighing some 2.72 kg), a silver alms pot (for liquids, weighing 2.05 kg) and a silver alms nef (a vessel for alms in the shape of a ship, weighing 2.17 kg); three spice plates with silver spoons, and three pairs of bowls for washing, along with two further bowls. Together these suggest entertainment for some 48 people – everyone would have had a silver cup, two dishes and two

1 Sir Geoffrey Luttrell at dinner with his family. From the Luttrell Psalter, England, *c.*1325–35.

2 Jesus and the twelve disciples at the Last Supper. From the Taymouth Hours, England, *c.*1330.

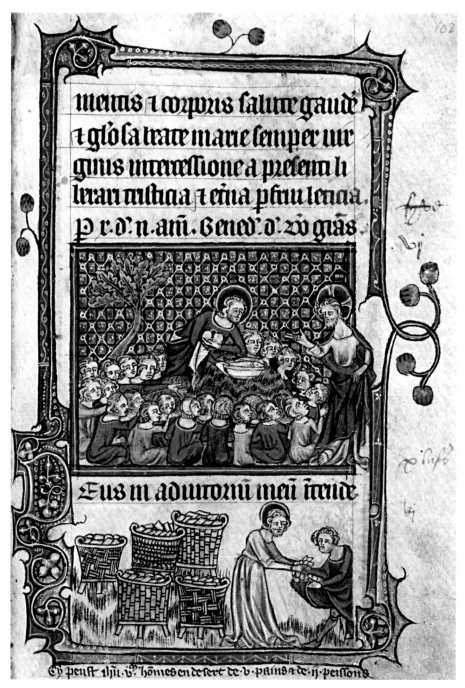

3 The miracle of the Feeding of the Five Thousand (John 6:9–13). The upper image shows the distribution of five barley loaves and two fishes: the two fishes are in a dish together, and two round loaves are visible in the left hand of the disciple making the distribution. In the lower image are five baskets of broken meats left over at the end of the meal. This miracle formed the archetype for large-scale distribution of alms: poor were fed on a special diet of barley bread and herring; and, beyond this, broken meats were collected up for distribution as alms. From the Taymouth Hours, England, c.1330.

4 The moral qualities and consequences of food and drink were never far from medieval minds. In a scene that combines drunkenness with lechery, a hermit, who has been tempted by the Devil, lasciviously handles the wife of the miller he is about to kill; the broom is a sign that the house is a tavern. The miller's wife has put down her bowl and jar or water container. From the Taymouth Hours, England, *c*.1330.

5 A bittern, from the wall paintings in the north-west corner of the first floor of the Longthorpe Tower, near Peterborough, *c*.1320–50. Common in the nearby fens, bitterns were a prestigious addition to the foods on elite tables.

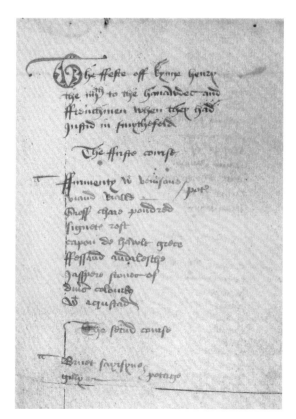

6 A medieval menu, from a collection of 'royal feasts', late fifteenth century: a record of a feast given by Henry IV for the men of Hainault and the Frenchmen who had jousted in Smithfield. The first course consists of furmenty with venison; 'viand rialle' (royal meat, sweetened wine, spiced and thickened with rice flour, coloured red with mulberries); 'gross chare, poudred' (meat: beef, mutton, pork, spiced); roast cygnets; fattened capon; pheasant with slices of a set dish, such as a tart or pudding; and a custard, with stones of jasper of assorted colours.

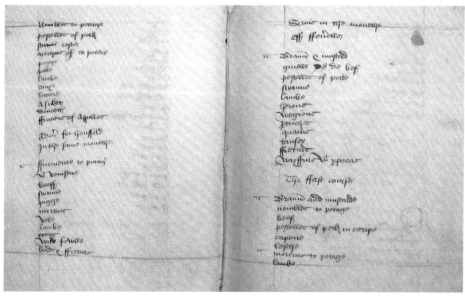

7 An awareness of seasonality: this late fifteenth-century text, from the same manuscript as Plate 6, would have allowed kitchen clerks and household stewards to plan their menus. It offers here a specimen menu for service in the month of February. Foods might include brawn and mustard, gruel of beef, pestles of pork, swan, lamb, herons, widgeon, partridges, quails, tansey, fritters and wafers with hippocras.

8 Stokesay Castle, Shropshire, built in the 1280s and 1290s for Laurence de Ludlow, a Shrewsbury wool merchant. Here is the impressive great hall, solar block and south tower, seen from the east. The comfortable accommodation provided by the chambers of the towers would ultimately displace halls as the location for the lord's daily meals.

9 Stokesay Castle, Shropshire: the interior of the timber-framed chamber at the top of the north tower, built in the 1280s and 1290s. Well lit and generously proportioned, rooms like this became the principal living space – and dining area – for the gentry and nobility.

10 The Studley bowl, silver, with some gilt, *c.*1400.

11 A large brass pot, now at Lacock Abbey, *c.*1500. Like many metal pots and cauldrons, it was made on the Continent, in this case at Mechlin.

12 Kenilworth Castle: the kitchens. A fireplace from the fourteenth century, with an oven set into it on one side, and an area, probably fifteenth-century, for a boiler or similar vessel. Outside large establishments, ovens would have produced too much for individual households to consume.

13 Sheep are milked and looked after in a fold by two women, while other women carry away a basket and a pot on their heads. From the Luttrell Psalter, England, c.1325–35.

14 The tomb of a cider maker, Andrew Jones (d.1497), and his wife in Hereford Cathedral.

15 A late medieval salting trough at Haddon Hall, Derbyshire.

16 A medieval pewter saucer, c.1290, from Cuckoo Lane, Southampton.

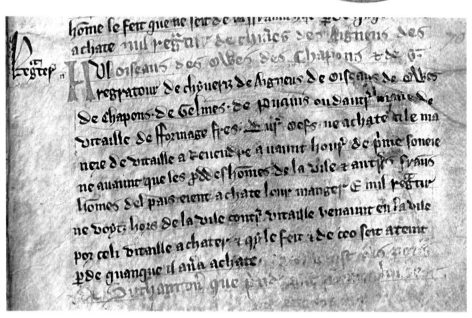

17 Municipal regulations, such as these from Southampton, c.1300, controlled the town's markets. Here, the regulations cover the sale of goats, sheep, birds, geese, capons, chickens, chicks, fresh cheese, butter and eggs, as well as times of sale, allowing the good men of the town and other men from outside to purchase their food before regrating was allowed.

18 Three women unmake a red deer, while a fourth sounds her hunting horn, proclaiming the kill. This manuscript is distinctive for the ways in which women are shown taking part in hunts of various kinds. From the Taymouth Hours, England, *c.*1330.

19 An aristocratic woman hunting hares with a dog. From the Taymouth Hours, England, *c.*1330.

20 Guild buildings at Stratford-upon-Avon: the chapel of the Holy Cross, with the fraternity's alms-houses stretching along Church Street.

21 St Augustine's Abbey, Canterbury. One of the oldest monastic houses in the British Isles, St Augustine's had a distinctive pattern of food allowances. Here are the remains of the hexagonal kitchen that was constructed in 1287–91; it survived in use until the sixteenth century, and was re-roofed in 1543 when Henry VIII used the site, especially the Abbot's lodgings, as a palace.

22 The Abbot's Kitchen at Glastonbury, constructed under Abbot John de Breynton (1334–42), is one of the best surviving examples of an elite kitchen. Internally octagonal in form, fireplaces were set across the corners of the structure.

23 The Abbot's Kitchen at Glastonbury: two of the fireplaces across the corners of the building.

24 The Prior's Kitchen: the octagonal kitchen built for the Prior of Durham in 1366–74.

25 Norwich Cathedral: the fifteenth-century washing place, or lavatorium, for the monks of the Cathedral Priory, just outside the entry to the refectory from the cloister.

26 The refectory at Fountains Abbey, rebuilt in the 1170s. The reader at meals had a lectern set into the thickness of the wall on the right-hand side.

27 Mary Magdalen anoints the feet of Christ as he sits at supper in the house of Simon at Bethany. From the Taymouth Hours, England, c.1330.

28. The head of St John the Baptist brought in to table on a charger, like the principal foods. This was the reward requested by Salome, dancing before Herodias. Roof boss, Norwich Cathedral cloister, mid fourteenth century.

29 The Burghley nef, partly silver gilt, with a nautilus shell. This nef has a detachable dish on the poop deck, suggesting that it was a salt. It was probably a special commission, perhaps intended as a gift, made 1527–8 in Paris.

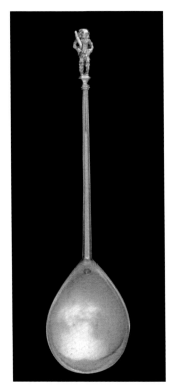

30 A late fifteenth-century English silver spoon, with a wild man, or 'woodwose', as a knop.

31 The west gable of the Abbey Barn, Glastonbury. Stone barns like this speak of the great investment that was made by major institutions in their food supply. One of the emblems of the four evangelists appears on each side of the barn: here, on the west side, is the eagle of St John. The barn was constructed in the fourteenth century, and dendrochronology now places its roof timbers in a felling period of 1334–44. A thatched roof may have been replaced with tiles in the period 1365–89.

32 Late medieval and sixteenth-century food chests and aumbries (cupboards) at Haddon Hall, Derbyshire.

saucers, although not everything might have been on the table at once. The Countess's husband was given 24 cups, along with 36 each of dishes and saucers – that is, with access to three dishes and saucers each per two diners, implying that dishes, or at least saucers, would be shared.[28]

Others had larger scale resources but, as time went by, several services might be in use together, or used for dining with smaller groups. The dinner services of Queen Philippa can be seen from her accounts for 1331–2 (Table 9.1).[29] Excluded from this analysis are the great cups, some with ewers, along with what may be table centrepieces – or pieces for display on a buffet – and salts. While spoons appear, there are no knives listed as these were not made of precious metals. The accounts show that the Queen had three principal groups of silver tableware, distinguished by their decoration: a comparatively small service, marked with the letter 'P'; a second group, marked with the arms of England and Hainault; and a third, marked with the arms of France and Hainault (her mother's arms). It would be a mistake to perceive these as 'sets' or 'services' in an exclusive sense: it is possible that they were, but there would not have been enough in any one set to furnish a meal – that saucers are found in only one set suggests the services must have been combined at table. In addition, some of the more prominent pieces could have been used with all three groups: the silver gilt alms nef, for example, and the gold ewer with the arms of England and Hainault on its cover. The dishes came in three general sizes: large, weighing around 0.81 kg (£2 10s), probably intended as chargers or serving dishes; medium, with weights in the range 0.356 kg to 0.437 kg (£1 2s to £1 7s); and small, for fruit, weighing 0.207 kg (12s 10d). Beyond this, there were saucers, at 0.097 kg to 0.129 kg (6s to 8s). There had been 22 dishes belonging to the set with the arms of England and Hainault, but the third service was the largest numerically, and had comprised at least 58 dishes. The 32 saucers also suggest a maximum size for the group dining (although saucers may have been shared). The presence of at least 35 silver drinking cups, decorated simply with an escutcheon of arms – that is, not the principal and ceremonial cups, but ones for individuals to use for drinking themselves rather than for a ritual of sharing, suggests a further limit on numbers dining. Given the way dishes and platters like this were commonly grouped by the dozen (as we shall see below), it is probable that the original intention was for there to be

Table 9.1: Dinner services: gold and silver tableware of Queen Philippa, 1331–2

Alms nef (an alms boat)

A silver gilt nef, with molets (stars with straight rays) and wheels, weighing 9.936 kg
(£30 13s 4d), worth £51

Cup and ewer sets

1 silver gilt cup, pounced, and enamelled, with a ewer of the same suit, weighing 0.964 kg
(£2 19s 6d), worth £5 19s (Given away)

1 silver gilt and enamel cup, with a ewer of the same suit, weighing 0.972 kg (£3),
worth £6 (Given away)

1 silver gilt cup, pounced and enamelled in part inside with the arms of England and Hainault
and outside on the cover, weighing 0.734 kg (£2 5s 4d), worth £4 10s 8d
(No ewer present with this cup in 1331–2)

1 silver gilt cup, without arms, with a silver ewer of the same suit, weighing 0.756 kg (£2 6s 8d),
worth £4 13s 4d; the ewer weighing 0.412 kg (£1 5s 5d), worth £2 10s 10d

1 silver gilt cup, with foot and cover, enamelled on the bottom and the cover with birds,
weighing 0.616 kg (£1 18s), worth £3 16s. 1 silver ewer of the same suit, weighing 0.34 kg
(£1 1s), worth £2 2s

Cups

14 silver cups, signed on the base with an escutcheon of arms, each weighing 0.216 kg (13s 4d)
(of these, 6 were sold and 3 lost)

21 silver cups, similar, 2 at 0.219 kg (13s 6d), 3 at 0.216 kg (13s 4d), the others varying
between 0.208 kg (12s 10d) and 0.229 kg (14s 2d)

Ewers

1 gold ewer enamelled with the arms of England and Hainault on the cover, weighing
0.405 kg (£1 5s), worth £21 7s 6d

1 ewer, silver gilt and enamelled, marked on the cover with the same arms (England and
Hainault, divided), weighing 1.045 kg (£3 4s 6d)

Pots for ewers

2 silver pots (olle) for ewers (for holding water for filling the ewers), weighing 1.006 kg
(£3 2s 1d)

1 silver gilt pot (olla) signed with the arms of France and Hainault, with a cover, weighing
1.042 kg (£3 4s 4d) (lost)

5 other silver pots, two of which were broken, weighing between 0.972 kg (£3) and 1.118 kg
(£3 9s)

Dishes and saucers

8 silver dishes signed with a letter P at the bottom, weighing between 0.794 kg (£2 9s)
and 0.814 kg (£2 10s 3d) (These were chargers)

32 silver saucers signed with a letter P, 2 weighing 0.131 kg (8s 1d); 3 weighing 0.128 kg
(7s 11d); 1 weighing 0.127 kg (7s 10d); 2 weighing 0.126 kg (7s 9d); 3 weighing
0.124 kg (7s 8d); 1 weighing 0.121 kg (7s 6d); 20 weighing 0.111 kg (6s 10d) to 0.105 kg
(6s 6d) (A further one had been lost and three slightly smaller ones had been sold)

12 silver spoons (no weight given)

Table 9.1 (*continued*)

Dishes and saucers (*continued*)

2 silver dishes marked on the outside on the bottom with an escutcheon with the arms of
England and Hainault, each weighing 0.443 kg (£1 7s 4d)

8 silver dishes, similar, each weighing 0.437 kg (£1 7s)

8 silver dishes, similar, each weighing 0.427 kg (£1 6s 4d) (A further one at this weight had
been lost)

1 silver dish, similar, weighing 0.421 kg (£1 6s)

4 silver dishes, similar, each weighing 0.425 kg (£1 6s 3d)

45 silver dishes, as follows:

  1 silver dish marked outside on the bottom with the arms of France and Hainault
  divided, weighing 0.389 kg (£1 4s)

  3 silver dishes, similar, each weighing 0.386 kg (£1 3s 10d)

  7 silver dishes, similar, each weighing 0.385 kg (£1 3s 9d)

  8 silver dishes, similar, each weighing 0.382 kg (£1 3s 7d)

  17 silver dishes, similar, each weighing 0.380 kg (£1 3s 6d)

  3 silver dishes, similar, each weighing 0.383 kg (£1 3s 8d)

  6 silver dishes, similar, each weighing 0.378 kg (£1 3s 4d)

With 13 further dishes:

  4 silver dishes, similar, weighing 0.375 kg (£1 3s 2d) (1) and 0.378 kg (£1 3s 4d)
  (3): lost

  2 silver dishes, similar, each weighing 0.375 kg (£1 3s 2d)

  6 silver dishes, similar, each weighing 0.373 kg (£1 3s)

  1 silver dish, similar, weighing 0.367 kg (£1 2s 8d)

Basins

1 basin with a silver gilt border and enamel in the bottom, with the arms of Hainault and
Valois, with a towel, weighing 1.320 kg (£4 1s 6d)

3 similar basins, without towels, weighing from 1.204 kg (£3 14s 4d) to 1.272 kg (£3 18s 6d)

1 pair, silver gilt and enamelled with an escutcheon at the bottom with the arms of England,
weighing 3.421 kg (£10 11s 2d)

1 pair, enamelled at the bottom, with the arms of England and France, weighing 2.376 kg
(£7 6s 8d)

1 round basin, silver, weighing 1.102 kg (£3 8s)

1 basin, silver gilt, enamelled in the bottom with the arms of England and Hainault, divided,
weighing 1.247 kg (£3 17s)

Spice plates and spoons

1 silver gilt spice plate, enamelled on the base (inside) with an armed knight and outside with
diverse images, weighing 1.282 kg (£3 19s 2d)

A silver gilt spoon made for the same plate, weighing 0.024 kg (1s 6d)

1 silver spice plate with a great silver spoon for the same plate, weighing, plate, 0.857 kg
(£2 12s 11d), spoon, 0.057 kg (3s 6d)

1 silver spice plate with a great silver spoon, weighing, plate, 0.857 kg (£2 12s 11d), spoon,
0.057 kg (3s 6d)

Fruit plates

12 small silver plates for fruit, each weighing 0.208 kg (12s 10d)

Table 9.1 (*continued*)

Spoons

24 white silver spoons, weighing 0.597 kg (£1 16s 10d)

Alms pot

1 white silver alms pot (*olla*), with 2 casks (*tenelle*), weighing 1.35 kg (£4 3s 4d)

Source: JRULM, MS Latin 235, ff. 23r–30v.

sufficient for 36 diners: there had once been that many saucers. The detailed record of weights of the vessels tells us, as well, that there were variations in size, albeit small, within each class of vessel, and there may also have been some small differences in decoration, as each piece was made individually: it is a reminder that we must not assume homogeneity in vessels of this sort, even if these distinctions might have been hard to detect visually.

A similar structure to a silver dinner service can be seen in the household of Philippa's mother-in-law, Queen Isabella, c.1358. She had a series of nine great dishes, or chargers, ranging in weight between 1.166 kg and 1.512 kg (£3 12s and £4 13s 4d) (Plate 28). About the same size – 1.539 kg (£4 15s) – was a great silver dish for 'interfercula'. There was a further broken dish that had served the same purpose, weighing 1.172 kg (£3 12s 4d). There was then a group of 15 dishes weighing between 0.54 kg and 0.567 kg (£1 13s 4d and £1 15s). Some of these were described as 'small', and they may have been intended as smaller versions of the chargers. The next group – 58 dishes weighing between 0.421 kg and 0.502 kg (£1 6s and £1 11s) – may have been intended as platters. Isabella then had smaller silver saucers: six weighing 0.194 kg (12s) each, 10 weighing 0.178 kg (11s) each, and two groups that were much smaller, three weighing 0.119 kg (7s 4d) each, and eight weighing 0.108 kg (6s 8d) each. Beyond this, she had eight fruit platters of silver, each weighing 0.283 kg (17s 6d).[30] The numbers of fruit platters in the services of both Philippa and Isabella are small compared to the other dishes, and the intention must have been that the fruit they contained was for groups of diners. Part of Queen Isabella's service may have been old: items appeared with the arms of England and France bipartite, which might have been made at any point after her marriage to

Edward II up to 1340; others with the arms of England and France quadri-
partite must have dated from 1340 or after. Close to 1358, Isabella had
purchased a range of silver cups, pots, basins, chargers, dishes – distinguished by their weight, between 0.405 kg and 0.448 kg (£1 5s and £1 7s 8d)
– and saucers, smaller than her others, at on average 0.081 kg (5s).[31]

These examples help us delineate how food came to table, with the large
and small serving dishes, platters and saucers, and small bowls for the
pottages. In looking at the plate, it is useful to bear in mind the structure of
meals as set out, for example, in the specimen menu in Table 1.1 – although
this is a fifteenth-century example, the meal a century earlier had the same
outlines – and to think of the elements of the food that would have been
brought to table on the plate. Most diners would have had before them a
silver platter and saucer – perhaps saucers of different sizes for different
sauces – and menus show us the range of foods that came to table together
as part of each course. In elite circles, French practice – well known to both
Philippa and Isabella – was to use shallow dishes known as 'écuelles' for
both liquids and solids, and the custom seems to have been that these
should be dishes for sharing, typically between two.[32] Diners ate from their
trenchers, transferring to them (or having it set out for them by carvers and
servers) the food from the chargers, platters and saucers. The great dishes
for 'entremes' punctuated the courses.

A further comparison to Philippa's dinner service can be made by
looking at the goods of Richard II in use in his household departments
c.1398–9, at the end of his reign.[33] These dining vessels were not decorated,
but there was a division in all the household departments between silver gilt
vessels and silver ones. In almost all cases the silver gilt vessels were larger
than the silver ones – or at least, their weights were on average more substantial, roughly in the proportion 2:1, which must have reflected a distinction
at table. The ratio in the buttery was, however, closer to 4:1: there were three
hanaps with covers and 18 without them, all of silver gilt, and 71 hanaps of
white silver. If these represent a single cup per diner – beyond the elaborate
drinking cups that feature elsewhere in the inventory – there was potential
for numbers of the elite dining with this service in Richard's household at
the end of his reign to reach two and a half times as many as those in the
household of Philippa in 1331. Some of this difference is doubtless the

result of this being the King's household, as opposed to that of the Queen. There is a further distinction, however. Dividing the number of cups into the number of chargers and dishes suggests that each person in Richard's household with a silver gilt cup could have had before him during the course of the meal a single charger, whereas those using white silver platters would have shared a charger, perhaps between two; there could have been up to five silver gilt dishes from the scullery (the 'esquillerye', the household department that looked after the 'esqueles' or dishes) per individual using the silver gilt service, but just under three white silver dishes for those using that part of the service. There were likewise more spice plates proportionately for the diners using silver gilt, perhaps one between two, each weighing about 2.59 kg (£8); those of white silver weighed approximately 0.864 kg (£2 13s 4d), and the numbers suggest they might have been shared by up to eight people. Chargers and dishes for spices and for fruit were separately identified.

There was therefore a clear distinction among the diners in Richard II's household in terms of the plate they might use, and the food that was expected to come before them. Those using the silver gilt service had access to more food, brought to them individually; those using the white silver were expected to share and had less variety. This division is not as apparent in Queen Philippa's dinner service, although some items will have been reserved for her own use. It suggests a sharper distinction at Richard's meals and a stronger emphasis on display and magnificence around the person of the monarch.

A distinction was also made in terms of alms of food and drink. In Richard II's almonry, there were only two alms dishes, one of silver gilt, and one of white silver: although the silver gilt one was smaller, at 2.97 kg (£9 3s 4d), it nonetheless could have held proportionately more alms per individual than those whose smaller meals were used to supply the white silver alms dish, at 4.117 kg (£12 14s 2d).[34] These alms dishes were doubtless supplemented by alms from the royal table as well, although it is less clear which dishes were in use at the time. The alms of a queen might be more significant, however. The goods of Queen Isabella included much more substantial vessels for alms: a great basin for the Queen's alms, weighing 6.364 kg (£19 12s 10d), a further dish or bowl for alms (possibly for general alms, rather than those of the Queen), of silver, weighing 7.617 kg (£23 10s 2d), and a large silver pot ('olla') for drink for alms, weighing 5.017 kg (£15 9s 8d).[35]

The listing of the silver kitchen goods of Richard II demonstrates the royal household's practice of using precious metal cooking utensils for the food of the monarch, and probably for that of his consort: four silver cauldrons; two silver pots, one with three legs – which must have been a sort of cauldron; a silver gridiron, like a grill, a silver ladle, skimmer and two silver spits.[36] The goods of Queen Isabella included two silver cauldrons (one broken), both with silver skimmers (one broken), and each with a great silver spoon, in one case identified as for vegetables.[37] Further silver 'cookware' can be identified in the household of Richard II, who had silver 'tost pains' (a toaster for bread), as had Edward III,[38] as well as a silver gridiron, ladle and fork.[39] At a lesser social level, Elizabeth, Lady Clifford (d.1424), had a roasting-iron – believed to be a griddle of some kind – but of silver, perhaps suggesting this was something used in her chamber, and that the practice of using silver cookware for the head of the house and his wife extended down the social scale into the nobility.[40]

Beyond the general dinner services, it is also possible to distinguish other equipment at table. A formal process of assaying food, testing it to make sure that it was good and had not been poisoned, was used extensively in great households. The testing extended beyond food and drink to tableware and table linen too. In a set of household ordinances probably for the Earl of Northumberland dating from the period 1500–15, assays – trials or tests – were taken from food and drink, as well as from napery. On Twelfth Night, the lord's table in hall was to have on it a great standing salt with a small salt, as well as a gold spoon for taking the assay and a pair of carving knives.[41] 'Serpents' tongues', fossil shells, often placed in ornamental metalwork settings, and believed to be a defence against poison, were found on elite tables; touching food with the serpent's tongue was sufficient to give the required protection (in an inversion of the normal effect of a serpent's bite). Five serpents' tongues in a case – which it was believed had belonged to St Richard, the former Bishop of Chichester – were among the goods of Edward I inventoried in the Tower of London in June 1296.[42] Some might appear hanging from 'trees': in 1322, among the goods of the late John de Sandall, Bishop of Winchester, there was one set in the manner of a frond.[43]

There was also equipment for food service to individuals. In 1357, the cofferer of Queen Philippa paid a cutler of London £5 for three pairs of knives for serving the Queen and her daughters Mary of Waltham (b.1344) and Margaret of Windsor (b.1346) at their tables on Christmas Day. James Martyn, a Bristol goldsmith, was paid for mending a posnet and spoon of silver in January, for her son, Thomas of Woodstock (b.1355). On 11 February 1358, the cofferer paid another goldsmith of Bristol for the repair of the Queen's salts, in the shape of an elephant, a falcon and, possibly, a female dancer ('tripera').[44] From this, we can see the pattern of service at Christmas, with the royal children probably at their own tables with their own carvers; the use of a silver posnet for preparing the food of the two to three year old Thomas suggests cooking in his chamber or close at hand; and the rich designs of the Queen's salts indicate the impressive quality of her dining arrangements.

These last – and special table pieces – were, in the greatest households, prestigious objects. The principal salts dominated the table settings of the medieval elite, providing centrepieces of elaborate and subtle work in precious metals, often making political and religious connections. Richard II had a gold salt in the shape of a hart, his heraldic badge, with 14 large pearls and a large sapphire, worth in total £53 6s 8d;[45] he also had one in the shape of a swan, sitting on a green base, with a livery collar of the Duke of Lancaster around its neck – among the goods that Richard seized which had belonged to his uncle, Thomas of Woodstock, murdered possibly on the King's orders in 1397, and which alluded to the descent of Thomas's wife from the Swan Knight.[46] Most salts like this are known to us now only from descriptions in inventories, but some survive from medieval England in Oxford and Cambridge colleges, presented by founders and benefactors – and hint at the striking impact these pieces must have made.[47] The Burghley nef, made in Paris in 1527–8 (Plate 29), has a detachable dish on the poop deck, suggesting that it was a salt. It was probably a special commission, perhaps intended as a gift. Nefs were less common in England than on the Continent and it was not unusual to import high-class table pieces like this into England, although English goldsmiths were also capable of fine work.

Plate was meant to be seen, and in dining areas the elite frequently had set up buffets or cupboards – literally boards on which cups might be displayed, cups of distinction rather than the undecorated silver and silver-gilt plate that was used for dining. These cups were indicators of the standing of the household. The number of tiers on a cupboard was carefully calibrated to the formal standing of the lord or lady. The Second Northumberland Household Book, from the early years of the sixteenth century, represents this at its most elaborate. In the chamber of the bride of an earl, where she was to take her meal, the cupboard was tiered according to her degree – the daughter of a duke had a cupboard with five tiers. At Twelfth Night, in hall, the cupboard in the earl's household was also to have five stages or shelves: the cupboard was covered with a diaper cloth, and each shelf with linen. The vessels on the shelves, all for drinking, were to be of gilt plate or parcel gilt: the first shelf had pots, the second flagons, the third bowls, the fourth goblets, and the fifth the standing cups, with the two cups that were to be brought by cupbearers from the cellar for the lord and lady once they had come into the hall.[48]

The pattern of dinner services was similar, although not as extensive, in most households of the gentry and aristocracy. In 1368, Sir Michael Poynings, first Baron Poynings, bequeathed to his wife Joan a pair of new basins and ewers of silver, two half gallon silver pots, a silver alms dish, 12 dishes ('esqueles') and 12 saucers of silver. He also give his heir a pair of silver basins and ewers, and a further dozen each of dishes and saucers, newly made of silver. It was very common for dishes and saucers to appear by the dozen: Thomas Beauchamp, eleventh Earl of Warwick, who died in 1369, left his son William two dozen each of silver dishes and saucers; Joan de Cobham, in the same year, left her son Reginald a dozen each of silver dishes and saucers, of which he had already received six dishes and four saucers when he went to Gascony. Joan had bought from the executors of Archbishop Simon Islip a dozen silver dishes, weighing on average 0.405 kg (£1 5s) and a dozen silver saucers weighing on average 0.101 kg (6s 3d). John de Swyneshevcd, a clerk, left the Archbishop of Canterbury 100 marks and a dozen silver dishes which had belonged to John Stratford, late the Archbishop of Canterbury, weighing on average 0.648 kg (£2) each: recycling goods through bequests like this reinforced connections and sustained memory.[49] When Sir Roger la Warre died, he left his wife Eleanor all the silver vessels, which she was to have for the term of her life and which were then to be passed to John la Warre, his first-born son, and thereafter to descend from heir to heir. The silverware became literally 'the family silver' – possessions to be maintained in the family. Sir Walter de Mauny in leaving all his silver vessels to his wife, Margaret Marshal, referred to 'all my silver vessels which we are in the habit of using continuously in our household service, both those I bought from Robinet Fraunceys as others there', although he further indicated that the vessels that he was accustomed to have with him when he was in London and elsewhere were to be used by his executors to satisfy his creditors.[50] The connections that might be expressed by these goods could be significant – the ties of family, friendship and lordship were especially important to medieval men.

Some of the most distinctive silver vessels were those that delineated elite dining experience by their focus on particular elements of ceremony, especially almsgiving and the consumption of spices at the end of the meal. The arrangements for alms were significant here. The vessels used reflected the standing and contribution of families. When Richard, tenth Earl of Arundel, made his will in December 1375, there was an extensive list of goods for the table, including an alms nef with four wheels, which he left to his son Richard; both his sons Richard and John received a silver pot with two casks for the alms of wine; the Countess of Kent, his daughter, had an alms nef with four wheels, and with battlements, which had belonged to the Bishop of Chichester; and Thomas Arundel, Bishop of Ely, was to have a large silver gilt alms charger, with assorted arms in bezants (roundels, like gold coins), and with an enamelled bezant with the Warenne arms in the middle.[51]

Spice plates and dishes had an important role in dining practice, for the spices that were brought in at the close of a meal, as a digestive, often with wine. The plates themselves were often highly decorated, prestigious pieces of metalwork.[52] In his will of 1370, a knight, Sir Roger de Norwich, left to Margaret, the relict of Sir Walter de Norwich, a silver plate with a foot, enamelled in the middle, for spices, weighing 0.648 kg (£2).[53] There were also spoons for these spices, such as the one bought for the chamber of the Prior of Norwich in 1310–11.[54]

As we have seen from the illuminated manuscripts, there were two principal eating utensils for use at table in the later Middle Ages in England: knives and spoons. Occasional reference is made to forks, but these had specific uses only, for preserves, as we shall see below. Even with these utensils, fingers had to be used for eating food, and therefore there had to be arrangements for washing hands – hence the prominence of basins and ewers. There was also an important difference between the utensils supplied by a household, or an institution, which might have been specially made, decorated in some way, or of special materials, and those that individuals carried themselves. Knives were carried by almost all men and boys in the Middle Ages, but not all of these would have been used for dining or the service of food: knives were designed for particular functions. First, households were equipped with knives for culinary practices, from the chopping of vegetables to the rituals of formal carving. The knives for the latter were typically bought in pairs. John Cutiller supplied the cofferer of Queen Philippa with three pairs of knives at Windsor in October 1351, one for the service of the Lady Mary, another pair for the service of the children of the Duke of Brittany, and a further pair for the stock of the wardrobe.[55] The Master of the Cellar bought for the Prior of Norwich in the accounting year 1313–14 a knife with a crystal handle, for 10s; 12 knives and a large pair from Robert de Brok; and a further 13 large pairs of knives, along with nine with handles of jasper and 57 of ebony.[56] Knives were bought for the priory's bailiffs in 1318–19,[57] and they were also popular gifts[58] – Bishop Mitford of Salisbury bought eight for New Year's gifts for 1407, to be given to the boys and others of his chapel.[59] The inventory of the wardrobe in the Tower of London, under the keepership of John de Flete, 1324–38, includes among the flotsam and jetsam from the royal household a collection of knives that once must have been in use there, or in a similar household, great knives with silver and enamel handles, hanging knives, knives with handles of silver and jet, of crystal, large and small knives from Wales, as well as knives for war and others decayed with rust.[60] Functional knives included dressing knives, for preparing meats, for the kitchen,[61] vegetable knives ('wortknyves')[62] and trencher knives (more widely used than just for cutting bread, probably 'knives for slicing' in general).[63]

The knives placed on tables ready for diners, in illuminations of great household practice, probably belonged to the establishment. But not all

households functioned in this way, and it may well have been the expectation at some levels of society that people would bring with them their
utensils, or at least their knives. Spoons seem to have been more often the
property of the household or institution. Those that appear in illuminations, laid on the table, were less often set out as if for each diner. Beyond
their practical purpose, spoons may have had a special devotional significance or other association (Plate 30). Some clearly had links to the Virgin in
'maidenhead' spoons, and the design of 'apostle spoons' marked a further
connection.[64] The existence of some spoons in groups of 13 is suggestive of
the latter, and individuals perhaps had in mind that they could be seated at
food with Christ and the apostles (the disciples, less Judas, plus Matthias
and Paul). Robert, the parson of Fritton, for example, had 13 spoons to leave
to William atte Moore in 1375.[65] A tale told by John Bromyard may also
make a link to the devotional significance of spoons. A man had confessed,
and had given a silver spoon to the Devil in homage as a sign of the remission of his sins – the spoon had fallen between the man and his confessor
– and in a mark of the hatred of God for sin and in memory of the mercy of
God, the man always used that spoon to eat thereafter.[66]

Silver spoons were plate: they could be converted into specie, and while
they had a value that might be measured in pence, it was sufficient to
guarantee them a place in wills along with other domestic goods of value.
Simon atte Welle of Foxley, Norfolk, a chaplain, left a fellow chaplain a
mazer with a silver foot and three silver spoons in 1374; and in 1375,
Nicholas de Wylby, the rector of Nacton near Ipswich, left Thomas Jurdon
his silver cup and two silver spoons.[67] They might need maintenance: at
Norwich Cathedral Priory, the Master of the Cellar paid 1s 8d for the repair
of spoons in 1283–4;[68] and 7d in 1294–5.[69] Like other plate, they were
subject to depredation – especially so given their portability. John West,
confessing to his thefts, reported stealing a mazer and eight silver spoons at
Conningsby next Tattershall in Lincolnshire belonging to John Bramley,
just before Christmas 1377.[70]

Spoons were also made for special purposes. Richard II's pantry probably intended that each of its salts had a spoon to go with it.[71] An inventory
of the plate of William Paston, probably after 1479, identifies a little spoon
for eggs, as well as several spoons for ginger, that is, green ginger, which

reached England as a sugared preserve. The egg spoon weighed just over 10.5 grams (⅜ oz); the Pastons' ginger spoons seem to have been similar in weight to other spoons, at between 21 and 28 grams (¾ and 1 oz).[72] Other spoons for green ginger, such as the one that belonged to Master Robert Alne, examiner general of the ecclesiastical court of York in 1440, had a long stem to allow them to reach into a deep jar or other container.[73] Forks in medieval England were for sweet confections such as green ginger; one was owned by John de Scardeburgh, rector of Titchmarsh, in 1395.[74] William Duffield, a wealthy canon residentiary of York, Southwell and Beverley, had, in 1453, a hybrid – a long spoon with a fork for green ginger.[75] Queen Isabella had six silver gilt forks for apples, which after her death passed to her son, Edward III.[76]

The patterns of dining of the elite were emulated widely, even if there were different expectations about the quality and quantities of food that might reach table. The terminology and patterns of purchases suggest that even those dining services and utensils made of lesser materials were designed to fit the same pattern of consumption, for example, of large dishes for serving, platters of various sizes, and saucers – and these can be found in use well down the ranks of society, much as the linen that dressed the tables of the upper levels of the peasantry suggests that the overall environment of the meal there was modelled on that of the elite.

Pewter was in use for domestic plate from at least late in the thirteenth century (Plate 16) – large households had some, invariably for lesser members, and pewter vessels can be found in a great many wills and inventories of the later fourteenth and fifteenth centuries.[77] In 1459–60, the cellarer of Durham Cathedral Priory bought two marking irons, with a mitre and a crook, for the priory's pewterware.[78] In London, there were in 1438 standard weights for pewter vessels: for a dozen chargers, middle-sized chargers, and small hollow chargers; for platters in three sizes – large, middle, and small to middle; dishes weighing 18 lbs (8.17 kg) the dozen, and middle-sized dishes, 14 lbs (6.36 kg) the dozen; dishes for the King's household, which were to weigh more, at 16 lbs (7.26 kg) the dozen – an indication of greater food allowances in the royal household; and small dishes weighing 12 lbs (5.45 kg) the dozen. There were four categories of saucer and, in addition, what were possibly different designs of different weights, for example, Florentine dishes and saucers.[79] William Riche, a citizen and pewterer of York, in his will of September 1465, listed a series of moulds belonging to his trade: for chargers, a hollow basin, hollow dish, small dish and a small saucer – the different size dishes again echo those of elite tables.[80] For household dining at its best, there had to be sufficient dishes to come to table, and a great many serving dishes could be required. Margaret Paston anxiously asked her husband in preparation for Christmas 1461 – should he be there – to buy one or two garnishes (that is, dozen sets) of pewter vessels, two basins, two ewers and a dozen candlesticks as, she said, 'for you have too few of any of these to serve this place'.[81]

Table linen was a crucial element in the dining experience. Like textiles and soft furnishings in great households generally, it was of much more importance than the wooden furniture it covered, which was usually of straightforward carpentry. It might also be costly: its use was an important part of the table display – and it might make an impact at all levels of society that aspired to elite patterns of dining. Napery typically included table-cloths ('mappe'); sanaps or sauvenaps to protect the tablecloth; and towels or cloths for wiping hands ('manutergia'). These textiles told of the standing and honour of the household: they had always to be clean, and of the finest quality that might be afforded, although they ranged from the finest linens to coarse canvas, depending on their purpose. The descriptions of some of these textiles imply embroidery, or special designs in their weaving. The goods of John de Sandall, Bishop of Winchester, who died in 1319, exemplify napery at an elite level, with cloth in a range of grades for different purposes (Table 9.2). The cloth at Sandall was of a higher quality than at Southwark. At both, however, the principal uses were the same: coarse cloth, typically a canvas, for wrapping and protecting, and also to go as a base cloth on tables; sauvenaps, to protect undercloths; textiles that were associated with service, such as the manutergia, for wiping hands; and linens, for the elite, or for wrapping or covering their foods.[82]

The Second Northumberland Household Book, in a section dating to around 1515, exemplifies the full development of the use of textiles at table. The napery was typically in the charge of the pantry, but some was kept in another department, the ewery, for washing and drying hands. In its description of the ceremonies for Twelfth Night, the book notes the laying

Table 9.2: Textiles for the table of the Bishop of Winchester, 1319

At Sandall

72 ells of napery at 10d the ell
30 ells for manutergia at 4d the ell
150 ells of canvas for napery, worth £3
32 ells for manutergia, worth 12s
150 ells of coarse canvas worth £2 11s
38 ells of napery, worth £1 1s 7d

Linens

2 pieces of napery of Dinant, containing 95 ells, worth £2 15s
10 manutergia in one piece, worth 8s 9d
1 piece of sauvenaps containing 35 ells, worth 10s 2½d
2 pieces of manutergia, worth 5s 3d and 6s 8d

At Southwark

83 ells of canvas, 20s 9d
1 piece of napery of 14 ells, 7s
Material for tablecloths, containing five tablecloths, each of 7 ells, at 6d the ell, 18s 6d
1 piece of manutergia, containing three towels for wiping hands, each of 7 ells, 3s 6d
A piece of manutergia, containing four towels for wiping hands, two of 7 ells and two of
    3 ells, 5s 3d
4 ells of linen, 2s

Source: TREWE, pp. 208, 213.

of carpets – a sign of especial status – for the lord in hall (he only ever came to hall on days of the greatest ceremony, eating in his great chamber on other days), on the floor between the hearth and the fire screen. Each of the six tables in the hall was to be covered with a carpet, and on that, a diapered tablecloth – even though the tablecloths were to be taken up at the end of the meal, the carpets were to stay on the tables all the time the lord was in the hall. The cupboard, at the side of the hall, was to be covered by a great carpet and a cloth of diaper. The lord's board was to be covered with a table-cloth brought by a servant from the ewery: a gentleman usher and a yeoman usher were to lay it – or in default of a gentleman usher two yeomen ushers and a servant from the ewery were to set it out. The tablecloth for the lady's table was not to be set until the lord's was done.[83]

The cloths of the napery need to be distinguished from textiles used in food processing for straining liquids: jelly cloths, cream cloths, and so forth.

That said, the use of napery had practical implications for eating and diet. On one level, it was connected to what we might view as hygiene, wrapping bread and other foods, keeping flies off foodstuffs left on the table from one meal to another or protecting foods brought in early to await the diners. People ate from clean surfaces, and the linen also kept clothing clean. At the upper end of the social scale, towels were used to wipe mouths between courses; they were possibly also effective in keeping food warm. On another level, clean linen was essential for the honour of the household: dining well meant dining in as honourable a fashion as possible.

The importance of elite dining practice resonated far beyond the great household. It set the pattern to which many in society aspired, and which we can see in goods as far down as the upper tiers of the peasantry and urban workers. Not only were the foods that came to table in elite establishments the most desirable and the most costly, the manner in which they were served, the accoutrements, cups, serving dishes and the style of their servants were something to be copied. The proliferation of works of courtesy disseminated aspects of good manners that might be found at elite tables. Some, however, pointed to excess as an undesirable quality, claiming that the meals of upper-class tables should not be copied. As the early fifteenth-century text 'How the wise man taught his son' put it, advising against choosing a wife for her money, and instead choosing a woman who was meek, courteous and wise: 'For it is better to have with rest and peace a meal's meat with homely fare than to have a hundred dishes with grouching and much care.'[84] The hundred dishes would have needed an investment in the most important of kitchen servants, the cooks, and it is to these professionals and others in the food trades that the next chapter turns.

CHAPTER TEN

COOKS AND KITCHENS, DIETETICS AND FOODS

I N EARLIER CHAPTERS WE have seen many people cooking, from peasant families upwards. But what made a professional cook? There was a large pool of catering professionals, practising at different levels of ability. At one end of the scale were those working in urban cookshops, or who might work for hire. Among these in the *Canterbury Tales* was the pilgrims' aspirational cook, Hogge of Ware, who listed a range of dishes, designed to impress, with high-quality spices, but whose leg ulcer suggested unsavoury elements of the catering trades. Medieval stereotypes of cooks were not, on the whole, flattering. Chaucer also pointed to their drunkenness and their obesity.[1] Proverbial lore highlighted irascibility, explaining something of the 'hastiness of cooks' – 'Hot fire and smoke makes many an angry cook'[2] – and sometimes questionable competence: 'He is an evil cook that cannot lick his own lips.'[3] The state of kitchen scullions was a matter of concern and the subject of common tales – 'A boy came out of the kitchen, a lout, all filthy with grease.'[4] On an entirely different level were the master cooks of the great household, managing not only the kitchen, but also the pantry, buttery, cellar, bakehouse and brewhouse, larder, boiling house, scalding house and confectioncry – in a highly complex operation that embraced cooks, pottagers, saucerers, bakers, pantlers, butlers, cellarers and their servants, producing food to the highest quality for the lord and the elite of his household, as well as lesser dishes for the remainder of the establishment. There were, for example, at least 24 people associated with cooking and the supply and provisioning of food in the household of 147 that accompanied the Duchess of Clarence and her family to Normandy in November 1419.[5] No one would forget that the quality of entertainment and hospitality was a mark of the calibre of the establishment. In the monasteries, a distinction has to be made between monks, working as cellarers, refectorers and cooks, sometimes on a weekly rota, and not necessarily with any specialist training, on the one hand – and, on the other, those who were professionals, usually laymen, who might prepare food for the head of the house or, indeed, the convent more generally, as we have seen at St Augustine's, Canterbury.[6]

In the great household, cooks, especially master cooks, were handsomely rewarded. Stephen Gravesend, Bishop of London, in his will of 1337, left his two master cooks, William and John, £5 each.[7] The hallmarks of their cuisine appear in the kitchen goods sometimes bequeathed by bishops to their successors to ensure their standing, as in the case of John Sheppey of Rochester in 1360.[8] The master cooks of visiting great lords were treated with courtesy: they – rather than their hosts – cooked the food that their lord would eat, much as the monarch had a cook for what he would consume. On a visit like this, the cellarer of Durham Cathedral Priory in 1443–4 gave 3s 4d to the cook of the Bishop of Durham, along with 8d for linen for him, probably for an apron.[9] Among those who came to Durham Priory in 1460–1, the cooks accompanying the Earl of Northumberland and Duke of Exeter likewise had linen cloth bought for them; linen of a slightly higher quality was bought for the cook of the Earl of Warwick, but the cooks of the first two also received a cash reward of 6s 8d.[10] 'Rewards' were given to the king's cook in 1462–3.[11] Over the next 15 years, Durham Priory made similar payments and gifts of linen to the cooks of the Archbishop of York, the Earls of Northumberland, Warwick and Westmorland, the Duke of Gloucester (the future Richard III) and Lord St John.[12] This was a routine practice recognising the standing of cooks at an elite level.

Just occasionally we have sufficient references to tell a little of the careers of these individuals. Pierrot, the cook of Henry VII, appears in the king's household around 1505. He is described as 'Pierrot who was the King of Castille's cook';[13] 'Pierrot the French cook';[14] and 'the French pastry cook'.[15] He was paid substantial wages: £13 6s 8d a year, in addition to periodic payment of rewards. He continued in royal service under Henry VIII, as cook 'for the king's mouth', for as long as until 1538, when he received £10 towards his apparel – an elegant and well-dressed cook, who was responsible, under the ordinances of Eltham, for making sure that his subordinates, the scullions of the kitchen, were properly clothed while they worked (some £50 was allowed for this in 1538).[16] Other foreign servants were to be found in elite kitchens: in 1431–2, John de Vere, twelfth Earl of Oxford, had at least two Frenchmen in his kitchen.[17] John Gower, in his *Mirour de l'homme* of c.1390, had pointed to this international quality of cooks: just as Satan circled the earth, so did cooks, who travelled to all the palaces to learn in each place the right pottages to serve with delicacies – from whatever land he had come, the cook would be worth nothing unless he had learned these things.[18]

These connections indicate how ideas about cooking may have been transmitted. Information about the training of cooks at this elite level is very thin, but learning on the job was doubtless common and travelling to do so brought together dishes and sauces from across Europe. Levels of wages indicate that some kitchen staff were not especially skilled; indeed, some were children. In 1270, the 10-year-old William, the son of Herbert ate Stil of Stagsden, in Bedfordshire, was cutting vegetables in the kitchen of the Prior of Newnham's manor when he dropped the knife on to his foot – injuring himself badly. He was carried home by his mother, who was in the adjacent courtyard.[19] The kitchen at Durham Cathedral Priory in the mid fifteenth century had a comparatively small staff – some of them were expected to double up the roles they undertook; others were no more than boys. Beyond the monastery's cellarer, in overall charge, and taking a fee of £4 p.a.,[20] there were, in 1455–6, a purchaser of victuals (an 'emptor'), a man to roast and bake, two men for boiling food (seethers), and a man to work the spit (the turnbroach). Others were involved in looking after, and slaughtering, animals.[21] In 1459–60, a keeper of the flesh larder was identified, and another man – the kitchen workman – who also looked after the pots ('vase').[22] The pattern changed slightly over the years: in 1465–6 there was a purchasing official; John Preston was the keeper of the flesh larder and in charge of roasting (in 1446–7 the roasting had been combined with the work of the pastry cook, the 'pastillator');[23] Richard Preston was the 'pistillator' – the man in charge of the pounding in the mortar – and the boiling of food; John Witwange continued as the kitchen's workman, but Edward Batmanson now took over as the keeper of the pots and the kitchen windows; there were two fishermen, a turnbroach, and John Cowper was the child of the kitchen 'for its necessaries'. Others were in charge of animals.[24] In 1445–6, there was a child – probably a young man – of the fish-house, Richard Collom;[25] and in 1448–9, there were two boys of the kitchen.[26]

A key post was an administrative one, that of clerk of the kitchen. At Durham, the cellarer may have performed some of these functions. In 1476, Lord Hastings, the Lieutenant of Calais, was in search of a new clerk for his kitchen, and commissioned John Paston III to look out for a suitable candidate. Paston identified one Richard Stratton, who was then in service with Master Fitzwalter, and who had previously served a household at Guines as purveyor at the time when King Edward IV was there. Paston outlined his personal qualities: 'This man is of average stature, young enough, well witted, well mannered, a good young man both on horse and on foot. He speaks English well, French moderately and is perfect in Flemish. He can write and read.' He was willing to enter Hastings's service at short notice and he was happy to meet Hastings before he left for Calais. At Stratton's request, Paston had also spoken to Master Fitzwalter that he might be 'good lord' to him; and Fitzwalter was happy that Stratton should make this move: if his own son had been of age, he would happily have seen him in Hastings's household – and that his servants, if they were in any way acceptable to Hastings, might serve him.[27] Stratton had proven expertise, in practical terms carrying out a similar post, the accomplishments necessary for employment in such a prestigious household, and had the support of his current employer for the move.

As well as cooks on the establishment in elite households, there was a pool of additional labour readily available for major occasions – either for hire, or individuals who might be released for a short period of time from other households. The funeral feast of Bishop Mitford of Salisbury, held in that city on 7 June 1407, required a meal for 1,450 household members and guests.[28] Twenty-nine cooks were hired for three days, working in different departments of the household kitchen.[29] Temporary buildings were put up. Equipment and utensils were hired: from 30 iron spits and a great lead, to 4,200 platters, dishes and saucers (the charge included the costs for 300 of them that were lost).[30] In 1416–17, for the marriage of Master de Wellys, Robert Waterton of Methley hired cooks: one from Wakefield, for 6d; the cook of John, Lord Scrope, for 1s 8d; and the cook of the Prior of Nostell Priory for 2s.[31]

Almost all cooks in great households were male, but there are occasional references to women helping in the kitchen.[32] In an institutional context, this was particularly the case at nunneries and hospitals. At Marrick Priory, a Yorkshire nunnery in the fifteenth century, there was a male cook paid 12s a year, and he was assisted by a kitchen maid paid 2s per annum. There were further maids in the storeroom and bakehouse; there are no details of who staffed the brewhouse and malthouse, but this work was often done in secular households by women.[33] At the almshouse of St John the Baptist and St John the Evangelist at Sherborne in Dorset at its refoundation in 1438, there was a woman, known as the 'housewife of St John', who was to purchase and prepare the food, which she was also entitled to share.[34]

More can be discovered about the techniques of professional cooks from a study of cookbooks, and from kitchens and their equipment. About 4,000 recipes survive from medieval England: some of these are gathered into collections, in recipe books, but many survive in less formal groupings or as isolated examples.[35] What is apparent from an examination of the recipe books, however, is that these were not manuscripts that were used directly by cooks in the kitchen but guides, perhaps for stewards of the household or clerks of the kitchen – probably to inform the discussions that took place between cooks and household officials, like those in the household of the Abbot of St Augustine's planning the following day's menu.

The preservation of a good deal of information about food and drink in works like John Russell's *Boke of nurture* of the second half of the fifteenth century shows that knowledge of these elements of food practice was essential for those managing provisioning the departments of the great household and day-to-day aspects of ceremony and courtesy. Russell's work was couched as the advice of an usher to a prince – but in reality was intended for aspirant ushers, key officials in the household's organisation. Here can be found guidance on, for example, the number of knives there should be in the pantry – three, a knife to chop (possibly to chip, to remove the crust of the bread), one to pare, and one especially sharp to give a smooth cut to the trenchers – laying the table, the provision of fruit, cheese and wines, desirable behaviour, carving a wide range of foods, their qualities and sauces, along with specimen menus.[36] A mid fifteenth-century recipe book known as the Ordinance of Pottage includes instructions for preparing a side of deer 'in high grease', fat, in season, which encompasses much about a prestigious medieval foodstuff – but would not have sufficed to teach a novice how to prepare the meat. The carcass was to be washed, the fillets (the best pieces) were to be cut off and were to be roasted on a spit. The remaining flesh was then to be scored in a lozenge pattern and basted with wine and spices. A charger was to be placed underneath to catch the fat, which was then to be used for basting. The roasted meat was then to be cut and served. Practical experience was necessary for those who had to carry out this task, but there was sufficient guidance here for an overseer or interested servant to see the main elements of the process and to justify expenditure on it to an auditor.[37] Cookbooks refer to a wide range of techniques – boiling, roasting, frying, baking, basting, stuffing, blending, soaking, broiling, poaching and so on – but instructions on how to cook in these ways are very scarce. The books rarely give quantities. Making a dish was a question of judgement, and these judgements were made by several people in the medieval kitchen, not just the cook: quantities of spices, for example, might be controlled carefully and issued to the cooks, as at St Augustine's Abbey.[38]

Kitchens and their equipment are useful for the indications they give of the potential and development of professional work. The construction of kitchens at an elite level made a useful distinction between the activities: places for boiling, for roasting, for working with material in pans and for wet working, and areas for preparation and for baking were often clearly set apart.[39] Some of these are still evident in surviving medieval kitchens, such as that at Glastonbury Abbey (Plates 22 and 23). The structures were also designed with space for fires either in a central hearth, and/or in fireplaces and ranges around the walls – and with as much ventilation as possible. At Durham Cathedral Priory, the kitchen was built anew in 1366–74 (Plate 24); its windows were covered, at least in part, with wooden frames, possibly supporting a textile – and we can follow the development of the equipment in this kitchen in some detail through the fifteenth century.[40]

The inventories of elite kitchens provide useful information about the development of major pieces of kitchen equipment, and especially about the evolution of the cooking range. The kitchen goods of Walter de Stapeldon, Bishop of Exeter and former treasurer of England, brutally murdered in Cheapside in 1326, included a piece of ironwork with four feet on which pots and pans could be placed.[41] 'Brandreths', the iron framework for supporting pots and pans over the fire, appear to be important in the development of the range.[42] Long brandreths can be found more widely by the 1410s and 1420s, but they still seem to have been unusual. The will of John Streche, probably of Oxborough in Norfolk, 26 August 1418, describes goods at his manor of Ashe in Musbury, Devon. He left his wife a certain piece of ironwork on which the pots assigned for cooking could be placed, a fairly convoluted way of saying a brandreth, but that may have been because it was novel.[43] There was a long brandreth listed among the goods of John Talkan, a citizen of York in the 1420s, probably a taverner or vintner like his father.[44] In the kitchen of Henry Bowet, Archbishop of York in 1423, there was a long 'brandyryn pour le range' ('fire-iron for the range') on which the pots were to be placed.[45] These early kitchen ranges were probably a series of enclosed hearths – 'cookers' or 'cooking places' – with space for cooking on top. Other references to ranges come from shortly afterwards in upper-class establishments. The ranges in the kitchen of the Archbishop of Canterbury's palace at Canterbury were repaired in 1446–7 probably in anticipation of a visit by the queen.[46] The first reference to a range in the kitchen at Durham Cathedral Priory comes from 1445–6, when £3 12s 6d was received as kitchen fees from the range and the offal or waste from animal carcasses and fish – and entries for these profits of the range appear in the cellarer's accounts through into the 1480s.[47] The household ordinances of the Duke of Clarence of 1469 also specify perquisites from the range, from roasted meat.[48] The range must therefore be envisaged as an essential part of the main cooking area of the great household, providing not just ironwork for supporting pots and places for cooking at a convenient height, but also spits for roasting. At Durham in 1471–2 three iron cressets – lights – were bought for the range, for 6s;[49] and a brandreth, probably for the range, almost certainly of ironwork and weighing just over three-quarters of a ton, was made in 1475–6, for 17s.[50]

The equipment in the kitchen at Durham Cathedral Priory included a series of cookers, where activities such as frying might take place. The accounts of the cellarer describe these as 'furni' or 'fornace'. In 1455–6, three days' work was invested in repairing these, while others worked on one of the hearths in the kitchen.[51] A 'fornace' was also repaired in 1472–3.[52] In 1478–9, John Thomson was paid 12d for making one for frying.[53] The kitchen complex had a larder house, which was paved in 1460–1, along with the main area of the kitchen floor,[54] and a boiling house which, in 1459, had two large cauldrons ('olle') set up as boilers.[55] Other large pots and pans in the kitchen had names, probably that of the cellarer who had been in office when they were bought. In 1459 there were two cauldrons called 'Stockton' and 'Warde', two pans called 'Hesilden' and 'Stockton', two called 'Eden', and a further two named vessels[56] – Thomas Warde had been cellarer in 1438–9; William and John Eden had been cellarers together in 1444–5; and William Hesilden had also held office in 1444–5.[57] Giving names to cauldrons and pots had a wider currency in great households: in 1322, among the goods of Humphrey de Bohun, Earl of Hereford, were a brass pot called 'Humfrey', one called 'Wynter' and four known as 'holiday' pots.[58] Other cauldrons might have legends on them, sometimes indicating manufacturer and date of casting (Plate 11).

Items of kitchen equipment help delineate styles of cookery. The York kitchen of William Duffield, a canon of the minster in 1453, had two mortars set into the ground – pounding and grinding were major tasks. There were also a paste or pastry board, a striking board – for dividing out portions of food – and a dressing board, where the final preparations were made before service.[59] Frying pans were in use, especially in elite and mano-rial households. The kitchen of Bishop Stapeldon of Exeter had a brass pan for frying weighing 20 lbs.[60] A source of fat were the great cauldrons: the copper skimmers purchased for the Durham Cathedral Priory kitchen were for taking the fat from the surface of cauldrons and pots – a commodity, 'flocks', that was carefully conserved and used in the kitchen and for grease elsewhere in the household.[61] Fried foods, sometimes cooked with batter – 'fritures' – were popular as elements in elite meals. There was also an Anglo-Norman word, 'cretun', for the burnt and dried-up pieces of meat that remained in the pan after cooking.[62]

Occasionally there were pans for cooking particular meats or fish: the will of John Brompton of Beverley, a wealthy merchant, proved in 1444, included an iron bowl called a 'roasting pan', with a spout at either end, and a rectangular, iron, goose pan.[63] In 1445, Sir Giles Dawbeny, bequeathed to his son William a chafer for boiling fish; and Edward Atwell the younger, a butcher of Northampton, left to John Pruey, his brother's son, a chafing dish for eels.[64] Among the goods of Sir John Fastolf in the kitchen at Caister Castle at his death in 1459 were three pike pans of brass.[65] As well as spits for roasting meat, there were special spits for fish. In 1454, Margaret Daunay, a widow of York, left her daughter Katherine two iron spits, along with a small spit for roasting eels.[66] John Carter, a citizen and tailor of York, had in his kitchen at his death in 1485 three iron spits and two lampern-spits.[67]

Kitchen perquisites and traditional rewards for cooks and others working with food supply further information about cooks and cooking practices – and about practices of waste and its management. Household ordinances aimed at ensuring that the lord and his household had the benefit, wherever possible, of all items brought for consumption. To the extent that things might be useful, or might have value, there were routines in place to make sure that there was no waste or theft. Auditing practices and discussions of agricultural management in the *Husbandry* of *c.*1300 indicate that value was seen in a great many things, that there were rights of ownership that were worth asserting, and that without formal control of these things a good deal might be lost to the lord.[68] Customary practice also played a part: what could be reused or sold on was identified; waste was minimised and the opportunities for household officials to obtain personal benefits were controlled. The strength of these customary assumptions is occasionally apparent when standard procedures broke down. At Maxstoke Priory in 1449–50, nothing was received from fat and the skimmings from the cauldrons as the kitchener had secretly sold them and fled as an apostate. In the account for the balance of the year, mid May to the end of September 1450, the sale of fat and the skimmings was worth 4s 2½d – sufficient to encourage the kitchener to abscond.[69]

Perquisites and the rewards of service in the kitchen had a close relationship to work activities. The problem was to define what might be taken legitimately. *A myrour to lewde men and wymmen*, a fifteenth-century text, put the tension well: ' "Little theft" is when men's servants or others steal meat, drink, poultry, sheaves in harvest or other small things and think these may be taken as a custom.'[70] In the household of George, Duke of Clarence in 1469, a balance was struck between customary practices in terms of taking of perquisites or 'fees', and a desire to control waste and peculation. The ordinances set out exactly what those perquisites were to be, and enforced a range of activities, such as a stocktaking every Monday, to control expenditure and to supervise servants, as well as control at the gate by the porter, to prevent the embezzlement of foodstuffs out of the household. In the pantry, no fees were to be taken by those looking after the bread except the waste – the chippings and cuttings – cut from trencher bread. In Clarence's cellar, empty vessels – barrels and containers of assorted sizes – were not to be taken until the office had sufficient of the larger empty containers and no spilt wine or dregs were to be taken as fees without the supervision of the household's head officers. The only fees in the spicery were to be empty containers: pots of green ginger, bags and boxes of char de quince and of comfits.

In Clarence's kitchen, no fees were to be taken from the fat skimmed from the lead until the lord had sufficient for frying and for greasing carts and carriages, and the same was true of meat roasted on the range. The 'crags' (necks) of veal and sheep, along with the back legs and rump of mutton, were available as perquisites, under supervision; and the waste ('garbage' – entrails – and the feathers) of all poultry and wildfowl were also perquisites provided the lord had been served and all that was needed for his food had been taken. Empty barrels of herring, salt salmon, sturgeon, salt eels and oil, and skins from rabbits that came as presents, or from the lord's warrens or by his warrant, were to be feeable, as were the panniers in which sea fish were delivered. In the scullery and saucery, it was only the entrails of swans that might form fees, provided there was no use for them in cooking.

The slaughter and butchery of animals were occasions when perquisites were commonly taken. In Clarence's household, the slaughtermen might take nothing from the carcass of an ox except the head and the lower part of the neck (the sticking-piece), and they were to leave the chine (the breast-bone) complete and with flesh, and also the first joint of the tail (that is, the other joints of the tail might be taken as a fee). Ox tongues belonged to the household and were not to be taken as fees at all seasons of the year – a statement suggesting that a contrary practice might have been common in other circumstances – and between All Saints and the start of Lent, the main season for butchery, tripe and the feet were not to be considered as perquisites, implying that they might be taken at other seasons. In butchering sheep, the household was to have the whole carcass except the head and the henge – the heart, liver, lights, etc., of the animal – with some limited exceptions. Calves, pigs and lambs were to have no fees taken from their carcasses at any season of the year – the value of young meatstock was high.[71] The ordinances made a comprehensive assessment of the problem of perquisites, and showed the extent to which those employed with food in the household expected to benefit from the materials they handled. Nothing here was waste: it all had a value – the question was who was to benefit from it.

What happened to 'waste' materials? Recipes made extensive use of offal and waste parts of birds and animals. To make 'garbage', a broth, a fifteenth-century cook was to take 'fair garbage of chickens, that is, the head, feet, liver and gizzard', mixed with beef or mutton stock, and thickened with bread, along with pepper, saffron, mace and cloves.[72] But there was an implication that some offal, at least, was simply discarded: 'We have blasphemed, and we beseech and pray, for we are made as the offal of all this world, which is cast out of it', wrote the author of the *Orcherd of Syon*, around 1425.[73] The 'hogwash' that was tipped over the head of a humble nun, as related in *Jacob's Well*, c.1440 – as a jest – was the kitchen waste of the nunnery destined for the pigs.[74] Parts of food only occasionally used for human consumption might serve other purposes, for example, as medicines, for both humans and animals. To this end, bacon rind was used on horses' hooves.[75]

Waste of anything that might serve as alms was to be deprecated. When visiting Nun Coton Priory in 1440, the Bishop of Lincoln had a report from the prioress that she was concerned that the leftovers and fragments of food from the convent's table were not collected and distributed in alms, and that they were lost through carelessness or were otherwise consumed – he charged her and the other nuns that leftover food from the convent's meals and the prioress's board should not be wasted, but honestly kept and distributed to the poor.[76]

As well as food and drink and their by-products, cooks received rewards or favours more generally. The purchase of textiles for aprons has already been noted. At Durham Cathedral Priory, the cooks were given gloves at Christmas 1447 and possibly in other years.[77] Gloves were given to other household servants and workmen as well, for example, carpenters employed by the guild of the Holy Cross at Stratford-upon-Avon in 1430–1;[78] and this should be seen as a reward that was more typical of service in general rather than for kitchen staff in particular. Cooks in some great households received a customary payment – a 'wite' – at Easter;[79] and other practices such as tipping household staff generally must have brought cooks benefits as well.[80]

Supplying and provisioning

Supplying the great household or institution was a major logistical challenge, but it was not without pattern. The purchasing of food, on one level, might be carried out by the cook or his equivalent.[81] There were also purchasing officials sometimes known as 'caters', or 'caterers', and it was on their shoulders that much of the burden of making the arrangements to transport food will have fallen. The cellaresses of Campsey Priory in Suffolk, around 1300, employed one Robert Catour to make their purchases for them.[82] In the household of Bishop Mitford of Salisbury in 1406–7, one of the bishop's servants was Geoffrey Catour. October 1406 saw him at Bristol buying a pipe of salt salmon for the household; in January 1407, he bought 102 salt fish in London, three barrels of herring (probably white herring), four cades (barrels) of red herring, 240 stockfish and two firkins of sturgeon.[83]

Typically there were two types of activity: on the one hand, bulk purchases, known commonly as 'gross emptions' ('emption' from the Latin for a purchase, 'emptio'), 'provisions' and sometimes as 'purveyances', which were made a few times a year, at fairs, or in larger towns and cities – like those Geoffrey Catour made for Bishop Mitford; and on the other hand, day-to-day acquisitions, either by purchase, shopping locally in markets or in the neighbourhood generally, or by transfer of some kind, for example, from an estate. The gross emptions were often of large quantities of goods that were in preserved form, or could be put into a form that preserved well, or of specialist products, such as spices. These 'provisions' are frequently listed separately in accounts, along with their associated transport costs. These might be an annual, or semi-annual, purchase, for example, of fish at the great herring fairs in East Anglia, in late September or early October, or of meat for provisioning the larder in late October or early November. Whether purchased locally, or in bulk at a distance, goods had to be transported to the household or one of its depots.

The daily shopping was used to top up the bulk purchases, with fresh foods, or perishables, or to provide special products. Typically these acquisitions were made locally, an activity usually taking only a part of the day. There was an intermediate tier of activity between the daily shop and the gross emption, that of purchases 'in patria', that is, in the countryside roundabout. The purchasing officials of the household spent a good deal of time scouring the neighbouring countryside for provisions and securing them for the household; and households devoted logistical expertise and resource to moving provisions to the place of residence.

The gross emptions presented special challenges. How were goods moved? Goods could be carried by individuals themselves or by porters. They could be moved using carts and waggons, either owned by the household, borrowed or hired, or by using professional carting services. Goods might be moved on packhorses, either tied to saddles or in baskets. And they might also be moved by water. All this might be done directly by household servants, or use might be made of men, horses and equipment hired for the occasion, or manorial carting or carrying services might be used.

First, individuals might simply carry small quantities with them. Richard Cely in London, writing to his younger brother George in Bruges in November 1479, noted that their mother wanted a sugar loaf of 3 lbs or 4 lbs, 'and bring it with you this Christmas'.[84] Porters operated around docks, markets and in towns. Where shorter distances were involved, or the goods were special in some way, porters might be used to carry goods directly. They were sometimes used to carry gifts to the great household. On 5 April 1393, four porters brought two pike and two tench – one fish each – as a gift from the Abbot of Chertsey to William of Wykeham, Bishop of Winchester.[85] Porters are unlikely to have constituted a principal means of conveying provisions, although they may have been employed for smaller quantities purchased during the daily shopping. Individuals on foot were also responsible for driving cattle to the household. Some of these were hired workers. In 1407, the household of Bishop Mitford of Salisbury hired a man to drive cattle from Ramsbury to Potterne.[86] It was quite a common practice to move the larger livestock on the hoof close to the household, keeping animals alive in pastures until they were needed for consumption. It was harder to move deadstock – but livestock had to be fed.[87]

Packhorses were used extensively for moving some foodstuffs, especially fish. In the stable of Queen Isabella on her death in 1358 was a white horse for carrying fish: worth 13s 4d, it was almost certainly a packhorse.[88] In the household of Dame Alice de Bryene, most weeks on a Saturday bread was bought for a fish merchant's horse. On Saturday 12 November 1412, the merchant and his horse delivered 3d worth of oysters, 33 whiting and 6 haddock.[89] Margaret Paston, writing to her husband, John, perhaps in October 1453, reported that she had bought a horse-load of herring.[90] Other foodstuffs were carried on horseback. In January 1312, Queen Isabella, the wife of Edward II, sent John Moigne to the Earl of Lancaster with wild boar, on two hackneys. Two old saddles were bought for 18d, to which the boars were lashed, and another two hackneys were accompanied by a valet of the Queen's chamber taking further wild boar to the Earl of Hereford.[91]

Heavier loads were moved by wheeled transport: the standard transport for the great household was a four-wheeled waggon, or long cart, with two-wheeled carts for lesser quantities. It is not unusual to find the waggons pulled by six horses, sometimes more, and sometimes with oxen in addition. Two-wheeled carts might also be pulled by more than one horse. In January 1407, Bishop Mitford's household sent Geoffrey the waggoner with the waggon and seven horses from Potterne in Wiltshire to London, for salt fish, spices and other foodstuffs, a trip that took seven days. In April he and a groom, along with the waggon and seven horses, went from Potterne to Bristol for two pipes of wine, a return journey they completed in three days.[92] For moving six pipes of wine from Southampton to Potterne, the household needed six carters, three carts and 18 horses. The carters were those of the Prior of Mottisfont, who were paid a reward for taking care of the wine.[93] In other instances, carts from the bishop's manors were used to carry his goods.[94]

Another option for transport was to use a carrier. In the 1470s there was a system of carriers operating between London and Norwich. It was used for smaller quantities of higher value goods, such as the oranges and pots of salad oil sent by the Pastons.[95]

Water transport was important for some of the bulkier foodstuffs, such as the trade in corn into London.[96] As well as inland waterways, coastal shipping was employed: the London corn trade made use of the Thames and its estuary to bring supplies from Kent. Elsewhere, in the week of 7 February 1406, Sir Hugh Luttrell had a bulk purchase of fish shipped from Bristol to Dunster on the Somerset coast: 150 hake, 600 whiting, 15 gallons of olive oil, and two baskets of figs and raisins, all bought by his steward, during an eight-day trip. The following week cod was carried to the household from another ship arriving at Dunster.[97]

Not all food had to be moved to its final destination at once. Purveyors for the Crown assembled goods in warehousing of various shapes and sizes, from cellars and rooms in houses, to granaries and barns.[98] Great barns for storage were a major investment made by large estates (Plate 31), but lesser accommodation was widely available for hire. Besides the Crown, other households also established depots for household goods, either in major towns or at points where some form of processing may have taken place, and from where foods could be distributed when needed. The household of Ralph of Shrewsbury, Bishop of Bath and Wells, while in Somerset in 1337–8, drew heavily on marine fish from Compton Bishop, close to the Severn estuary, which was perhaps a centre for processing or for holding fish in store until the bishop wanted them.[99] In 1409–10, the Duke of York's establishment at Hanley Castle was a substantial one, reaching a peak at Twelfth Night in 1410 when 281 people were present. The effort of supplying the household was substantial: a granary was rented in Bristol, from where wine was also shipped up the Severn.[100] The amount of time goods were held in storage may have had an impact on the quality of food: there are examples of grain in storage for royal purveyance for more than 12 months, although grain must regularly have been kept from one harvest to next.

Most examples of the use of depots, however, were comparatively short-term, easing logistical efforts.

Beyond bulk storage in barns and granaries, there was a range of options for storage in the household itself. We have seen buildings for apples, spices, larders and so on. Within domestic buildings there were also wooden food chests and aumbries (cupboards, sometimes with apertures for ventilation, for food) (Plate 32), for keeping food as safe as possible against vermin or depredation. Odo of Cheriton had these in mind in a tale of *c*.1220, targeting the rapacity of the clergy. He recounted how the head of a household put a cat in the food chest to catch the rat that was eating the cheese, and the cat ate both.[101]

Dietetics and foods

The connection between foods, their characteristics and health was one that was commonly made. People made links to the long-established theories of the four humours and to academic medicine, giving consideration to the properties of foods and lifestyles, and matching them together. John Lydgate, in a dietary setting out practices for healthy eating, advised that over-consumption at supper and drinking late in the evening caused a superfluity of phlegm, one of the humours. All illness came from eating either too much or too little: a temperate mean was desired: 'a moderate diet against all sickness is the best physician to temper your stomach.' Food was to be taken according to one's complexion (we might say 'constitution'), to achieve the balance of the humours.[102]

The link between dietetics and health was made at an elite level: regimens for health circulated across Europe in the later Middle Ages. These took advantage of the medical tracts translated in southern Italy, particularly at Salerno and Monte Cassino in the eleventh century, such as the work of a physician and philosopher from Kairouan in present-day Tunisia, Isaac Israëli (d.*c*.932), *On universal and particular diets* – which came to form a part of the curriculum of medical schools, as at Montpellier. Texts of this kind were fundamental to works such as Aldebrandin of Siena's *Livre de physique*, the first dietetic treatise in the vernacular, dating from before 1257.[103] The ideas from these works were influential and circulated widely among professional physicians: there was a crucial link to diet, and an understanding that dietary practices had an influence on health.[104] John of Gaddesden (d.1348/9), for example, in his 'Rosa Anglica', of *c*.1313, pointed to foodstuffs that might cause the condition known as 'hydrops', particularly by warming the complexion of the liver – salted, fried and roast foods, and foods with a strong flavour of garlic, chives and leeks.[105] His advice on eating fruit noted the different effects its consumption would have on those of different complexions, that is, different individuals would need to consume different foods:

> Some eat more [fruit] than other food, wherein they do not well, for all fruits make watery useless blood, and prone to putrefaction. But yet styptic fruits should be eaten after dinner by those who are inclined to looseness of the belly, and such are pears, figs and apples. But these when roasted and taken by sufferers from colic before dinner are laxative. When eaten raw, however, they are constipating, though not all equally, for the sweet are less so and the sour more.

John concluded that it would be better to do without fruit altogether, following Galen's advice – Galen's father had lived to be 100, because he never ate fruit.[106]

There is some evidence of the use of different diets for the sick: at a general level, one might point to the use of meat in the monastic infirmary and hospitals.[107] Occasionally we can see a different regimen employed for an individual. At God's House, Southampton, William de Wygeton, a relative of the warden of the house, was ill for a period of at least three weeks from 19 October 1328. He had pork bought for him specially that day; on 23 October there was a small chicken, fish on Tuesday 25 October, a pomegranate the following day, and sprats and bread on Saturday 29 October. The following Thursday he again had a small chicken. The pattern suggests light meats, with fish on a day when others ate meat, but we have no indication what his illness was.[108] At an elite level, these ideas were drawn upon directly: the *Forme of cury*, from the court of Richard II, claimed to have been drawn up by the King's chief master cooks with the assent and advice of the physicians and philosophers at the court.[109] While most people, most of the time, however, would not have sought physicians who were trained in this way, many would nonetheless have made a connection between foodstuffs and health.

Many medical recipes incorporated foodstuffs, but one approach to health was simply to ensure good food. At St Augustine's Abbey, c.1330–40, if a monk were sick, the day he took his medicine the custom was, with the prior's licence, that he should have from the cellarer a good, fat capon and a gallon of wine beyond the daily food given to those that had rooms in the infirmary.[110] Others looked to provide sweet, palliative medicines, such as electuaries and syrups – for which locally sourced fruits and berries were a common ingredient. One fifteenth-century prescription for the flux and prolonged menstruation made a syrup from myrtle berries and sugar: if it was well prepared it would last for 12 months and it might be made with honey if there were no sugar available.[111] Medicines, however, might address the imbalance of the complexion through the consumption of calefactives (warming) or cooling mixtures, or desiccants, for those with a superfluity of moistness.[112] Prescriptions might make use of seeds, gathered in gardens and woods. 'Dauke', wild carrot, for example, was a diuretic, and used as part of a treatment for kidney stones.[113] As a remedy for a cough, one prescription was to drink wine in which dauke seed had been boiled, along with figs and barley water; a further recipe, for those sick with cancer, was for goats' milk which had been boiled with powdered dauke seed.[114]

Medicinal waters were also enlisted. The infirmarer at Norwich Cathedral Priory had a still-house, where herbs from the infirmary garden might be turned into waters like this.[115] Margaret Paston offered waters that she had made herself and recommended those of Dame Elizabeth Callethroppe to her relation John Bernay in 1473 – waters of mint, of milfoil (yarrow) or of other plants.[116] The connection to women in the preparation of the waters may have been significant: these plants will have been in their gardens. Women certainly went out gathering plants and herbs, and the distinction between what was for food and what for medicine will have been opaque. Their skill, however, in making waters and medicinal preparations was not in doubt.

If there were professional cooks, there were also many people for whom cooking was an integral part of their daily lives and who will not have made their living from this task. Elite cooks will have had an international training; peasant women in their villages would have watched their mothers at work, and learned the importance of nurturing foodstuffs in their gardens and what might be gathered in woods. There was a well-established connection between what one ate and well-being – on one level, one might eat a diet that aimed to bring health, and on another there were many plants that were cultivated or collected for their medical benefits. Getting sufficient to eat, however, was an essential part of health. Hunger was a persistent problem in late medieval England and that, along with measures to relieve it, are the focus of the next chapter.

CHAPTER ELEVEN

HUNGER AND FAMINE

THERE IS CONSENSUS AMONG historians that many people in England in the period up to 1375 did go hungry, and that up to that point, especially in the years 1290 to 1325, there were major crises of subsistence, which led to serious mortality through starvation and the effects of disease on a population poorly equipped to resist it. In 1315–18, during the Great Famine, some 10 to 15 per cent of the population perished, and the English experience was much like that of the rest of Northern Europe. After 1375, although there may have been food shortages – as in the 1430s – the English did not suffer starvation in the way that the populations of continental European countries long continued to do.[1] Serious hunger, however, was a constant concern of the peasantry.[2] Three proverbs – 'Winter eats what summer provides'; 'When you are full you do not know the meaning of hunger'; and 'Hunger makes hard beans honey sweet' – all appear in a mid fifteenth-century collection of proverbs from southern England.[3] A further collection, of a similar date, which repeats the last sentiment, adds 'Hunger breaks stone and wall.'[4] These proverbs are a reminder that even if in the English countryside in the late medieval period famine might be unknown, there were still periods of dearth, and some of them might be serious for individuals. Hunger was a general phenomenon in the worst years of bad harvests – given the dependence of the population on corn – and it might also have regional and seasonal dimensions: it can never have been far from the late medieval peasant mind.

This chapter considers how people thought about food in these circumstances, from the very poorest to the elite; how notions of social obligation related to the food supply, and how these were made manifest through systems of almsgiving; and how other groups dependent on such charity, such as the mendicant friars, might be treated. The different resources available to different sections of society occasioned important social comment: those who composed the political songs of the early fourteenth century were outraged at the levels of consumption in aristocratic households and especially by the way in which low-status guests were fed poor-quality foods (an offence against traditions of hospitality).[5] At the same time, these elite institutions made a virtue of giving food, of entertaining the poor, and often doing so with extravagant ceremony and elaborate plate. There was also major change in the pattern and scale of charitable support over the later Middle Ages.

Social responsibility was woven into medieval mentalities – and those who failed in charitable works might expect consequences in the life to come. John Bromyard, writing shortly before the Black Death, was clear the law of nature was that one should do as one would wish to be done by. Therefore the wealthy sitting at an abundant table, warmed by the fire and clothed, satiated with diverse foods and drinks, hearing the cries of the poor, exposed to the cold and poorly clothed, should think of what they were suffering and what in a similar case they would wish others to do for them.[6] But it was rare that the rich did such things, because they fed their dogs more freely than the poor, and more abundantly and with more delicate foods. Where the poor were hungry and would voraciously eat bread made from beans, the dogs would refuse such fare, wanting the most delicate meats and the first piece of every dish.[7] The words of Christ in Matthew's Gospel, read on the second Sunday in Lent, 'it is not right to take the bread of children and give it to dogs to eat', had resonances that all would have known.[8]

Feeding the poor was a Christian duty, one of the seven works of mercy. As John Mirk put it in the late 1380s, in his sermon for Sexagesima Sunday (the second Sunday before Ash Wednesday): 'The which works are to give meat to the hungry; to give drink to the thirsty; to clothe those who are cold for default of clothing; to give shelter to those that have none; and to help the sick with whatever they need.' He also drew attention to the need to visit prisoners and succour them with meat and drink and supply their other needs.[9] Charitable almsgiving was a key component in this relief: there was a belief that the individual could, and should, do something. Almsgiving was like the sower casting his seed in good earth: it would yield a hundredfold and would give the donor everlasting food in Heaven. 'Thus he who does deeds of alms prudently shall have his food in heaven perpetually.'[10]

Almost anyone might have the misfortune to become a beggar. *Dives and Pauper*, a long treatise on the meaning of the Ten Commandments, written between 1405 and 1410, commented on folk customs. Some believed that if one saw a kite flying over the road before them that they would fare well that day, for which benefit they thanked the kite and not God; but these fools did not consider that the kite would have been seen most often by those who begged their food from door to door.[11] Before the Black Death, the margin between having enough to survive and not was very thin. It has been argued that those households of four or five members who held a yardland (30 acres or more) probably had enough, but that those who held half-yardlands (15 acres or less) might easily find themselves without sufficient.[12] However necessary, we can see begging as a hazardous and desperate activity in the English countryside, both before the great plague and for years afterwards, and these beggars must have been vulnerable in many ways. In February 1335, Vincent Makourneys of Hinxton in Cambridgeshire, aged about 60, frail of body, went begging for his food; because of the great snow and the scale of the tempest and the darkness, even though it was around midday, he was unable to see a well that was next to the windmill that belonged to the chapel of All Saints in Hinton (now Cherry Hinton), and he fell in and was drowned.[13] Beatrice Thacker of Kingsley in Staffordshire went begging for bread in various villages in the county: she was found dead from cold in December 1397.[14] Some beggars took food from the fields, bringing them directly into conflict with the owners of the crops. At the start of September 1346, Matthew the servant of William le Reeve of Findern in Derbyshire found William the Welshman, a poor beggar, in the field of Findern, in William le Reeve's peas – and struck him on the head with a staff.[15]

Incidents with dogs argue that despite biblical injunctions for charity, begging was not seen as a neutral activity in all quarters. From Bicker, in

Lincolnshire south-west of Boston, in February 1353, Thomas Cony went to nearby Donington, searching for food, and he asked at the house of Robert Phelip there. Robert's dog, without any encouragement – and without restraint – bit Thomas on the right leg and he died. It would have been of little consolation to Thomas that the coroner's jury recorded that the dog did not usually cause harm.[16] Alice, the wife of William Kidde of Wainfleet, came to the manor that had belonged to John Caltoft in Thoresby in Lincolnshire in July 1355, about 20 km from her home village, seeking bread. A dog came out of the hall and Alice struck the dog on the back with her staff, whereupon the dog seized Alice by the belly – she was pregnant with twins. Alice continued begging nearby at Belleau and Claythorpe, then came to Swaby, where she gave birth, and died 13 days later. The dog was declared to be the cause of her death.[17] John Bromyard, in pointing to the predatory nature of great lords when the poor came to them to redeem tallies for goods they had handed over, requiring them to forego a large portion, often half of their rightful claim, drew an analogy with beggars who encountered vicious dogs while seeking alms – that it was necessary to give dogs like this part of the bread if one was to enjoy the rest in peace.[18]

Some of the beggars were elderly or unwell. Alice Berdholf of Donington, aged 70, poor and a beggar, drowned while drunk in Donington in Lincolnshire, in July 1377.[19] In January 1380, Thomas Kede of Whaplode, going around begging his food at Moulton in Holland, Lincolnshire, fell into water and drowned. He was said to have the falling sickness.[20] Accidents happened to beggars travelling around their neighbourhoods. In May 1341, at Great Wilbraham, near Newmarket, Cambridgeshire, another beggar, going across the marsh from Wilbraham to Fulbourn, was drowned.[21] A Hampshire beggar, Heloise of Swarraton (near Northington), was found dead: she had been going from Alresford to nearby Abbotstone in December 1378 when she slipped on a bridge and fell into the water, where she drowned.[22] These beggars were mainly known to their communities – these were the poor neighbours Bromyard had in mind, and they were in some cases clearly well known. Their illnesses were familiar to the jurors; some were elderly. They were at the margins, vulnerable and exposed in bad weather; or in poor, rented accommodation, as at Spalding in Lincolnshire in February 1355, where Matilda Scherlok of Pinchbeck, a beggar, along with her three children, was burned in the house she was renting from John Hervy of Spalding: she was drunk and had gone to bed with her children leaving a candle alight.[23] Just occasionally these individuals are described as 'unknown', or as 'strangers'. A beggar, looking for bread, found the body of an infant in Hougham in Loveden Wapentake in Lincolnshire, in October 1354. Unusually, the coroner's jury did not know the beggar's name.[24] Charity was forthcoming in some instances; but in other cases ale was the downfall of the poor. Their lives were itinerant, although they did not on the whole move far from their villages of origin.

Despite the arguments for charity, there was a suspicion that had long attached to those begging for food. A fable of Odo of Cheriton, c.1220, recounts how a fox thirsty and cold went to a hen house and asked to be let in – which the hens declined, 'because you are our enemy and always have harmed us'. The fox protested that he was dying of hunger and cold, and the hens, led by piety, opened the door. When the fox had rested and warmed up, his promise was forgotten, and he took, killed and ate a hen. To Odo, the fox was like a fraudulent pauper, who, in order that he might eat well, begged to be let into the cloister in order that he might live simply like monks, yet in reality remained in the secular world; he was quiet during his time of probation, but once he had been professed he disturbed his fellows, demanding more food, more clothing, as well as inducing the others to sin.[25] Beyond virtue in giving food, there was also a hint of exasperation, more than a suggestion that those who begged food were undeserving, if not threatening. The fifteenth-century sermon cycle *Jacob's Well* warned against 'latchdrawers', beggars who undid men's doors. If they find a good man at home, they say that their own goods have been burned, or stolen – 'and if the wife be alone, they follow her into the foodstore, with the intent that out of fear she will give them what she may'.[26] These suspicions were to find their articulation more widely in the fifteenth century.

If giving food and drink was enjoined upon everyone, relieving the needy, it was expressed in particular ways, institutionalised and given a ritual pattern in medieval life. In some aspects it merged with practices of hospitality and the gifts of food which were common currency. There was regular provision of food alms in hospitals, monasteries and friaries, in great households and guilds. But why was food given? Beyond charity, we should identify a special characteristic. A section of a customary from the abbey of Bury St Edmunds, written after 1248, sets out punishments for a monk who had committed a serious offence. The monk was to be excluded from all blessings. He was to come into the refectory after the blessings of food had been given, and he was to leave before other prayers and blessings were given. The consequence of this was that his food was not blessed, and that nothing from it was to belong to the almonry. Any waste from the monk's portion was to be given to dogs, pigs or elsewhere, because it lacked a blessing. Humans would not usually have eaten unblessed food, and waste food that had been blessed had to be given to humans. It could not be given to animals as the blessing had changed the nature of the food: it now had a spiritual quality and, as animals lacked souls, it was not appropriate for them to consume it.[27] Food was routinely blessed in every institutional context, in households great and small – the daily bread had a sacred quality that could not be, or should not have been, set aside. Aside from the physical importance of foodstuffs in an age when the food supply was vulnerable, it had a spiritual dimension as well, and this explains some of the ritual accompanying its distribution: this was not simply charity that was seen to be done; what was at stake was a commodity that had to be treated with reverence and had special characteristics.

Who was to be given food alms, how much and when? A distinction had to be made between food given to strangers, generally, like hospitality, almost at random, to the needy at the household gate, the 'naked poor'; and the institutionalised and ritualised forms of giving, for example, to poor invited into the great household, even residing there, as well as in almonries in some monastic institutions, in hospitals and almshouses. The latter categories were in effect targeted distributions of food, which might extend to the poor and needy who might not be able to find their way to the household gate. Giving food in alms was a routine part of life in the great household. The Rules composed by Robert Grosseteste Bishop of Lincoln for the Countess of Lincoln between 1245 and 1253, give a useful example.[28] The fourteenth rule ordered how alms, by the Countess's commandment, should be faithfully kept and collected, and not sent from the table to the grooms of the household ['garcuns' – largely adolescent males, one of the largest groups in the great household], nor carried out of the hall, nor wasted in suppers or dinners of the grooms; but freely, wisely and temperately, without dispute and strife, divided between the poor, the sick and beggars ['mendiaunz' – probably also intending to include the mendicant friars].[29]

This was a system that was well understood and ordered, a common pattern of operation, with food gathered up from the table and given to three groups. The intention was that food from the table should not be wasted in the household, but used to the lady's honour and profit. The exercise might be carried out in the great household by an almoner, usually a cleric – although not identified in this case. In Grosseteste's Rules, there was some ambiguity about how the food was to be given: the instruction was that it should not be carried out of the hall – but divided between the poor, the sick and the beggars. The Rules imply therefore that individuals identified as in need of alms were physically brought into the hall to receive food. This might not always be the case, and almoners might distribute food roundabout to needy people – but the provision of food for a group of people within the hall, sometimes the same group of people, almost an almshouse within the household, was a feature before the Black Death of some households of the great, especially those of widows and bishops.

Some aspects of this practice can be seen in the households of the kings of England. In that of Henry III, the great halls of his castles and palaces had images of Dives (the rich man) and Lazarus: there were wall paintings of this parable (Luke 16:19–31) opposite the King's dais at Ludgershall and Guildford, and images in the glazing at Northampton – they were an especially prominent part of the decoration, to remind the King of the duty of the rich man to the poor.[30] There were areas immediately outside royal halls where the poor might gather: the porches to the halls were a significant feature, for example, at Winchester and Woodstock.[31] Almonries were also linked to the great hall: there are mentions of construction or repairs to them at no fewer than 15 of Henry III's residences. At Winchester Castle, a pentice – a covered walkway with a lean-to roof – was constructed specifically for the use of the poor.[32] The King fed hundreds of poor each day, reputedly as many as 500, and the subsidiary households associated with the Crown, those of the Queen and their children, fed a further 100. On exceptional occasions the King fed as many as 10,000 poor. The standard capacity of the great hall at Westminster was between 2,000 and 3,000, although it might stretch to 4,000, and there was also a smaller hall, which could accommodate about half that number.[33] That feeding the poor was a regular practice, beyond any distribution of leftovers from the meal, can be seen in the accounts of the almoner of Edward I. At Windsor, on the feast of St Lucy (13 December) 1276, the almoner spent 12s 6d feeding 100 poor;[34] and in 1299–1300, the almoner often fed 666 poor on a Sunday, with varying numbers on other days, for example, 1,000 on Christmas Day 1299.[35] Between July 1338 and May 1340, the almoner of Edward III fed 150 poor every Friday, with varying numbers on feast days.[36] These examples show the persistence of the custom and its variation based on different devotional interests. The feeding of thousands puts one in mind of Christ's miracle (Plate 3): a monarch might not achieve the miraculous, but he might emulate it in practical terms, handing out a sanctified commodity, and on a similar scale.

Groups of poor were probably resident in at least some great households. In 1336–7, Dame Katherine de Norwich, the widow of a prominent Exchequer official, fed 13 poor, almost certainly the same group of people, each day.[37] The options for charitable support are also apparent from a remarkable series of vignettes that we have for another great household, in the replies of witnesses at the enquiry of 1307 into the sanctity of Thomas Cantilupe, Bishop of Hereford, who died in 1282. Nicholas de Warewik, a judge and one of Cantilupe's counsellors, reported as evidence of Cantilupe's great charity that, when he ate, he was accustomed to give great alms to the poor coming to the gate. There were also other poor who used to eat every day in his presence in his hall, one for each year he had been a bishop and five to seven beyond that number. Nicholas was asked whether Thomas ministered with his own hands to those poor eating in his hall, or whether he gave them anything else – but the witness did not know.[38] Adam de Kyngesham reported he had often seen Cantilupe give alms to the poor, both in bread and silver (that is, silver pennies), and that he used to have poor people eat in his presence.[39] Robert Deynte, a servant in the pantry and buttery of Cantilupe's household and subsequently his chamberlain, recorded that he fed many poor, at least 12 every day and sometimes more, in addition to giving alms at the gate, using his stewards to give to the poor on his properties and lending them corn when they lacked it.[40] Brother Robert of St Martin, sacrist of St Bartholomew's in London, reported that he had seen Cantilupe have 15 poor eat in his presence every day and nonetheless gave substantial alms at the gate.[41] Brother Walter de Knulle had seen many poor eat in Cantilupe's presence every day and that he gave much in the way of alms at the gate – and he frequently fed poor religious, and that he had seen this frequently at the Franciscan friary in Hereford.[42] Brother Nicholas de Wich, a monk of Worcester, noted that it was Cantilupe's custom not to eat the delicate foods that had been prepared for him, but to send them to the poor and the sick – Nicholas and others had been emissaries with these foods. Cantilupe himself ate the pottage that had been prepared for the grooms of the household.[43]

These passages provide evidence for the poor at the gate and those eating with Cantilupe every day: both the naked poor and the religious poor, the friars. There was a group who customarily ate in the bishop's presence. Two practices had wider resonances. The first was that of increasing by one the number of poor eating with the bishop for every year of his episcopate – which was similar to other practices of Maundy, where the numbers receiving payment matched the age of the donor. Secondly, although the numbers fed varied, there was a repeated occurrence of 13 poor dining together in the household, a number evoking the apostles as we have already seen with spoons and other household practices, a mirror of the first Christian community. But there was also variation between households here, driven by particular devotional practice. In the household of Joan de Valence Countess of Pembroke in 1296–7, there were never fewer than 20 poor, with 27 on many Saturdays, rising to 61 for the feast of St Katherine (25 November).[44]

The mendicant orders of friars had no goods of their own and were entirely dependent on alms, and great households were both a welcome source and one with which they were familiar through their activities as confessors. Support for the mendicant orders in the thirteenth century commonly featured gifts of food and drink, not only within the household, but also directly to friaries, for example, gifts of corn. In 1273, the Earl of Oxford gave wine, herring and a bushel of wheat to the Franciscans of Colchester.[45] Eleanor of Castile gave the Oxford Dominicans salmon baked in pastry in 1290, and she also made contributions to them in cash for the purchase of food, giving that year £10 towards the order's sustenance ('putura') at two of its chapters general.[46] In 1331, Queen Philippa travelled with her sister-in-law through Kent, eastern England and the east Midlands. Rather than food itself, her gifts were of cash to purchase a day's sustenance, or a pittance – that is, a dish and drink extra to the ordinary meal – to religious houses on her route. In May, the Dominicans in Cambridge were given funds for a pittance, as were the Carmelites there and the nuns of St Radegund.[47] The Prior of Norwich Cathedral Priory, in the late thirteenth and early fourteenth centuries, fed the local Franciscans at Christmas.[48] In the search for food alms, however, friars would cast their net widely – if we are to believe Chaucer's 'Summoner's tale'. After preaching in Holderness, the friar went forth: 'He went on his way; no longer would he rest. With scrip and tipped staff, his coat tucked up, in every house he began to look and peer, and begged meal and cheese, or else corn.' The quantities that he sought – a bushel of wheat, malt or rye – were not modest. He also sought 'a Goddes kechyl' – a little cake given in alms, probably a common practice – but he was prepared to have a bit of cheese and meat, especially bacon and beef; and he was followed by his man who had a sack to gather it all up.[49]

To mark the importance of almsgiving, many of the greatest households had special alms-dishes – or in some cases, alms-boats – into which the food was placed. In elite households, these could be very expensive productions, typically of silver, just like other vessels on the high table. We have seen the one in use by Queen Philippa (Table 9.1): she was also given another one by her mother-in-law, worth some £23, which was disposed of during the course of 1331–2.[50] Simon Langham, the cardinal and formerly Archbishop of Canterbury, had two silver alms-boats among his goods at this death in 1376.[51] Bishop Stephen Gravesend of London, who died in 1338, bequeathed to Elizabeth de Burgh, Lady of Clare, his silver alms-dish, which weighed 1.458 kg (£4 10s). This was a very substantial piece of plate: among the vessels for dinner service he bequeathed, a group of 12 dishes,

12 saucers and two ewers weighed 6.156 kg (£19) – the alms-dish was there-fore the equivalent in size to a quarter of this group of vessels.[52] These elab-orate vessels speak of the importance of the rituals associated with food alms. Like everything else associated with elite living, this was a practice connected to display; alms were given in a way that developed connections of lordship and personal links. Decoration with heraldic devices, for example, brought these ties to mind.

These elaborate alms-dishes and vessels should not lead us to think that the alms themselves were presented to the poor in these costly vessels. Food for the poor might be placed in great alms-buckets or tubs, or carried out in bags.[53] Eleanor, sister of Edward III, travelling to her wedding in Nijmegen in 1332, paid her almoner 2s 3d for the making and binding of two buckets for alms.[54] The consequence was that the food must have been all mixed together, as slops. Consecrated it may have been, and once it might have been finely prepared and sauced, but it did not normally reach the poor in any form that might have encouraged reflection on this. One should note, perhaps, that Bishop Cantilupe, as part of his campaign against sensory stimulation, made a practice of mixing together all the spiced sauces which accompanied his food, perhaps to cancel each other out.[55] The diet the poor acquired in this way, therefore, had none of the refinements of service and taste which accom-panied elite dining, nor did it not suffer from the spiritual disadvantages which resulted from stimulation by finely sauced and spiced food.

The rituals of giving food alms can be established most clearly from monastic institutions and their customaries. The poor were not far from the thoughts of many diners and were even present in the monastic refectory – but this was only one of a number of separate elements in monastic charity involving food. Monasteries, especially Benedictines, had almon-ries, with a specific income assigned to them for this form of charity. There was in addition food from the monastic table. This included food offered on a daily basis, and food for special commemorations. The daily alms would have included the full portion of three monks, to be given to three poor, after their feet had been washed, evoking Christ's Maundy and the washing of the feet of the disciples. There were also the portions of deceased monks: these were traditionally earmarked for the poor for 30 days after a monk's death; and those of a deceased abbot might be set aside in this way for a whole year. Anniversaries of deaths might also be marked – although possibly not with a full portion of food, sometimes simply with a loaf.[56]

Some idea of the scale of this daily relief can be seen from the distributions made at Norwich Cathedral Priory. In 1282–3 the granator (who looked after the priory's grain) gave 5 qrs of wheat directly in alms, before handing 734 qrs to the baker. Of the baker's portion, the prior then gave more than 58 qrs at the castle, to those in prison there, and at the priory's manors. The baker then provided loaves for the refectory, cellar, guest hall and hall. A proportion of these would also have been given away in food alms. These figures suggest that in this year between 8 and 10 per cent was given in alms. What is remarkable here, too, is that these charitable distributions were of bread made from wheat, rather than lesser grains.[57]

Beyond the daily routine distribution, institutions made special handouts a feature of their commemorations at the major liturgical feasts of the year and at those particular to the institution; it was also a way of marking the personal connections of individual religious. There were certain days when these rituals of alms-giving were prominent – the most important, in both religious and secular establishments, was Maundy Thursday. At Christ Church, Canterbury, the Monastic Constitutions of Lanfranc of c.1070–89, the base for much later practice, set out that on Good Friday the monks were not to eat food except for bread, water and uncooked greens; but their meals were cooked as usual and were given to the poor.[58] At Norwich Cathedral Priory, c.1260, on Maundy Thursday after chapter, the cellarer and almoner selected 24 paupers, who then heard Mass. The 24 were then taken to the hospital and given bread, vegetables and drink, before the ritual of washing their feet.[59] The duty of the almoner at Eynsham Abbey, outlined in its thirteenth-century customary, was to collect the alms in the abbot's chamber. On the day celebrating the obits of deceased brethren, he was to have for the poor as many loaves and jugs as there were names of the departed recited in chapter. The loaves were to be put on the abbot's table and the servers were to place the portions of 'pulmentum' for the dead monks on the loaves.[60] At Lacock Abbey in the late thirteenth or early fourteenth century, distributions on ordinary almsdays were to be made to a number of poor equal to the number of nuns; those that were made on feasts that were special to the nunnery were more substantial, on one anniversary reaching 500 portions; on occasions connected to the individual lives of nuns, such as the obits of a father or former husband, 13 poor were to be fed. A very substantial donation was made on Maundy Thursday, including food not only for that day, but to be taken away for subsequent meals: dough for bread, and half a bushel of beans (Table 11.1).[61] The domestic accounts of Lacock show large quantities of wheat baked at these feasts: at Pentecost 1348, 5 qrs of wheat were baked, as compared with the normal weekly levels of just over 3 qrs.[62] On Shrove Tuesday 1347, a customary distribution to the waged servants and the poor saw the abbey give out bacon – a foodstuff that, while forbidden in Lent, appears to have been permitted as an exception for the poor.[63] At Battle Abbey in Sussex, the almoner provided 18s 6d for the use of the poor on Maundy Thursday 1343,[64] and made payments of 15s for meat, fish and ale for alms in 1365–6, probably also on special occasions.[65] In 1426–7, there were payments for repairing the almoner's hall, which tells us about the continuous nature of the relief that was offered to pilgrims there – and Battle had indeed been famed for the provision of its charity in this regard.[66]

There were distinctive and individual elements to the process of distributing food alms at each monastery. In 1315, from Canterbury Cathedral Priory, there is a record of the annual baking and distribution of 'Lanfranc' loaves – named after the late eleventh-century archbishop – from a varying mixture of wheat, rye, barley and peas, a bread reserved for the poor and distributed to 36 hospitals. The Cathedral Priory and its servants also celebrated this largesse, but with loaves made from good wheat alone, according to the 'Lanfranc' measure.[67] At St Augustine's, Canterbury, in the 1330s and 1340s, the almoner went to the almonry after lunch and supper to organise the distribution of food.[68] By right and ancient custom, twice in every week throughout the year, he was to make a distribution to all the poor coming to the almonry of the leftovers of the monks in the refectory and the misericord, and from the abbot's chamber, the hall and all other places frequented by the monks; and, if the monks' leftovers did not suffice, a distribution of bread was to be made. He had a granary, so that all might be fed on these days – known locally as the 'dolhus', the 'dole house'.[69] Even the leftovers from the infirmary were taken for the poor, but it was expected that the monastic sick would eat their whole ration if possible.[70]

Table 11.1: Lacock Abbey: memorandum on food alms, late thirteenth or early fourteenth century

We give food on an almsday, for as many poor as there are nuns, each poor person to have a 'pricked loaf' ('un payn fyche') and 'relish' ('companage') to accompany it, two herrings or a slice of cheese ('une leche de formage'). The convent to have that day two courses ('mes')

At the anniversary of 'la Wone', each year 500 poor, each to have a wheat loaf and two herrings, whether it is a flesh day or not; and the convent will have simnels and wine and three courses at lunch and two at supper

At the anniversary of her father each year, 13 poor

At the anniversary of her husband ('sun baron'), 13 poor and the convent half a mark for a pittance

At the anniversary of Nicholas de Hedinton, the poor to share 8s 4d or corn (wheat, barley and beans) to the same amount, and the convent to have half a mark for a pittance

The day of the burial of a nun 100 poor to have each a halfpenny or a 'pricked loaf'

It is the custom to have pain-demaine at Christmas Day, Easter, Pentecost, the Assumption of the Virgin and at St Bernard (21 August)

[...]

On Maundy Thursday after the maundy has been given, each poor person is to be given a loaf of the weight of a conventual loaf, and dough ('past') equivalent to an ordinary loaf and a half, a gallon of ale and two herrings and half a bushel of beans for pottage

Source: BL, Add. MS 88973, f. 88v.

Charitable institutions known for their distributions of alms were an obvious resort of the poor. Agnes Love of Waterbeach in Cambridgeshire was killed at nearby Denny Abbey on Passion Sunday in 1348: she had gone there to seek alms from the abbess, and she was going into the precinct by the east gate, when a leaf of the gate was caught by the wind and struck her.[71] Less than a year later, in January 1349, John Cros of Waterbeach, about the hour of Vespers, also went begging at Denny. He was given alms, and he ate and drank to the extent that he was drunk, and unfortunately fell in the river.[72] Sometimes the poor gathered in large numbers to receive alms, as on 25 February 1367 at the Dominican friary in Lincoln. Among them was a 12-year-old, Roger the son of Roger de Bellewode of Lincoln. He was sitting under a stone slab or table, perhaps the counter at which alms were being given out, when it fell on his stomach and shattered the bone in his leg, from which injuries he later died.[73]

These examples show how food alms formed an essential part of the life of the monasteries, part of the daily routine and a part of special commemoration. The distributions were effected with ritual solemnity and purpose; the benefits for the poor were given in honourable fashion, and in the largest monasteries these must have made a significant difference to the quality of life, or, indeed, to sustaining life itself for the least well off. The doles that were given out in almonries attached to hospitals and monasteries were an important and reliable source of charity.

As well as post mortem commemoration through food alms in an institutional context, there were many appearances of this form of charity in individual wills, and it formed a part of civic, parochial and guild life. Besides feasting, at wakes, the month's mind (the commemoration of the departed, with a requiem, a month after death) and anniversaries, provision was made for gifts of food to the poor as part of many funeral arrangements and bequests. A sample of wills from the 1370s, from Norfolk and Suffolk, shows how clergy left food for their parishioners. Geoffrey, the vicar of Brooke, in March 1371, left 2 qrs of barley to those in his parish begging, and four bushels of beans to other poor.[74] William Ely, parson of Crostwight, in October 1373 left 1 qr of wheat to be distributed as bread between the day of his death and his burial.[75] John, rector of Kennett on the Suffolk/Cambridgeshire border west of Bury, in late September 1375 left his parishioners in general 5 qrs of barley, along with 2 qrs of wheat to distribute to the poor of his parish.[76] And Richard Deudeney of East Barsham left 10s for a distribution of bread among the parishioners (but not necessarily the poor ones) of East Barsham between the day of his burial and the eighth day after, in equal amounts.[77]

What food was given to the poor? First, the poor were given food from the table, that is, they might have anything that was being eaten – and in the case of Bishop Cantilupe that might include the finest prepared dishes. In other cases, particularly with poor resident in the household, they had a distinctive pattern of diet. Those in Dame Katherine de Norwich's household were fed in a pattern of almost perpetual abstinence: herring in one of its preserved forms and bread.[78] The poor of her household had a different loaf, one that was smaller in size to the others, and made from barley rather than wheat. Barley loaves, as we have seen from the miracle of the Feeding of the Five Thousand, had a special resonance.[79] The one exception to the dietary pattern was its reversal on the day when everyone else abstained from everything except bread and ale: Good Friday. On this day, the poor did not have their herring, but wastel bread – that is, the finest;[80] in the household of Joan de Valence, in 1296–7, on some fish days which fell on major festivals, the poor were given mutton.[81]

The virtuous pattern of diet can be seen too in the food for the poor in the household of Henry III in 1242, with a good deal of the herring acquired for the household while it was in Gascony destined for the poor; and the special instructions for provisions for the poor during his reign feature bread and fish, but not meat. That some of the king's almonries had ovens attached suggests, too, that the poor fed in the royal household had a different loaf to the household.[82] Special alms loaves featured in other institutions. At St Augustine's Abbey Canterbury in the 1330s, the almoner had barley bread – while, in this case, it was to be given to a monk who had been imprisoned as punishment, the implication was that the almoner's loaves were different from those consumed elsewhere in the monastery.[83]

The demographic changes that came with the Black Death brought a recalibration of almsgiving – and it was one that came about perhaps faster than the food supply stabilised. No longer was it common to feed the poor indiscriminately, or in large numbers; few households made regular provision in this way. Indeed, provision of food for the poor at table within the great household was highly unusual after the mid fourteenth century, and its disappearance as a charitable act should be counted as one of the social adjustments resulting from the great plague. To have the poor dining in the household had been an especial feature of the establishments of widows and bishops. The alms payments in the household account roll of William of Wykeham, Bishop of Winchester, for six months in 1393, record only one occasion when 13 poor were given bread and ale as alms.[84] This does not mean that no provision was made for the poor – the use of food gathered from the table continued with, if anything, evidence for a more elaborate ritual.

A sense of the changes is apparent in testamentary records. Although the clerks of Norfolk and Suffolk made distributions to the poor of their parishes in the 1370s, the poor were not necessarily first in their minds. Comparatively few others followed their lead: a rare example was John Palmer the elder of Barnham who, in his will of September 1373, made provision for seven of the poorest of his village to have 7 bushels of any sort of corn for bread.[85] Large-scale or indiscriminate feeding of the poor was very unusual after the Black Death. When the fourth Earl of Salisbury made his will in 1427, his insistence that his widow give by her own hand food alms – a dish of food, a loaf and a quart of drink – to three paupers each day was exceptional; even the Earl suspected his widow might not do it, and therefore made provision for one of his executors to do it in her stead.[86] There is more evidence for the use of food alms at funerals, the month's mind and anniversaries; but even here charity was reshaped. When William Derby, archdeacon of Bedford, made his will in June 1438, he envisaged gifts to the poor on the day of his funeral – to the poor of his parish praying for his soul that day – of a loaf, a dish of meat or fish depending on the diet for the day, and a quart of ale. He also asked that his parishioners and neighbours be honestly served with food that day.[87] Wills have an increasing tendency to avoid indiscriminate poor relief: there was instead an emphasis on community, on commensality, with neighbours and parishioners, and even where there was nothing stated in a will, executors often considered it their duty to fund food for the funeral. Charity increasingly focused on friends and neighbours. Funeral and guild meals were for friends: food was not so much 'alms' as a commemorative occasion, and a chance to create community. From this, the vagrant poor were now excluded. Civic ordinances at Chester from the 1390s, for example, forbade vagrants within the city unless they possessed the wherewithal to live.[88]

In parallel to this, late medieval benefactions, for almshouses and hospitals, focused on the poor of the area with a new sense of purpose, directed at a dignified way of managing the poverty of old age for the local, and deserving, population. At the almshouse of St John the Baptist and St John the Evangelist at Sherborne in Dorset, refounded in 1438 by Bishop Neville of Salisbury and others, the statutes established a fraternity of 20 brothers, and arrangements for the support of 12 poor, feeble and helpless men and four poor women, drawn from the householders of the town, or, in default of them, those living within the parish. There was to be an allowance of 10s a week for the food and drink of the 16, along with an annual allowance for their clothing.[89] The beadsmen and beadswomen of Leicester New College petitioned the Bishop of Lincoln in 1440, alleging that 'our gracious founders of the almshouse of Leicester ordained that when a quarter of wheat cost 10s, then every beadsman and beadswoman of the said almshouse should have 10½d a week during the dearth': implicit was the sentiment that these were reasonable and decent people, and alms should enable them to live respectable lives without hunger.[90]

General distributions from monastic gates were also reduced to token levels. This had started to happen earlier, in the thirteenth century, at houses of both Benedictines and Cistercians – and canon lawyers had set out to distinguish the 'deserving poor' in the twelfth century. At Westminster Abbey, the alms from the table of the abbot or the refectory were appropriated to the support of monastic servants, possibly elderly, a group of poor who were specially deserving.[91] In the fifteenth century there was a range of responses which suggests this focusing of food alms was widespread. At the visitation of Thornton Abbey in Lincolnshire in 1423, the injunctions forbade the conversion of the portion of a dead monk to other purposes than feeding the poor – the abbey's plans for a more targeted distribution were set aside.[92] In Leicestershire, at Laund Priory, visited in 1440, it was reported that the portions provided for dead canons as alms were used first as a supplement to the food of the servants of the priory, and then for other, enclosed poor, as well as for poor former servants of the priory. The injunctions required that these alms be distributed to the poorest, especially those confined to bed in the neighbourhood and that they should not be given to others, provided that those who had served the house were not exposed to poverty and especially in cases where they might not seek food by their own hands they were to be preferred in any distribution.[93] Other injunctions, such as those for Bradwell Priory in Buckinghamshire required that the fragments of food from the monastic table be used to support children who might benefit from teaching and, if suitable, in due course be admitted as monks.[94] This use of broken meats to support children was found more widely.

At the same time, where we can see the ceremonies and rituals associated with food alms, their operation in the fifteenth century is much more elaborate than the events we know about from an earlier date. This paralleled the increase in ceremoniousness of great household life in the fifteenth century more generally. The description of the arrangements to be made for the Earl of Northumberland for Maundy Thursday, around 1500, fill some 10 pages in the household book that was probably prepared for the guidance of gentlemen ushers.[95]

In the later Middle Ages, therefore, these patterns – of hunger and of the provision of food as alms – show a broad change. One reason may be that after the Black Death the match between population and food supply was a much closer one. After 1349, a great many demands from workers were for the provision of better food, for wheat bread, or better ale. The absolute provision of food was no longer the central question: there was sufficient food it was a question of its quality. This did not mean that there was no poverty. The naked poor, clustered at the abbey or household gates, had always been there, especially in an urban environment.[96] But there was here an underlying change in attitude. Celebrations that once had been indiscriminate might now be managed. There were responsible and respectable guilds catering for the needs of their brethren, most of whom had contributed to the common purse. People had to work harder for a living in a plague-ridden world; and new groups of people were drawn into the world of work, for example, women performing heavy manual labour, at least in the second half of the fourteenth century.

In the medieval great household, the feeding of the poor at meals, almost as an almshouse within the household, ceased. Alms-dishes and the domestic ritual for food alms were still there, if anything, with an increasingly elaborate ritual developing in the fifteenth century – but the poor no longer sat in groups of 13 at table. Household accounts now have only occasional references to meals for travellers, or wayfarers, or perhaps a prisoner. There was a notion of the deserving poor: a judgement was made. We are, however, still some way from the 'sturdy beggars' of Tudor England and the idea of state responsibility for the poor. The naked poor must still have been present in quantity, especially in the great conurbations, but they were not as valued as those with connections, poor parishioners, friends and neighbours, or as those who could not physically come to the abbeys and great houses, whom almoners needed to seek out.

CHAPTER TWELVE

FOOD AND POPULAR MENTALITIES

FOOD FEATURED IN A great many ways in the lives of medieval English people. Across society, they were deeply engaged in growing crops, gathering foodstuffs, raising livestock and poultry, and in preparing sauces and special foods – or in paying for the best cooks possible to do so on their behalf. These activities required time, labour and investment. The nuances of foodstuffs themselves help us in understanding the ramifications of their consumption, the ways in which food was important to the fabric of society, and its role in creating social obligation. People enjoyed food and spent time and effort ensuring it was good; they looked forward to food at its best and to welcome, and convivial occasions on which it might be shared. At the same time no one can have failed to appreciate how the good times depended on the food supply, and how close starvation might be.

Almost all daily actions in the Middle Ages might be expressed in metaphors and similes linked to food and drink, giving a timelessness to their interest and linking us through turns of phrase to deeper perspectives on medieval society. When Langland's figure of Good Faith praised poverty – and penance – for the sweetness that was to come after suffering, 'As a walnut has a bitter shell, but after that bitter shell is removed, there is a kernel of comfort to restore strength', she had in mind a common country food, one that might be gathered by the peasantry – a resort in hard times as well as an annual crop; and she tells us too about the condition of the poor, as well as how this common food was eaten, that people cracked walnuts with their teeth.[1] In another phrase, the importance of social connection could be expressed in the bonds arising from gifts of food: 'It is better to give the apple than to eat it.'[2] Those gifts, however, might link to eternal responsibilities and obligations: 'God will not give you a pear or an apple as one does a child, but greater things, and he will expect greater things from you too', was the sentiment of the *Ayenbit of Inwyt*.[3] But apples might also indicate the falseness of outward appearances: 'Many an apple is green on the outside and bitter within.'[4] A group of proverbs refers to foodstuffs that were so common they were a synonym for something of little value. These were major components of diet, especially at a peasant level – and the fact that they included garden and field crops, as well as foods that might commonly be gathered, is suggestive of the importance of these items. Peas and beans come high on this list. Piers Plowman dismisses an indulgence with the words, 'I set by this pardon not a pea nor a pie crust.'[5] That something was not worth a bean was an expression found from the 1320s on.[6] Food and drink were never far from people's thoughts.

Food and its consumption provided a framework for society, a structure to the day, to the week and to the year. It was a pattern shaped by religion, with its demands for abstinence and for conformity, from mealtimes to what was eaten. The implications of eating, of taking pleasure in, or avoiding, particular foods, were much in mind. Food was inseparably linked in its consumption to personal behaviour, and the honour and standing of the individual. How a person ate or drank told their neighbours the measure of their companion. 'So brew, so drink' and 'brew sour, drink sour' express the sentiment 'reap as you sow'. There was sound, proverbial comment: 'Often drink makes your head spin';[7] or 'Drink afterwards less, and go home by daylight.'[8] Yet this was also much more than practical advice: it had a moral charge. The stimulation in diet that came especially through sauces was closely bound up with the use of sweeteners, such as honey; the comparisons with sour taste, and with spices, and the connections of morality were never far away. Two proverbs from a mid fifteenth-century collection express the same sentiment: 'It is hard to lick honey from a thorn'; 'Dear is honey bought that on thorns is sought.'[9] The sweetness of honey might make it a desirable substance, but it was not always easily obtainable – and, in some circumstances, it was to be avoided. Proffered sweetness might come with a barb, with consequences. The corrupting sweetness of sugar might conceal poison: 'Each man beware, of wisdom and reason, of sugar strewed that hides false poison.'[10] The strewing of sugar and other spices as powder brought a further caution: this was effort, perhaps vanity, that might be wasted, for powder – a most precious substance – might be blown away by the wind.[11] Riches were not to be wasted: there were proper social and divine purposes for them.

Despite moral strictures – or perhaps because of them – these foodstuffs became highly desirable and food quickly crossed social boundaries. The dishes, spices and sauces of elite cookery were copied, as far as possible, elsewhere in society – they were a common passion. The idea of 'petty cury' was predicated on facilitating, for those without access to expensive spices, the preparation of dishes that might have associations with elite cuisine. The boundaries between an elite and a demotic cuisine were infinitely permeable, however: the anthropological model of distinct cookeries is one that requires a great deal of nuance as far as late medieval England is concerned. Aristocrats might recognise the qualities of good country foods, such as peasecods. The best demotic foods, the puddings and preserved meats, were highly sought after, and the women by whose skill these foods were prepared had outstanding reputations. Even male monastic houses made sure they had skilled female labour for this purpose. In 1363, in the fluid social environment of the post-plague years, an attempt was made to restrict consumption of foodstuffs on a sumptuary basis by statute, on the initiative of the Commons. It was inappropriate for lesser servants, 'grooms', to eat a main meal more than once a day. But this was quickly recognised as an unrealistic way of restraining social aspiration and, with its repeal less than two years later, people were free to eat what they could afford.[12] Those who could afford it might still make statements with foodstuffs. Even at an elite level, consumption could be shaped for the greatest effect. Bishop Mitford of Salisbury, one-time secretary of Richard II, had the most impressive foodstuffs appear on the most significant occasions: for example, venison and other game, such as rabbits, were prominent in his household's meals during the Christmas season of 1406–7; there was pike on New Year's Day 1407 and on the eve of Easter that year.[13]

The international connections of cookery, embodied in the cooks themselves at the highest levels, journeying through the courts of Europe to learn new dishes, might also be felt in the English countryside. Food brought new horizons. Even peasants might consume a little of foodstuffs such as pepper, that had travelled halfway around the world. To eat a sauce, even a common sauce like mustard, was essential to the enjoyment of a food. When the citizens of Meaux complained to Henry V about the behaviour of English soldiers during the siege of that city in 1421–2, the King is said to have replied that 'war without fire was not worth anything, as worthless as sausages ("andouilles") without mustard.'[14]

There is much more to be learned about cooks and cooking, and we cannot now do so without understanding the importance of women in this process. Many had a close involvement in the preparation of food and drink, in its marketing and retail. From their gardens to livestock, they gave food their care and attention. Food in the countryside was as pleasurable as it was because of their interest. The distractions of domesticity might, at times, be at the forefront of their minds, as in *Hali meiðhad*; but at others, ensuring foodstuffs were 'housewifely made' said all that was necessary about their high quality. It was not accidental that the worthy knight in Chaucer's 'Merchant's tale' should think of food at the same time as he contemplated wedded bliss: 'No other life is worth a bean, for wedlock is so easy and so clean, that in this world it is a paradise.' Moving from the crops of the field to the vegetable garden, he continued his theme: 'That every man who considers himself worth a leek upon his bare knees ought to thank God all his life that he has sent him a wife.'[15] As well as drawing on dishes from continental Europe, elite cuisine was inspired by country foods, from gardens and hedgerows, with preparations using flowers, berries and vegetables.

It was more than just foodstuffs that were desirable; it was also the patterns of behaviour and customs that were linked to eating them. Wherever possible, the structure of elite meals was copied at lower levels of society, as was the equipment that went with them. When guilds had feasts, they expected to have either their members or hired individuals who would act out the rituals of service as if they were in an aristocratic household. The ways in which people were seated, tables laid and attended to by stewards, pantlers, butlers and carvers, with cooks hired from local elite households, all pointed to a common expectation: people aspired to the rituals of food service, of ceremonial and courtesy of the elite, as well as their food. They had chargers, platters and saucers and common cups in much the same way as the upper classes. Equally, the abbots of leading monasteries sought to present a dining experience that was as impressive and honourable as that of lay establishments of the first rank. Great monastic institutions made sure that the constraints of their way of life should not unduly affect the appreciation of advances in secular cuisine within the cloister. The structure of the elite meal itself, with its subtleties and 'entremes', might also be copied. But there was also a medieval sense of realism, as a proverb put it, 'It is better to lack the cloth than the loaf', it is better to have the essentials than the trimmings, in this case the napery that might go with a more elevated style of dining.[16] If the upper levels of the peasantry might aspire to dine in the style of those above them, they had better make this choice with care.

Food was a way of creating community among the living on these convivial occasions. And it was also an important way of creating community with the dead, through commemoration and memorial practice. Acts of maundy, the Mass and miraculous tales of food cannot have been far from mind as kings and others fed the poor, or shared drink and food at funerals, the month's mind and anniversaries. Cups might recall past owners or family, or the community of a guild; and the formalities of drinking together, the sharing of large vessels, might also resemble in some ways the central act of Christian worship, the Eucharist. These occasions might bring citizens and parishioners together, and act as a focus for charitable giving. Giving alms from the table, or with specially prepared alms loaves, might echo the Last Supper and its act of maundy, or miracles, such as the Feeding of the Five Thousand. The food was important both in providing for the poor and in building up rewards for the donor in the life to come. The rations that came to table in the monasteries in memory of deceased monks continued gifts of food from beyond the grave, as did the special provisions made for the commemoration of benefactors. Yet these were not always common sentiments, and there was a marked in change in almsgiving in the later part of our period, with a concentration on friends and neighbours. When Langland's Covetousness was asked by Repentance if he was charitable towards his neighbours in food and drink, his reply was disdainful: 'I am held to be as courteous as a hound is in a kitchen.'[17] His words may also have been a reflection of new judgements in charitable giving, of worthiness, even if they did not accord with those of Repentance.

Sharing food might create other bonds. Choice foods taken from the dish of the head of the household, given to those eating with him or her, were marks of favour and connection. A fourteenth-century proverb noted that good service brought a worthy reward, pain-demaine, additional rations of the bread of the great household – rewards of bread are sometimes noted in the daily accounts of these establishments.[18] More generally, food was one of the few commodities that anyone might give: a country-woman might give an apple, a pudding or a cheese to a queen, communities might offer provisions to their lords or those from whom they sought influence, and kings and queens might supply their guests, or religious houses, with substantial quantities of provisions.[19]

Food in the period 1200–1500 was not unchanging, and we can point to differences in terms of the range of foodstuffs, the ways in which they were prepared and in the aspirations of individuals. The later Middle Ages was a period of dietary change. After the Black Death, those in the countryside hoped for better quality foods: from bread made with wheat, ale malted from the best barley, to the consumption of more meat. There was a parallel change in the possibilities for cooking, in the development of culinary equipment and in the scale of possessions related to preparing food and its consumption which many people might now hold. These were not necessarily great changes in terms of the technology itself, but their spread through society was significant. The change in potential for cooking in the countryside between 1200 and 1500 was striking. From frying pans to pewter saucers, the possibilities for food and its presentation for consumption opened up new lifestyles in the countryside and among the burgess classes in the towns. In great institutions we can see the development of kitchens, of the provision of new arrangements for cooking with ranges and 'cookers'. These changes speak of a different type of investment in food preparation, of gradual advances and change in technique, facility in practice and increasing expectations from the cooks of the great households. That some of them were individually recognised – and handsomely rewarded – underlines the importance of the leading members of the profession.

One might also conjecture that these changes extended to the ways in which foods were eaten. This is much harder to document, even at an elite level, as the records are much thinner. Poetic descriptions of feasts, of which the 'Vows of the heron' ('Les voeux du heron') of *c.*1337 is a typical example, and which might tell us more of what transpired on these occasions, are very reticent about what was eaten and how it was served. At this ceremony at the English royal court, vows were taken on a heron (a symbol of cowardice) in an act in which Edward III was led to declare war on France at the instigation of Robert of Artois, who was in exile at the English court. Beyond the heron, no foodstuffs are mentioned, and the poem says very little about how the food comes to table. We are told, however, how the heron was caught by Robert of Artois with his falcon, and how he took it to the kitchen, where it was roasted, stuffed and dressed again in its feathers, and then brought into the hall ('the vaulted palace', 'ou palais vautis') between two silver platters ('Entre deux plats d'argent fu li hairons assis').[20] And if we lack this detail in general for aristocratic feasts like this, there is even less available for those of others. We can see, however, in texts like the Harleian household ordinances, from the second half of the fifteenth century, how elaboration of ceremony extended to the ways in which servants were expected to behave around those eating and drinking in the great household.[21] How this was emulated elsewhere in society is a question that asks for more research, but it is clear that it had an influence – the example of the accident at St Mary Bourne in Hampshire, in July 1385, where John Brounrobyn was laying out the bread for the vicar's table, suggests as much,[22] as do the garnishes of pewter platters and saucers that are increasingly found in the households at all social levels, and the tablecloths that covered boards in the houses of the upper ranks of the peasantry.

Food and drink therefore demonstrate important cultural links across society. They were of much more importance than nutritional value alone. Meals show tastes, patterns of eating and ways of behaviour; there were links to morality and religion, to commemoration and to aspiration, and to pleasure and enjoyment. Eating and drinking together connected men and women with each other in myriad ways. It is through these insights into daily life and mentalities that we can see the importance of food, in all its associations, to late medieval people.

GLOSSARY

Advent the four weeks preceding Christmas, starting on the Sunday nearest to 30 November

alkanet a red dye like henna, extracted from the roots of dyer's bugloss (*Anchusa tinctoria*)

amaroke amarusca, mayweed, maithe, also known as stinking camomile (*Anthemis cotula*)

assay to taste or test food or household items for poison or danger

avens the wood avens or herb bennet (*Geum urbanum*); gives a clove-like flavour to ale; also used in medicine

beadsman, beadswoman an inmate of an almshouse bound to pray for its benefactors

beast of the chase animal permitted to be hunted in a chase: red deer, fallow deer and roe deer (until Edward III's reign), fox and marten

brandreth grate, or iron framework, to go on the fire, from the Old Norse 'brand-reið', a 'fire-carriage'

brawn flesh meat

bullace a wild plum (*Prunus insititia*), sometimes in semi-cultivation; larger than a sloe, with black/blue and white varieties

butt a joint of meat: the back flanks of cattle and pigs

cade a cask or barrel; a liquid measure, sometimes 12 gallons; as a measure of herrings, usually 720 (six long hundreds), but later 600 (five long hundreds)

cater, catour a caterer, an official in charge of purchasing, from the French 'achater', to buy; 'achats', purchases

chervil a garden herb (*Anthriscus cerefolium*), used in cooking

comfit a sweetmeat, usually something preserved in sugar, such as ginger

comfrey a plant (*Symphytum officinale*) used in medicine, especially for healing wounds

Corpus Christi   the Thursday after Trinity Sunday (which falls a week after Pentecost)

crop   as meat, the dewlap of cattle

crumb   the soft interior of the loaf, protected by the crust

cubeb   the berry of *Piper cubeba* or *Cubeba officinalis*, a climbing plant from Indonesia, with a pungent flavour

demesne   property held and managed directly by a landowner, rather than being leased out

electuary   a medicinal syrup, often spices or herbs with sugar

entremes   literally 'between the courses' (Anglo-Norman French; 'interfercula': Latin) in the thirteenth century a dish with a contrasting or special food, which had by the fifteenth century evolved into the 'subtlety', a special set piece, sometimes a model, with a political or religious message

ferculum   a portion or course of food (Latin); *pl.* 'fercula'

firkin   a small barrel for liquids or other goods, as a measure, a quarter of a barrel and half a kilderkin, but of varying capacity

flitch   a cured side of meat from a pig or from cattle

forestalling   the practice of traders intercepting goods before they can come to market and buying them up for resale at a higher price

franklin   a freeman holding land, below the level of the gentry

furmenty   a dish based on boiled wheat

galentine   a sauce, originally made with jellied juices of meat or fish, but with variant spicing and thickeners (*CI*, pp. 190–1)

galingale   an aromatic root, from the East Indies, from the genera *Alpinia* and *Kæmpferia*, used for cooking and medicines

grain   a red colourant, a dyestuff (later cochineal), from the kermes (an insect)

grout   infused malt, before or during the process of fermentation

haw   the fruit of the hawthorn (*Cratægus oxyacantha* and related plants)

hippocras   wine flavoured with spices

latten   a metal alloy, either brass or similar

Lent   the 40 days preceding Easter, starting on Ash Wednesday

long hundred   120

malmsey   a sweet white wine, from the Mediterranean, especially from the Morea (the Peloponnese)

Martinmas   11 November (feast of St Martin)

mease   a barrel of fish, usually preserved herrings or sprats; as a measure of herring, usually 600 (five long hundreds)

medlar   the fruit of the medlar tree (*Mespilus germanica*), eaten when the flesh has become soft through decay

mes   a course of food (Anglo-Norman French)

Michaelmas   29 September (feast of St Michael)

mordant   a sharp, biting constituent (of sauces), cutting the taste

nef   a vessel shaped like a ship (Anglo-Norman French)

newel   a wafer or light cake (Anglo-Norman French 'neule')

obedientiary   the holder of an office (or 'obedience') in a monastery

obit   the commemoration of the anniversary of a death

Octave   a date eight days from the date that is named, counting that day, i.e. a week later

the 'O's   the antiphons sung at Vespers before and after the Magnificat, between 16 and 23 December, each 'O' preceding one of the titles of the Messiah as prophesied in the Old Testament, e.g. 'O sapientia'

Osey   a sweet white wine, from Portugal

pain-demaine   white bread of high quality, usually associated with the great household ('pain de meine', i.e. possibly 'de mesnee'; also 'lord's bread', 'panis dominicus')

pantler   the household officer in charge of the pantry, typically looking after bread, sometimes cheese, and table linen

peasecod   peas in the pod, especially young ones, eaten whole like mangetout

peel   implement, like a large spade, for putting goods to be baked into an oven

pestle   meat from the leg of an animal: often a haunch or ham, sometimes the foreleg; the instrument for pounding food in a mortar

pipe   a large cask, for wine or similar liquids; as a measure of wine, some variation but usually half a tun, containing 2 hogsheads (4 barrels or 126 old wine gallons)

pipkin   a handled pot, like a modern saucepan but with three feet

pittance   an additional dish of food and/or drink given to a religious institution, school or college, out of charity

posnet   a handled saucepan, usually with three feet

pulmentum   a cooked dish of pottage, mainly cereals and vegetables, but sometimes with fat and other foods, such as eggs and fish (Latin); also 'pulmentaria'

quern   a hand-mill, consisting of a pair of stones; the upper one is turned to grind corn, pepper, mustard or something similar

regrating   retailing; buying up goods for resale in a market, typically for a higher price

rissole   a dish of ground meat, or fruit and fish in Lent, shaped and fried in a batter

sack   a wine from Spain

salt-cote   a building where salt is made through boiling and evaporation, a salt-house

sanap   a cloth to go over a tablecloth, a 'sauvenap', to save the cloth

sanders   red sanders, used for food colouring; a form of sandalwood, but not an aromatic form

service tree   a fruit tree (*Pyrus domestica*), with small pear-shaped or round edible fruit

simnel   a white loaf or bun of the finest wheat flour, cooked twice (boiled before baking, or baked twice) and therefore weighing less than a wastel

sloe   the fruit of the blackthorn, a wild plum (*Prunus spinosa*)

spikenard   an aromatic substance, from a plant of the Valerian order; used in ointments

squab   a young pigeon

table dormant   a table with fixed legs, as opposed to a board on trestles

tally   a wooden stick, cut with notches as a receipt, and divided into two parts, a stock and a foil

tansy   a herbaceous plant, with a strong aromatic and bitter taste (*Tanacetum vulgare* or related plants)

tun   a cask or brewing vessel; a measure of wine and other liquids, containing 2 pipes (252 old wine gallons)

usher   a household officer, originally a door-keeper, but also more generally an attendant

verjuice   a sour juice from unripened, acidic grapes and other fruits, notably crab apples

warren   an enclosure for breeding and keeping game; free warren, the right to hunt this game

wastel   a white loaf made of the finest wheat flour, ranked in quality immediately below simnels and baked in much larger quantities

wey   a measure of weight of dry goods, varying by commodity and locality

wort   unfermented or partly fermented ale

zedoary   an aromatic tuber, with properties similar to ginger; sometimes described as white turmeric, from a species of *Curcuma*, especially *Curcuma zedoaria*

ABBREVIATIONS

The place of publication is London unless otherwise stated. All biblical references are taken from the Vulgate – *Biblia sacra iuxta vulgatam versionem*, ed. R. Weber and others (4th edition, Stuttgart, 1994) – unless otherwise noted.

AHEW III	*The agrarian history of England and Wales*, vol. 3: *1348–1500*, ed. E. Miller (Cambridge, 1991)
AND	*The Anglo-Norman Dictionary*, ed. W. Rothwell and others (2nd edition, online at http://www.anglo-norman.net/)
BA	*On the properties of things: John Trevisa's translation of Bartholomaeus Anglicus De proprietatibus rerum*, ed. M. C. Seymour (3 vols, Oxford, 1975–88)
BAV	Biblioteca Apostolica Vaticana, The Vatican
BL	British Library, London
Bozon	*Les contes moralisés de Nicole Bozon frère mineur publiés pour la première fois d'après les manuscrits de Londres et de Cheltenham*, ed. L. Toulmin Smith and P. Meyer (Paris, 1889)
BSP	John Bromyard, *Summa predicantium* (Nuremberg: Anton Koberger, 1485)
CClR	*Calendar of Close Rolls preserved in the Public Record Office* (47 vols, 1900–63)
Chaucer	*The Riverside Chaucer*, ed. L. D. Benson (3rd edition, Oxford, 1988)
CI	*Curye on Inglysch*, ed. C. Hieatt and S. Butler (EETS, ES, 8; 1985)
CO	*A collection of ordinances and regulations for the government of the royal household . . .*, ed. Anon. for the Society of Antiquaries (1790)
CS	*Councils and synods with other documents relating to the English Church. II A.D. 1205–1313*, ed. F. M. Powicke and C. R. Cheney (2 vols, Oxford, 1964)

CSACSPW	*Customary of the Benedictine monasteries of Saint Augustine, Canterbury, and Saint Peter, Westminster*, ed. E. M. Thompson (2 vols, Henry Bradshaw Society, 23, 28; 1902–4)
DCP	Muniments of Durham Cathedral Priory
DUL	Durham University Library
EARD I	*Extracts from the account rolls of the Abbey of Durham*, vol. 1, ed. J. T. Fowler (Surtees Society, 99; 1898)
EARD II	*Extracts from the account rolls of the Abbey of Durham*, vol. 2, ed. J. T. Fowler (Surtees Society, 100; 1899)
EARD III	*Extracts from the account rolls of the Abbey of Durham*, vol. 3, ed. J. T. Fowler (Surtees Society, 103; 1901)
EETS	Early English Text Society
EHR	*English Historical Review*
ERT	*Richard II and the English royal treasure*, ed. J. Stratford (Woodbridge, 2012)
ES	Extra series
Executors	*Account of the executors of Richard, Bishop of London, 1303, and of the executors of Thomas, Bishop of Exeter, 1310*, ed. W. H. Hale and H. T. Ellacombe (Camden Society, new series, 10; 1874)
FL	*Les fabulistes latins depuis le siècle d'Auguste jusqu'à la fin du moyen âge*, ed. L. Hervieux (5 vols, Paris, 1893–9)
FME	*Food in medieval England: diet and nutrition*, ed. C. M. Woolgar, D. Serjeantson and T. Waldron (Oxford, 2006)
GH	C. M. Woolgar, *The great household in late medieval England* (New Haven, 1999)
HAME	*Household accounts from medieval England*, ed. C. M. Woolgar (2 vols, British Academy, Records of Social and Economic History, new series, 17–18; 1992–3)
HKW	*The history of the king's works*, ed. H. M. Colvin (6 vols, 1963–82)
HMC	Historical Manuscripts Commission
JRULM	John Rylands University Library of Manchester
LPL	Lambeth Palace Library
LV I	*Visitations of religious houses in the diocese of Lincoln: injunctions and other documents from the registers of Richard Flemyng and William Gray, Bishops of Lincoln, A.D. 1420 to A.D. 1436*, ed. A. H. Thompson (Lincoln Record Society, 7; 1914)
LV II	*Visitations of religious houses in the diocese of Lincoln: II. Records of visitations held by William Alnwick, Bishop of Lincoln, A.D. 1436 to A.D. 1449 (part I)*, ed. A. H. Thompson (Lincoln Record Society, 14; 1918)
LV III	*Visitations of religious houses in the diocese of Lincoln: III. Records of visitations held by William Alnwick, Bishop of Lincoln, A.D. 1436 to A.D. 1449 (part II)*, ed. A. H. Thompson (Lincoln Record Society, 21; 1929)

MED	*Middle English Dictionary*, ed. H. Kurath, S. M. Kuhn and others (Ann Arbor, 1956–2001)
Mirk	*John Mirk's Festial*, ed. S. Powell (2 vols, EETS, OS, 334–5; 2009, 2011)
MM	*Manners and meals in olden time: the Babees Book . . .*, ed. F. J. Furnivall (EETS, OS, 32; 1868)
MO	*Mirour de l'omme*, in *The complete works of John Gower: the French works*, ed. G. C. Macaulay (Oxford, 1899), pp. 1–334
MRC	*Manorial records of Cuxham, Oxfordshire, c.1200–1359*, ed. P. D. A. Harvey (HMC, Joint Publications series, 23; 1976)
NHB	*The regulations and establishment of the household of Henry Algernon Percy, the fifth Earl of Northumberland at his castles of Wressle and Leckonfield, in Yorkshire. Begun Anno Domini MDXII*, ed. T. Percy (new edition, 1905) [Northumberland Household Book]
ODNB	*Oxford Dictionary of National Biography*, ed. H.C.G. Matthew and B. Harrison, online edition, at http://www.oxforddnb.com/
OED	*Oxford English Dictionary*
OS	Original series
PLP	*Paston letters and papers of the fifteenth century*, ed. N. Davis, R. Beadle and C. Richmond (3 vols, Oxford, 1971–2005)
PP	William Langland, *Piers Plowman: a parallel-text edition of the A, B, C and Z versions*, ed. A. V. C. Schmidt (2nd edition, 2 vols in 3, Kalamazoo, 2011)
RO	Record Office
SBTRO	Shakespeare Birthplace Trust Record Office, Stratford-upon-Avon
SCRO	Southampton City Record Office
SS	Supplementary series
TE I	*Testamenta Eboracensia . . .*, vol. 1, ed. J. Raine (Surtees Society, 2; 1836)
TE II	*Testamenta Eboracensia . . .*, vol. 2, ed. J. Raine (Surtees Society, 30; 1855)
TE III	*Testamenta Eboracensia . . .*, vol. 3, ed. J. Raine (Surtees Society, 45; 1865)
TE IV	*Testamenta Eboracensia . . .*, vol. 4, ed. J. Raine (Surtees Society, 53; 1869)
TFCCB	*Two fifteenth-century cookery-books*, ed. T. Austin (EETS, OS, 91; 1888)
TNA	The National Archives, Kew
TREWE	*Testamentary records of the English and Welsh episcopate 1200–1413: wills, executors' accounts and inventories, and the probate process*, ed. C. M. Woolgar (Canterbury and York Society, 102; 2011)

NOTES

1 Food Cultures

1. A list with 'a hastynes of cookes' appears at the end of Caxton's second printing, in 1477, of John Lydgate's 'Horse, goose and sheep'. For lists like this, see R. Corner, 'More fifteenth-century terms of association', *Review of English Studies*, new series, 13 (1962), pp. 229–44; and L. M. Cooper, 'Recipes for the realm: John Lydgate's "soteltes" and the Debate of the horse, goose and sheep', in *Essays on aesthetics in medieval literature in honor of Howell Chickering*, ed. J. M. Hill, B. Wheeler and R. F. Yeager (Toronto, 2013), pp. 194–215. A similar listing, 'The compaynys of beestys and fowlys', but without the cooks, appears in the facsimile of *The Boke of Saint Albans by Dame Juliana Berners*, ed. W. Blades (1901), sig. F6r–7r, at the end of the book on hawking.
2. For which, see *FME*.
3. F. Swabey, 'The household of Alice de Bryene, 1412–13', in *Food and eating in medieval Europe*, ed. M. Carlin and J. T. Rosenthal (1998), pp. 133–44, at pp. 135–6.
4. *GH*, pp. 111–13; for other examples, C. Dyer, *Standards of living in the later Middle Ages* (2nd edition, Cambridge, 1998), p. 70.
5. *Mirk*, i, p. 70; for a listing of the clean beasts, those fit for food, and those that might not be eaten: Deut. 14:3–20.
6. *PP*, i, p. 260 (B V, l. 603).
7. *MO*, pp. 91–2, especially ll. 7945–56.
8. P. Freedman, 'Introduction: a new history of cuisine', in *Food: the history of taste*, ed. P. Freedman (2007), pp. 11–12.
9. C. M. Woolgar, D. Serjeantson and T. Waldron, 'Conclusion', in *FME*, p. 271.
10. Ramón A. Banegas López, *Europa carnívora. Comprar y comer carne en el mundo bajomedieval* (Gijón, 2012), pp. 18–20.
11. C. Horstmann, 'Des MS Bodl. 779 jüngere Zusatzlegenden zur südlichen Legendensammlung', *Archiv für das Studium der neueren Sprachen und Litteraturen* 82 (1889), pp. 335–6, ll. 85–116.
12. C. M. Woolgar, 'Group diets in late medieval England', in *FME*, pp. 191–3; B. Laurioux, *Manger au moyen âge: pratiques et discours alimentaires en Europe aux XIVe et XVe siècles* (Paris, 2002), pp. 105–10; Banegas López, *Europa carnívora*, pp. 63–84, especially p. 71.
13. *GH*, pp. 90–2.
14. *Mirk*, i, pp. 77–8.

15. *The records of the city of Norwich*, ed. W. Hudson and J. C. Tingey (2 vols, Norwich, 1906), i, pp. lxxxviii–xc, 340–6.
16. *BSP*, L vii Luxuria, Art. vii: xxvii.
17. *BSP*, A xxiii Anima, Art. iiii: xvii.
18. *A myrour to lewde men and wymmen: a prose version of the Speculum Vitae, ed. from BL MS Harley 45*, ed. V. Nelson (Heidelberg, 1981), pp. 205–11.
19. *BSP*, F iii Ferie, Art. ii: viii, 'sicut pomum puero ostensum facit eum venire ridentem'.
20. *BSP*, I i Ieiunium, Art. ii: iiii.
21. See, for example, Gratian, *Decretum*, Prima Pars, Distinctio IV, cap. VI, printed in *Corpus iuris canonici*, ed. E. Friedberg (2nd edition, 2 vols, Leipzig, 1922), i, cols 6–7, with the comment at IV.
22. *Mirk*, i, p. 79.
23. *An edition of the Judica me Deus of Richard Rolle*, ed. J. P. Daly (Salzburg Studies in English Literature, 92: 14; 1984), pp. iv, liii, 50 (my translation), 104.
24. BL, Add. MS 88974, f. 146v, 'unde caro cadaverum'; f. 147r, first week of the account, Tuesday, 2 Oct 1347: 'Item i bos necatum de stauro de Lak' quia debilis et infirmus cuius caro quasi cadaver et remanet in lardario.'
25. Adam Murimuth, *Continuatio Chronicarum*, Robertus de Avesbury, *De gestis mirabilibus regis Edwardi tertii*, ed. E. M. Thompson (Rolls series, 93; 1889), p. 386.
26. J. Marvin, 'Cannibalism as an aspect of famine in two English chronicles', in *Food and eating in medieval Europe*, ed. M. Carlin and J. T. Rosenthal (1998), pp. 73–86; W. C. Jordan, *The great famine: Northern Europe in the early fourteenth century* (Princeton, 1996), pp. 148–50; P. Bonnassie, 'Consommation d'aliments immondes et cannibalisme de survie dans l'occident du haut moyen âge', *Annales: Économies, Sociétés, Civilisations* 44 (1989), pp. 1035–56.
27. Rule of St Benedict: chapters 39 and 40 cover food and drink; chapters 35–8 and 41, service and timing of meals. *RB 1980: the Rule of St Benedict*, ed. T. Fry and others (Collegeville, MN, 1981), pp. 232–41.
28. R. M. Clay, *The mediaeval hospitals of England* (1909), pp. 168–9, quoting from the God's House account rolls, which I have not been able to trace among the surviving manuscripts.
29. One thinks too of the Cathar *perfecti*, but they ate fish as well as vegetables. See also K. Albala, *Eating right in the Renaissance* (Berkeley, 2002), p. 70.
30. N. J. Sykes, 'The impact of the Normans on hunting practices in England', in *FME*, pp. 162–75.
31. *NHB*, pp. 102–8.
32. *Statutes of the realm*, ed. A. Luders, T. E. Tomlins, J. Raithby and others (11 vols, 1810–28), i, p. 380; discussed in C. M. Woolgar, 'The Cook', in *Historians on Chaucer: the 'General Prologue' to the Canterbury Tales*, ed. S. H. Rigby, with A. J. Minnis (Oxford, 2014), p. 274.
33. C. M. Woolgar, 'Feasting and fasting: food and taste in Europe in the Middle Ages', in *Food: the history of taste*, ed. Freedman, pp. 162–95.
34. J. Goody, *Cooking, cuisine and class: a study in comparative sociology* (Cambridge, 1982), pp. 1–9, 97–153; C. M. Woolgar, 'Food and the Middle Ages', *Journal of Medieval History* 36 (2010), pp. 7–14.
35. B. Laurioux, *Gastronomie, humanisme et société à Rome au milieu du XVe siècle. Autour du De honesta voluptate de Platina* (Florence, 2006), pp. 302–23.
36. *Liber cure cocorum, copied and edited from the Sloane MS. 1986*, ed. R. Morris (Berlin, 1862), p. 1: 'Fyrst to ʒow I wylle schawe / Þo poyntes of cure, al by rawe, / Of potage, hastery, and bakun mete, / And petecure, I nylle forʒete.'
37. *Liber cure cocorum*, ed. Morris, pp. 42–6; B. A. Henisch, *The medieval cook* (Woodbridge, 2009), pp. 28–70, for cooking by peasant women.
38. J. L. Flandrin, *Arranging the meal: a history of table service in France*, trans. J. E. Johnson, with S. Roder and A. Roder (Berkeley, 2007); J. L. Flandrin, 'Structure des menus français

et anglais aux XIVe et XVe siècles', in *Du manuscrit à la table: essais sur la cuisine au moyen âge et répertoire des manuscrits médiévaux contenant des recettes culinaires*, ed. C. Lambert (Montreal, 1992), pp. 173–92.

39. *FL*, iv, pp. 447–8. Cf. *Chaucer*, p. 206, ll. 251–4.
40. TNA, JUST 2/18, mem. 8r.
41. *CSACSPW*, i, pp. 163–4; ii, p. 104; P. B. Griesser, 'Die "Ecclesiastica Officia Cisterciensis Ordinis" des Cod. 1711 von Trient', *Analecta Sacri Ordinis Cisterciensis* 12 (1956), pp. 239–40; *Reading gild accounts 1357–1516*, ed. C. Slade (2 vols, Berkshire Record Society, 6–7; 2002), i, pp. lxxxviii–xc, 8, 16, 74, 106; C. M. Woolgar, 'Fast and feast: conspicuous consumption and the diet of the nobility in the fifteenth century', in *Revolution and consumption in late medieval England*, ed. M. Hicks (Woodbridge, 2001), p. 10.
42. *GH*, pp. 84–9.
43. BAV, MS Vat. Lat. 4015, ff. 158r–v.
44. *Materials for the history of Thomas Becket, Archbishop of Canterbury*, ed. J. C. Robertson (7 vols, Rolls series, 67; 1875–85), i, pp. 258–60.
45. *NHB*, *passim*.
46. *BSP*, I i Ieiunium, Art. i: iii.
47. TNA, JUST 2/78, rot. 2, mem. 1r: 'in tempore dormiscionis post nonam'.
48. *TREWE*, p. xxxii.
49. *GH*, p. 85.
50. TNA, JUST 2/66, mem. 3d: 'hora vesper'.
51. Walter de Bibbesworth, *Le tretiz*, ed. W. Rothwell (Aberystwyth, 2009; online edition, at www.anglo-norman.net), p. 70.
52. *Lydgate's Fall of princes*, ed. H. Bergen (4 vols, EETS, ES, 121–4; 1924–7), i, p. 264.
53. *A myrour to lewde men and wymmen*, ed. Nelson, p. 207: 'right so he may synne in over-late soupers; wherfore þilke men & wommen þat useþ to soupe late and longe to wake on þe nyght and waste þe tyme in ydelnes & vanitee, wast & nycete, late goþ to bedde & late aryseþ, þei synneþ in many maneres.'
54. Dorset History Centre, Dorchester, D/SHA/CH2 (read from Ph 233).
55. *The fabric rolls of York Minster . . .*, ed. J. Raine (Surtees Society, 35; 1859), pp. 181–2.
56. BL, MS Harley 6815 ff. 40r/37r: 'Strangeres, as men of worships servantes, and such other as be honest personages of the contrey, after they have dyned or supped and done their reverence to the head officers [of the household], the ussher is commanded by on of the said head officers to have them to the cellour barre and there to geve them wyne.'
57. *LV II*, p. 8.
58. *GH*, p. 85.
59. *The receyt of the Ladie Kateryne*, ed. G. Kipling (EETS, OS, 296; 1990), p. 58.
60. Flandrin, 'Structure des menus français et anglais', pp. 173–92.
61. *Walter of Henley and other treatises on estate management and accounting*, ed. D. Oschinsky (Oxford, 1971), pp. 404–5 (Rules of St Robert). For the date, L. J. Wilkinson, 'The *Rules* of Robert Grosseteste reconsidered: the lady as estate and household manager in thirteenth-century England', in *The medieval household in Christian Europe, c.850–c.1550*, ed. C. Beattie, A. Maslakovic and S. Rees Jones (Turnhout, 2003), pp. 299–300.
62. e.g. BL, MS Harley 6815, f. 33r.
63. TNA, JUST 2/164, mem. 7r; *Chaucer*, p. 180, ll. 901–6.
64. *BSP*, A xxvii Avaricia, Art. x.
65. TNA, JUST 2/113, mem. 38r (Nortoft, 26 Jun 1356), goods of the vicar of Guilsborough; see also Chapter 9.
66. *CS*, i, p. 54, c. 3.
67. Norfolk RO, Norwich Consistory Court Records, Will Register 1 Heydon (1370–82), f. 29v.
68. Will Register 1 Heydon (1370–82), f. 96r.
69. TNA, JUST 2/155, mem. 12d.

70. *The pipe roll of the bishopric of Winchester 1301–2*, ed. M. Page (Hampshire Record Series, 14; 1996), p. 65.
71. *MRC*, pp. 152–3.
72. H. W. Saunders, *An introduction to the obedientiary and manor rolls of Norwich Cathedral Priory* (Norwich, 1930), image opposite p. 42.
73. *GH*, pp. 145–6. For Stokesay Castle (Plates 8 and 9), A. Emery, *Greater medieval houses of England and Wales* (3 vols, Cambridge, 1996–2006), ii, pp. 574–6.
74. Bodleian Library, Oxford, MS Eng. hist. b. 208, f. 72v: 'Ande that the saide uschar taike good heed that no man wype or rubb their handes uppon arras or any outhir stuf hanginge in the said chambre whereby the said stuf might be hurtid wheir his lord or maister is.'
75. *HKW*, iv, p. 12.
76. *HKW*, iv, pp. 30–1.
77. L. F. Salzman, *Building in England down to 1540: a documentary history* (Oxford, 1952), pp. 432–6.
78. TNA, JUST 2/67, mem. 12r.
79. *PLP*, ii, pp. 594–5.
80. East Sussex RO, MS RYE 60/3, f. 81r.
81. M. E. Mate, *Women in medieval English society* (Cambridge, 1999), pp. 14–15, 28, 31–2, 38–46; *The Fountains Abbey lease book*, ed. D. J. H. Michelmore (Yorkshire Archaeological Society Record Series, 140; 1981), p. 208: 'housewyffly handelede'.
82. *Catholicon Anglicum, an English-Latin wordbook, dated 1483*, ed. S. J. H. Herrtage and H. B. Wheatley (Camden Society, new series, 30; 1882), pp. 336, 361. Cf. M. Segalen, *Love and power in the peasant family: rural France in the nineteenth century*, trans. S. Matthews (Oxford, 1983), p. 68. I am grateful to Dr Jeremy Goldberg for drawing Segalen's work to my attention.
83. M. G. Muzzarelli and F. Tarozzi, *Donne e cibo: una relazione nella storia* (n.p., 2003), pp. 41–9; C. Walker Bynum, *Holy feast, holy fast: the religious significance of food to medieval women* (Berkeley, 1987); C. Mazzoni, *The women in God's kitchen: cooking, eating and spiritual writing* (New York, 2005).
84. *Heresy trials in the diocese of Norwich, 1428–31*, ed. N. P. Tanner (Camden Society, 4th series, 20; 1977), p. 121: 'Also that no man ne woman is bounde to faste in Lenton, Ymbre Days, Fridays, vigiles of seyntes ne other tymes whyche ar commaunded of the Churche to be fasted, but it is leful to every persone all suche days and tymes to ete flessh and all maner of metis indifferently at hys owyn lust.'
85. Albala, *Eating right in the Renaissance*, pp. 151–4.
86. *The myroure of oure Ladye containing a devotional treatise on divine service, with a translation of the offices used by the sisters of the Brigittine monastery of Sion . . .*, ed. J. H. Blunt (EETS, ES, 19; 1873), pp. xx–xxi.
87. E. Power, *Medieval English nunneries c.1275 to 1535* (Cambridge, 1922), p. 141, quoting G. J. Aungier, *History and antiquities of Syon* (1840), pp. 393–4.
88. *Mirk*, i, p. 12.
89. *Merlin*, ed. H. B. Wheatley (4 vols, EETS, OS, 10, 21, 36, 112; 1865, 1866, 1869, 1899), i, p. 15: 'Therfore was the moder suffred to norishe it tell it was x monthes of age.'
90. M. P. Richards, S. Mays and B. Fuller, 'Stable carbon and nitrogen isotope values of bone and teeth reflect weaning age at the medieval Wharram Percy site, Yorkshire, U.K.', *American Journal of Physical Anthropology* 119, no. 3 (2002), pp. 205–10.
91. *Calendar of inquisitions post mortem*, vol. 3: *Edward I* (1912), p. 323; J. T. Rosenthal, *Telling tales: sources and narration in late medieval England* (University Park, PA, 2003), p. 32.
92. *Speculum sacerdotale*, ed. E. H. Weatherly (EETS, OS, 200; 1936), p. 200.
93. *The life and miracles of St William of Norwich by Thomas of Monmouth . . .*, ed. A. Jessopp and M. R. James (Cambridge, 1896), pp. 12–13. Cf. Genesis 21:8.
94. C. M. Woolgar, *The senses in late medieval England* (2006), pp. 109–10.
95. *CS*, i, p. 473 and n. 4.

96. TNA, JUST 2/67, mem. 12d.
97. *BSP*, E ii Electio, Art. ii: ii.
98. *BSP*, R v Religio, Art. xi: xxxiii.
99. TNA, JUST 2/18, mem. 2r.
100. JUST 2/82, mem. 9r.
101. 'But som men for wynnynge of worldes goodes conne [gladliche] faste al þe day to þe nyght, but for þe love of God and for wynnynge of everlastynge [goodes] þei wole not faste to none of þe day, but fareþ as wantoun children þat woleþ alwey have brede in here hond': *A myrour to lewde men and wymmen*, ed. Nelson, p. 207.
102. Walter de Bibbesworth, *Le tretiz*, ed. Rothwell, pp. 8–9, ll. 195–205; pp. 60–1, ll. 164–75.
103. *GH*, p. 101; *HAME*, i, pp. 214–25.
104. T. F. Kirby, *Annals of Winchester College from its foundation in the year 1382 to the present time* (1892), pp. 78, 80.
105. TNA, JUST 2/82, mem. 6d.
106. *Gothic: art for England 1400–1547*, ed. R. Marks and P. Williamson (2003), p. 315.
107. TNA, JUST 2/78, rot. 3, mem. 5r.

2 Cooking in the Countryside

1. C. Dyer, *Standards of living in the later Middle Ages: social change in England c.1200–1520* (new edition, Cambridge, 1989), pp. 151–60, 287–96.
2. *FL*, iv, pp. 190–1: 'mus domestica'; 'mus campestrina'.
3. *Hali meiðhad*, ed. B. Millett (EETS, OS, 284; 1982), pp. xxii–xxiii, 19.
4. e.g. Walter Map, *De nugis curialium. Courtiers' trifles*, ed. M. R. James, rev. C. N. L. Brooke and R. A. B. Mynors (Oxford, 1983), pp. 20–1.
5. W. de Wadington, *Le manuel des pechez*, in Robert of Brunne's *Handlyng Synne*, ed. F. J. Furnivall (2 vols, EETS, OS, 119, 123; 1901–3), i, p. 58, ll. 2407–10: 'Meus vaudreint descuplé, / Car il ne paient Dampne Dé. / Pur ceo, poi de gent a custum lealment / gaynent le bacon.'
6. *Peter Idley's instructions to his son*, ed. C. D'Evelyn (Modern Language Association of America, monograph series, 6; Boston and London, 1935), p. 143: 'a litell bacon flycche ... long hanged and is resty and toughe'; *Chaucer*, p. 108, ll. 215–18.
7. 'Meuz unce de porc, que bacun de adne'; 'Ja n'iert trové bacon en lit de guaignon': E. Stengel, 'Die beiden Sammlungen altfranzösischer Sprichwörter in der Oxforder Handschrift Rawlinson C 641', *Zeitschrift für französische Sprache und Litteratur* 21 (1899), p. 5, no. 51, and p. 12, no. 329.
8. 'Childe is pigge, and fader is the flicche'; 'When me profereth þe pigge, opon [open] þe pogh; For when he is an olde swyn, thow tyte hym now3ht': M. Förster, 'Die mittelenglische Sprichwörtersammlung in Douce 52', in *Festschrift zum XII. allgemeinen deutschen Neuphilologentage in München, Pfingsten 1906*, ed. E. Stottreither (Erlangen, 1906), p. 54, nos 113–14.
9. 'Qui sert baron, manjue braon': Stengel, 'Die beiden Sammlungen', p. 12, no. 306.
10. 'What so ever 3e brage ore boste, My mayster 3et shall reule the roste': E. Wilson, 'The debate of the carpenter's tools', *Review of English Studies*, new series 38, no. 152 (1987), p. 459, ll. 175–6; the note on p. 467 argues that this could be 'roost', and *OED* is ambivalent; MnE 'Hrost', hen-house.
11. *The Middle English metrical romances*, ed. W. H. French and C. B. Hale (2 vols, New York, 1930), ii, p. 995, l. 136: ' "I vow to God," quod Perkyn, "þou spekis of cold rost!" '
12. *Heresy trials in the diocese of Norwich, 1428–31*, ed. N. P. Tanner (Camden Society, 4th series, 20; 1977), pp. 50–1; 135.
13. *Heresy trials in the diocese of Norwich*, ed. Tanner, pp. 75–6.
14. Cf. the role of peasant women in giving food: C. M. Woolgar, 'Gifts of food in late medieval England', *Journal of Medieval History* 37 (2011), p. 9.
15. P. Brears, *Cooking and dining in medieval England* (Blackawton, 2008), pp. 64, 66.

16. TNA JUST 2/25, rot. 1, mem. 1r; rot. 2, mem. 2r; rot. 2, mem. 2d; *MRC*, p. 433.
17. JUST 2/25, rot. 1, mem. 1r.
18. *TE I*, pp. 108, 110.
19. *The inventories and account rolls of the Benedictine houses or cells of Jarrow and Monk-Wearmouth in the County of Durham*, ed. J. Raine (Surtees Society, 29; 1854), p. 152.
20. *TE I*, pp. 172–3.
21. TNA, JUST 2/18, mem. 42r.
22. JUST 2/209, mem. 7r.
23. JUST 2/113, mem. 47r.
24. JUST 2/113, mem. 25r.
25. *GH*, pp. 76–7.
26. TNA, JUST 2/211, mem. 16d.
27. JUST 2/116, mem. 11r.
28. G. C. Homans, *English villagers of the thirteenth century* (New York, 1970), pp. 258–9.
29. R. K. Field, 'Worcestershire peasant buildings, household goods and farming equipment in the later Middle Ages', *Medieval Archaeology* 9 (1965), pp. 105–45, especially p. 121.
30. M. R. McCarthy and C. M. Brooks, *Medieval pottery in Britain AD 900–1600* (Leicester, 1988), pp. 101–2; B. Jervis, *Pottery and social life in medieval England: towards a relational approach* (Oxford, 2014), pp. 66–9.
31. TNA, JUST 2/25, mem. 1r.
32. JUST 2/194, mem. 2r.
33. JUST 2/195, mem. 5d.
34. JUST 2/114, mem. 8r.
35. JUST 2/116, mem. 5r: 'urciolus'.
36. McCarthy and Brooks, *Medieval pottery*, p. 23.
37. McCarthy and Brooks, *Medieval pottery*, pp. 55–6, 102.
38. K. J. Barton, *Medieval Sussex pottery* (Chichester, 1979), pp. 75–7.
39. TNA, JUST 2/82, mem. 1r.
40. Norfolk RO, Le Strange NH6 (recte 7), mem. 3d, week commencing Sunday 15 Jun 1348; NH8, mem. 2r, week commencing Sunday 15 Mar 1349.
41. S. Moorhouse, 'Documentary evidence for the uses of medieval pottery: an interim statement', *Medieval Ceramics* 2 (1978), pp. 3–21; Jervis, *Pottery and social life*, pp. 36–50; McCarthy and Brooks, *Medieval pottery*, pp. 104–10.
42. McCarthy and Brooks, *Medieval pottery*, p. 114, citing *TFCCB*, p. 73; Moorhouse, 'Documentary evidence', p. 6.
43. Barton, *Medieval Sussex pottery*, p. 71.
44. TNA, JUST 2/18, mem. 42d.
45. JUST 2/67, mem. 2r.
46. JUST 2/17, mem. 11d.
47. JUST 2/113, mem. 11r.
48. JUST 2/82, mem. 6r.
49. JUST 2/66, mem. 12r.
50. JUST 2/203, mem. 1r.
51. JUST 2/67, mem. 33r, rot. 3r.
52. JUST 2/113, mem. 43r.
53. JUST 2/18, mem. 41r.
54. JUST 2/113, mem. 34r.
55. JUST 2/113, mem. 47r.
56. e.g. J. M. Bennett, *Ale, beer and brewsters in England: women's work in a changing world, 1300–1600* (Oxford, 1996).
57. TNA, JUST 2/18, mem. 20r.
58. JUST 2/18, mem. 42r.
59. JUST 2/18, mem. 44r; JUST 2/113, mem. 3r.
60. JUST 2/113, mem. 37r.

61. JUST 2/113, mem. 46r.
62. JUST 2/114, mem. 25r.
63. JUST 2/155, mem. 7d.
64. Caldecote, Cambs, 1347: pan and tripod, 6d (JUST 2/18, mem. 20r); Lolworth, Cambs, 1353: pan and ale, 2d (JUST 2/18, mem. 42r); Haslingfield, Cambs, 1356: pan and grout, 6d (JUST 2/18, mem. 44r); Wilby, Northants, 1344: pan and wort ('ciromellum'), 12d (JUST 2/113, mem. 3r); Rushton, Rothwell Hundred, Northants, 1346: pan and wort ('ciromellum'), 18d (JUST 2/113, mem. 6r); Rushden, Higham Ferrers Hundred, Northants, 1356: pan and wort ('granomellum'), 14d (JUST 2/113, mem. 37r).
65. JUST 2/209, mem. 8d.
66. JUST 2/194, mem. 7r.
67. JUST 2/194, mem. 5r.
68. JUST 2/67, mem. 23r.
69. JUST 2/209, mem. 5r.
70. JUST 2/209, mem. 5r.
71. JUST 2/116, mem. 10r.
72. JUST 2/49, mem. 1d.
73. The word may be related to 'coomb' as a measure: 4 bushels; but it is a diminutive, and is used for liquids.
74. TNA, JUST 2/67, mem. 40, rot. 1d.
75. JUST 2/69, mem. 4d.
76. JUST 2/67, mem. 11d.
77. e.g. JUST 2/78, rot. 1, mem. 1d.
78. JUST 2/82, mem. 12, rot. 1r: 'plumbum geymynellum'.
79. JUST 2/78, rot. 3, mem. 2d.; JUST 2/113, mem. 6r.
80. JUST 2/66, mem. 1d.
81. JUST 2/67, mems 10r–d.
82. JUST 2/67, mem. 49r.
83. JUST 2/194, mem. 2r.
84. JUST 2/113, mem. 11r.
85. JUST 2/116, mem. 10r.
86. JUST 2/194, mem. 5r.
87. JUST 2/18, mem. 15r.
88. *Select cases from the coroners' rolls A.D. 1265–1413 with a brief account of the history of the office of coroner*, ed. C. Gross (Selden Society, 9; 1896), pp. 39–40.
89. Although some of these were probably for splitting wood: *TE III*, p. 49.
90. TNA, JUST 2/113, mem. 38r.
91. JUST 2/194, mem. 7r.
92. JUST 2/116, mem. 9r.
93. *TE I*, p. 110; *OED* yetling *sb.* 1.
94. *The priory of Finchale: the charters of endowment, inventories, and account rolls . . .*, ed. J. Raine (Surtees Society, 6; 1837), p. xxxvii.
95. *EARD III*, p. 588.
96. *TE II*, pp. 96–103, at pp. 99, 101.
97. *TE III*, p. 161.
98. TNA, JUST 2/50, mem. 1r.
99. JUST 2/66, mem. 6d.
100. JUST 2/155, mem. 3d.
101. JUST 2/18, mem. 13r: 'tyneam ligneam'.
102. Norfolk RO, DCN 1/1/4, Norwich Cathedral Priory, Master of the Cellar, 1278–9, mem. 2r.
103. e.g. DCN 1/1/7, Master of the Cellar, 1283–4, mem. 2d; DCN 1/1/14, Master of the Cellar, 1298–1300, mem. 3r; DCN 1/1/19, Master of the Cellar, 1308–9, mem. 2r; DCN 1/1/23, Master of the Cellar, 1313–14, mem. 2r.

104. TNA, JUST 2/78, rot. 3, mem. 5d.

105. JUST 2/193, mem. 1r.

106. JUST 2/74, mem. 8r.

107. JUST 2/160, mem. 2d.

108. *TE I*, pp. 267–8; *OED* rackan *sb.* 2; and rackan-crook, *sb.*

109. *TE II*, pp. 22–3: 'unum par furcarum pro dependencia ollarum in leʒ rakkes et cruks'.

110. *Early Northampton wills preserved in Northamptonshire Record Office*, ed. D. Edwards, M. Forrest, J. Minchinton, M. Shaw, B. Tyndall and P. Wallis (Northamptonshire Record Society, 42; 2005), pp. 63, 75–6, 86–7, 106.

111. *Early Northampton wills*, ed. Edwards and others, pp. 239–40.

112. N. J. Sykes, 'From cu and sceap to beefe and mouton: the management, distribution, and consumption of cattle and sheep in medieval England', in *FME*, pp. 56–71; C. M. Woolgar, 'Meat and dairy products in late medieval England', in *FME*, pp. 88–101.

113. TNA, JUST 2/113, mem. 45r.

114. *Early Northampton wills*, ed. Edwards and others, pp. 63–4.

115. McCarthy and Brooks, *Medieval pottery*, p. 73.

3 The Culture of Drink and Drinking

1. E. Power, *Medieval English nunneries* (Cambridge, 1922), p. 166.

2. *PP*, i, p. 201 (C VI, ll. 173–4), 'Drynke but with þe doke and dyne but ones'; 'goose' in some manuscripts of the A version: *Piers Plowman: the A Version, Will's Visions of Piers Plowman and Do-Well*, ed. G. Kane (1960), p. 276 (A V, l. 58).

3. e.g. *CSACSPW*, i, pp. 233–4, 240, 250; ii, p. 200.

4. *FL*, iv, pp. 190–1.

5. *PP*, i, p. 720 (C XXII, l. 19).

6. TNA, JUST 2/18, mem. 9r.

7. JUST 2/18, mem. 16r.

8. JUST 2/116, mem. 14r, rot. 2.

9. JUST 2/17, mem. 7d.

10. JUST 2/18, mem. 1d.

11. JUST 2/18, mem. 4d.

12. In the miracle of turning the water into wine at the marriage at Cana, *The mirrour of the blessed lyf of Jesu Christ . . . made before the year 1410 by Nicholas Love*, ed. L. F. Powell (Oxford, 1908), p. 106: 'They ful filleden the stenes that there were ful of water; and anone at his blissynge all the water of hem was torned in to wyne.'

13. *Charters and records of Hereford Cathedral*, ed. W. W. Capes (Hereford, 1908), p. 237, c.1375: 'Quandam cameram vocatam cycternechaumbre . . . situatam infra communem mansionem dictorum vicariorum'.

14. DUL, DCP Cellarer's account, 1466–7 (A), mem. 1d.

15. Bitters and bittes, ordinances of Worcester, 1467: *English gilds: the original ordinances of more than one hundred early English gilds . . .*, ed. L. T. Smith (EETS, OS, 40; 1870), p. 382; *The minor poems of John Lydgate*, part 2, ed. H. N. MacCracken (EETS, OS, 192; 1934), p. 545, ll. 141–2 ('Debate of the horse, goose and sheep'): 'Bi draught of hors, fro rivers & fro wellis bowges be brouht to brewers for good ale.'

16. 'The hermit and the outlaw', in M. Kaluza, 'Kleinere Publikationen aus me. Handschriften', *Englische Studien* 14 (1890), pp. 165–88, at p. 174, ll. 199–206: 'On her hed sche bar a canne; / The watyr over the brerde ran, / That seemed hym fayre and cler. / "Wenche," he sayde, "me thyrsteth sore. / If that watyr thou berest thare, / Set thonne thy pot ryght here!" / "Syr," sche sayde, "at thy wyl / Here may thou drynke thy fylle!" '

17. TNA, JUST 2/67, mem. 12r.

18. JUST 2/67, mem. 12r.

19. JUST 2/67, mem. 40r, rot. 4d.

20. H. C. M. Lambert, *History of Banstead in Surrey* (Oxford, 1912), pp. 321–36.

21. *The cartulary of the priory of St Denys near Southampton*, ed. E. O. Blake (2 vols, Southampton Records Series, 24–5; 1981), ii, pp. 213–14.

22. TNA, JUST 2/113, mem. 41r.

23. H. P. Cholmeley, *John of Gaddesden and the Rosa medicinae* (Oxford, 1912), pp. 52–5, especially p. 55; M. Carlin, 'Gaddesden, John', in *ODNB*: http://www.oxforddnb.com/view/article/10267 (accessed 25 April 2015).

24. *BA*, ii, p. 895.

25. 'A potu ante prandium mirum in modum abstinuit. In estate vero, cum nimius estus et sitis aridior cum urgeret, aquam coctam, que "cisona" dicitur, in poculum sumpsit': C. H. Lawrence, *St Edmund of Abingdon: a study in hagiography and history* (Oxford, 1960), p. 193. The word may refer to King Cissa of Upper Wessex, who was buried at Abingdon Abbey.

26. *Records of the wardrobe and household 1286–1289*, ed. B. F. Byerly and C. R. Byerly (1986), p. 20, no. 165.

27. *Lydgate's Siege of Thebes*, part 1, ed. A. Erdmann (EETS, ES, 108; 1911), p. 166, l. 3533: 'He first sett allay on wynys, Meynte water whan they were to strong.'

28. *BA*, ii, p. 1080: 'is most stronge & grieveþ moche þe heed and smyteþ þe witte'.

29. D. J. Stone, 'The consumption of field crops', in *FME*, pp. 15–26.

30. J. M. Bennett, *Ale, beer, and brewsters in England: women's work in a changing world, 1300–1600* (Oxford, 1996).

31. *PLP*, i, p. 14, no. 7: 'Pur faire holsom drynk of ale, Recipe sauge, avence, rose maryn, tyme, chopped right small, and put þis and a newe leyd hennes ey in a bage and hange it in þe barell. Item, clowys, maces, and spikenard grounden and put in a bagge and hanged in þe barell. And nota þat þe ey of þe henne shal kepe þe ale fro sourynge.'

32. *Chaucer*, p. 214, l. 763: 'And notemuge to putte in ale'.

33. *BSP*, A v Absconsio, Art. vi.

34. A. G. Rigg, ' "Descriptio Northfolchie": a critical edition', in *Nova de veteribus: Mittel- und neulateinische Studien für Paul Gerhard Schmidt*, ed. A. Bihrer and E. Stein (Munich, 2004), pp. 585–6, 593.

35. *Bozon*, pp. 170–1.

36. Bennett, *Ale, beer, and brewsters*, pp. 100–3.

37. *CSACSPW*, i, p. 135: good malt: 'bene granata'; good flavour: 'boni saporis'.

38. *CSACSPW*, i, p. 160.

39. e.g. *Calendar of the plea and memoranda rolls preserved among the archives of the corporation of the city of London at the Guildhall, A.D. 1364–1381*, ed. A. H. Thomas (Cambridge, 1929), p. 147 and n. 1 (1372); *The overseas trade of Boston in the reign of Richard II*, ed. S. H. Rigby (Lincoln Record Society, 93; 2005), pp. 38, 39, 41–3, etc.

40. Norfolk RO, NCR Case 16d/1, f. 41v.

41. *Calendar of letter-books preserved among the archives of the corporation of the city of London at the Guildhall*, vol. 11: *Letter-Book L, temp. Edward IV–Henry VII*, ed. R. R. Sharpe (1912), pp. 52–3: 'Forasmoche as the comon people for lacke of experience can not knowe the perfitnesse of bere aswele as of the ale.'

42. G. Fransson, *Middle English surnames of occupation 1100–1350* (Lund Studies in English, 3; 1935), p. 79.

43. *FL*, iv, pp. 227–8, 425–6. C. M. Woolgar, 'The language of food and cooking', in *The language of the professions: proceedings of the 2013 Harlaxton Symposium*, ed. M. Carruthers (Donington, 2015), p. 46.

44. Norfolk RO, DCN 1/1/1, Master of the Cellar, 1263–4, mem. 1r; mem. 1d.

45. DCN 1/1/18, Master of the Cellar, 1307–8, mem. 2r.

46. TNA, JUST 2/73, mem. 4r.

47. *Records of the borough of Nottingham . . .*, vol. 1: *King Henry II to King Richard II, 1155–1399*, ed. W. H. Stevenson (1882), pp. 313–14.

48. TNA, JUST 2/82, mem. 2r.

49. JUST 2/17, mem. 7d.

50. JUST 2/74, mem. 10r.

51. *PP*, i, p. 24 (B, Prologue, ll. 229–30): 'Whit wyn of Oseye and red wyn of Gascoigne, / Of þe Ryne and of þe Rochel the roste to defye!'

52. *MO*, p. 289, ll. 26078–112, quotes at ll. 26104–7: 'Et si leur dist, "O mes treschieres, / Mes dames, faitez bonnes cheres, / Bevetz trestout a vo plaisir, / Car nous avons asses laisir." '

53. S. Rose, *The wine trade in medieval Europe 1000–1500* (2011), p. 54.

54. *Jacob's Well: an Englisht treatise on the cleansing of man's conscience*, part 1, ed. A. Brandeis (EETS, OS, 115; 1900), p. 291, 'Levyth ʒoure rennyng on holy-dayes to wrestelynges . . . & dauncys, to bed-alys, bede-wynes, & schetynges.'

55. J. Dyer, 'Bede ale', *Notes and Queries*, 3rd series, 8 (1865), p. 436.

56. East Sussex RO, MS RYE 60/3, f. 30v.

57. MS RYE 60/3, f. 37r.

58. MS RYE 60/3, f. 81r.

59. *OED* wassail *sb.*

60. Geoffrey of Monmouth, *Historia regum Britanniae: a variant version*, ed. J. Hammer (Cambridge, MA, 1951), p. 113; *Le Roman de Brut de Wace*, ed. I. Arnold (2 vols, Paris, 1938, 1940), i, pp. 369–70: ll. 6963–6: 'Custume est, sire, en lur pais, / Quant ami beivent entre amis, / Que cil dit "Wesheil" qui deit beivre, / & E "Drincheheil" ki deit receivre.'

61. *Middle English metrical romances*, ed. W. H. French and C. B. Hale (2 vols, New York, 1930), ii, p. 961, ll. 317–20: 'When þou seest þe cuppe anon, But þou sei "passilodion", Þou drynkis not þis day. Sely Adam shall sitt þe hende, And onswere with "berafrynde" '; ll. 325–30: 'Passilodyon, þat is þis: Whoso drynkys furst, iwys, Wesseyle þe mare dele! Berafrynde also, i wene, Hit is to make þe cup clene, And fylle hit ofte full wele.'

62. HMC, *The manuscripts of Lincoln, Bury St Edmund's, and Great Grimsby Corporations, and of the Dean and Chapters of Worcester and Lichfield* . . . (1895), p. 124.

63. *CO*, p. 121.

64. *MM*, p. 171, ll. 816–18.

65. 'Ounk n'i out damaisele / Qui regard esquiele, / Ne taunt cointe eschançun / Qui serve de beissun, Ne ki port mazerin / Ne grant coupe d'or fin / D'art vin ne [de] claré, / Burgerastre n'erbé': *The Anglo-Norman text of 'Le lai du cor'*, ed. C. T. Erickson (Anglo-Norman Text Society, 24; 1973), p. 34, ll. 85–92.

66. C. B. Hieatt and R. Jones, 'Culinary collections edited from British Library Manuscripts Additional 32085 and Royal 12.C. xii', *Speculum* 61 (1986), p. 866.

67. *A leechbook, or a collection of medical recipes of the fifteenth century*, ed. W. R. Dawson (1934), p. 92, no. 243.

68. *The English works of John Gower*, ed. G. C. Macaulay (2 vols, EETS, ES, 81–2; 1900–1), i, pp. 173–4 (Confessio Amantis, Book 6, ll. 249–51): 'In cold I brenne and frese in hete: And thanne I drinke a biter swete With dreie lippe and yhen wete.'

69. *Chaucer*, p. 750, The Romaunt of the Rose, ll. 6028–30: 'Ladyes shullen hem such pepir brewe, / If that they fall into her laas, / That they for woo mowe seyn "allas!" '

70. *The Cyrurgie of Guy de Chauliac*, ed. M. S. Ogden (EETS, OS, 265; 1971), p. 95. See Chapter 10, below, for medicinal waters.

71. *CI*, pp. 142–3, no. 197; p. 186.

72. *CSACSPW*, ii, pp. 77–9, 179–80.

73. *A talkyng of þe loue of God*, ed. M. S. Westra (The Hague, 1950), pp. xiii, 26: 'Swettore art þou þen hony or milk in mouþe, meode, meþ or piʒement maad wiþ spices swete, or eny lykinde licour þat ouʒwher may be founden.'

74. *LV I*, pp. 109, 112.

75. Fransson, *Middle English surnames of occupation*, p. 79.

76. *The pipe roll of the bishopric of Winchester 1210–1211*, ed. N. R. Holt (Manchester, 1964), pp. 16, 30, 38, 60, 120.

77. *PP*, i, p. 685 (C XX, ll. 409–10): 'May no pyement ne pomade ne preciouse drynkes / Moiste me to þe fulle in my furst slokke'; *HAME*, ii, p. 677.

78. E. Kölbing, 'Kleine Publicationen aus der Auchinleck-hs', *Englische Studien* 7 (1884), p. 105, ll. 170–4: 'Piment, clare, no no licour, / Milke, perre, no no meþ; / & who so loveþ hem wiþ honour, / No dye he never schamely deþ / Þurch gilt!' Although glossed on p. 110 as a dish of peas, onions and spices, it is a drink of perry here.

79. *GH*, pp. 101, 128.

80. B. J. Whiting and H. W. Whiting, *Proverbs, sentences, and proverbial phrases from English writings mainly before 1500* (Cambridge, MA, 1968), pp. 402–3.

81. J. C. Hodgson, *A history of Northumberland*, vol. 7: *The parish of Edlingham, with the chapelry of Bolton . . .* (Newcastle-upon-Tyne, 1904), p. 426.

82. *The customary of the Cathedral Priory Church of Norwich: MS 465 in the Library of Corpus Christi College, Cambridge*, ed. J. B. L. Tolhurst (Henry Bradshaw Society, 82; 1948), p. 243, immediately before an entry dated 1379.

83. *PP*, i, p. 308 (Z VII, ll. 285–6).

84. *TFCCB*, pp. 15, 36.

85. *Anglo-Norman medicine*, ed. T. Hunt (2 vols, Cambridge, 1994–7), ii, p. 162 (no. 106).

86. *Liber quotidianus contrarotulatoris garderobae anno regni regis Edwardi primi vicesimo octavo A.D. MCCXCIX & MCCC*, ed. Anon. (1787), p. 57.

87. Rose, *Wine trade in medieval Europe*, pp. 14–17.

88. *A roll of the household expenses of Richard de Swinfield, Bishop of Hereford*, ed. J. Webb (2 vols, Camden Society, old series, 59, 62; 1854–5), i, p. 59.

89. *HAME*, ii, pp. 526, 540.

90. *BSP*, A xxiiii Arma.

91. *BSP*, E i Ebrietas, Art. ii: iiii.

92. Rose, *Wine trade in medieval Europe*, pp. 14, 61–4.

93. *PLP*, i, pp. 652–4, no. 409: 'Wherfore ȝe had nede to warne Wylliam Gogyne and hys felawes to purvey them off wyne inow, for every man berythe me on hande that þe towne schalbe dronkyn drye as Yorke was whan the Kynge was there.'

94. TNA, E 101/79/1, mem. 5r, 7r.

95. E 101/79/3, mem. 3–4r (1339–40); E 101/79/5, mem. 2r (1340–1); Rose, *Wine trade in medieval Europe*, pp. 101–2.

96. TNA, E 101/79/1, mem. 17r; E 101/79/5, mem. 8r.

97. *CSACSPW*, ii, pp. 77–9.

98. Norfolk RO, DCN 1/1/1, Master of the Cellar, 1263–4, mem. 1r.

99. DCN 1/1/25, Master of the Cellar, 1315–16, mem. 1r.

100. DCN 1/1/5, Master of the Cellar, 1279–80, mem. 1d.

101. DCN 1/1/7, Master of the Cellar, 1283–4, mem. 2d.

102. DCN 1/1/11, Master of the Cellar, 1291–2, mem. 2r.

103. DCN 1/1/22, Master of the Cellar, 1310–11, mem. 1r.

104. DCN 1/1/16, Master of the Cellar, 1303–4, mem. 1r; DCN 1/1/23, Master of the Cellar, 1313–14, mem. 1r.

105. J. Bellis, 'The dregs of trembling, the draught of salvation: the dual symbolism of the cup in medieval literature', *Journal of Medieval History* 37 (2011), pp. 47–61.

106. For the display of plate on great occasions, see *The receyt of the Ladie Kateryne*, ed. G. Kipling (EETS, OS, 296; 1990), pp. 66, 75; the Second Northumberland Household Book, Oxford, Bodleian Library, MS Eng. hist. b. 208, f. 34v; for the connections of plate, C. M. Woolgar, 'Treasure, material possessions and the bishops of late medieval England', in *The prelate in England and Europe, 1300–1560*, ed. M. Heale (York, 2014), pp. 173–190, especially pp. 185–6.

107. JRULM, MS Latin 235, f. 23r.

108. MS Latin 235, f. 28r.

109. MS Latin 235, ff. 28r–29r.

110. R. W. Lightbown, *Secular goldsmiths' work in medieval France: a history* (Reports of the Research Committee of the Society of Antiquaries of London, 36; 1978), pp. 20–1; *The register of Henry Chichele, Archbishop of Canterbury 1414–1443*, vol. 2: *Wills proved*

before the Archbishop or his commissaries, ed. E. F. Jacob and H. C. Johnson (Canterbury and York Society, 42; 1937), pp. 82, 90; see also M. Campbell, 'Gold, silver and precious stones', in *English medieval industries: craftsmen, techniques, products*, ed. J. Blair and N. Ramsay (1991), pp. 156–8.

111. Cf. *AND* bolle 1.
112. LPL, Register of William Courtenay, ff. 203v–204r.
113. Register of William Courtenay, f. 200v, presumably like the bowl left by Beatrice, Lady de Roos, in 1414, to her daughter, Elizabeth, Lady Clifford: *TE I*, p. 375, 'unam magnam peciam cum vii peciis introclusis vocatum magnum boll'.
114. LPL, Register of Simon Sudbury, f. 86r.
115. *OED* beaker *sb.*; LPL, Register of William Whittlesey, ff. 111v–112v.
116. LPL, Register of William Courtenay, f. 214v.
117. Register of William Courtenay, f. 200r.
118. *Register of Henry Chichele*, vol. 2, ed. Jacob and Johnson, p. 517.
119. LPL, Register of Thomas Arundel, I, f. 210r.
120. LPL, Register of Simon Sudbury, f. 97r.
121. *TE I*, pp. 410–11.
122. LPL, Register of Simon Sudbury, f. 108v; also *TE I*, pp. 113–14.
123. *A consuetudinary of the fourteenth century for the refectory of the house of S. Swithun in Winchester*, ed. G. W. Kitchin (Hampshire Record Society 6, i; 1886), pp. 7, 20–1.
124. *Register of Henry Chichele*, vol. 2, ed. Jacob and Johnson, p. 323.
125. BL, Add. MS 60584, f. 14r; C. M. Woolgar, *The senses in late medieval England* (New Haven, 2006), pp. 56–7.
126. *ERT*, pp. 42, 214–15 (R760–2), 327.
127. Norfolk RO, Norwich Consistory Court Records, Will Register 1 Heydon (1370–82), f. 42r.
128. LPL, Register of William Whittlesey, f. 123v.
129. Norfolk RO, Norwich Consistory Court Records, Will Register 1 Heydon (1370–82), ff. 3r–v.
130. *Register of Henry Chichele*, vol. 2, ed. Jacob and Johnson, pp. 560, 562.
131. *CS*, ii, p. 787.
132. BL, Add. MS 88973, f. 90 i, recto.
133. Norfolk RO, DCN 1/8/48, inventory of the refectory, 1393–4; and DCN 1/8/56, 1410–11.
134. Weight calculated as if using Tower pounds, but there is no related evidence for which system of weight for precious metals was in use at Norwich at this point. 'Heaven ale' is perhaps self-explanatory; 'runnale' less so – perhaps from ME rinel, a brook (AN rinnelle); or ME rininge, 'touching'; or 'rimale', perhaps something to do with poetry.
135. *CSACSPW*, i, pp. 162, 180, 184–5.
136. Norfolk RO, DCN, 1/8/119.
137. S. Sweetinburgh, 'Remembering the dead at dinner-time', in *Everyday objects: medieval and early modern material culture and its meanings*, ed. T. Hamling and C. Richardson (Farnham, 2010), pp. 257–66; W. J. St John Hope, 'Of the English medieval drinking bowls called mazers', *Archaeologia* 50 (1887), pp. 176–81.
138. *TREWE*, p. 254.

4 Bread, Meat and Dairy Foods

1. *Mirk*, i, p. 91 (loaves and fishes); ii, pp. 199 (St Laurence), 265 (Lord's Prayer).
2. *Llandaff episcopal acta 1140–1287*, ed. D. Crouch (South Wales Record Society, 5; 1988), p. 92, no. 101.
3. P. Binski, 'Function, date, imagery, style and context of the Westminster Retable', in *The Westminster Retable: history, technique, conservation*, ed. P. Binski and A. Massing (Cambridge, 2009), pp. 16–44, especially pp. 28–9; M. A. Michael, 'The *Bible moralisée*, the *Golden Legend* and the *Salvator mundi*: observations on the iconography of the Westminster Retable', *Antiquaries Journal* 94 (2014), pp. 101, 109.

4. See C. M. Woolgar, 'The language of food and cooking', in *The language of the professions: proceedings of the 2013 Harlaxton Symposium*, ed. M. Carruthers (Donington, 2015), pp. 36–43.
5. *Hali meiðhad*, ed. B. Millett (EETS, OS, 284; 1982), p. 19.
6. TNA, JUST 2/18, mem. 3r.
7. See, for example, a London court case of 1327: H. T. Riley, *Memorials of London and London life, in the XIIIth, XIVth and XVth centuries . . .* (1868), pp. 162–5.
8. *MM*, p. 301, the 'Boke of Curtasye', ll. 59–60.
9. *An alphabet of tales: an English fifteenth century translation of the Alphabetum narrationum of Étienne de Besançon*, ed. M. M. Banks (2 vols, EETS, OS, 126–7; 1904–5), i, pp. 203–4.
10. D. J. Stone, 'The consumption of field crops', in *FME*, pp. 11–26.
11. John 6:9: 'Est puer unus hic qui habet quinque panes hordiacios et duos pisces.' For alms loaves, see Chapters 8 and 11; also Woolgar, 'Language of food and cooking', p. 42.
12. *Dan Michel's Ayenbite of Inwyt, or remorse of conscience*, ed. R. Morris, rev. P. Gradon (EETS, OS, 23; 1965), p. 205: 'Þe levayne zoureþ þet doȝ and hit draȝþ to smac.'
13. *BA*, ii, p. 959: 'Sour-dowe hatte fermentum, for it makeþ paste ferment and makeþ it also arise'; 'to heve past and bred, and to chaunge and amende þe savour þerof'.
14. *BA*, ii, p. 938: 'Mele is ygrounde at mylle and sifted wiþ a syfe, and ymedlid with hoot water and wiþ sour dowe to have the bettre savour, and yknedde and ymoldid to þe schap of loves, and ybake þerafter.'
15. See Woolgar, 'Language of food and cooking'.
16. *The book of the knight of La Tour-Landry*, ed. T. Wright (EETS, OS, 33; 1868), pp. 140–1: 'Notwithstonding this woman a litelle before, for her playser and disporte, toke upon her to make levein for brede of whete, and with her hondes as thei were, pasted with the levein that she handeled, al floury, in the estate as she was, she comithe forthe with gret ioye and enbraced hym plesauntly betwene her armes . . .'
17. Walter de Bibbesworth, *Le tretiz . . .*, ed. W. Rothwell (Aberystwyth, 2009) pp. 18–19, ll. 368–409 (and rubric before l. 368).
18. *TE III*, pp. 106, 112.
19. J. Greenstreet, 'Early Kentish wills', *Archaeologia Cantiana* 11 (1877), p. 380: 'Also I wylle that my wyff shalnot take awey oute of my mesuage the querne nor the knedyng trowe in no wyse.'
20. *TE III*, p. 112.
21. Norfolk RO, DCN 1/4/75, Sacrist's inventory, Michaelmas 1436, mem. 1r.
22. *CI*, p. 52, no. 43.
23. SBTRO, BRT 1/3/50, mem. 2r.
24. J. Davis, 'Baking for the common good: a reassessment of the assize of bread in medieval England', *Economic History Review*, second series, 57 (2004), pp. 465–502; J. Davis, *Medieval market morality: life, law and ethics in the English marketplace, 1200–1500* (Cambridge, 2012), pp. 233–41.
25. 'Mui de furment a dener, guay celui qui denier n'a': 'mui' here in the general sense of 'a measure' rather than 4 bushels. E. Stengel, 'Die beiden Sammlungen altfranzösischer Sprichwörter in der Oxforder Handschrift Rawlinson C 641', *Zeitschrift für französische Sprache und Litteratur* 21 (1899), p. 8, no. 167.
26. Davis, *Medieval market morality*, pp. 312–14.
27. *The Oak Book of Southampton*, ed. P. Studer (3 vols, Southampton Record Society, 10–12; 1910–11), i, pp. 68–9.
28. Norfolk RO, NCR Case 16d/1, f. 27r.
29. 'Suef eut pain en altrui forn': Stengel, 'Die beiden Sammlungen', p. 8, no. 164.
30. Stengel, 'Die beiden Sammlungen', p. 5, no. 36: 'Bel servise trait pain de main.'
31. W. A. Pantin, 'A medieval collection of Latin and English proverbs and riddles from the Rylands Latin MS 394', *Bulletin of the John Rylands Library* 14 (1930) pp. 81–104: p. 94, nos 16 and 18, 'Hotte wortes make harde crustes nesche', 'The more cruste the lasse cromme.'

32. M. Förster, 'Die mittelenglische Sprichwörtersammlung in Douce 52', in *Festschrift zum XII. allgemeinen deutschen Neuphilologentage in München, Pfingsten 1906*, ed. E. Stottreither (Erlangen, 1906), p. 57, no. 142.
33. e.g. *The cartulary of the priory of St Denys near Southampton*, ed. E. O. Blake (2 vols, Southampton Records Series, 24–5; 1981), ii, p. 213.
34. *PP*, i, p. 25 (A, Prologue, ll. 105–6): 'Hote pyes, hote! / Goode geese and gris! Go we dyne, go we!'
35. D. L. Farmer, 'Marketing the produce of the countryside, 1200–1500', in *AHEW III*, pp. 388–95; D. J. Stone, 'The consumption and supply of birds in late medieval England', in *FME*, pp. 152–61.
36. SBTRO, BRT 1/3/80, mem. 1r.
37. *A myrour to lewde men and wymmen: a prose version of the Speculum Vitae, ed. from BL MS Harley 45*, ed. V. Nelson (Heidelberg, 1981), p. 147: 'Þe oxe þat men wole holde to lyf men fediþ him wiþ harde fode & putteþ him under ʒok, but þat oxe þat schal be slayn to larder hit schal be fedde wiþ þe beste fode & fele no travaile.'
38. U. Albarella, 'Pig husbandry and pork consumption in medieval England', in *FME*, pp. 72–87; C. M. Woolgar, 'Meat and dairy products in late medieval England', in *FME*, pp. 88–101; East Sussex RO, Add. MS 4903, mem. 1r; *Accounts of the cellarers of Battle Abbey 1275–1513*, ed. E. Searle and B. Ross (Sydney, 1967), pp. 49, 59.
39. *The Plumpton letters and papers*, ed. J. Kirby (Camden Society, 5th series, 8; 1996), p. 152.
40. E. Smirke, 'Notice of the custumal of Bleadon, Somerset, and of the agricultural tenures of the thirteenth century', in *Memoirs illustrative of the history and antiquities of Wiltshire and the City of Salisbury, communicated to the annual meeting of the Archaeological Institute of Great Britain and Ireland, held at Salisbury, July, 1849* (1851), p. 206.
41. *FL*, iv, pp. 207–8; G. R. Owst, *Literature and pulpit in medieval England: a neglected chapter in the history of English letters and of the English people* (Cambridge, 1933): p. 37 talks of the cries from the village slaughterhouse, citing BL, MS Harley 2398, f. 25b, probably derived from *BSP*, Mors – but this is to anticipate the existence of these buildings.
42. See below, Chapter 10.
43. DUL, DCP Cellarer's account, 1438–9 (A), mem. 2r, 3d.
44. Cellarer's account, 1443–4 (A), mem. 3r.
45. Norfolk RO, DCN 1/4/75, Sacrist's inventory, Michaelmas 1436, mem. 1r; mentioned in many Durham cellarers' accounts, e.g. DUL, DCP Cellarer's account, 1467–8 (A), mem. 1r.
46. *MO*, p. 290, ll. 26210–32.
47. *Lydgate's Fall of princes*, ed. H. Bergen (4 vols, EETS, ES, 121–4; 1924–7), i, p. 264, book 2, l. 2271: 'Boistous bocheris, al bespreynt with blood'.
48. Edward of Norwich, *The master of game*, ed. W. A. Baillie-Grohman and F. N. Baillie-Grohman (1909), p. 118.
49. *Jacob's Well, an Englisht treatise on the cleansing of man's conscience . . .*, ed. A. Brandeis (EETS, OS, 115; 1900), p. 262; *The Coventry Leet Book or mayor's register*, ed. M. D. Harris (4 parts in 1; EETS, OS, 134, 135, 138, 146; 1907–13), p. 361; *Beverley town documents*, ed. A. F. Leach (Selden Society, 14; 1900), pp. lvi, 29.
50 *The pilgrimage of the lyf of the manhode*, ed. W. A. Wright (Roxburghe Club, 91; 1869), p. 129: 'Thow seye nevere in thi lyfe mastyf ne bicche in bocherye that so gladliche wolde ete raw flesh as I ete it.'
51. P. Dunn, 'Trade', in *Medieval Norwich*, ed. C. Rawcliffe and R. Wilson (2004), pp. 230–3; Norfolk RO, NCR Case 16d/1, f. 17v.
52. NCR Case 16d/1, f. 40r: 'a shepis hed and þe brede'.
53. Ramón A. Banegas López, *Europa carnívora. Comprar y comer carne en el mundo bajomedieval* (Gijón, 2012), p. 146; P. E. Jones, *The butchers of London: a history of the Worshipful Company of Butchers of the City of London* (1976), pp. 106–8.
54. *EARD I*, p. 38; *NHB*, p. 135.
55. East Sussex RO, MS RYE 60/2, ff. 43v, 68r.

56. MS RYE 60/3, f. 7r.
57. *CI*, p. 110; hocks: *TFCCB*, pp. 25, 37, 51, 86; sirloin: *The Stonor letters and papers 1290-1483*, vol. 1, ed. C. L. Kingsford (Camden Society, 3rd series, 29; 1919), p. 40; SBTRO, BRT 1/3/32, mem. 1r; BRT 1/3/49, mem. 1r.
58. Norfolk RO, Le Strange NH5 (recte 6), mem. 1r; NH6 (recte 7), mem. 4r.
59. LPL, MS 1213, p. 315.
60. *Historiae Dunelmensis scriptores tres: Gaufridus de Coldingham, Robertus de Graystanes, et Willielmus de Chambre*, ed. J. Raine (Surtees Society, 9; 1839), p. 57.
61. DUL, DCP Cellarers' accounts, 1438–9 (A), mem. 2r; 1440–1 (A), mem. 2r, 3d.
62. Cellarer's account, 1443 (A), mem. 2d.
63. Cellarer's account, 1444–5, mem. 3d.
64. Cellarers' accounts, 1445–6 (A), mem. 1r; 1446–7 (A), mem. 1r; 1447–8, mem. 1r; 1448–9 (A), mem. 1r.
65. Cellarer's account, 1455–6, mem. 1r.
66. Cellarers' accounts, 1459–60, mem. 1r; 1460–1 (A), mem. 1r; 1461–2 (A), mem. 1r; 1462–3, mem. 1r.
67. Cellarers' accounts, 1465–6 (A), mem. 1r; 1466–7 (A), mem. 1r; 1467–8 (A), mem. 1r; 1468–9 (A), mem. 1r; 1469–70, mem. 1r; 1471–2 (A), mem. 1r; 1472 (A), mem. 1r; 1472–3 (A), mem. 1r; 1473–4 (A), mem. 1r; 1475–6, mem. 1r; 1476–7, mem. 1r; 1477–8, mem. 1r; 1478–9 (A), mem. 1r; 1479–80, mem. 1r.
68. *Privy purse expenses of Elizabeth of York: wardrobe accounts of Edward the Fourth, with a memoir of Elizabeth of York, and notes*, ed. N. H. Nicolas (1830), p. 64.
69. There are recipes for filled 'mawe' of swine, 'franche-mol', a filled sheep's stomach, and filled bladders: *TFCCB*, pp. 38, 39; *CI*, p. 112.
70. M. Carlin, 'Fast food and urban living standards in medieval England', in *Food and eating in medieval Europe*, ed. M. Carlin and J. T. Rosenthal (1998), pp. 27–51; M. Carlin, 'Putting dinner on the table in medieval London', in *London and the kingdom: essays in honour of Caroline M. Barron. Proceedings of the 2004 Harlaxton Symposium*, ed. M. Davies and A. Prescott (Donington, 2008), p. 68; C. M. Woolgar, 'The cook', in *Historians on Chaucer: the 'General Prologue' to the Canterbury Tales*, ed. S. H. Rigby, with A. J. Minnis (Oxford, 2014), pp. 262–76.
71. *The English works of Wyclif*, ed. F. D. Matthew (EETS, OS, 74; 1880), p. 82: 'Þei sillen a faat goos for litel or nouȝt, but þe garlek costiþ many shillyngis.'
72. *AND*: agis; hagis; hagiz (*pl.* hegges), *s.*; Walter de Bibbesworth, *Le tretiz*, ed. Rothwell, p. 47, ll. 1035–6.
73. *HAME*, i, p. 244; *TFCCB*, p. 39; *OED* haggis sb.
74. *CI*, p. 100.
75. A. Hussey, 'Calf's gadyr', *Notes and Queries*, 10th series, 2, no. 50 (1904), pp. 467–8.
76. Norfolk RO, DCN 1/4/75, Sacrist's inventory, Michaelmas 1436, mem. 1r.
77. DUL, DCP Cellarer's account, 1443–4 (A), mem. 3r.
78. Cellarer's account, 1447–8, mem. 1r.
79. Cellarer's account, 1465–6 (A), mem. 1r.
80. L. Keen, 'Coastal salt production in Norman England', *Anglo-Norman Studies* 11 (1988), pp. 133–79; *Salt: the study of an ancient industry: report on the Salt Weekend held at the University of Essex, 20, 21, 22 September 1974*, ed. K. W. de Brisay and K. A. Evans (Colchester, 1975); witness also the frequency of Salter as a surname: G. Fransson, *Middle English surnames of occupation 1100–1350* (Lund Studies in English, 3; 1935), pp. 70–1.
81. TNA, JUST 2/67, mem. 20d.
82. *The pipe roll of the bishopric of Winchester 1210–1211*, ed. N. R. Holt (Manchester, 1964), pp. 9, 119–20.
83. *The proverbs of Alfred: an emended text*, ed. O. Arngart (Lund: Scripta minora regiae societatis humaniorum litterarum Lundensis, 1979–1980, 1; 1978), pp. 5, 15, 27.
84. *HAME*, ii, p. 545.

85. *CI*, p. 73.
86. See the discussion of salting deer: J. Birrell, 'Procuring, preparing, and serving venison', in *FME*, pp. 180–4.
87. *CO*, p. 466: 'Pouder hom with salt al a nyght, and on the mornynge wash of the salte.'
88. *Wynnere and Wastoure*, ed. S. Trigg (EETS, OS, 297; 1990), p. 9, l. 250: 'The bemys bended at the rofe, siche bakone there hynges'; also flitches in *TE II*, p. 261.
89. *LV II*, pp. 95, 98, 104–5.
90. W. Dugdale, *Monasticon Anglicanum*, ed. J. Caley, H. Ellis and B. Bandinel (new edition, 6 vols in 8, 1846), i, pp. 443–5; also discussed in E. Power, *Medieval English nunneries, c.1275 to 1535* (Cambridge, 1922), pp. 563–8.
91. *HAME*, i, pp. 192, 193, 204.
92. *HAME*, i, p. 232.
93. *HAME*, i, pp. 360–1.
94. A. Paravicini-Bagliani, *The pope's body*, trans. D. S. Peterson (Chicago, 2000), pp. 75–81.
95. Unavailable to Piers Plowman in his hunger: *PP*, i, p. 308 (B VI, ll. 283–4): 'And yet I seye, by my soule, I have no salt bacon / Ne no cokeney, by Crist, coloppes to maken!'
96. D. Owen, 'Bacon and eggs: Bishop Buckingham and superstition in Lincolnshire', in *Popular belief and practices*, ed. G. J. Cuming and D. Baker (Studies in Church History, 8; Cambridge, 1972), p. 141.
97. J. Laughton and C. Dyer, 'Seasonal patterns of trade in the later Middle Ages: buying and selling at Melton Mowbray, Leicestershire, 1400–1520', *Nottingham Medieval Studies* 46 (2002), pp. 162–84, especially pp. 173–80.
98. TNA, JUST 2/18, mem. 67d.
99. DUL, DCP Cellarer's account, 1443–4 (A), mem. 3r.
100. *Three receptaria from medieval England: the languages of medicine in the fourteenth century*, ed. T. Hunt (Medium Aevum Monographs, new series 21, Oxford, 2001), p. 140, no. 585.
101. B. F. Harvey, *Living and dying in England, 1100–1540: the monastic experience* (Oxford, 1993), p. 56.
102. Norfolk RO, DCN 1/2/1, mem. 1r; DCN 1/2/14.
103. *LV II*, p. 90.
104. *A noble boke off cookry ffor a prynce houssolde or eny other estately houssolde*, ed. R. Napier (1882), p. 55: 'Take salt lard of pork and dice it smale.'
105. *TFCCB*, p. 49.
106. BL, Add. MS 21480 f. 23v.
107. Woolgar, 'Meat and dairy products', in *FME*, pp. 94–101. There were some egregious exceptions: see Chapter 8 and Abingdon Abbey.
108. D. L. Farmer, 'Marketing the produce of the countryside, 1200–1500', in *AHEW III*, pp. 401–4.
109. J. Laughton, *Life in a late medieval city: Chester 1275–1520* (Oxford, 2008), p. 43.
110. *Catholicon Anglicum: an English-Latin wordbook*, ed. S. J. H. Herrtage and H. B. Wheatley (EETS, OS, 75; 1881), p. 50.
111. *Plumpton letters*, ed. Kirby, p. 41.
112. *The household book of Queen Isabella of England for the fifth regnal year of Edward II 8th July 1311 to 7th July 1312*, ed. F. D. Blackley and G. Hermansen (University of Alberta, Classical and Historical Studies, 1; 1971), p. 132.
113. *The parliament rolls of medieval England, 1275–1504*, vol. 11: *Henry VI, 1432–1445*, ed. A. Curry (2005), p. 290.
114. *The Cely letters 1472–1488*, ed. A. Hanham (EETS, OS, 273; 1975), p. 78.
115. C. Dyer, 'Alternative agriculture: goats in medieval England', in *People, landscape and alternative agriculture: essays for Joan Thirsk*, ed. R. W. Hoyle (*Agricultural History Review*, supplement series, 3; 2004), pp. 20–38.
116. *AHEW III*, pp. 875–7.
117. TNA, JUST 2/67, mem. 34r, rot 1r.

118. *Walter of Henley and other treatises on estate management and accounting*, ed. D. Oschinsky (Oxford, 1971), pp. 200–1, 208–9, 430–1.
119. *Walter of Henley*, ed. Oschinsky, pp. 144–5, 180–1, 332–5, 373–6.
120. *Old English homilies of the twelfth century*, series 2, ed. R. Morris (EETS, OS, 53; 1873), p. 163: talking of the clerk, 'Ac his daie þe is his hore'; *The Simonie: a parallel-text edition,* ed. D. Embree and E. Urquhart (Heidelberg, 1991), p. 81: 'He taketh al that he may ... And leveth thare behinde a theef and an hore, A serjaunt and a deie that leden a sory lif: Al so faire hii gon to bedde as housebonde and wif.'
121. *Walter of Henley*, ed. Oschinsky, pp. 39, 208, 462; new edition and commentary in M. Carlin, 'Cheating the boss: Robert Carpenter's embezzlement instructions (1261×1268) and employee fraud in medieval England', in *Commercial activity, markets and entrepreneurs in the Middle Ages: essays in honour of Richard Britnell,* ed. B. Dodds and C. D. Liddy (Woodbridge, 2011), pp. 183–97.
122. *Walter of Henley*, ed. Oschinsky, pp. 179–82, 334–5.
123. *Robert of Brunne's Handlyng synne . . .,* ed. F. J. Furnivall (2 vols, EETS, OS, 119, 123; 1901, 1903), i, pp. 19–21, ll. 501–56.
124. *Chaucer,* p. 253, ll. 2843–6: 'Hir bord was served most with whit and blak – / Milk and broun breed, in which she foond no lak, / Seynd [broiled or smoked] bacoun, and somtyme an ey or tweye, / For she was, as it were, a maner deye.' 'White and black', i.e. as opposed to coloured (and suspect) food and drink, such as wine.
125. SBTRO, BRT 1/3/105, mem. 2d.
126. *EARD II,* p. 525; *EARD III,* p. 577; DUL, DCP Cellarer's account, 1446–7 (A); *Wellingborough manorial accounts A.D. 1258–1323 from the account rolls of Crowland Abbey,* ed. F. M. Page (Northamptonshire Record Society, 8; 1935), p. 124; *TFCCB,* p. 36.
127. *Materials for the history of Thomas Becket, Archbishop of Canterbury,* ed. J. C. Robertson (7 vols, Rolls series, 67; 1875–85), ii, pp. 153–4.
128. TNA, JUST 2/203, mem. 1r; JUST 2/66, mem. 12r.
129. *Lanfrank's 'Science of Cirurgie',* ed. R. V. Fleischhacker (EETS, OS, 102; 1894), p. 21: 'Riȝt as þe rundelis [rennet] & þe mylk maken a chese, so boþe the spermes of man & womman maken generacioun of embrioun.'
130. *OED* cheeselip *sb.*[1]
131. Pantin, 'Medieval collection of Latin and English proverbs', p. 92, no. 19: 'Fowle salte is good inow for foule butter'.
132. *A noble boke off cookry,* ed. Napier, p. 32.
133. *Ein mittelenglisches Medizinbuch,* ed. F. Heinrich (Halle, 1896), pp. 178–9, 186: 'Tak May butter, mad of raw crayme, & ewe mylke wyþ dew water, & gyf þou may noo buttre gete of ewe mylke, take buttre of cow mylke'; 'raw cramyn of ewe mylke in May'.
134. *Ein mittelenglisches Medizinbuch,* ed. Heinrich, p. 217.
135. *Walter of Henley*, ed. Oschinsky, pp. 332–5.
136. *HAME,* i, p. 153; for the date, J. R. Maddicott, 'Follower, leader, pilgrim, saint: Robert de Vere, Earl of Oxford, at the shrine of Simon de Montfort, 1273', *English Historical Review* 109 (1994), pp. 641–53.
137. *PP,* i, p. 190 (B V, ll. 91–2): 'I wold be gladder, by God! þat Gybbe hadde meschaunce / Than þouȝ I hadde þis woke ywonne a weye of Essex chese.'
138. Dugdale, *Monasticon,* i, p. 444.
139. *MM,* part 1, p. 155, ll. 558–9.
140. DUL, DCP Cellarer's account, 1438–9 (A), mem. 2r.
141. Cellarer's account, 1443–4 (A), mem. 3r.
142. *Bozon,* pp. 14–15; *FL,* iv, pp. 242, 419.
143. *Bozon,* p. 215; also in 'Nicolai Bozon exempla quaedam', in *FL,* iv, p. 261: 'For was hyt never myn kynd, Chese in well to fynd.'
144. *Ten fifteenth-century comic poems,* ed. M. M. Furrow (New York, 1985), p. 39, ll. 43–4: 'as red as any scarlette'.
145. *BA,* ii, pp. 1324–38, especially pp. 1332–4; for later analyses, see K. Albala, *Eating right in the Renaissance* (Berkeley, 2002), pp. 93, 105, 229–30, 256, 260.

146. *MM*, part 1, pp. 123–4, ll. 81–95.
147. *CO*, pp. 447, 463.
148. See Chapter 8.
149. *Modus cenandi*, in *MM*, part 2, pp. 40–1.
150. BL, Add. MS 34213, ff. 22r, 29r.
151. Add. MS 34213, f. 36r.
152. Add. MS 34213, f. 50v.
153. C. Dyer, 'Changes in diet in the late Middle Ages: the case of harvest workers',
     Agricultural History Review 36 (1988), pp. 21–37; M. Müller, 'Food, hierarchy, and class
     conflict', in *Survival and discord in medieval society: essays in honour of Christopher
     Dyer*, ed. R. Goddard, J. Langdon and M. Müller (Turnhout, 2010), pp. 231–48.
154. *The Southampton steward's book of 1492–93 and the terrier of 1495*, ed. A. Thick
     (Southampton Records Series, 38; 1995), pp. 53–7.
155. East Sussex RO, MS RYE 60/3, f. 70r.
156. *Rolls of the justices in eyre, being the rolls of pleas and assizes for Lincolnshire, 1218–19,
     and Worcestershire, 1221*, ed. D. M. Stenton (Selden Society, 53; 1934), p. 229.
157. *Inquisitions and assessments relating to feudal aids . . .*, vol. 6, ed. H. C. Maxwell Lyte
     (1920), p. 152.
158. *Calendar of the Patent Rolls preserved in the Public Record Office: Edward II*, vol. 3:
     A.D. 1321–1324 (1904), p. 87.
159. *Supplications from England and Wales in the registers of the Apostolic Penitentiary
     1410–1503*, vol. 2: *1464–1492*, ed. P. D. Clarke and P. N. R. Zutshi (Canterbury and York
     Society, 104; 2014), p. 26, no. 1361; p. 29, no. 1372.
160. C. M. Woolgar, 'Group diets in late medieval England', in *FME*, p. 192.

5 Sauces and Spices, Sugars and Preserves

1. *BA*, ii, pp. 875–6.
2. *BA*, ii, p. 1109: 'Som tyme in þe water in þe which fleissh is y-sode is spicerye y-do, and
   þer of is y-made dyverse sauce; and kepeþ and saveþ þe fleissh in his kynde and good-
   nesse; and amendeþ it boþe in smelle and in savour . . .'
3. The earliest recipes for sauces in use in medieval England can now be dated to the
   second half of the twelfth century: G. E. M. Gasper and others, *Zinziber: sauces from
   Poitou. Twelfth-century culinary recipies from Sidney Sussex College, Cambridge, MS
   51* (2015). I am very grateful to Dr Giles Gasper for letting me see the text of his contributions to this volume in advance of publication.
4. *FL*, iv, p. 313.
5. *A myrour to lewde men and wymmen: a prose version of the Speculum Vitae*, ed. from BL
   MS Harley 45, ed. V. Nelson (Heidelberg, 1981), p. 209: 'For all manere mete þat is foode
   to man is good to hem þat beþ goode, and specialiche to hem þat wole use hit wiþ skile
   & mesure, and ete it wiþ þe sauce of þe drede of God; for men schulde alwey drede God
   so þat he ne schulde not use þat God sent but in mesure wiþoute outrage, & love God
   & þanke him of his sone.'
6. P. Freedman, *Out of the East: spices and the medieval imagination* (New Haven, 2008),
   pp. 50–75.
7. P. Spufford, *Power and profit: the merchant in medieval Europe* (2004), pp. 309–15.
   Rents of nugatory value – cloves: *The English register of Godstow Nunnery, near Oxford*,
   ed. A. Clark (2 vols, EETS, OS, 130, 142; 1906, 1911), ii, pp. 117, 449; peppercorn rents:
   Calendar of the Patent Rolls preserved in the Public Record Office: Edward III, vol. 4:
   A.D. 1338–1340 (1898), p. 127 (1338); *Calendar of the Patent Rolls preserved in the
   Public Record Office: Edward III*, vol. 12: *A.D. 1361–1364* (1912), p. 460 (1364).
8. *HAME*, i, pp. 108–9.
9. *HAME*, i, p. 126; *Manners and household expenses of England in the thirteenth and
   fifteenth centuries*, ed. T. H. Turner (Roxburghe Club, 1841), p. 7.

10. P. Nightingale, *A medieval mercantile community: the Grocers' Company and the politics and trade of London 1000–1485* (New Haven, 1995), pp. 7, 75, 95–6, 104–6.

11. *HAME*, ii, pp. 765–6. Note that not all spices were destined for the table, but may have been used in other domestic contexts, e.g. bathing, for perfuming clothes and bedding, and as cosmetics.

12. Freedman, *Out of the East*, p. 43.

13. *Walter of Henley and other treatises on estate management and accounting*, ed. D. Oschinsky (Oxford, 1971), pp. 398–9 (Rules of St Robert): the 'wardrobe' of the text encompasses both clothing and spices.

14. Norfolk RO, DCN 1/1/3, Master of the Cellar, 1273–4, mem. 2d.

15. DCN 1/1/4, Master of the Cellar, 1278–9, mem. 1r.

16. P. Nightingale, 'The London pepperers' guild and some twelfth-century English trading links with Spain', *Bulletin of the Institute of Historical Research* 58 (1985), pp. 123–32.

17. G. E. Trease, 'The spicers and apothecaries of the royal household in the reigns of Henry III, Edward I and Edward II', *Nottingham Medieval Studies* 3 (1959), pp. 19–38; Nightingale, *Medieval mercantile community*, p. 53.

18. D. Keene, *Survey of medieval Winchester* (2 vols, Oxford, 1985), i, pp. 262–4.

19. Nightingale, *Medieval mercantile community*, pp. 95–6.

20. *Mirk*, ii, p. 223.

21. Nightingale, *Medieval mercantile community*, pp. 490–552.

22. East Sussex RO, MS RYE 60/2, f. 49r.

23. MS RYE 60/2, f. 55r.

24. See the inventory of John Brodocke, apothecary of Southampton, of 1571: *Southampton probate inventories, 1447–1575*, ed. E. Roberts and K. Parker (2 vols, Southampton Records Series, 34–5; 1992), ii, pp. 290–306.

25. *Facsimile of first volume of MS. archives of the Worshipful Company of Grocers of the City of London . . .*, ed. J. A. Kingdon (1886), p. 73; Nightingale, *Medieval mercantile community*, pp. 337–8, 368–9.

26. *CI*, pp. 153, 208–9; powder Lombard: *EARD I*, p. 91.

27. C. Rawcliffe, *Leprosy in medieval England* (Woodbridge, 2006), pp. 220–1; *PLP*, i, pp. 242–3, 512, 614.

28. *PLP*, i, p. 541: 'he shold never have my good wyll for to make my sustyr to selle kandyll and mustard in Framlyngham.'

29. *Bozon*, p. 22, no. 16: 'gentil moustard'.

30. *NHB*, p. 63: 'Whereas mustard hath beyn boght of the sawce-maker affore tyme that now it be made within in my lordis house and that one be providit to be grome of the skullery that can make it.'

31. *Ancrene Wisse: a corrected edition of the text in Cambridge, Corpus Christi College, MS 402, with variants from other manuscripts*, ed. B. Millett (2 vols, EETS, OS, 325–6; 2005–6), i, p. 59.

32. DUL, DCP, Cellarer's status 1488, mem. 1r.

33. Packet: Norfolk RO, DCN 1/1/21, Master of the Cellar, 1309–10, mem. 2r; paper, possibly for wrapping spice purchases, SBTRO, BRT1/3/28, mem. 1r, paragraph starting 'In speciebus', and concluding, penultimate item, 'in paupiro i d.'

34. Norfolk RO, DCN 1/1/11, Master of the Cellar, 1291–2, mem. 2r.

35. *TREWE*, p. 213.

36. *The local port book of Southampton for 1439–40*, ed. H. S. Cobb (Southampton Records Series, 5; 1961), p. 76; *HAME*, ii, p. 677; *GH*, p. 157.

37. *TREWE*, pp. 207–8.

38. M. Carlin, 'Putting dinner on the table in medieval London', in *London and the kingdom: essays in honour of Caroline M. Barron. Proceedings of the 2004 Harlaxton Symposium*, ed. M. Davies and A. Prescott (Donington, 2008), p. 61.

39. *TE III*, pp. 132–3.

40. *TE III*, p. 113.

41. *ERT*, pp. 209 (R702), 324.
42. *A dialogue between reason and adversity: a late Middle English version of Petrarch's De remediis*, ed. F. N. M. Diekstra (Assen, 1968), p. 39: 'Seyntes couden ete wel inow þoow þe powder box bleuȝ not on here sawser.'
43. *TE I*, p. 186.
44. G. Fransson, *Middle English surnames of occupation, 1100–1350, with an excursus on toponymical surnames* (Lund Studies in English, 3; 1935), p. 65.
45. *CSACSPW*, i, p. 33.
46. *Executors*, pp. 11, 43.
47. *The inventories and account rolls of the Benedictine houses or cells of Jarrow and Monk-Wearmouth, in the county of Durham*, ed. J. Raine (Surtees Society, 29; 1854), p. 158 (pepper-quern); H. T. Riley, *Memorials of London and London life, in the XIIIth, XIVth and XVth centuries . . .* (1868), p. 284 (mustard-quern).
48. DUL, DCP Cellarer's status 1488, mem. 1r.
49. *TE I*, pp. 172–3.
50. 'Whan hantlopes sermountes eglys in flyght ... And musketes [sparrowhawks] mak vergese of crabbes sower ... Than put women in trust and confydens.' *The early English carols*, ed. R. L. Greene (2nd edition, Oxford, 1977), p. 238.
51. *TE III*, p. 261; *OED* brake *sb.*[3]
52. *The priory of Saint Radegund Cambridge*, ed. A. Gray (Cambridge Antiquarian Society, Octavo Publications, 31; 1898), p. 167: 'pro salsagio vocato vergewes'.
53. DUL, DCP Cellarers' accounts, 1467–8 (A), mem. 1d; 1474–5, mem. 1r; 1475–6, mem. 1r.
54. *PLP*, i, p. 325, no. 195; DUL, DCP Cellarer's status 1488, mem. 1r.
55. *Statutes of the realm*, ed. A. Luders, T. E. Tomlins, J. Raithby and others (11 vols, 1810–28), i, p. 279: 'et si homme voet avoir sawes pur messe les eit, siqe ils ne soient pas faitz des grantz coustez' (10 Edward III, cap. 3).
56. *Before the mast: life and death aboard the Mary Rose*, ed. J. Gardiner, with M. J. Allen (2 vols, Portsmouth, 2005), i, pp. 444–5; but the rims of some were much narrower, e.g. from Southampton, *c*.1290 (Plate 16); R. Brownsword and W. E. H. Pitt, 'Some examples of medieval domestic pewter flatware', *Medieval Archaeology* 29 (1985), pp. 152–5.
57. Norfolk RO, DCN 1/1/21, Master of the Cellar, 1309–10, mem. 3r.
58. Norfolk RO, Norwich Consistory Court Records, Will Register 1 Heydon (1370–82), f. 29v.
59. Norwich Consistory Court Records, Will Register 1, f. 96r.
60. R. F. Michaelis, 'The pewter saucer', in *Excavations in medieval Southampton 1953–1969*, ed. C. Platt and R. Coleman-Smith (2 vols, Leicester, 1975), ii, p. 250.
61. *TE I*, p. 183.
62. Oxford, Bodleian Library, MS Eng. hist. b. 208, ff. 42v–43r.
63. Norfolk RO, DCN 1/1/22, Master of the Cellar, 1310–11, mem. 1r.
64. LPL, Register of William Whittlesey, ff. 112v (Ufford), 119r (Vere); TNA, E 101/400/6 (1378–9), 'deux coillers d'or, l'un pur espices'; Norfolk RO, DCN 1/1/22, Master of the Cellar, 1310–11, mem. 1r.
65. *MM*, pp. 151–2, ll. 529–32: 'Also to know youre sawces for flesche conveniently, / hit provokithe a fyne apetide if sawce youre mete be bie; / to the lust of youre lord looke þat ye have þer redy / suche sawce as hym likethe to make hym glad & mery.'
66. *MM*, pp. 152–3, 172–5.
67. *CI*, e.g. p. 39.
68. *CI*, pp. 102–3, 129.
69. *CI*, pp. 131, 213.
70. *CI*, p. 129.
71. *CI*, pp. 117 (Sarazin), 131 (green and black).
72. *CI*, pp. 41, 128.
73. *CI*, p. 104.
74. *TFCCB*, p. 39.

75. J.-L. Flandrin, 'Le goût et la nécessité: sur l'usage des graisses dans les cuisines d'Europe occidentale (XIVe–XVIIIe siècle)', *Annales: Économies, Sociétés, Civilisations*, 38 (1983), pp. 369–401.

76. Cited by Flandrin, 'Le goût et la nécessité', p. 382 and n. 81, from B. J. Whiting and H.W. Whiting, *Proverbs, sentences and proverbial phrases from English writings mainly before 1500* (Cambridge, MA, 1968), p. 439, O21.

77. Flandrin, 'Le goût et la nécessité', p. 399, n. 78; *The forme of cury, a roll of ancient English cookery*, ed. S. Pegge (1780), pp. 96, 103 (appulmos); 115 (sowpys dorry).

78. *HAME*, i, pp. 186, 233.

79. *PLP*, i, p. 448, no. 268.

80. Nightingale, *Medieval mercantile community*, p. 530, citing W. Childs, 'Anglo-Portuguese trade in the fifteenth century', *Transactions of the Royal Historical Society*, 6th series, 11 (1992), pp. 204–7.

81. e.g. *A leechbook, or a collection of medical recipes of the fifteenth century*, ed. W. R. Dawson (1934), *passim*.

82. *EARD I*, p. 51; Fransson, *Middle English surnames of occupation*, p. 70.

83. *BA*, ii, p. 1034; N. S. B. Gras, *The early English customs system* (Cambridge, MA, 1918), pp. 504, 610.

84. *Calendar of plea and memoranda rolls preserved among the archives of the corporation of the city of London at the Guildhall, A.D. 1413–1437*, ed. A. H. Thomas (Cambridge, 1943), p. 32.

85. *MED* mete *n*. 1 (1 (b) (d)).

86. *The customs accounts of Hull, 1453–1490*, ed. W. R. Childs (Yorkshire Archaeological Society Record Series, 144; 1986), *passim* (seal-smear); pp. 99, 248 (train-oil).

87. *Chaucer*, pp. 74–5, ll. 3698–9: 'What do ye, hony-comb, sweete Alisoun, / My faire bryd, my sweete cynamome?'

88. R. W. Tryon, 'Miracles of Our Lady in Middle English verse', *Proceedings of the Modern Language Association of America* 38 (1923), p. 321, ll. 19–20: 'loved oure lady evere elyke / His lufe was swettur þen hony of byke'.

89. *Chaucer*, p. 410: Book 2, Prosa 3, ll. 8–10.

90. *Cursor mundi*, ed. R. Morris (7 vols, EETS, OS, 57, 59, 62, 66, 68, 99, 101; 1874–93), v, p. 1432, ll. 25037–8: ' "Pilate" . . . And he bitakens feind of hell, For bok him clepis muth of mell.'

91. *Rolls of the fifteenth of the ninth year of the reign of Henry III for Cambridgeshire, Lincolnshire and Wiltshire and rolls of the fortieth of the seventeenth year of the reign of Henry III for Kent*, ed. F. A. Cazel, Jr., and A. P. Cazel (Pipe Roll Society, new series, 45; 1983), pp. 46–9.

92. DUL, DCP, Locellus 8, no. 2, Inventory of Thomas Birdale, f. 1v, col. 1; DUL, DCP, Locellus 8, no. 1, Inventory of William Capes, mem. 2r.

93. *TE IV*, pp. 174–5.

94. British Beekeepers' Association, 'Honey', at http://www.bbka.org.uk/learn/general_information/honey (accessed 4 January 2015).

95. Norfolk RO, DCN 1/1/10, Master of the Cellar, 1290–2, mem. 2r; DCN 1/1/17, Master of the Cellar, 1303–4, mem. 1r; DCN 1/1/24, Master of the Cellar, 1314–15, mem. 2r.

96. Norfolk RO, DCN 1/1/13, Master of the Cellar, 1297–8, mem. 3r; DCN 1/1/17, Master of the Cellar, 1303–4, mem. 2r.

97. DUL, DCP Cellarer's account, 1438–9 (A), mem. 3r.

98. Cellarer's status 1488, mem. 1r.

99. Cellarer's status 1488, mem. 1r.

100. SBTRO, D37/2 Box 114/2, mem. 3r.

101. Pokerounce: *TFCCB*, p. 41.

102. *CI*, p. 113, recipe 68 (and p. 204).

103. e.g. in medical recipes: *Lanfrank's 'Science of Cirurgie'*, ed. R. V. Fleischhacker (EETS, OS, 102; 1894), p. 55, l. 5: 'take up a drope þerof wiþ þy fyngur and do it in a litel water, and loke if it hong togydre.'

104. M. Ouerfelli, *Le sucre: production, commercialisation et usages dans la Méditerranée médiévale* (Leiden, 2008), pp. 503–67.

105. See, for example, R. Newhauser, 'John Gower's sweet tooth', *Review of English Studies*, new series, 64 (2013), pp. 752–69, especially 764–9.

106. Ouerfelli, *Le sucre*, pp. 2, 39, 435, 438, 484–5, 497.

107. *EARD I*, p. 11 (Cypre); *EARD II*, pp. 510 (Marrok), 518 (Babilon); 'Alisaundre', see Table 5.1.

108. *TFCCB*, p. 21, recipe 83.

109. *TFCCB*, p. 73 (white); *HAME*, i, pp. 205, 227 (Cafatyn); ii, pp. 507, 521 (potsugre); *Liber cure cocorum copied and edited from the Sloane MS 1986*, ed. R. Morris (Berlin, 1862), p. 7: 'With sugur candy, þou may hit dowce, / If hit be served in grete lordys howce. / Take black sugur for mener menne; / Be ware þer with, for hit wylle brenne.'

110. *PLP*, i, p. 569.

111. *HAME*, i, p. 227 (loaf), 209, 232–3 (tablet); *EARD I*, pp. 13 (rock), 125 (plate); *Medical works of the fourteenth century together with a list of plants recorded in contemporary writings, with their identifications*, ed. G. Henslow (1899), pp. 120–1 (plate, with flowers and flavoured with rose-water); *Liber cure cocorum*, ed. Morris, p. 39 (powder, added to flans).

112. Norfolk RO, DCN 1/1/24, Master of the Cellar, 1314–15, mem. 2r, sugar and honey; DCN 1/1/25, Master of the Cellar, 1315–16, no sugar or honey.

113. H. W. Saunders, *An introduction to the obedientiary and manor rolls of Norwich Cathedral Priory* (Norwich, 1930), pp. 160–3. Numbers fluctuated around 50 by the end of the fourteenth century.

114. Ouerfelli, *Le sucre*, pp. 629–30.

115. *Elizabeth de Burgh, Lady of Clare (1295–1360): household and other records*, ed. J. Ward (Suffolk Records Society, 57; 2014), p. 59; F. A. Underhill, *For her good estate: the life of Elizabeth de Burgh* (New York, 1999), p. 74.

116. *HAME*, i, p. 227.

117. *Expeditions to Prussia and the Holy Land made by Henry Earl of Derby ...*, ed. L. T. Smith (Camden Society, new series, 52; 1894), p. 219.

118. *HAME*, ii, p. 677.

119. *Lydgate's Fall of princes*, ed. H. Bergen (4 vols, EETS, ES, 121–4; 1924–7), i, p. 185, ll. 6571–3: 'That ther colour outward appeire nouht / With wynd or sonne, which sholde hem steyne or fade, / For onkynde heetis thei [women] use citrynade.'

120. *Ein mittelenglisches Medizinbuch*, ed. F. Heinrich (Halle, 1896), p. 171.

121. *TREWE*, p. lvi.

122. *HAME*, ii, p. 680.

6 Gardens, Wild Foods, Fish and Hunting

1. *A Middle English translation of Macer Floridus De viribus herbarum*, ed. G. Frisk (The English Institute in the University of Upsala, Essays and studies on English language and literature, 3; 1949); B. P. Flood, Jr., 'The medieval herbal tradition of Macer Floridus', *Pharmacy in History*, 18, no. 2 (1976), pp. 62–6.

2. *The Holy Bible ... by John Wycliffe and his followers*, ed. J. Forshall and F. Madden (4 vols, Oxford, 1850), iii, pp. 39–40 (Proverbs 24:31): 'I passide bi the feeld of a slow man, and bi the vyner of a fonned man; and lo! nettlis hadden fillid al, thornes hadden hilid the hiȝere part therof, and the wal of stoonys with out morter was distried.'

3. *BSP*, C v Contritio, Art. i; F i Falsitas, Art. ii: v.

4. *BA*, ii, p. 1088.

5. *BA*, ii, pp. 788–9.

6. *MO*, p. 100, ll. 8569–80.

7. A. M. T. Amherst, 'A fifteenth-century treatise on gardening by "Mayster Ion Gardener"', *Archaeologia* 54 (1894), pp. 157–72; J. H. Harvey, 'The first English garden book: Mayster John Gardener's treatise and its background', *Garden History* 13 (1985), p. 92.

8. Amherst, 'Fifteenth-century treatise on gardening', pp. 163–4: 'Wurtys we most have / Both to mayster & to knave'; 'wurtys yong al tyme of þe yere'.
9. Amherst, 'Fifteenth-century treatise on gardening', pp. 164–6.
10. C. Dyer, 'Gardens and orchards in medieval England', in C. Dyer, *Everyday life in medieval England* (1994), pp. 118–19; C. Dyer, 'Gardens and garden produce in the later Middle Ages', in *FME*, pp. 27–40, especially p. 36.
11. See the discussion in C. Noble, 'Norwich Cathedral Priory gardeners' accounts, 1329–1530', in *Farming and gardening in late medieval Norfolk*, ed. C. Noble and C. Moreton (Norfolk Record Society, 61; 1996), pp. 5–11: although focused on monastic gardens, much of it holds good for other institutions.
12. 'The churl and the bird', in *The minor poems of John Lydgate*, part 2: *Secular poems*, ed. H. N. MacCracken (EETS, OS, 192; 1934), p. 470, ll. 43–56.
13. *Manières de langage (1396, 1399, 1415)*, ed. A. M. Kristol (Anglo-Norman Text Society, 53; 1995), p. 17.
14. TNA, JUST 2/66, mem. 11d.
15. JUST 2/18, mem. 61d.
16. JUST 2/70, mem. 10r.
17. DUL, DCP Cellarer's account, 1443 (A), mem. 2d.
18. Cellarer's account, 1467–8 (A), mem. 1r; for sowing rates, J. H. Harvey, 'Vegetables in the Middle Ages', *Garden History* 12 (1984), p. 94: onion seed, 10 lbs for an acre.
19. Cellarer's account, 1471–2 (A), mem. 1r.
20. Cellarer's account, 1474–5, mem. 1r.
21. Cellarer's account, 1445–6 (A), mem. 1d.
22. Cellarer's account, 1459–60, mem. 1r–1d.
23. Cellarer's account, 1461–2 (A), mem. 1d.
24. Cellarer's account, 1465–6 (A), mem. 1d.
25. Cellarer's account, 1474–5, mem. 1r.
26. Walter de Bibbesworth, *Le tretiz*, ed. W. Rothwell (Aberystwyth, 2009), pp. 18–19, ll. 410–16.
27. *The inventories and account rolls of the Benedictine houses or cells of Jarrow and Monk-Wearmouth in the County of Durham*, ed. J. Raine (Surtees Society, 29; 1854), p. 153.
28. HMC, *Report on the manuscripts of Lord de L'Isle and Dudley preserved at Penshurst Place*, vol. 1, ed. C. L. Kingsford (1925), p. 207.
29. Norfolk RO, DCN 1/1/11, Master of the Cellar, 1291–2, mem. 1d; D. Yaxley, *The Prior's manor-houses: inventories of eleven of the manor-houses of the Prior of Norwich made in the year 1352 A.D.* (Dereham, 1988), pp. 10–11.
30. Harvey, 'Vegetables in the Middle Ages', p. 99, n. 43.
31. *PP*, i, pp. 308–9 (B VI, l. 285; C VIII, ll. 309–10).
32. *The works of Sir Thomas Malory*, ed. E. Vinaver, rev. P. J. C. Field (3 vols, 3rd edition, Oxford, 1990), ii, p. 945: 'saw a poore house, and besyde the chapell a litill courtelayge where Nacien the ermyte gadred wortis to hys mete'.
33. Dyer, 'Gardens and orchards', pp. 119–21.
34. *The Stonor letters and papers, 1290–1483*, ed. C. L. Kingsford (2 vols, Camden, 3rd series, 29–30; 1919), i, p. 135.
35. TNA, JUST 2/77, mem. 4r.
36. JUST 2/165, mem. 1r.
37. JUST 2/18, mem. 20r.
38. JUST 2/18, mem. 49r.
39. E 36/214, f. 134v.
40. BL, Add. MS 21480, ff. 15r, 16r, 21r, 25v.
41. Walter de Bibbesworth, *Le tretiz*, ed. Rothwell, p. 77, ll. 507–20.
42. *BSP*, E vi Eucharistia, Art. i.
43. D. Stevens, 'A Somerset coroner's roll, 1315–1321', *Somerset and Dorset Notes and Queries* 31 (1985), p. 459.

44. *FL*, iv, p. 323.
45. JRULM, MS Latin 235, f. 19r.
46. *PLP*, i, pp. 554, 589, 612–13; *Chaucer*, p. 167, ll. 2330–7.
47. C. M. Woolgar, 'Gifts of food in late medieval England', *Journal of Medieval History* 37 (2011), pp. 6–18.
48. *The early South-English Legendary or Lives of saints, I, MS Laud, 108, in the Bodleian Library*, ed. C. Horstmann (EETS, OS, 87; 1887), p. 140, ll. 1189–91.
49. Blaunderels: *HAME*, ii, pp. 506–7; pippins: *MM*, p. 166, l. 714; red stars and Ricardons: *A leechbook, or collection of medical recipes of the fifteenth century*, ed. W. R. Dawson (1934), pp. 154–5, no. 462; costards and quenings: 'Henry VI's triumphal entry into London, 21 Feb., 1432', in *The minor poems of John Lydgate*, part 2, ed. MacCracken, p. 642, l. 357.
50. Pear Jonette: *Secular lyrics of the XIVth and XVth centuries*, ed. R. H. Robbins (2nd edition, Oxford, 1955), pp. 15–16, ll. 8, 24; pearmains: *CClR, 1313–18*, p. 357; wardens: *HAME*, ii, pp. 507–20.
51. *An anonymous short English metrical chronicle*, ed. E. Zettl (EETS, OS, 196; 1935), p. 42, l. 999.
52. *The Coventry leet book, or, mayor's register . . .*, ed. M. D. Harris (4 parts in 1; EETS, OS, 134, 135, 138, 146; 1907–13), p. 300.
53. *MED* jonette *n.*; *PP*, i, p. 473 (C XII, ll. 223–5): 'And þat rathest rypeth, rotieth most sonnest.'
54. *The customary of the Cathedral Priory Church of Norwich: MS 465 in the Library of Corpus Christi College, Cambridge*, ed. J. B. L. Tolhurst (Henry Bradshaw Society, 82; 1948), p. 153.
55. *CSACSPW*, ii, pp. 90–1.
56. *The ormulum*, ed. R. Holt (2 vols, Oxford, 1878), i, p. 281, l. 8118.
57. *CO*, p. 448.
58. *The Laud Troy Book, a romance of about 1400 A.D.*, ed. J.E. Wülfing (2 vols, EETS, OS, 121–2; 1902–3), i, p. 266, l. 9010.
59. *Chaucer*, p. 69, l. 3622; barrels: *HAME*, ii, pp. 506–7.
60. *Stonor letters and papers*, ed. Kingsford, i, p. 135.
61. *BSP*, C xiii Conversatio, Art. iiii.
62. *TFCCB*, pp. 51–2.
63. *AHEW III*, pp. 322–3.
64. *The place-names of Surrey*, ed. J. E. B. Gover, A. Mawer and F. M. Stenton (English Place-Name Society, 11; 1934), pp. 132, 144, 296; *The place-names of Oxfordshire*, vol. 1, ed. M. Gelling and D. M. Stenton (English Place-Name Society, 23; 1953), pp. 188, 192.
65. *The place-names of Sussex*, vol. 2, ed. A. Mawer and F. M. Stenton (English Place-Name Society, 7; 1930), pp. 160, 177, 277; *The place-names of Wiltshire*, ed. J. E. B. Gover, A. Mawer and F. M. Stenton (English Place-Name Society, 16; 1939), p. 111.
66. *Select documents of the English lands of the abbey of Bec*, ed. Marjorie Chibnall (Camden Society, 3rd series, 73; 1951), pp. 59, 103–4.
67. H. C. M. Lambert, *History of Banstead in Surrey* (Oxford, 1912), pp. 321–36.
68. *The local port book of Southampton for 1439–40*, ed. H. S. Cobb (Southampton Records Series, 5; 1961), p. 117.
69. E. Wilson, 'An unpublished alliterative poem on plant-names from Lincoln College, Oxford, MS Lat. 129(E)', *Notes and Queries* 224, new series 26 (1979), p. 508, l. 53.
70. *EARD II*, p. 574.
71. *An ordinance of pottage: an edition of the fifteenth-century culinary recipes in Yale University's MS Beinecke 163*, ed. C. B. Hieatt (1988), p. 90, no. 138.
72. *BA*, ii, p. 1000.
73. *The forme of cury, a roll of ancient English cookery . . .*, ed. S. Pegge (1780), p. 121.
74. T. Hunt, 'Anglo-Norman medical receipts', in *Anglo-Norman anniversary essays*, ed. I. Short (Anglo-Norman Text Society, Occasional Publications series, 2; 1993), pp. 179–233, at p. 187, l. 47.

75. *HAME*, i, p. 227.

76. *EARD II*, p. 527.

77. P. Nightingale, *A medieval mercantile community: the Grocers' Company and the politics and trade of London 1000–1485* (New Haven, 1995), pp. 66, 68, 74–5.

78. *CSACSPW*, i, p. 178.

79. *CSACSPW*, i, pp. 172–3.

80. Tony Hunt, *Plant names of medieval England* (Cambridge, 1989), pp. xiii–xviii, xxxvii–li.

81. TNA, E 36/214, ff. 33r–35r.

82. BL, Add. MS 34213, ff. 21v, 27r 30r, 31r, 32r, 32v, 34v, 36r, 41v, 42r, 42v, 45r, 46r, 46v.

83. *Mum and the Sothsegger*, ed. M. Day and R. Steel (EETS, OS, 199; 1936), p. 53, ll. 889–908.

84. *Kyng Alisaunder*, ed. G. V. Smithers (2 vols, EETS, OS, 227, 237; 1952–7), i, p. 273, ll. 4971–4.

85. *Libellus de vita et miraculis S. Godrici, heremitae de Finchale auctore Reginaldo monacho Dunelmensi. Adjicitur appendix miraculorum*, ed. J. Stevenson (Surtees Society, 20; 1845), pp. 71, 80–1.

86. *PP*, i, p. 589 (C XVII, l. 21).

87. *CSACSPW*, ii, p. 200.

88. Walter de Bibbesworth, *Le tretiz*, ed. Rothwell, p. 76, l. 498; dauke: *Ein mittelenglisches Medizinbuch*, ed. F. Heinrich (Halle, 1896), p. 134; lettuce: Lanfrank's *'Science of Cirurgie'*, ed. R. V. Fleischhacker (EETS, OS, 102; 1894), pp. 277, 351.

89. C. Horstmann, 'Des MS Bodl. 779 jüngere Zusatzlegenden zur südlichen Legendensammlung', *Archiv für das Studium der neueren Sprachen und Litteraturen* 82 (1889), pp. 307–422, at p. 335, ll. 67–8: 'Al his lif to penaunce þis goodman haþ i-dyȝt: / xv nepus he et echday & þat a-ȝen þe nyȝt.'

90. *The Brut or the Chronicles of England*, ed. F. W. D. Brie (EETS, OS, 136; 1908), p. 400: 'And thanne hem failid bothe whete, and mele, and alle othir graynys that thei myght make of eny brede; but branne and broken wortis, and nepe-rotis, and lekis, was to hem mete of grete valewe …'

91. Walter de Bibbesworth, *Le tretiz*, ed. Rothwell, p. 76, ll. 504–6.

92. *PP*, i, pp. 312–13, e.g. C VIII, ll. 330–1.

93. TNA, JUST 2/116, mem. 4r.

94. A. S. C. Ross, 'The Middle English poem on the names of a hare', *Proceedings of the Leeds Philosophical and Literary Society (Literary and Historical Section)* 3, part 6 (1935), pp. 350–1.

95. *An alphabet of tales*, ed. M. M. Banks (EETS, OS, 126, 127; 1904–5), i, p. 78: 'Allas! Whatt hafe I done? I satt opon þe letes, & sho came & tuke me up & ate me'; also *FL*, iv, p. 303.

96. *MM*, p. 124, ll. 97–8: 'Beware of saladis, grene metis, & of frutes rawe / For þey make many a man have a feble mawe.' Cf. K. Albala, *Eating right in the Renaissance* (Berkeley, 2002), pp. 164–5.

97. *CI*, p. 115, no. 78.

98. TNA, JUST 2/113, mem. 33r.

99. *PP*, i, p. 215, C VI, ll. 291–2: 'ȝut were me leuer, by Oure Lord, lyve al by welle-cresses / Then have my fode and my fyndynge of fals menne wynnynges.'

100. *Liber cure cocorum, copied and edited from the Sloane MS. 1986*, ed. R. Morris (Berlin, 1862) p. 42: 'Þou take þe crop of þo rede brere, … town cresses, and cresses þat growene in flode'.

101. *CI*, p. 100, no. 12. Note how few entries there are in *MED* funge *n.* and musheron *n.*

102. *BSP*, F ii Fama, Art. i: i.

103. C. B. Hieatt, 'Medieval Britain', in *Regional cuisines of medieval Europe: a book of essays*, ed. M. Weiss Adamson (2002), pp. 19–45, e.g. p. 35.

104. *TFCCB*, p. 29.

105. *CI*, p. 138.

106. *CI*, p. 91.

107. *CI*, p. 117.

108. *Liber cure cocorum*, ed. Morris, p. 42.
109. A. J. Frantzen, *Food, eating and identity in early medieval England* (Woodbridge, 2014), pp. 232–45; D. Serjeantson and C. M. Woolgar, 'Fish consumption in medieval England', in *FME*, pp. 102–30.
110. Matt. 4:18–22.
111. *Customary of the Cathedral Priory Church of Norwich*, ed. Tolhurst, p. 18.
112. *Mirk*, i, pp. 173–4; ii, p. 389.
113. *CSACSPW*, ii, p. 103.
114. Norfolk RO, DCN 1/1/13, Master of the Cellar, 1297–8, mem. 4r; DCN 1/1/15, Master of the Cellar, 1302–3, mem. 2r; DCN 1/1/16, Master of the Cellar, 1303–4, mem. 1r; DCN 1/1/19, Master of the Cellar, 1308–9, mem. 2r; DCN 1/1/21, Master of the Cellar, 1309–10 (22 Henry de Lakenham), mem. 2r; DCN 1/1/22, Master of the Cellar, 1310–11, mem. 2r; DCN 1/1/23, Master of the Cellar, 1313–14, mem. 2r; DCN 1/1/24, Master of the Cellar, 1314–15, mem. 2r; DCN 1/1/25, Master of the Cellar, 1315–16, mem. 1r.
115. C. M. Woolgar, ' "Take this penance now, and afterwards the fare will improve": seafood and late medieval diet', in *England's sea fisheries: the commercial sea fisheries of England and Wales since 1300*, ed. D. J. Starkey, C. Reid and N. Ashcroft (2003), pp. 36–44.
116. *BSP*, O vi Ordo clericalis, Art. vii: lxi.
117. *CI*, p. 54, no. 50.
118. *CI*, pp. 121, 178, and *CO*, p. 449 ('chisanne'); *CI*, pp. 119, 192 ('gin-gaudre'); *CO*, p. 446.
119. Hake: *Laud Troy Book*, ed. Wülfing, i, p. 231, ll. 7847–8; herring: *The pilgrimage of the lyf of the manhode*, ed. W. A. Wright (Roxburghe Club, 91; 1869), p. 68; herring tails: *Laud Troy Book*, ed. Wülfing, ii, p. 512, ll. 17398–401; oysters: *Chaucer*, p. 26 (General Prologue to the Canterbury Tales, l. 182).
120. *Mirk*, i, p. 125, l. 98.
121. *Cursor mundi*, ed. R. Morris (7 vols, EETS, OS, 57, 59, 62, 66, 68, 99, 101; 1874–93), ii, p. 470, l. 8150; ii, p. 682, l. 11884.
122. Pike: K. I. Sandred, *A Middle English version of the Gesta Romanorum, edited from Gloucester Cathedral MS 22* (Uppsala: Studia Anglistica Upsaliensis, 8; 1971), p. 46; pickerel: *Laud Troy Book*, ed. Wülfing, ii, p. 431, ll. 14627–8.
123. *Chaucer*, p. 156, ll. 1418–20: ' "Oold fissh and yong flessh wolde I have fayn. / Bet is", quod he, "a pyk than a pykerel, / And bet than old boef is the tendre veel." '
124. J. Hall, 'Short pieces from MS. Cotton Galba E.IX', *Englische Studien* 21 (1895), p. 202, l. 37: 'When þou lyes bonden als hering dos in maies'.
125. *The book of Margery Kempe*, ed. W. Butler-Bowdon (EETS, OS, 212; 1940), pp. 17, 91: 'Þow xalt ben etyn & knawyn of þe pepul of þe world as any raton knawyth þe stok-fysch'; 'Dowtyr, for þu art so buxom to my wille & clevyst as sore on-to me as þe skyn of stokfysche clevyth to a mannys handys whan it is sothyn'.
126. *Minor poems of John Lydgate*, part 2, ed. MacCracken, p. 781, ll. 12–13 (no. 63, 'As a mydsomer rose'): 'Al is not gold that outward shewith bright; / A stokfyssh boon in dirknesse yevith a light.'
127. *A common-place book of the fifteenth century*, ed. L. T. Smith (1886), p. 13.
128. Serjeantson and Woolgar, 'Fish consumption in medieval England'.
129. Woolgar, 'Take this penance now'.
130. TNA, E 101/351/1, nos 1–15; E 101/351/1/7: barrels with lock and chain; E 101/351/1/13: 16s each; E 101/351/1/15: 3d each.
131. *TFCCB*, p. 99: 'Take a lamprey poudred, and stryke away the salt with thi honde.'
132. *Liber cure cocorum*, ed. Morris, p. 25.
133. TNA, JUST 2/12, mem. 26r.
134. JUST 2/18, mem. 19d.
135. *Cursor mundi*, ed. Morris, iii, p. 763, l. 13285.
136. *Die Kildare-gedichte: die ältesten mittelenglischen Denkmäler in anglo-irischer Überlieferung*, ed. W. Heuser (Bonner Beiträger zur Anglistik, 14; 1904), p. 157: liver, 'tromcheri'.

137. TNA, JUST 2/52, mem. 8r.
138. JUST 2/67, mem. 5r.
139. JUST 2/67, mem. 9r.
140. JUST 2/67, mem. 21r.
141. *CI*, p. 185.
142. e.g. BL, Add. MS 34213, f. 101v.
143. *HAME*, i, pp. 171 (large), 247 (shaft), 249 (pimpernols); ii, pp. 509 (roasting, stick); *Calendar of letter-books preserved among the archives of the corporation of the city of London at the Guildhall*, vol. 11: *Letter-Book L*, ed. R. R. Sharpe (1912), p. 47 (kemp, red).
144. *HAME*, i, p. 100; ii, pp. 509, 519, 562. *OED* tolling *vbl. sb.*[1]
145. *Yorkshire writers: Richard Rolle of Hampole and his followers*, ed. C. Horstmann (2 vols, 1895–6), i, p. 311 (Rolle, 'Our daily work'): 'Þay are faylande & noghte lastande ay, & slepir als ane eele, þat whene mene wenys he hase hym faste, als fantome he fra hyme glyddys, & tynys hym for ay.'
146. *The epistle of Othea translated from the French text of Christine de Pisan by Stephen Scrope*, ed. C. F. Bühler (EETS, OS, 264; 1970), p. 56: 'An evil kepte tong glydith as an ele'; *The Towneley plays*, ed. M. Stevens and A. C. Cawley (2 vols, EETS, SS, 13; 1994), i, p. 141, Play 13, ll. 513–14: 'Lord! what I have slept weyll; As fresh as an eyll.'
147. TNA, JUST 2/67, mem. 10d.
148. SBTRO, DR37/2/Box 107/2, mem. 2r.
149. *PLP*, ii, p. 426.
150. DUL, DCP Cellarers' accounts, 1459–60, mem. 1d; 1469–70, mem. 1r.
151. 'The treatise of fishing with an angle attributed to Dame Juliana Berners', in J. McDonald, *The origins of angling* (New York, 1963), p. 165.
152. TNA, JUST 2/113, mem. 6r.
153. *FL*, iv, pp. 245–6.
154. TNA, JUST 2/67, mem. 22d.
155. JUST 2/78, rot. 3, mem. 5r.
156. *EARD I*, p. 10.
157. *PP*, i, p. 329 (C IX, ll. 94–5): 'Fridays and fastyng days a ferthing-worth of moskeles / Were a fest with suche folk, or so fele cockes.'
158. TNA, JUST 2/67, mem. 19d.
159. JUST 2/67, mem. 19d.
160. *MM*, p. 171, ll. 821–2.
161. *MM*, p. 166, l. 719.
162. *HAME*, ii, pp. 482, 484.
163. *EARD II*, pp. 402 (1408), 452 (1401).
164. See the example of the Northumberland Household Book in Chapter 1.
165. N. J. Sykes, 'The impact of the Normans on hunting practices in England', in *FME*, pp. 162–75; J. Birrell, 'Procuring, preparing, and serving venison in late medieval England', in *FME*, pp. 176–88.
166. J. Birrell, 'Deer and deer farming in medieval England', *Agricultural History Review*, 40 (1992), pp. 112–26.
167. Birrell, 'Procuring, preparing, and serving venison', pp. 180–4.
168. N. J. Sykes, 'The animal bones', in *A medieval royal complex at Guildford: excavations at the castle and palace*, ed. R. Poulton (Guildford, 2005), pp. 116–28; Sykes, 'Impact of the Normans on hunting practices', pp. 170–5.
169. *Sir Gawain and the Green Knight*, ed. W. R. J. Barron (Manchester, 1974), pp. 98–9.
170. Birrell, 'Procuring, preparing, and serving venison', p. 184; Sykes, 'Impact of the Normans on hunting practices', p. 171.
171. East Sussex RO, SAS CP/148–9, 151.
172. TNA, JUST 2/17, mem. 13r.
173. JUST 2/156, mem. 2r.

174. K. A. Smith, *The Taymouth Hours: stories and the construction of the self in late medieval England* (2012). I follow her argument, pp. 9–27, that the work was intended for Eleanor rather than another female member of the royal family. I am grateful to Dr Naomi Sykes for her thoughts on the scene in Plate 18.
175. *BSP*, B ii Bellum, Art. iiii: xxxiii.
176. J. T. Rosenthal, *Telling tales: sources and narration in late medieval England* (University Park, PA, 2003), p. 51.
177. *PLP*, i, p. 189, no. 108; ii, pp. 421, 423, 487, nos 778–9, 850.
178. DUL, DCP Cellarer's account, 1465–6 (A), mem. 1d.

7 Civic Food Culture and the Guilds

1. *Wynnere and Wastoure*, ed. S. Trigg (EETS, OS, 297; 1990), p. 16, l. 482: 'Hotte for þe hungry.' See also *PP*, i, p. 24 (B, Prologue, ll. 226–30).
2. See Chapters 3, 4, 10 and 12.
3. C. M. Woolgar, 'Gifts of food in late medieval England', *Journal of Medieval History* 37 (2011), pp. 6–18.
4. *The stewards' books of Southampton from 1428*, vol. 2: *From 1434 to 1439*, ed. H. W. Gidden (Southampton Record Society, 1939), pp. 80–1.
5. East Sussex RO, MS RYE 60/3, f. 31v.
6. SCRO, SC 5/1/6, pp. 42–3.
7. SCRO, SC 5/1/6, p. 25.
8. SCRO, SC 5/1/6, pp. 13–14. See also the remarks of J. S. Davis, *A history of Southampton, partly from the MS of Dr Speed in the Southampton archives* (Southampton, 1883), pp. 422–6.
9. SCRO, SC 5/1/7, pp. 38–40.
10. SBTRO, BRT 1/3/51, mem. 1r.
11. *The records of the guild of the Holy Trinity, St Mary, St John the Baptist and St Katherine of Coventry*, ed. G. Templeman (Dugdale Society, 19; 1944), p. 153.
12. *Records of the guild of the Holy Trinity . . . Coventry*, ed. Templeman, p. 155.
13. East Sussex RO, MS RYE 60/3, f. 70r; for what is almost certainly the *Regent* depicted in a local wall painting, G. Nesbitt-Wood, 'Wall painting of a 16th-century great ship in St Dunstan's church, Snargate, Romney Marsh', *Archaeologia Cantiana* 87 (1972), pp. 208–9.
14. e.g. East Sussex RO, MS RYE 60/3, f. 22r, Christmas term 1471.
15. J. S. Bothwell, 'Making the Lancastrian capital at Leicester: the battle of Boroughbridge, civic diplomacy and seigneurial building projects in fourteenth-century England', *Journal of Medieval History* 38 (2012), pp. 335–57.
16. East Sussex RO, MS RYE 60/2, f. 36v, 'ad essendum bonum virum nobis in materia de Tenderden'.
17. SCRO, SC 5/1/6, p. 18.
18. SCRO, SC 5/1/7, p. 6.
19. SCRO, SC 5/1/6, pp. 15–16.
20. *English gilds. The original ordinances of more than one hundred early English gilds . . .*, ed. T. Smith and L. T. Smith (EETS, OS, 40; 1870), pp. 54–5: 'in time of drynck or of morwespeche unskylfulleche'.
21. *English gilds*, ed. Smith and Smith, pp. 2, 14–19.
22. *English gilds*, ed. Smith and Smith, pp. 446–7: 'all the bretheren and sustren schul honestly gon to her mete to place assigned be the aldirman and þe maistres and there for to ete togidre every brother and sister payng for her mete wax and minstrales x [d.] And qwat brother or sister absente hem fro her messe and mete, if thei be within xii mile on ony quarter about Norwich thei . . . up peyne ii li. wax.'
23. Hants RO, W/H1/204, mem. 9r.
24. SBTRO, BRT 1/3/25. The earlier account rolls run from Michaelmas to Michaelmas: from 1410–11, they run from the morrow of the translation of St Thomas, 8 July.

25. *Reading gild accounts 1357–1516*, ed. C. Slade (2 vols, Berkshire Record Society, 6–7; 2002), i, pp. 18, 22.
26. SBTRO, BRT 1/3/28.
27. BRT 1/3/37.
28. Hants RO, W/H1/205, recto.
29. *Records of the guild of the Holy Trinity, . . . Coventry*, ed. Templeman, p. 151.
30. *Records of the guild of the Holy Trinity, . . . Coventry*, ed. Templeman, pp. 148–51.
31. *English gilds*, ed. Smith and Smith, pp. 3–4, 'þe brethren and sustren of þe bretherhede at on assent in suyt . . . shul every ȝer come and hold to-geder for to norish more knowelech and love a fest; which fest schal be þe Soneday after þe day of Seint Jame apostle. And every paye þerto xx d.'
32. SBTRO, BRT 1/3/29.
33. BRT 1/3/29.
34. BRT 1/3/27.
35. BRT 1/3/39.
36. BRT 1/3/29.
37. BRT 1/3/30.
38. BRT 1/3/89; BRT 1/3/100, mem. 2r; BRT 1/3/105, mem. 2d.
39. BRT 1/3/106, mem. 1r.
40. *Select cases from the ecclesiastical courts of the province of Canterbury c.1200–1301*, ed. N. Adams and C. Donahue (Selden Society, 95; 1981), pp. 103, 106: 'ad quamdam potacionem faciendam que vocatur gylde'; 'Johannes Hodde de Hampslape . . . dicit quod dictus R. de quo agitur eorum senescallus fuit.' Feast of St Edmund the Martyr: 20 November, or the translation, 29 April.
41. G. Rosser, 'Going to the fraternity feast: commensality and social relations in late medieval England', *Journal of British Studies* 33 (1994), p. 422.
42. SBTRO, BRT 1/3/22.
43. BRT 1/3/28.
44. BRT 1/3/38.
45. *The register of the guild of the Holy Cross, St Mary and St John the Baptist, Stratford-upon-Avon*, ed. M. Macdonald (Dugdale Society, 42; 2007), pp. 22–30.
46. SBTRO, BRT 1/3/37.
47. BRT 1/3/44, mem. 1r.
48. BRT 1/3/30; BRT 1/3/37.
49. BRT 1/3/28.
50. M. Macdonald, 'The guild of the Holy Cross and its buildings', and K. Giles and J. Clark, 'The archaeology of the guild buildings of Shakespeare's Stratford-upon-Avon', in *The guild and guild buildings of Shakespeare's Stratford: society, religion, school and stage*, ed. J. R. Mulryne (Farnham, 2012), pp. 13–30, 135–69.
51. SBTRO, BRT 1/3/30.
52. BRT 1/3/34.
53. BRT 1/3/22, BRT 1/3/23, BRT 1/3/30 and BRT 1/3/49, mem. 1r.
54. BRT 1/3/30.
55. BRT 1/3/51, mem. 1r.
56. BRT 1/3/19, mem. 1r; BRT 1/3/20, mem. 1r.
57. BRT 1/3/57, mem. 2r.
58. BRT 1/3/82, mem. 1r.
59. BRT 1/3/22, hemming, sanaps; BRT 1/3/16, BRT 1/3/25, BRT 1/3/89, washing napery.
60. BRT 1/3/20, mem. 1r.
61. BRT 1/3/64, mem. 1r.
62. BRT 1/3/26, mem. 3r, paragraph 5.
63. BRT 1/3/52, mem. 2r.
64. BRT 1/3/33, mem. 2r, custus domorum, paragraph 2.
65. BRT 1/3/184.

66. BRT 1/3/19, mem 1r; BRT 1/3/26, mem. 3r, paragraph 5.
67. BRT 1/3/63, mem. 1r.
68. BRT 1/3/52, mem. 2r; BRT 1/3/62, mem. 1r; BRT 1/3/63, mem. 1r; BRT 1/3/67, mem. 1r.
69. BRT 1/3/20, mem. 1r.
70. BRT 1/3/184.
71. BRT 1/3/18, mem. 1r.
72. BRT 1/3/49, mem. 1r.
73. BRT 1/3/80, mem. 1r.
74. BRT 1/3/82, mem. 1r.
75. BRT 1/3/28, 36.
76. Hants RO, W/H1/204, mem. 9r, 1411 feast on a day of abstinence; mem. 10r, 1414 feast on a meat day.
77. SBTRO, BRT 1/3/37, 39; BRT 1/3/50, mem. 2r; BRT 1/3/53, mem. 1r.
78. BRT 1/3/30.
79. BRT 1/3/28, BRT 1/3/29, BRT 1/3/36; BRT 1/3/77, mem. 1r.
80. BRT 1/3/12, mem. 2d; BRT 1/3/27, BRT 1/3/28, BRT 1/3/36.
81. e.g. BRT 1/3/52, mem. 2r; BRT 1/3/82, mem. 1r.
82. BRT 1/3/13, mem. 1r.
83. BRT 1/3/39.
84. B. F. Harvey, *Living and dying in England, 1100–1540: the monastic experience* (Oxford, 1993), p. 58.
85. SBTRO, BRT 1/3/52, mem. 2r.
86. BRT 1/3/36.
87. BRT 1/3/22 (the dried malt is more expensive, 5½*d* a bushel, as opposed to 5*d* for the undried).
88. BRT 1/3/23.
89. BRT 1/3/53, mem. 1r.
90. BRT 1/3/22.
91. BRT 1/3/52, mem. 1r.
92. P. Slavin, 'Goose management and rearing in late medieval eastern England, *c*.1250–1400', *Agricultural History Review* 58 (2010), pp. 6–8, 15, 24; SBTRO, BRT 1/3/43: 165 pullets at 1*d* each; four of the geese died of disease.
93. BRT 1/3/25.
94. BRT 1/3/28.
95. BRT 1/3/30.
96. BRT 1/3/27, BRT 1/3/28, BRT 1/3/29, BRT 1/3/30.
97. BRT 1/3/53, mem. 1r.
98. BRT 1/3/27.
99. BRT 1/3/36.
100. BRT 1/3/27.
101. BRT 1/3/52, mem. 2r.
102. BRT 1/3/53, mem. 1r.
103. BRT 1/3/25, BRT 1/3/43.
104. BRT 1/3/100, mem. 2r.
105. BRT 1/3/23, 30.
106. BRT 1/3/25.
107. BRT 1/3/39.
108. BRT 1/3/105, mem. 2d.
109. BRT 1/3/50, mem. 2r.
110. BRT 1/3/65, mem. 1r.
111. BRT 1/3/89, mem. 1r.
112. BRT 1/3/105, mem. 2d.
113. BRT 1/3/25, BRT 1/3/27.
114. BRT 1/3/40, mem. 2r.

115. BRT 1/3/34, BRT 1/3/36; BRT 1/3/44, mem. 1r; BRT 1/3/82, mem. 1r.
116. BRT 1/3/37, BRT 1/3/39.
117. BRT 1/3/12, mem. 2d; BRT 1/3/50, mem. 2r; BRT 1/3/86, mem. 1r.
118. BRT 1/3/40, mem. 2r; BRT 1/3/42, mem. 1r; BRT 1/3/47, mem. 1r; BRT 1/3/51, mem. 2r.
119. BRT 1/3/14, mem. 1d.
120. BRT 1/3/28; BRT 1/3/40, mem. 2r; BRT 1/3/43; BRT1/3/50, mem. 2r.
121. BRT 1/3/106, mem. 1r.
122. BRT 1/3/25.
123. BRT 1/3/34.
124. BRT 1/3/43.
125. Fat: BRT 1/3/50, mem. 2r; BRT 1/3/52, mem. 2r; marrowbones: BRT 1/3/50, mem. 2r; BRT 1/3/52, mem. 2r.
126. BRT 1/3/55, mem. 1r.
127. BRT 1/3/51, mem. 1r.
128. BRT 1/3/53, mem. 1r.
129. BRT 1/3/27.
130. BRT 1/3/28.
131. BRT 1/3/36.
132. BRT 1/3/50, mem. 2r.
133. Rosser, 'Going to the fraternity feast', pp. 435–6.
134. SBTRO, BRT 1/3/22.
135. BRT 1/3/26, mem. 2r.
136. BRT 1/3/39, mem. 1d.
137. BRT 1/3/43, mem 1d.
138. BRT 1/3/52, mem. 2r.; BRT 1/3/80, mem. 1r; BRT 1/3/82, mem. 1r; BRT 1/3/85, mem. 1r.
139. BRT 1/3/60, mem. 1r; BRT 1/3/80, 82, 85, 86 and 89.
140. BRT 1/3/13, mem. 1r; BRT 1/3/43, mem 1d; BRT 1/3/105, mem. 2d.
141. BRT 1/3/39, mem. 1d.
142. BRT 1/3/44, mem. 1d.
143. BRT 1/3/43, mem. 1r.
144. BRT 1/3/30.
145. BRT 1/3/105, mem. 2d; BRT1/3/106, mem. 1r.
146. BRT 1/3/44, mem. 1r–1d.
147. BRT 1/3/80, mem. 1r.
148. BRT 1/3/50, mem. 2r; BRT 1/3/53, mem. 1r.
149. BRT 1/3/28.
150. BRT 1/3/37.
151. BRT 1/3/39; BRT 1/3/82, mem. 1r.
152. BRT 1/3/30.
153. BRT 1/3/34.
154. BRT 1/3/37.
155. Rosser, 'Going to the fraternity feast', p. 436.
156. SBTRO, BRT 1/3/4, mem. 2r.
157. BRT 1/3/47, mem. 1r, paragraphs 2, 7.
158. e.g, BRT 1/3/25, 1410–11, audit of the accounts before the master and aldermen and election of John Leke to office of master; BRT 1/3/27, 1412–13, audit of accounts; one other set of food expenses in hall.
159. BRT 1/3/61, mem. 1r.
160. BRT 1/3/16, mem. 1r.
161. BRT 1/3/49, mem. 1r.
162. BRT 1/3/42, mem. 1r.
163. BRT 1/3/54, mem. 1r.
164. BTR 1/3/38.
165. BTR 1/3/38, mem. 5d.

166. BRT 1/3/39.
167. BRT 1/3/36.
168. BRT 1/3/21, mem. 1r.
169. BRT 1/3/56, mem. 1r.
170. BRT 1/3/60, mem. 1r.
171. BRT 1/3/61, mem. 1r.
172. BRT 1/3/67, mem. 1r.
173. BRT 1/3/23.
174. BRT 1/3/82, mem. 1r.
175. BRT 1/3/105, mem. 2d.
176. Rosser, 'Going to the fraternity feast', pp. 440, 446.
177. Hants RO, W/H1/204, mem. 9r.

8 Foodways and Monastic Institutions

1. *FL*, iv, pp. 178–9.
2. Or 'grooms', i.e. 'garsons': 'Bibendo ad garsacil', cf. *AND* garsçuaile. *Statuta capitulorum generalium Ordinis Cisterciensis ab anno 1116 ad annum 1786* (8 vols, Louvain, 1933–41), i, p. 445. I am grateful to Professor Nicholas Vincent for this reference.
3. B. F. Harvey, *Living and dying in England, 1100–1540: the monastic experience* (Oxford, 1993), pp. 36–71, 108–11.
4. P. Patrick, *The 'obese medieval monk': a multidisciplinary study of a stereotype* (Oxford, British Archaeological Reports, British series, 590; 2014), pp. 63–76, 128–53.
5. Rule of St Benedict: chapters 39 and 40 cover food and drink, chapters 35–8 and 41, service and timing of meals. *RB 1980: the Rule of St Benedict*, ed. T. Fry and others (Collegeville, MN, 1981), pp. 232–41. For a summary and a description of pittances, B. F. Harvey, 'Monastic pittances in the Middle Ages', in *FME*, pp. 220–1.
6. *The customary of the Benedictine abbey of Bury St Edmunds in Suffolk ...*, ed. A. Gransden (Henry Bradshaw Society, 99; 1973), pp. xxix, xxxix, 96–9.
7. B. F. Harvey, *Westminster Abbey and its estates in the Middle Ages* (Oxford, 1977), pp. 340, 404.
8. *CSACSPW*, ii, pp. 75–7.
9. *CSACSPW*, i, pp. 389, 394–6; Harvey, 'Monastic pittances', pp. 220–1; D. Postles, 'The regular canons and the use of food, *c*.1200–1350', in *The regular canons in the medieval British Isles*, ed. J. Burton and K. Stober (Turnhout, 2011), pp. 233–49.
10. Cf. P. Slavin, *Bread and ale for the brethren: the provisioning of Norwich Cathedral Priory 1260–1536* (Hertford, 2012), pp. 147–55.
11. *Customary of the Benedictine abbey of Bury St Edmunds*, ed. Gransden, pp. 39–40.
12. See Chapter 4; Abingdon Abbey: *Historia ecclesie Abbendonensis. The history of the church of Abingdon*, vol. 2, ed. J. Hudson (Oxford, 2002), pp. 332–8; weys of 18 and 22 stone both appear in Abingdon sources, and it is uncertain how many ounces there were to the pound: calculation based on 22 stones to a wey, 14 lbs to a stone, 16 oz to a pound. C. M. Woolgar, 'Meat and dairy products in late medieval England', in *FME*, pp. 96–9: the Beaulieu Abbey wey was 15 stones of 12 lbs of 16 oz. Even using this figure it is still an impressive amount at the abbot's table: 411 oz a day, or 34 lbs.
13. *Historia ecclesie Abbendonensis*, vol. 2, ed. Hudson, pp. 358, 368–70.
14. *Chronicon monasterii de Abingdon*, ed. J. Stevenson (2 vols, Rolls series, 2; 1858), ii, pp. 398, 403–4.
15. *A consuetudinary of the fourteenth century for the refectory of the house of S. Swithun in Winchester*, ed. G. W. Kitchin (Hampshire Record Society, 6, i; 1886), pp. 15–16.
16. Norfolk RO, DCN 1/8/48, 56, inventories of the refectory, 1393–4, 1410–11.
17. *Chronicon monasterii de Abingdon*, ed. Stevenson, ii, p. 402.
18. *Consuetudinary ... S. Swithun in Winchester*, ed. Kitchin, pp. 18–19, 23. See Chapter 6 for the blessing of apples at St James at Norwich.

19. *CSACSPW*, i, p. 34.
20. See the essays in *English Heritage book of St Augustine's Abbey, Canterbury*, ed. R. Gem (1997).
21. T. Tatton-Brown, 'The Abbey precinct, liberty and estate', in *English Heritage book of St Augustine's Abbey*, ed. Gem, pp. 123–42, at pp. 127–9.
22. The abbey's main customary of 1330–40 notes that the subcellarer was to help oversee the service of bread and ale to the convent, as well as to guests, and what is due to the paid servants (*famuli*) in the offices, whether by hereditary right or as arranged by the convent. *CSACSPW*, i, p. 134, refers to the subcellarer's customary, three states of which are now in LPL MS 1213 (p. 309, 'Hic notantur consuetudines que pertinent ad subcelerarium dare de celario sancti Augustini Cantuariensis'). The three customaries are LPL, MS 1213, pp. 309–20 (mid to late thirteenth century), and pp. 321–3 and pp. 323–6, the first probably 1310×40, the second possibly contemporary, or just a few years later.
23. LPL, MS 1213, p. 309.
24. *Statutes of the Realm*, ed. A. Luders, T. E. Tomlins, J. Raithby and others (11 vols, 1810–28), i, pp. 199–200; for a summary of the arguments for the date of *c*.1256, see J. Davis, 'Baking for the common good: a reassessment of the assize of bread in medieval England', *Economic History Review*, 2nd series, 57 (2004), pp. 465–502, at p. 468, n. 15.
25. LPL, MS 1213, p. 322.
26. MS 1213, pp. 313–14.
27. MS 1213, p. 310.
28. *CSACSPW*, i, pp. 57–8.
29. LPL, MS 1213, p. 314.
30. MS 1213, p. 315.
31. MS 1213, p. 316.
32. MS 1213, pp. 315–16.
33. MS 1213, p. 313.
34. MS 1213, pp. 309–10.
35. MS 1213, p. 316.
36. It looks as if a pound of 12 oz is used here for cheese, rather than 16 oz; at 16, the weight of cheese per flan is 0.62 kg (2^1/$_5$ oz). LPL, MS 1213, p. 322.
37. MS 1213, p. 321.
38. MS 1213, p. 321.
39. MS 1213, p. 322.
40. MS 1213, p. 325.
41. MS 1213, p. 322.
42. MS 1213, p. 322.
43. MS 1213, pp. 316–17.
44. MS 1213, pp. 317–18.
45. Compare those tenants described as 'avertrull' and 'averhors' and their services from Minster in *The register of St Augustine's Abbey, Canterbury, commonly called the Black Book*, ed. G. J. Turner and H. E. Salter (2 vols, British Academy, Records of Social and Economic History, 2–3; 1915, 1924), i, pp. 46–58.
46. LPL, MS 1213, pp. 318–19.
47. *CSACSPW*, i, p. 134.
48. *CSACSPW*, i, p. 64.
49. *CSACSPW*, i, p. 62.
50. *CSACSPW*, i, pp. 57–8.
51. *CSACSPW*, i, p. 53.
52. *CSACSPW*, i, pp. 54–5.
53. *CSACSPW*, i, pp. 55–6.
54. Cf. BL, MS Harley 6815, ff. 29r–33r.
55. *CSACSPW*, i, p. 56.
56. *CSACSPW*, i, p. 56.

57. *CSACSPW*, i, pp. 56–7.
58. *CSACSPW*, i, pp. 58–62.
59. *CSACSPW*, i, pp. 121, 125–6, 130–3.
60. *CSACSPW*, i, p. 136.
61. *CSACSPW*, i, p. 136.
62. *CSACSPW*, i, p. 136.
63. *CSACSPW*, i, p. 137.
64. *CSACSPW*, i, p. 149.
65. J. Greatrex, *The English Benedictine cathedral priories: rule and practice, c.1270–c.1420* (Oxford, 2011), pp. 243–6.
66. *CSACSPW*, i, pp. 361–2, 387–8.
67. *CSACSPW*, i, pp. 7–8.
68. *CSACSPW*, ii, pp. xvii–xviii, 101–2.
69. W. Dugdale, *Monasticon Anglicanum*, ed. J. Caley, H. Ellis and B. Bandinel (new edition, 6 vols in 8, 1846), i, pp. 443–5; BL, MS Cotton Julius D VIII, ff. 40–8, for the 'charge' of the cellaress of Barking, and ff. 88–108 for the *Forme of cury*; discussed in E. Power, *Medieval English nunneries, c.1275 to 1535* (Cambridge, 1922), pp. 563–8. Cf. the taste for peasant dishes in some aristocratic circles: B. Laurioux, *Gastronomie, humanisme et société à Rome au milieu du XVe siècle. Autour du De honesta voluptate de Platina* (Florence, 2006), pp. 302–23.
70. Suffolk RO, Ipswich, HD 1538/174/3/2–3, 5–7.
71. C. Walker Bynum, *Holy feast and holy fast: the religious significance of food to medieval women* (Berkeley, 1987); M. G. Muzzarelli and F. Tarozzi, *Donne e cibo: una relazione nella storia* (n.p., 2003), pp. 41–9; C. Mazzoni, *The women in God's kitchen: cooking, eating and spiritual writing* (New York, 2005).
72. *CS*, ii, pp. 789–90.
73. *PP*, i, p. 198 (B V, ll. 151–63): 'I have an aunte to nonne and an abbesse: / Hir were levere swowe or swelte þan suffre any peyne. / I have be cook in hir kichene and þe covent served / Many monþes wiþ hem, and wiþ monkes boþe. / I was þe prioresse potager and oþer pouere ladies, / And maad hem ioutes of ianglyng – ... / Of wikkede wordes I Wraþe hire wortes made.'
74. *PP*, i, p. 200 (B V, ll. 174–7): 'Forþi no likyng have I wiþ þo leodes to wonye; / I ete þere unþende fissh and feble ale drynke. / Ac ouþer while whan wyn comeþ, and whan I drynke wel at eve, / I have a flux of a foul mouþ wel fyve dayes after.'
75. M. Oliva, 'The French of England in female convents: the French kitcheners' accounts of Campsey Ash Priory', in *Language and culture in medieval Britain: the French of England c.1100–c.1500*, ed. J. Wogan-Browne (York, 2009), p. 90, for a survey of domestic accounts of nunneries; J. H. Tillotson, *Marrick Priory: a nunnery in late medieval Yorkshire* (York, Borthwick Paper, 75; 1989), pp. 1–2 and n. 7.
76. Tillotson, *Marrick Priory*, pp. 1–2; A. Savine, *English monasteries on the eve of the Dissolution* (Oxford, 1909), pp. 269–88.
77. *The register of Thomas de Cobham, Bishop of Worcester, 1317–1327*, ed. E. H. Pearce (Worcestershire Historical Society, 40; 1930), p. 162.
78. *LV III*, pp. 248–9.
79. *LV II*, pp. 217–18: 'there be fysshe or white mete or other lyke as is usede in your place of olde tyme.'
80. *LV I*, pp. 44–5.
81. *LV II*, pp. 46–52.
82. *LV II*, pp. 89–90.
83. *LV II*, p. 89, n. 8.
84. *LV I*, pp. 48–9.
85. *LV II*, pp. 248, 250–1.
86. *LV II*, pp. 183–4.
87. *LV II*, pp. 356–7.

88. *LV III*, pp. 347–8.
89. Similar conclusions about the diet of nuns can be drawn from the accounts of St Radegund's, Cambridge, and from those of Carrow, in Norfolk: A. Gray *The priory of Saint Radegund Cambridge* (Cambridge Antiquarian Society, Octavo Publications, 31; 1898); and L. J. Redstone, 'Three Carrow account rolls', *Norfolk Archaeology* 29 (1946), pp. 41–88. The comments of Marilyn Oliva, 'French of England in female convents', p. 98, argue for the same, but the nuns of Wilton whom she uses in her comparison had a diet closer to the elite.
90. Dugdale, *Monasticon*, i, pp. 436–46.
91. Dugdale, *Monasticon*, i, pp. 443–5.
92. E. Crittall, 'Fragment of an account of the cellaress of Wilton Abbey, 1299', in *Collectanea*, ed. N. J. Williams (Wiltshire Archaeological and Natural History Society, Records Branch, 12; 1956), pp. 142–56; R. B. Pugh, 'Fragment of an account of Isabel of Lancaster, nun of Amesbury, 1333–4', in *Festschrift zur Feier des zweihundertjährigen Bestandes des Haus-, Hof- und Staatsarchivs*, ed. L. Santifaller (2 vols, Vienna, 1949–51), i, pp. 487–98.

9 The Elite Table

1. BL, MS Harley 6815, ff. 28r–33r.
2. For a survey of elite dining practices, see *GH*, pp. 145–65.
3. M. Camille, *Mirror in parchment: the Luttrell Psalter and the making of medieval England* (1998), pp. 89–90.
4. C. M. Woolgar, *The senses in late medieval England* (New Haven, 2006), pp. 117–26.
5. John 13:26: 'Et cum intinxisset panem dedit Iudae Simonis Scariotis'.
6. 'Rules of St Robert', in *Walter of Henley and other treatises on estate management and accounting*, ed. D. Oschinsky (Oxford, 1971), pp. 404–5.
7. *BSP*, E vi Eucharistia, Art. viii: xxxii.
8. C. M. Woolgar, 'Queens and crowns: Philippa of Hainaut, possessions and the Queen's chamber in mid XIVth-century England', *Micrologus* 22 (2014), pp. 219–23.
9. Norfolk RO, Norwich Consistory Court Records, Will Register 1 Heydon (1370–82), f. 21v.
10. *Mirk*, i, p. 79.
11. Camille, *Mirror in parchment*, pp. 88–9. The tribulations of Sir Geoffrey and his wife had included the deaths of at least two children and the discovery that they were too closely related to have married without formal dispensation, which they acquired retrospectively in 1332–4; Camille, *Mirror in parchment*, pp. 93–107.
12. Camille, *Mirror in parchment*, pp. 84–107. The argument that this is a late autumn/winter meal because pigs (in an earlier image) were often killed then, is to take the evidence too far. Pigs were in fact slaughtered at any age, from suckling pigs, a delicacy, upwards; and Walter of Henley at least expected pigs to produce two litters in a year. U. Albarella, 'Pig husbandry and pork consumption in medieval England', in *FME*, pp. 82–7.
13. For the illustrations, see *GH*, pp. 138–9.
14. For the family, Camille, *Mirror in parchment*, pp. 94–5.
15. *Azure a bend between six martlets argent.*
16. *ERT*, p. 210, R716; p. 325. Cf. R. W. Lightbown, *Secular goldsmiths' work in medieval France: a history* (Research Reports of the Society of Antiquaries of London, 36; 1978), p. 18, for trenchers.
17. C. Welch, *History of the Worshipful Company of Pewterers of the city of London* (2 vols, 1902), i, pp. 14–15.
18. P. Brears, *Cooking and dining in medieval England* (Totnes, 2008), p. 399.
19. SBTRO, BRT 1/3/100, mem. 2r.
20. I misidentified this in *GH*, p. 138, caption to plate 52: see D. A. Hinton, *Gold and gilt, pots and pins* (Oxford, 2005), p. 358, n. 10.
21. C. M. Woolgar, 'Group diets in late medieval England', in *FME*, pp. 191–200.

22. *BSP*, N iii Nobilitas, Art. v: xiii: 'quod membrorum corporis magis sumptuosum fuisset.'

23. C. M. Woolgar, 'Treasure, material possessions and the bishops of late medieval England', in *The prelate in England and Europe, 1300–1560*, ed. M. Heale (York, 2014), pp. 178–81, 190.

24. *BSP*, A xxvii Avaricia, Art. xi; M xi Mors, Art. xvii. For giving away plate at a major wedding, *The receyt of the Ladie Kateryne*, ed. G. Kipling (EETS, OS, 296; 1990), pp. 74–6.

25. JRULM, MS Latin 235, ff. 20v, 21r.

26. *BSP*, T v Tribulatio, Art. iiii: xvii.

27. *The political songs of England, from the reign of John to that of Edward II*, ed. T. Wright (Camden Society, old series, 6; 1839), p. 186: 'Est vitii signum pro victu solvere lignum.'

28. M. Vale, *The princely court: medieval courts and culture in north-west Europe 1270–1380* (Oxford, 2001), pp. 360–1. I am grateful to Dr Jenny Stratford for a discussion of the systems of recording the weight of plate in the royal household.

29. JRULM, MS Latin 235, ff. 24r–30v.

30. TNA, E 101/393/4, ff. 1r–3r.

31. E101/393/4, ff. 3v–4r.

32. Lightbown, *Secular goldsmiths' work*, pp. 16–17.

33. *ERT*, pp. 14–15, 20–7, and 217–20 for the listing of mem. 27 of the inventory, 'Vessell d'argent en diverses offices de l'hostiell' du roy'.

34. *ERT*, pp. 217–20.

35. TNA, E 101/393/4, f. 1r.

36. *ERT*, p. 218.

37. TNA, E 101/393/4, ff. 3r–4r.

38. *ERT*, pp. 205 (R656–7), 322.

39. *ERT*, p. 205 (R658–60).

40. *TE III*, pp. 85–6.

41. Bodleian Library, Oxford, MS Eng. hist. b. 208, f. 35r.

42. TNA, E 101/353/30, mem. 2d.

43. *TREWE*, p. 213; Lightbown, *Secular goldsmiths' work*, pp. 29–30; A. Paravicini-Bagliani, *The pope's body*, trans. D. S. Peterson (Chicago, 2000), pp. 225–6.

44. JRULM, MS Latin 236, f. 5v.

45. *ERT*, pp. 147 (R14), 266. It is possible Richard inherited this from Edward III.

46. *ERT*, pp. 147 (R18), 266.

47. H. M. Clifford, *A treasured inheritance: 600 years of Oxford college silver* (Oxford, 2004), pp. 72–5.

48. Bodleian Library, Oxford, MS Eng. hist. b. 208, ff. 31v, 34v.

49. LPL, Register of William Whittlesey, ff. 99r–v, 110r, 114r–115r, 125v.

50. Register of William Whittlesey, ff. 116v, 121r ('toute ma vessell dargent qest acustume continuelment de servir en nostre hostiel si ce qe ie achataie de Robinet Fraunceys come autre illeoqes').

51. LPL, Register of Simon Sudbury, ff. 94v–95v.

52. Lightbown, *Secular goldsmiths' work*, pp. 18–19.

53. Norfolk RO, Norwich Consistory Court Records, Will Register 1 Heydon (1370–82), f. 14v.

54. Norfolk RO, DCN 1/1/22, Master of the Cellar, 1310–11, mem. 1r.

55. London, Society of Antiquaries, MS 208, f. 7v.

56. Norfolk RO, DCN 1/1/23, Master of the Cellar, 1313–14, mem. 1r.

57. DCN 1/1/27, Master of the Cellar, 1318–19, mem. 1r.

58. DCN 1/1/16, Master of the Cellar, 1303–4, mem. 1r.

59. *HAME*, i, p. 423.

60. BL, Add. MS 60584, f. 12r.

61. *HAME*, ii, p. 512.

62. *TREWE*, p. 95.

63. TNA, JUST 2/74, mem. 11r; JUST 2/156, mem. 2d.

64. P. J. P. Goldberg, 'The fashioning of bourgeois domesticity in later medieval England: a material culture perspective', in *Medieval domesticity: home, housing and household in medieval England*, ed. M. Kowaleski and P. J. P. Goldberg (Cambridge, 2008), pp. 134–5, 139–44.

65. Norfolk RO, Norwich Consistory Court Records, Will Register 1 Heydon (1370–82), f. 96r.

66. *BSP*, C vi Confessio, Art. x: xli.

67. Norfolk RO, Norwich Consistory Court Records, Will Register 1 Heydon (1370–82), ff. 38r, 99v.

68. Norfolk RO, DCN 1/1/7, Master of the Cellar, 1283–4, mem. 1r.

69. DCN 1/1/12, Master of the Cellar, 1294–5, mem. 1r.

70. TNA, JUST 2/80, mem. 3r.

71. *ERT*, p. 217.

72. *PLP*, ii, pp. 601–4.

73. *TE II*, pp. 78–9.

74. *TE III*, pp. 1–3.

75. *TE III*, p. 131.

76. TNA, E 101/393/4, f. 4v.

77. J. Hatcher and T. C. Barker, *A history of British pewter* (1974), pp. 41–59.

78. DUL, DCP Cellarer's account, 1459–60, mem. 1r.

79. Welch, *History of the Worshipful Company of Pewterers*, i, pp. 11–12.

80. *TE II*, p. 270. See also the list of moulds in a London pewterer's workshop, 1427, that had belonged to Thomas Filkes: R. F. Homer, 'Tin, lead and pewter', in *English medieval industries: craftsmen, techniques, products*, ed. J. Blair and N. Ramsay (1991), pp. 71–2.

81. *PLP*, i, p. 275, no. 166: 'for ye have to few of any of these to serve this place'.

82. *TREWE*, pp. 208, 213.

83. Bodleian Library, Oxford, MS Eng. hist. b. 208, ff. 34r–v.

84. *MM*, pp. 50–1: 'For it is betere with reste and pees, / A melis meete of hoomeli fare, / Þan for to have an hundrid mees / With grucchinge & wiþ myche care.'

10 Cooks and Kitchens, Dietetics and Foods

1. C. M. Woolgar, 'The cook', in *Historians on Chaucer: the 'General Prologue' to the Canterbury Tales*, ed. S. H. Rigby, with A. J. Minnis (Oxford, 2014), pp. 262–76.

2. *The minor poems of John Lydgate*, vol. 2, ed. H. N. MacCracken (EETS, OS, 192; 1934), p. 836, l. 36: ' 'Hoot ffir and smoke makith many an angry cook.'

3. B. J. Whiting and H. W. Whiting, *Proverbs, sentences, and proverbial phrases from English writings mainly before 1500* (Cambridge, MA, 1968), p. 97 (C418): 'He is an evyll coke that can not lycke his owne lyppes.'

4. *Mirk*, i, p. 133: 'þere come a boy owte off þe kychon, a broþell alle bawded wit gresse.'

5. *HAME*, ii, pp. 651–5.

6. e.g. 'ebdomadarii coquine', *The customary of the Cathedral Priory Church of Norwich: MS 465 in the Library of Corpus Christi College, Cambridge*, ed. J. B. L. Tolhurst (Henry Bradshaw Society, 82; 1948), pp. xxviii (blessing of cooks), 27, 29, 30; P. B. Griesser, 'Die "Ecclesiastica Officia Cisterciensis Ordinis" des Cod. 1711 von Trient', *Analecta Sacri Ordinis Cisterciensis* 12 (1956), pp. 267 70. For specialist cooks at St Augustine's Abbey, see Chapter 8.

7. *TREWE*, p. 121.

8. *TREWE*, p. 220.

9. DUL, DCP Cellarer's account, 1443–4 (A), mem. 3r.

10. Cellarer's account, 1460–1 (A), mem. 1r.

11. Cellarer's account, 1462–3, mem. 1r.

12. Cellarers' accounts, 1465–6 (A), mem. 1r (Archbishop of York, Earls of Northumberland, Warwick and Westmorland); 1467–8 (A), mem. 1r (Robert Ruke, cook of the Earl of

Northumberland); 1473–4 (A), mem. 1r; 1475–6, mem. 1r; 1478–9 (A), mem. 1r (Duke of Gloucester, Lord St John).

13. TNA, E 36/214, f. 42r: 'Perowe that was þe king of Castell's coke'.

14. E 36/214, f. 58v: 'Perowe the ffrenche coke'.

15. E 36/214, f. 58v: 'the Frenche pasteler'.

16. C. M. Woolgar, *The senses in late medieval England* (2006), p. 270; Pierrot was the same person as Piero le Doux: *Dress at the court of King Henry VIII: the wardrobe book of the Wardrobe of the Robes . . .*, ed. M. Hayward (Leeds, 2007), pp. 271–2. For short biographies of some other cooks, C. M. Woolgar, 'Feasting and fasting: food and taste in Europe in the Middle Ages', in *Food: the history of taste*, ed. P. Freedman (2007), pp. 186–8.

17. *HAME*, ii, p. 536–7.

18. *MO*, p. 92, ll. 7873–81.

19. *Bedfordshire coroners' rolls*, ed. R. F. Hunnisett (Bedfordshire Historical Record Society, 41; 1961), p. 52, no. 119.

20. DUL, DCP Cellarer's account, 1459–60, mem. 1r.

21. Cellarer's account, 1455–6, mem. 1r.

22. Cellarer's account, 1459–60, mem. 1r.

23. Cellarer's account, 1446–7 (A), mem. 1r.

24. Cellarer's account, 1465–6 (A), mem. 1r.

25. Cellarer's account, 1445–6 (A), mem. 1r.

26. Cellarer's account, 1448–9 (A), mem. 1r.

27. *PLP*, i, p. 599, no. 370: 'Thys man is meane of stature, yonge inough, well wittyd, well manerd, a goodly yong man on horse and foote. He is well spokyn in Inglyshe, metly well in Frenshe, and verry parfite in Flemyshe. He can wryght and reed.'

28. *HAME*, i, p. 400.

29. *HAME*, i, p. 405.

30. *HAME*, i, p. 406.

31. *HAME*, ii, p. 513.

32. *GH*, p. 36.

33. J. H. Tillotson, *Marrick Priory: a nunnery in late medieval Yorkshire* (York: Borthwick Paper, 75; 1989), p. 14.

34. Dorset History Centre, Dorchester, D/SHA/CH2 (original now returned to Sherborne, read from Ph233).

35. C. B. Hieatt, *A gathering of medieval English recipes* (Turnhout, 2008), pp. 9–20; C. B. Hieatt, T. Nutter and J. H. Holloway, *Concordance of English recipes: thirteenth through fifteenth centuries* (Tempe, 2006).

36. *MM*, pp. 115–99; pantry knives at p. 120.

37. *An ordinance of pottage: an edition of the fifteenth century culinary recipes in Yale University's MS Beinecke 163*, ed. C. B. Hieatt (1988), p. 95, recipe 159.

38. For techniques, see e.g. *TFCCB*, pp. 1–64.

39. P. Brears, *Cooking and dining in medieval England* (Blackawton, 2008), pp. 173–214, is especially good at defining the functions of the kitchen.

40. DUL, DCP Cellarer's account, 1465–6 (A), mem. 1r. M. G. Snape, 'Documentary evidence for the building of Durham Cathedral and its monastic buildings', in *Medieval art and architecture at Durham Cathedral*, ed. N. Coldstream (British Archaeological Association Conference Transactions, 3; 1980), pp. 27–8.

41. *The register of Walter de Stapeldon, Bishop of Exeter (A.D. 1307–1326)*, ed. F. C. Hingeston-Randolph (1892), p. 568.

42. See Chapter 2 for brandreths generally.

43. *The register of Henry Chichele, Archbishop of Canterbury 1414–1443*, vol. 2: *Wills proved before the Archbishop or his commissaries*, ed. E. F. Jacob and H. C. Johnson (Canterbury and York Society, 42; 1937), pp. 140–1: 'ad supponendum ollas deputatum ad coquendum'.

44. *TE III*, pp. 87–8.

45. *TE III*, p. 79.

46. LPL, ED 297, mem. 1r.
47. DUL, DCP Cellarers' accounts, 1445–6 (A), mem. 1r; 1479–80, mem. 1r.
48. *CO*, p. 95.
49. DUL, DCP Cellarer's account, 1471–2 (A), mem. 1r.
50. Cellarer's account, 1475–6, mem. 1r: 125 stone.
51. Cellarer's account, 1455–6, mem. 1r.
52. Cellarer's account, 1472–3 (A), mem. 1r.
53. Cellarer's account, 1478–9 (A), mem. 1r: 'pro factura fornacis pro le friyng in coquina'.
54. Cellarer's account, 1460–1 (A), mem. 1r.
55. Cellarer's status, 1459, mem. 1r.
56. Cellarer's status, 1459, mem. 1r.
57. Cellarers' accounts, 1438–9 (A); 1444–5; 1444–5, month 1 (Friday next after feast of St Martin).
58. HMC, *Report on manuscripts in various collections* [*HMC* 55], part 7 (1914), p. 334.
59. *TE III*, pp. 136–7.
60. *Register of Walter de Stapeldon*, ed. Hingeston-Randolph, p. 568.
61. DUL, DCP Cellarer's account, 1459–60, mem. 1r.
62. *AND* cretun *n*.
63. *TE II*, pp. 96, 99, 101.
64. *TE II*, pp. 110, 112; *Early Northampton wills preserved in Northamptonshire Record Office*, ed. D. Edwards, M. Forrest, J. Minchinton, M. Shaw, B. Tyndall and P. Wallis (Northamptonshire Record Society, 42; 2005), pp. 112–13.
65. *The Paston letters, A.D. 1422–1509*, vol. 3, ed. J. Gairdner (new edition, 1904), p. 189.
66. *TE II*, p. 194.
67. *TE III*, p. 300.
68. e.g. *MRC*, pp. 35–57; *Walter of Henley and other treatises on estate management and accounting*, ed. D. Oschinsky (Oxford, 1971), pp. 200–57, 417–45, 469–75.
69. SBTRO, DR37/2/Box 114/1, mem. 1r and 2r.
70. *A myrour to lewde men and wymmen: a prose version of the Speculum Vitae, ed. from BL MS Harley 45*, ed. V. Nelson (Heidelberg, 1981), p. 134: 'Letel þefte is whan menis servantes or oþer steleþ mete, drinke, polayle, scheves in heruest or oþre smale þinges and þinkeþ it is noght to charge for it is a custome.'
71. *CO*, pp. 95–6.
72. *TFCCB*, p. 9.
73. *The orcherd of Syon*, ed. P. Hodgson and G. M. Liegey (EETS, OS, 258; 1966), p. 170: 'We ben blasphemyd, and we biseche and preye, for we ben maad as orfayle [offal] of al þis world, þe which is icast out þerof.'
74. *Jacob's Well, an Englisht treatise on the cleansing of man's conscience …*, ed. A. Brandeis (EETS, OS, 115; 1900), p. 81.
75. *Of hawks and horses: four late Middle English prose treatises*, ed. W. L. Braekman (Brussels, 1986), p. 76.
76. *LV III*, pp. 249, 252.
77. DUL, DCP Cellarer's accounts, 1447–8, mem. 1r; a similar entry for Christmas 1448 is deleted in cellarer's account, 1448–9 (A), mem. 1r.
78. SBTRO, BRT 1/3/40, mem. 2r.
79. *GH*, p. 31. St John's College, Cambridge, muniments D91.21, pp. 15, 107 (household of Lady Margaret Beaufort). I am grateful to Professor Sue Powell for this reference.
80. *GH*, p. 26.
81. *GH*, pp, 120, 136.
82. Suffolk RO, Ipswich, HD1538/174/3/3.
83. *HAME*, i, p. 410.
84. *The Cely letters 1472–1488*, ed. A. Hanham (EETS, OS, 273; 1975), p. 63, letter 71: 'and bryng hyt wyth yow at thys Kyrstemes …'
85. Winchester College Muniments 1: dorse, Dona.

86. *HAME*, i, p. 426.
87. See, for example, *GH*, pp. 112–14.
88. TNA, E 101/393/4, f. 13r.
89. *Household book of Dame Alice de Bryene of Acton Hall, Suffolk, Sept. 1412–Sept. 1413*, ed. M. K. Dale and V. B. Redstone (Ipswich, 1931), p. 14.
90. *PLP*, i, p. 251, no. 148.
91. *The household book of Queen Isabella of England for the fifth regnal year of Edward II 8th July 1311 to 7th July 1312*, ed. F. D. Blackley and G. Hermansen (University of Alberta, Classical and Historical Studies, 1; 1971), pp. 136, 214.
92. *HAME*, i, pp. 428–9.
93. *HAME*, i, p. 409.
94. *HAME*, i, p. 426.
95. *PLP*, i, p. 412, no. 248; p. 448, no. 268; p. 554, no. 339.
96. B. M. S. Campbell, J. A. Galloway, D. Keen and M. Murphy, *A medieval capital and its grain supply: agrarian production and distribution in the London region c.1300* (Institute of British Geographers, Historical Geography Research Series, 30; 1993).
97. Somerset RO, DD/L P37/7, part 1, mem 6r.
98. J. Claridge and J. Langdon, 'Storage in medieval England: the evidence from purveyance accounts, 1295–1349', *Economic History Review*, 2nd series, 64 (2011), pp. 1242–65.
99. J. A. Robinson, 'Household roll of Bishop Ralph of Shrewsbury 1337–8', in *Collectanea I*, ed. T. F. Palmer (Somerset Record Society, 39; 1924), pp. 94–5, 97, 100, 103, 105–6, 110–13, 117, 123, 125–6, 130, 132.
100. Northants RO, Westmorland (Apethorpe) 4/XX/4, ff. 20, 24a.
101. *FL*, iv, p. 194.
102. *Minor poems of John Lydgate*, part 2, ed. MacCracken, pp. 704–5, quote at ll. 87–8: 'Moderat diet ageyns al seekenesse, / Is best phisicien to mesur thyn entraile.'
103. M. Nicoud, *Les régimes de santé au moyen âge* (2 vols, Rome, 2007), i, pp. 17–18, 87; ii, p. 699.
104. Nicoud, *Les régimes de santé*, i, pp. 171–5, 401–524; C. Rawcliffe, *Medicine and society in later medieval England* (Far Thrupp, 1995), pp. 37–40; C. Rawcliffe, *Urban bodies: communal health in late medieval English towns and cities* (Woodbridge, 2013), pp. 232–4.
105. H. P. Cholmeley, *John of Gaddesden and the Rosa medicinae* (Oxford, 1912), pp. 32–3; M. Carlin, 'Gaddesden, John (d.1348/9), physician', in *ODNB*, at http://www.oxforddnb.com/view/article/10267?docPos=1 (accessed 11 June 2015).
106. Cholmeley, *John of Gaddesden and the Rosa medicinae*, pp. 66–7.
107. C. Rawcliffe, *Medicine for the soul: the life, death and resurrection of an English medieval hospital. St Giles's, Norwich, c.1249–1550* (Woodbridge, 1999), pp. 176–86.
108. *The cartulary of God's House, Southampton*, ed. J. M. Kaye (2 vols, Southampton Records Series, 19–20; 1976), i, pp. xlvi–li; Bodleian Library, Oxford, muniments of Queen's College, Oxford, R257, mem. 1r.
109. *CI*, p. 20.
110. *CSACSPW*, i, p. 300.
111. H. Schöffler, 'Practica Phisicalia Magistri Johannis de Burgundia', *Beiträge zur mittelenglischen Medizinliteratur, Sächsische Forschungsinstitut in Leipzig, Forschungsinstitut für neuere Philologie. III. Anglistische Abteilung*, Heft I (1919), p. 244.
112. *The Cyrurgie of Guy de Chauliac*, ed. M. S. Ogden (EETS, OS, 265; 1971), e.g. pp. 113–14.
113. *Lanfrank's 'Science of Cirurgie'*, ed. R. V. Fleischhacker (EETS, OS, 102; 1894), p. 276.
114. Schöffler, 'Practica Phisicalia Magistri Johannis de Burgundia', pp. 206, 217.
115. *Farming and gardening in late medieval Norfolk*, ed. C. Noble and C. Moreton (Norfolk Record Society, 61; 1996), p. 9.
116. *PLP*, i, pp. 370–1.

11 Hunger and Famine

1. W. C. Jordan, *The great famine: Northern Europe in the early fourteenth century* (Princeton, 1996); C. Dyer, 'Did the peasants really starve in medieval England?', in *Food and eating in medieval Europe*, ed. M. Carlin and J. T. Rosenthal (1998), pp. 53–71.

2. e.g. E. Stengel, 'Die beiden Sammlungen altfranzösischer Sprichwörter in der Oxforder Handschrift Rawlinson C 641', *Zeitschrift für französische Sprache und Litteratur* 21 (1899), p. 8, no. 167: see chapter 4.

3. S. B. Meech, 'A collection of proverbs in Rawlinson MS D.328', *Modern Philology* 38 (1940), pp. 117–26, at p. 118, no. 17: 'Whynter etyt þat somer getyt'; p. 121, no. 45: 'Lytill wote þe full what þe hongre eylyth'; p. 123, no. 63: 'Hungger makyth arde benis honi suete.'

4. M. Förster, 'Die mittelenglische Sprichwörtersammlung in Douce 52', in *Festschrift zum XII. allgemeinen deutschen Neuphilologentage in München, Pfingsten 1906*, ed. E. Stottreither (Erlangen, 1906), p. 46, no. 28: 'Hungur brekyth stone and walle'; and no. 29, hard beans.

5. *The political songs of England from the reign of John to that of Edward II*, ed. T. Wright (Camden Society, old series, 6; 1839), pp. 237–40.

6. *BSP*, E iii Elemosyna, Art ii: ii.

7. *BSP*, E iii Elemosyna, Art. ix: xxxvi.

8. *Mirk*, i, p. 83; Matt. 15:26, 'Non est bonum sumere panem filiorum et mittere canibus.'

9. These six works were derived from the account of the Last Judgement in Matthew's Gospel, 25:31–46, and a further work – the burial of the poor – was derived from the Book of Tobit: *Mirk*, i, pp. 6, 67; ii, p. 274: 'þe wheche werkes be: for to ȝev mete to hongry; to ȝeve drynk to hem þat ben thrusty; to cloþe hem þat ben akolde for defaute of cloþus; for to ȝeve hem herbar þat han none; to helpon hem þat ben seke of þat hem nedeth.'

10. *Mirk*, i, p. 68: 'Þus he þat doth almys-dede discretely schal have hys fode in heven perpetualy.'

11. *Dives and Pauper*, ed. P. H. Barnum (3 vols, EETS, OS, 275, 280, 434; 1976, 1980, 2004), i, p. 182; ii, p. 76.

12. Dyer, 'Did the peasants really starve in medieval England?', pp. 59–60.

13. TNA, JUST 2/17, mem. 2r.

14. JUST 2/166, mem. 1r.

15. JUST 2/25, rot. 1, mem. 3r.

16. JUST 2/67, mem. 11r.

17. JUST 2/67, mem. 40, rot. 4d.

18. *BSP*, R i Rapina, Art. v: xxi.

19. TNA, JUST 2/82, mem. 3r.

20. JUST 2/82, mem. 10r.

21. JUST 2/18, mem. 1d.

22. JUST 2/155, mem. 2r.

23. JUST 2/67, mem. 15r.

24. JUST 2/66, mem. 14d.

25. *FL*, iv, pp. 221–2: 'quia es inimicus noster et semper nobis nocuisti.'

26. *Jacob's Well, an Englisht treatise on the cleansing of man's conscience*, ed. A. Brandeis (EETS, OS, 115, 1900), p. 134: 'And ȝif þe wyif be alone, þei folwyn here into þe spense, þat for dreed sche is fayn to ȝyven hem what sche may.'

27. *The customary of the Benedictine abbey of Bury St Edmunds in Suffolk (from Harleian MS. 1005 in the British Museum)*, ed. A. Gransden (Henry Bradshaw Society, 99; 1973), pp. 82–3.

28. *Walter of Henley and other treatises on estate management and accounting*, ed. D. Oschinsky (Oxford, 1971), pp. 402–5.

29. *Walter of Henley*, ed. Oschinsky, pp. 400–1, rule 19/14: 'Comaundez ke vostre almone seyt lealment garde e coylly, ne pas envee de la table a garcuns, ne pas hors de sale porte, ne a supers, ne a diners de garcuns wastroyle; mes fraunchement, sagement e atempreement, saunz tencer e batre parti a poveres, malades, e mendiaunz.'

30. S. Dixon-Smith, 'The image and reality of alms-giving in the great halls of Henry III', *Journal of the British Archaeological Association* 152 (2000), pp. 79–96.

31. Dixon-Smith, 'Image and reality of alms-giving', p. 81.

32. Dixon-Smith, 'Image and reality of alms-giving', p. 86.

33. Dixon-Smith, 'Image and reality of alms-giving', pp. 86–7.

34. TNA, E 101/350/23, mem. 1r.

35. *Liber quotidianus contrarotulatoris garderobae anno regni regis Edwardi primi vicesimo octavo A.D. MCCXCIX & MCCC*, ed. Anon. (1787), pp. 17–25.

36. *The wardrobe book of William de Norwell 12 July 1338 to 27 May 1340*, ed. M. Lyon, B. Lyon, H. S. Lucas and J. de Sturler (Brussels, 1983), pp. 210–11.

37. *HAME*, i, pp. 179–227.

38. BAV, MS Vat. Lat. 4015, f. 16v.

39. MS Vat. Lat. 4015, f. 32r.

40. MS Vat. Lat. 4015, f. 109r.

41. MS Vat. Lat. 4015, f. 49v.

42. MS Vat. Lat. 4015, f. 79r.

43. MS Vat. Lat. 4015, f. 121r.

44. *GH*, p. 54. On feeding the poor in hall, see also *BSP*, P iii Paupertas, Art. iii: iiii.

45. *HAME*, i, p. 158.

46. *The court and household of Eleanor of Castile in 1290: an edition of British Library Additional Manuscript 35294*, ed. J. C. Parsons (Toronto, 1977), pp. 96–7, 130.

47. JRULM, MS Latin 235, ff. 7v–8v; B. F. Harvey, 'Monastic pittances in the Middle Ages', in *FME*, pp. 215–27.

48. Norfolk RO, DCN 1/1/11, Master of the Cellar, 1291–2, mem. 1r; DCN 1/1/14, Master of the Cellar, 1298–1300, mem. 3r; DCN 1/1/15, Master of the Cellar, 1302–3, mem. 2r; DCN 1/1/16, Master of the Cellar, 1303–4, mem. 1r; DCN 1/1/17, Master of the Cellar, 1303–4, mem. 2r; DCN 1/1/18, Master of the Cellar, 1307–8, mem. 2r; DCN 1/1/19, Master of the Cellar, 1308–9, mem. 2r; DCN 1/1/21, Master of the Cellar, 1309–10, mem. 2r.

49. *Chaucer*, p. 129, ll. 1736–9 (quote), and ll. 1746–56: 'He wente his wey; no lenger wolde he reste. / With scrippe and tipped staf, ytukked hye, / In every hous he gan to poure and prye, / And beggeth mele and chese, or elles corn.'

50. JRULM, MS Latin 235, ff. 5v, 23r, 29r.

51. *TREWE*, pp. 143–4.

52. *TREWE*, pp. 121, 125.

53. C. M. Woolgar, 'Gifts of food in late medieval England', *Journal of Medieval History* 37 (2011), p. 15.

54. E. W. Safford, 'An account of the expenses of Eleanor, sister of Edward III, on the occasion of her marriage to Reynald, Count of Guelders', *Archaeologia* 77 (1927), p. 128.

55. BAV, MS Vat. Lat. 4015, ff. 56r–57v.

56. B. F. Harvey, *Living and dying in England 1100–1540: the monastic experience* (Oxford, 1993), pp. 9–23.

57. The granator may have handed over as much as 874 qrs: the calculations are not consistent and sometimes use the long hundred of 120. Norfolk RO, DCN 1/1/6 Norwich Cathedral Priory, Master of the Cellar, 1282–3, mem. 2d (the granator's account). These figures suggest a different balance for this year to those abstracted in P. Slavin, *Bread and ale for the brethren: the provisioning of Norwich Cathedral Priory, 1260–1536* (Hertford, University of Hertfordshire Press, Studies in Regional and Local History, 11; 2012), pp. 156–7, table 7.8.

58. *The monastic constitutions of Lanfranc*, ed. D. Knowles, rev. C. N. L. Brooke (Oxford, 2002), pp. xxviii, 64.

59. *The customary of the Cathedral Priory Church of Norwich: MS 465 in the Library of Corpus Christi College, Cambridge*, ed. J. B. L. Tolhurst (Henry Bradshaw Society, 82; 1948), pp. 79–80.
60. *The customary of the Benedictine abbey of Eynsham in Oxfordshire*, ed. A. Gransden (Siegburg, 1963), pp. 189–90.
61. BL, Add. MS 88973, f. 88v.
62. BL, Add. MS 88974, f. iv verso, 3 qrs 1 bus. Also f. iv recto, Vigil of All Saints, 3 qrs 1 bus.
63. BL, Add. MS 88973, f. 90v.
64. East Sussex RO, Add. MS 4901, mem. 1d.
65. East Sussex RO, Add. MS 4905, mem. 1r.
66. East Sussex RO, Add. MS 4909, mem. 1r; Harvey, *Living and dying*, p. 17.
67. Canterbury Cathedral Archives, Archives of the Dean and Chapter, DE/26.
68. *CSACSPW*, i, p. 148.
69. *CSACSPW*, i, pp. 220–1.
70. *CSACSPW*, i, p. 329.
71. TNA, JUST 2/18, mem. 19r.
72. JUST 2/18, mem. 18r.
73. JUST 2/67, mem. 50r.
74. Norfolk RO, Norwich Consistory Court Records, Will Register 1 Heydon (1370–82), f. 6r.
75. Will Register 1 Heydon (1370–82), f. 32v.
76. Will Register 1 Heydon (1370–82), f. 102r.
77. Will Register 1 Heydon (1370–82), f. 109r.
78. *HAME*, i, pp. 173–227.
79. Above, Chapter 4. Also C. M. Woolgar, 'The language of food and cooking', in *The language of the professions: proceedings of the 2013 Harlaxton Symposium*, ed. M. Carruthers (Donington, 2015), p. 42.
80. *HAME*, i, p. 223.
81. *GH*, p. 91.
82. Dixon-Smith, 'Image and reality of alms-giving', pp. 86–7 and n. 107.
83. *CSACSPW*, i, p. 250.
84. Winchester College Muniments 1: 1 September.
85. Norfolk RO, Norwich Consistory Court Records, Will Register 1 Heydon (1370–82), f. 32r.
86. *The register of Henry Chichele, Archbishop of Canterbury 1414–1443*, vol. 2: *Wills proved before the Archbishop or his commissaries*, ed. E. F. Jacob and H. C. Johnson (Canterbury and York Society, 42; 1937), pp. 390, 392, 665.
87. *Register of Henry Chichele*, vol. 2, ed. Jacob and Johnson, pp. 562–3; see also the examples in Woolgar, 'Gifts of food', pp. 15–16.
88. Cheshire RO, Chester City archives Z/MB/1, ff. 16r, 19v.
89. Dorset History Centre, D/SHA/CH2.
90. *LV II*, p. 195: 'our gracyous foundours of the bedehouse of Leycestre ordeyned that when a quarter of whete were at x s. that thenne every bedeman and bedewoman of the saide bedehouse shulde have every weke x d. ob. duryng the derthe.'
91. Harvey, *Living and dying*, pp. 21–2.
92. *LV I*, pp. 120–1.
93. *LV II*, pp. 179–81.
94. *LV I*, pp. 22–3.
95. Bodleian Library, Oxford, MS Eng. hist. b. 208, ff. 45r–49v.
96. Harvey, *Living and dying*, p. 17.

12 Food and Popular Mentalities

1. *PP*, i, p. 467 (C XII, ll. 143–52): 'As on a walnote withoute is a bittere barke, / And aftur þat bittere barke, be þe shale aweye, / Is a cornel of confort kynde to restore.'

2. E. Stengel, 'Die beiden Sammlungen altfranzösischer Sprichwörter in der Oxforder Handschrift Rawlinson C 641', *Zeitschrift für französische Sprache und Litteratur* 21 (1899), p. 5, no. 52, 'Meuz valt pome dunee, que mangie', and p. 17, 'Betere is appel ygeve than yete.'
3. *Dan Michel's Ayenbite of Inwyt, or remorse of conscience*, ed. R. Morris, rev. P. Gradon (EETS, OS, 23; 1965), p. 208: 'God þe wyle wel gratter þinges yeve. He nele þe yeve pere ne eppel ase me deþ ane childe, ac greate þinges he wile þet þou him acsi.'
4. B. J. Whiting and H. W. Whiting, *Proverbs, sentences, and proverbial phrases from English writings mainly before 1500* (Cambridge, MA, 1968), pp. 11–12, A155.
5. *PP*, i, p. 353 (C IX, l. 345): 'Y sette by pardon nat a pese ne nat a pye hele!'
6. *MED* ben (*n.*(1)), 2(b).
7. M. Förster, 'Die mittelenglische Sprichwörtersammlung in Douce 52', in *Festschrift zum XII. allgemeinen deutschen Neuphilologentage in München, Pfingsten 1906*, ed. E. Stottreither (Erlangen, 1906), p. 52, no. 96: 'Ofte drynke maketh þy wyttes renne'; no. 97: 'So brewe, so drynke'; H. Varnhagen, 'Zu mittelenglischen Gedichten: XI. Zu den Sprichwörtern Hending's', *Anglia* 4 (1881), p. 185: 'First sour brewit, sit sour drinkit.'
8. *Early English proverbs, chiefly of the thirteenth and fourteenth centuries* ..., ed. W. W. Skeat (Oxford, 1910), p. 37, no. 94: 'Drynk eft lasse, and go by lyhte hom.'
9. Förster, 'Die mittelenglische Sprichwörtersammlung in Douce 52', pp. 50–1, nos 79–80: 'Hit is harde to lykke hony fro the thorne'; 'Dere is þe hony bouȝt, / Þat on thornes is souȝt.'
10. *The minor poems of John Lydgate*, part 2: *Secular poems*, ed. H. N. MacCracken (EETS, OS, 192; 1934), p. 476: 'Eche man beware, of wisdam & resoun, / Of sugre strowid that hidith fals poisoun.'
11. *The early English version of the Gesta Romanorum*, ed. S. J. H. Herrtage (EETS, ES, 33; 1878), p. 42: 'Who so ever þat berith othir vertues withoute humilite, he berith hem as in to þe wynde, or as men berith pouder in þe wynde.'
12. C. M. Woolgar, 'The cook', in *Historians on Chaucer: the 'General Prologue' to the Canterbury Tales*, ed. S. H. Rigby, with A. J. Minnis (Oxford, 2014), p. 274.
13. *HAME*, i, pp. 311–20, 359; J. Birrell, 'Deer and deer farming in medieval England', *Agricultural History Review* 40 (1992), pp. 112–26.
14. 'Et quant aux feux qu'on disoit qu'ils boutoient au plat pays, il respondit que ce n'estoit que usance de guerre, et que guerre sans feu ne valoit rien, non plus que andouilles sans moutarde': chronicle attributed to Jean Juvenal des Ursins, in *Choix de chroniques et mémoires relatifs à l'histoire de France avec notices biographiques*, ed. J. A. C. Buchon (Paris, 1875), p. 565. I am grateful to Dr Rémy Ambühl for this reference.
15. *Chaucer*, p. 154, Merchant's Tale, ll. 1263–5: ' "Noon oother lyf", seyde he, 'is worth a bene, / For wedlok is so esy and so clene, / That in this world it is a paradys." '; p. 155, ll. 1350–2: 'That every man that halt hym worth a leek / upon his bare knees ought al his lyf / Thanken his God that hym hath sent a wyf ...'
16. S. B. Meech, 'A collection of proverbs in Rawlinson MS D.328', *Modern Philology* 38 (1940), p. 119, no. 21: 'Melius est vere mappa quam pane carere'; 'Hyt ys beter to lake þe clothe than þe love.'
17. *PP*, i, p. 210 (B V, ll. 256–7): ' "I am holden", quod he, "as hende as hounde is in kichene.'
18. E. Stengel, 'Die beiden Sammlungen altfranzösischer Sprichwörter', p. 5, no. 36: 'Bel servise trait pain de main'; 'Obsequium pronum trahit ex manibus grave donum.' *HAME*, i, pp. 264–405, entries under the pantry in the daily accounts of Bishop Mitford.
19. C. M. Woolgar, 'Gifts of food in late medieval England', *Journal of Medieval History* 37 (2011), pp. 6–18.
20. *Political poems and songs relating to English history composed during the period from the accession of Edward III to that of Richard III*, ed. T. Wright (2 vols, Rolls series, 14; 1859–61), i, pp. 1–26; B. J. Whiting, 'The Vows of the Heron', *Speculum* 20 (1945), pp. 261–78; N. J. Lacy, 'Warmongering in verse: Les voeux du heron', in *Inscribing the Hundred Years' War in French and English cultures*, ed. D. N. Baker (Albany, NY, 2000), pp. 17–26.
21. BL, MS Harley 6815, ff. 16r, 25r–41v.
22. TNA, JUST 2/155, mem. 12d.

BIBLIOGRAPHY

Manuscripts: United Kingdom

Brighton: East Sussex Record Office
Add. MSS 4901, 4903, 4905, 4909
Rye Corporation archives, MS RYE 60/2–3
Sussex Archaeological Society, SAS CP/148–9, 151

Cambridge: St John's College, muniments
D91.21

Canterbury: Canterbury Cathedral Archives
Archives of the Dean and Chapter, DE/26

Chester: Cheshire Record Office
Chester City archives, Z/MB/1

Dorchester: Dorset History Centre
D/SHA/CH2

Durham: University Library
Muniments of Durham Cathedral Priory
   Cellarers' accounts
   Locellus 8

Ipswich: Suffolk Record Office
HD 1538/174/3/1–7

Kew: The National Archives (Public Record Office)
E 36   Exchequer, Treasury of Receipt, miscellaneous books
E 101   Exchequer, accounts various
JUST 2 Coroners' rolls

London: British Library
Add. MS 21480
Add. MS 34213

Add. MS 60584
Add. MS 88973
Add. MS 88974
MS Harley 6815

London: Lambeth Palace Library
MS 1213
Register of Thomas Arundel
Register of William Courtenay
Register of Simon Sudbury
Register of William Whittlesey

London: Society of Antiquaries
MS 208
MS 287

Manchester: John Rylands University Library of Manchester
MS Latin 235

Northampton: Northamptonshire Record Office
Westmorland (Apethorpe) 4/XX/4

Norwich: Norfolk Record Office
Le Strange of Hunstanton muniments, NH
Muniments of the Dean and Chapter of Norwich
    DCN 1/1, accounts of the Master of the Cellar of Norwich Cathedral Priory
    DCN 1/4, accounts and inventories of the Sacrist of Norwich Cathedral Priory
    DCN 1/8, accounts and inventories of the Refectorer of Norwich Cathedral Priory
Norwich City Records, NCR
Norwich Consistory Court Records, Will Register 1 Heydon (1370–82)

Oxford: Bodleian Library
MS Eng. hist. b. 208
Muniments of Queen's College, Oxford, R257

Southampton: Southampton City Record Office
Southampton City archives, SC 5/1, stewards' books

Stratford-upon-Avon: Shakespeare Birthplace Trust Record Office
Accounts of the guild of the Holy Cross, BRT 1/3
DR37

Taunton: Somerset Record Office
DD/L P37/7, part 1

Winchester: Hampshire Record Office
Winchester City archives, W/H1/204–5

Winchester: Winchester College
Muniments 1

Manuscripts: overseas

The Vatican: Biblioteca Apostolica Vaticana
MS Vat. Lat. 4015

Printed primary sources

Account of the executors of Richard, Bishop of London, 1303, and of the executors of Thomas, Bishop of Exeter, 1310, ed. W. H. Hale and H. T. Ellacombe (Camden Society, new series, 10; 1874)

Accounts of the cellarers of Battle Abbey 1275–1513, ed. E. Searle and B. Ross (Sydney, 1967)

An alphabet of tales: an English fifteenth century translation of the Alphabetum narrationum of Étienne de Besançon, ed. M. M. Banks (2 vols, EETS, OS, 126–7; 1904–5)

Amherst, A. M. T., 'A fifteenth-century treatise on gardening by "Mayster Ion Gardener"', *Archaeologia* 54 (1894), pp. 157–72

Ancrene wisse: a corrected edition of the text in Cambridge, Corpus Christi College, MS 402, with variants from other manuscripts, ed. B. Millett (2 vols, EETS, OS, 325–6; 2005–6)

Anglo-Norman medicine, ed. T. Hunt (2 vols, Cambridge, 1994–7)

The Anglo-Norman text of 'Le lai du cor', ed. C. T. Erickson (Anglo-Norman Text Society, 24; 1973)

An anonymous short English metrical chronicle, ed. E. Zettl (EETS, OS, 196; 1935)

Bartholomew the Englishman, *On the properties of things: John Trevisa's translation of Bartholomaeus Anglicus De proprietatibus rerum*, ed. M. C. Seymour (3 vols, Oxford, 1975–88)

Bedfordshire coroners' rolls, ed. R. F. Hunnisett (Bedfordshire Historical Record Society, 41; 1961)

Berners, Juliana, 'The treatise of fishing with an angle attributed to Dame Juliana Berners', in J. McDonald, *The origins of angling* (New York, 1963), pp. 133–73

Beverley town documents, ed. A. F. Leach (Selden Society, 14; 1900)

Bibbesworth, Walter de, *Le tretiz*, ed. W. Rothwell (Aberystwyth, 2009; online edition, at www.anglo-norman.net)

Biblia sacra iuxta vulgatam versionem, ed. R. Weber and others (4th edition, Stuttgart, 1994)

The Boke of Saint Albans by Dame Juliana Berners, ed. W. Blades (1901)

The book of the knight of La Tour-Landry, ed. T. Wright (EETS, OS, 33; 1868)

The book of Margery Kempe, ed. W. Butler-Bowdon (EETS, OS, 212; 1940)

Bozon, Nicolas, *Les contes moralisés de Nicole Bozon frère mineur publiés pour la première fois d'après les manuscrits de Londres et de Cheltenham*, ed. L. Toulmin Smith and P. Meyer (Paris, 1889)

Bromyard, John, *Summa predicantium* (Nuremberg: Anton Koberger, 1485)

The Brut or the Chronicles of England, ed. F. W. D. Brie (EETS, OS, 136; 1908)

Calendar of Close Rolls preserved in the Public Record Office (47 vols, 1900–63)

Calendar of inquisitions post mortem, vol. 3: *Edward I* (1912)

Calendar of letter-books preserved among the archives of the corporation of the city of London at the Guildhall, vol. 11: *Letter-book L, temp. Edward IV–Henry VII*, ed. R. R. Sharpe (1912)

Calendar of the Patent Rolls preserved in the Public Record Office: Edward II, vol. 3: *A.D. 1321–1324* (1904)

Calendar of the Patent Rolls preserved in the Public Record Office: Edward III, vol. 4: *A.D. 1338–1340* (1898)

Calendar of the Patent Rolls preserved in the Public Record Office: Edward III, vol. 12: *A.D. 1361–1364* (1912)

Calendar of the plea and memoranda rolls preserved among the archives of the corporation of the city of London at the Guildhall, A.D. 1364–1381, ed. A. H. Thomas (Cambridge, 1929)

The cartulary of God's House, Southampton, ed. J. M. Kaye (2 vols, Southampton Records Series, 19–20; 1976)

The cartulary of the priory of St Denys near Southampton, ed. E. O. Blake (2 vols, Southampton Records Series, 24–5; 1981)

Catholicon Anglicum, an English-Latin wordbook, dated 1483, ed. S. J. H. Herrtage and H. B. Wheatley (Camden Society, new series, 30; 1882)

The Cely letters 1472–1488, ed. A. Hanham (EETS, OS, 273; 1975)

Charters and records of Hereford Cathedral, ed. W. W. Capes (Hereford, 1908)

Chaucer, Geoffrey, *The Riverside Chaucer*, ed. L. D. Benson (3rd edition, Oxford, 1988)

Chauliac, Guy de, *The Cyrurgie of Guy de Chauliac*, ed. M. S. Ogden (EETS, OS, 265; 1971)

Choix de chroniques et mémoires relatifs à l'histoire de France avec notices biographiques, ed. J. A. C. Buchon (Paris, 1875)

Cholmeley, H. P., *John of Gaddesden and the Rosa medicinae* (Oxford, 1912)

Chronicon monasterii de Abingdon, ed. J. Stevenson (2 vols, Rolls series, 2; 1858)

A collection of ordinances and regulations for the government of the royal household . . ., ed. Anon. for the Society of Antiquaries (1790)

A common-place book of the fifteenth century, ed. L. T. Smith (1886)

A consuetudinary of the fourteenth century for the refectory of the house of S. Swithun in Winchester, ed. G. W. Kitchin (Hampshire Record Society, 6, i; 1886)

Councils and synods with other documents relating to the English Church. II A.D. 1205–1313, ed. F. M. Powicke and C. R. Cheney (2 vols, Oxford, 1964)

The court and household of Eleanor of Castile in 1290: an edition of British Library Additional Manuscript 35294, ed. J. C. Parsons (Toronto, 1977)

The Coventry leet book or mayor's register, ed. M. D. Harris (4 parts in 1; EETS, OS, 134, 135, 138, 146; 1907–13)

Crittall, E., 'Fragment of an account of the cellaress of Wilton Abbey, 1299', in *Collectanea*, ed. N. J. Williams (Wiltshire Archaeological and Natural History Society, Records Branch, 12; 1956), pp. 142–56

Cursor mundi, ed. R. Morris (7 vols, EETS, OS, 57, 59, 62, 66, 68, 99, 101; 1874–93)

Curye on Inglysch, ed. C. Hieatt and S. Butler (EETS, ES, 8; 1985)

The customary of the Benedictine abbey of Bury St Edmunds in Suffolk . . ., ed. A. Gransden (Henry Bradshaw Society, 99; 1973)

The customary of the Benedictine abbey of Eynsham in Oxfordshire, ed. A. Gransden (Siegburg, 1963)

Customary of the Benedictine monasteries of Saint Augustine, Canterbury, and Saint Peter, Westminster, ed. E. M. Thompson (2 vols, Henry Bradshaw Society, 23, 28; 1902–4)

The customary of the Cathedral Priory Church of Norwich: MS 465 in the library of Corpus Christi College, Cambridge, ed. J. B. L. Tolhurst (Henry Bradshaw Society, 82; 1948)

The customs accounts of Hull, 1453–1490, ed. W. R. Childs (Yorkshire Archaeological Society Record Series, 144; 1986)

A dialogue between reason and adversity: a late Middle English version of Petrarch's De remediis, ed. F. N. M. Diekstra (Assen, 1968)

Dives and Pauper, ed. P. H. Barnum (3 vols, EETS, OS, 275, 280, 323; 1976, 1980, 2004)

Dress at the court of King Henry VIII: the wardrobe book of the Wardrobe of the Robes . . ., ed. M. Hayward (Leeds, 2007)

Dugdale, W., *Monasticon Anglicanum*, ed. J. Caley, H. Ellis and B. Bandinel (new edition, 6 vols in 8, 1846)

The early English carols, ed. R. L. Greene (2nd edition, Oxford, 1977)

Early English proverbs, chiefly of the thirteenth and fourteenth centuries . . ., ed. W. W. Skeat (Oxford, 1910)

Early Northampton wills preserved in Northamptonshire Record Office, ed. D. Edwards, M. Forrest, J. Minchinton, M. Shaw, B. Tyndall and P. Wallis (Northamptonshire Record Society, 42; 2005)

The early South-English Legendary or Lives of saints, I, MS Laud, 108, in the Bodleian Library, ed. C. Horstmann (EETS, OS, 87; 1887)

Edward of Norwich, *The master of game*, ed. W. A. Baillie-Grohman and F. N. Baillie-Grohman (1909)

Elizabeth de Burgh, Lady of Clare (1295–1360): household and other records, ed. J. Ward (Suffolk Records Society, 57; 2014)

English gilds: the original ordinances of more than one hundred early English gilds . . ., ed. T. Smith and L. T. Smith (EETS, OS, 40; 1870)

The English register of Godstow Nunnery, near Oxford, ed. A. Clark (2 vols, EETS, OS, 130, 142; 1906, 1911)

The English works of Wyclif, ed. F. D. Matthew (EETS, OS, 74; 1880)

The epistle of Othea translated from the French text of Christine de Pisan by Stephen Scrope, ed. C. F. Bühler (EETS, OS, 264; 1970)

Expeditions to Prussia and the Holy Land made by Henry Earl of Derby . . ., ed. L. T. Smith (Camden Society, new series, 52; 1894)

Extracts from the account rolls of the Abbey of Durham, ed. J. T. Fowler (3 vols, Surtees Society, 99, 100, 103; 1898–1901)

The fabric rolls of York Minster . . ., ed. J. Raine (Surtees Society, 35; 1859)

Les fabulistes latins depuis le siècle d'Auguste jusqu'à la fin du moyen âge, ed. L. Hervieux (5 vols, Paris, 1893–9)

Facsimile of first volume of MS. archives of the Worshipful Company of Grocers of the City of London . . ., ed. J. A. Kingdon (1886)

Farming and gardening in late medieval Norfolk, ed. C. Noble and C. Moreton (Norfolk Record Society, 61; 1996)

The forme of cury, a roll of ancient English cookery, ed. S. Pegge (1780)

Förster, M., 'Die mittelenglische Sprichwörtersammlung in Douce 52', in *Festschrift zum XII. allgemeinen deutschen Neuphilologentage in München, Pfingsten 1906*, ed. E. Stottreither (Erlangen, 1906), pp. 40–60

The Fountains Abbey lease book, ed. D. J. H. Michelmore (Yorkshire Archaeological Society Record Series, 140; 1981)

Geoffrey of Monmouth, *Historia regum Britanniae: a variant version*, ed. J. Hammer (Cambridge, MA, 1951)

Gower, John, *The English works of John Gower*, ed. G. C. Macaulay (2 vols, EETS, ES, 81–2; 1900–1)

Gower, John, *Mirour de l'omme*, in *The complete works of John Gower: the French works*, ed. G. C. Macaulay (Oxford, 1899), pp. 1–334

Gratian, *Decretum*, in *Corpus iuris canonici*, ed. E. Friedberg (2nd edition, 2 vols, Leipzig, 1922), i

Greenstreet, J., 'Early Kentish wills', *Archaeologia Cantiana* 11 (1877), pp. 370–87

Griesser, P. B., 'Die "Ecclesiastica Officia Cisterciensis Ordinis" des Cod. 1711 von Trient', *Analecta Sacri Ordinis Cisterciensis* 12 (1956), pp. 153–288

Hali meiðhad, ed. B. Millett (EETS, OS, 284; 1982)

Hall, J., 'Short pieces from MS. Cotton Galba E.IX', *Englische Studien* 21 (1895), pp. 201–9

Heresy trials in the diocese of Norwich, 1428–31, ed. N. P. Tanner (Camden Society, 4th series, 20; 1977)

Hieatt, C. B., and Jones, R., 'Culinary collections edited from British Library Manuscripts Additional 32085 and Royal 12.C. xii', *Speculum* 61 (1986), pp. 859–82

Historia ecclesie Abbendonensis. The history of the church of Abingdon, vol. 2, ed. J. Hudson (Oxford, 2002)

Historiae Dunelmensis scriptores tres: Gaufridus de Coldingham, Robertus de Graystanes, et Willielmus de Chambre, ed. J. Raine (Surtees Society, 9; 1839)

HMC, *The manuscripts of Lincoln, Bury St Edmund's, and Great Grimsby Corporations, and of the Dean and Chapters of Worcester and Lichfield . . .* (1895)

HMC, *Report on manuscripts in various collections*, part 7 (1914)

HMC, *Report on the manuscripts of Lord de l'Isle and Dudley preserved at Penshurst Place*, vol. 1, ed. C. L. Kingsford (1925)

The Holy Bible . . . by John Wycliffe and his followers, ed. J. Forshall and F. Madden (4 vols, Oxford, 1850)

Horstmann, C., 'Des MS Bodl. 779 jüngere Zusatzlegenden zur südlichen Legendensammlung', *Archiv für das Studium der neueren Sprachen und Litteraturen* 82 (1889), pp. 307–422

Household accounts from medieval England, ed. C. M. Woolgar (2 vols, British Academy, Records of Social and Economic History, new series, 17–18; 1992–3)

Household book of Dame Alice de Bryene of Acton Hall, Suffolk, Sept. 1412–Sept. 1413, ed. M. K. Dale and V. B. Redstone (Ipswich, 1931)

The household book of Queen Isabella of England for the fifth regnal year of Edward II 8th July 1311 to 7th July 1312, ed. F. D. Blackley and G. Hermansen (University of Alberta, Classical and Historical Studies, 1; 1971)

Hunt, Tony, 'Anglo-Norman medical receipts', in *Anglo-Norman anniversary essays*, ed. I. Short (Anglo-Norman Text Society, Occasional Publications series, 2; 1993), pp. 179–233

Idley, Peter, *Peter Idley's instructions to his son*, ed. C. D'Evelyn (Modern Language Association of America, monograph series, 6; Boston, 1935)

Inquisitions and assessments relating to feudal aids . . ., vol. 6, ed. H. C. Maxwell Lyte (1920)

The inventories and account rolls of the Benedictine houses or cells of Jarrow and Monk-Wearmouth in the County of Durham, ed. J. Raine (Surtees Society, 29; 1854)

Jacob's Well: an Englisht treatise on the cleansing of man's conscience, part 1, ed. A. Brandeis (EETS, OS, 115; 1900)

Kaluza, M., 'Kleinere Publikationen aus me. Handschriften', *Englische Studien* 14 (1890), pp. 165–88

Die Kildare-gedichte: die ältesten mittelenglischen Denkmäler in anglo-irischer Überliferung, ed. W. Heuser (Bonner Beiträger zur Anglistik, 14; 1904)

Kölbing, E., 'Kleine Publicationen aus der Auchinleck-hs.', *Englische Studien* 7 (1884), pp. 101–25

Kyng Alisaunder, ed. G. V. Smithers (2 vols, EETS, OS, 227, 237; 1952–7)

Lanfrank's 'Science of Cirurgie', ed. R. V. Fleischhacker (EETS, OS, 102; 1894)

Langland, William, *Piers Plowman: a parallel-text edition of the A, B, C and Z versions*, ed. A. V. C. Schmidt (2nd edition, 2 vols in 3, Kalamazoo, 2011)

Langland, William, *Piers Plowman: the A Version, Will's Visions of Piers Plowman and Do-Well*, ed. G. Kane (1960)

The Laud Troy Book, a romance of about 1400 A.D., ed. J. E. Wülfing (2 vols, EETS, OS, 121–2; 1902–3)

Lawrence, C. H., *St Edmund of Abingdon: a study in hagiography and history* (Oxford, 1960)

A leechbook, or a collection of medical recipes of the fifteenth century, ed. W. R. Dawson (1934)

Libellus de vita et miraculis S. Godrici, heremitae de Finchale auctore Reginaldo monacho Dunelmensi. Adjicitur appendix miraculorum, ed. J. Stevenson (Surtees Society, 20; 1845)

Liber cure cocorum, copied and edited from the Sloane MS. 1986, ed. R. Morris (Berlin, 1862)

Liber quotidianus contrarotulatoris garderobae anno regni regis Edwardi primi vicesimo octavo A.D. MCCXCIX & MCCC, ed. Anon. (1787)

Llandaff episcopal acta 1140–1287, ed. D. Crouch (South Wales Record Society, 5; 1988)

The local port book of Southampton for 1439–40, ed. H. S. Cobb (Southampton Records Series, 5; 1961)

Love, Nicholas, *The mirrour of the blessed lyf of Jesu Christ . . . made before the year 1410 by Nicholas Love*, ed. L. F. Powell (Oxford, 1908)

Lydgate, John, *Lydgate's Fall of princes*, ed. H. Bergen (4 vols, EETS, ES, 121–4; 1924–7)

Lydgate, John, *Lydgate's Siege of Thebes*, part 1, ed. A. Erdmann (EETS, ES, 108; 1911)

Lydgate, John, *The minor poems of John Lydgate*, part 2: *Secular poems*, ed. H. N. MacCracken (EETS, OS, 192; 1934)

Manières de langage (1396, 1399, 1415), ed. A. M. Kristol (Anglo-Norman Text Society, 53; 1995)

Manners and household expenses of England in the thirteenth and fifteenth centuries, ed. T. H. Turner (Roxburghe Club, 1841)

Manners and meals in olden time: the Babees book . . ., ed. F. J. Furnivall (EETS, OS, 32; 1868)

Manorial records of Cuxham, Oxfordshire, c.1200–1359, ed. P. D. A. Harvey (HMC, Joint Publications series, 23; 1976)

Map, Walter, *De nugis curialium. Courtiers' trifles*, ed. M. R. James, rev. C. N. L. Brooke and R. A. B. Mynors (Oxford, 1983)

Materials for the history of Thomas Becket, Archbishop of Canterbury, ed. J. C. Robertson (7 vols, Rolls series, 67; 1875–85)

Meech, S. B., 'A collection of proverbs in Rawlinson MS D.328', *Modern Philology* 38 (1940), pp. 117–26

Merlin, ed. H. B. Wheatley (4 vols, EETS, OS, 10, 21, 36, 112; 1865, 1866, 1869, 1899)

Michel, *Dan Michel's Ayenbite of Inwyt, or remorse of conscience*, ed. R. Morris, rev. P. Gradon (EETS, OS, 23; 1965)

The Middle English metrical romances, ed. W. H. French and C. B. Hale (2 vols, New York, 1930)

A Middle English translation of Macer Floridus De viribus herbarum, ed. G. Frisk (The English Institute in the University of Upsala, Essays and studies on English language and literature, 3; 1949)

Mirk, John, *John Mirk's Festial*, ed. S. Powell (2 vols, EETS, OS, 334–5; 2009, 2011)

Ein mittelenglisches Medizinbuch, ed. F. Heinrich (Halle, 1896)

The monastic constitutions of Lanfranc, ed. D. Knowles, rev. C. N. L. Brooke (Oxford, 2002)

Mum and the sothsegger, ed. M. Day and R. Steel (EETS, OS, 199; 1936)

Murimuth, Adam, *Continuatio chronicarum*, Robertus de Avesbury, *De gestis mirabilibus regis Edwardi tertii*, ed. E. M. Thompson (Rolls series, 93; 1889)

A myrour to lewde men and wymmen: a prose version of the Speculum vitae, ed. from BL MS Harley 45, ed. V. Nelson (Heidelberg, 1981)

The myroure of Oure Ladye containing a devotional treatise on divine service, with a translation of the offices used by the sisters of the Brigittine monastery of Sion . . ., ed. J. H. Blunt (EETS, ES, 19; 1873)

A noble boke off cookry ffor a prynce houssolde or eny other estately houssolde, ed. R. Napier (1882)

The Oak Book of Southampton, ed. P. Studer (3 vols, Southampton Record Society, 10–12; 1910–11)

Of hawks and horses: four late Middle English prose treatises, ed. W. L. Braekman (Brussels, 1986)

Old English homilies of the twelfth century, series 2, ed. R. Morris (EETS, OS, 53; 1873)

The orcherd of Syon, ed. P. Hodgson and G. M. Liegey (EETS, OS, 258; 1966)

An ordinance of pottage: an edition of the fifteenth-century culinary recipes in Yale University's MS Beinecke 163, ed. C. B. Hieatt (1988)

The ormulum, ed. R. Holt (2 vols, Oxford, 1878)

The overseas trade of Boston in the reign of Richard II, ed. S. H. Rigby (Lincoln Record Society, 93; 2005)

Pantin, W. A., 'A medieval collection of Latin and English proverbs and riddles from the Rylands Latin MS 394', *Bulletin of the John Rylands Library* 14 (1930), pp. 81–104

The parliament rolls of medieval England, 1275–1504, vol. 11: *Henry VI, 1432–1445*, ed. A. Curry (2005)

The Paston letters, A.D. 1422–1509, vol. 3, ed. J. Gairdner (new edition, 1904)

Paston letters and papers of the fifteenth century, ed. N. Davis, R. Beadle and C. Richmond (3 vols, Oxford, 1971–2005)

The pilgrimage of the lyf of the manhode, ed. W. A. Wright (Roxburghe Club, 91; 1869)

The pipe roll of the bishopric of Winchester 1210–1211, ed. N. R. Holt (Manchester, 1964)

The pipe roll of the bishopric of Winchester 1301–2, ed. M. Page (Hampshire Record Series, 14; 1996)

The place-names of Oxfordshire, vol. 1, ed. M. Gelling and D. M. Stenton (English Place-Name Society, 23; 1953)

The place-names of Surrey, ed. J. E. B. Gover, A. Mawer and F. M. Stenton (English Place-Name Society, 11; 1934)

The place-names of Sussex, vol. 2, ed. A. Mawer and F. M. Stenton (English Place-Name Society, 7; 1930)

The place-names of Wiltshire, ed. J. E. B. Gover, A. Mawer and F. M. Stenton (English Place-Name Society, 16; 1939)

The Plumpton letters and papers, ed. J. Kirby (Camden, 5th series, 8; 1996)

Political poems and songs relating to English history composed during the period from the accession of Edward III to that of Richard III, ed. T. Wright (2 vols, Rolls series, 14; 1859–61)

The political songs of England from the reign of John to that of Edward II, ed. T. Wright (Camden Society, old series, 6; 1839)

The priory of Finchale: the charters of endowment, inventories, and account rolls . . ., ed. J. Raine (Surtees Society, 6; 1837)

The priory of Saint Radegund Cambridge, ed. A. Gray (Cambridge Antiquarian Society, Octavo Publications, 31; 1898)

Privy purse expenses of Elizabeth of York: wardrobe accounts of Edward the Fourth, with a memoir of Elizabeth of York, and notes, ed. N. H. Nicolas (1830)

The proverbs of Alfred: an emended text, ed. O. Arngart (Lund: Scripta minora regiae societatis humaniorum litterarum Lundensis, 1979–1980: 1; 1978)

Pugh, R. B., 'Fragment of an account of Isabel of Lancaster, nun of Amesbury, 1333–4', in *Festschrift zur Feier des zweihundertjährigen Bestandes des Haus-, Hof- und Staatsarchivs*, ed. L. Santifaller (2 vols, Vienna, 1949–51), i, pp. 487–98

RB 1980: the Rule of St Benedict, ed. T. Fry and others (Collegeville, MN, 1981)

Reading gild accounts 1357–1516, ed. C. Slade (2 vols, Berkshire Record Society, 6–7; 2002)

The receyt of the Ladie Kateryne, ed. G. Kipling (EETS, OS 296; 1990)

Records of the borough of Nottingham . . ., vol. 1, *King Henry II to King Richard II, 1155–1399*, ed. W. H. Stevenson (1882)

The records of the city of Norwich, ed. W. Hudson and J. C. Tingey (2 vols, Norwich, 1906)

The records of the guild of the Holy Trinity, St Mary, St John the Baptist and St Katherine of Coventry, ed. G. Templeman (Dugdale Society, 19; 1944)

Records of the wardrobe and household 1286–1289, ed. B. F. Byerly and C. R. Byerly (1986)

Redstone, L. J., 'Three Carrow account rolls', *Norfolk Archaeology* 29 (1946), pp. 41–88

The register of the guild of the Holy Cross, St Mary and St John the Baptist, Stratford-upon-Avon, ed. M. Macdonald (Dugdale Society, 42; 2007)

The register of Henry Chichele, Archbishop of Canterbury 1414–1443, vol. 2: *Wills proved before the Archbishop or his commissaries*, ed. E. F. Jacob and H. C. Johnson (Canterbury and York Society, 42; 1937)

The register of St Augustine's Abbey, Canterbury, commonly called the Black Book, ed. G. J. Turner and H. E. Salter (2 vols, British Academy, Records of Social and Economic History, 2–3; 1915, 1924)

The register of Thomas de Cobham, Bishop of Worcester, 1317–1327, ed. E. H. Pearce (Worcestershire Historical Society, 40; 1930)

The register of Walter de Stapeldon, Bishop of Exeter (A.D. 1307–1326), ed. F. C. Hingeston-Randolph (1892)

The regulations and establishment of the household of Henry Algernon Percy, the fifth Earl of Northumberland at his castles of Wressle and Leckonfield, in Yorkshire. Begun Anno Domini MDXII, ed. T. Percy (new edition, 1905)

Richard II and the English royal treasure, ed. J. Stratford (Woodbridge, 2012)

Rigg, A. G., ' "Descriptio Northfolchie": a critical edition', in *Nova de veteribus: Mittel- und neulateinische Studien für Paul Gerhard Schmidt*, ed. A. Bihrer and E. Stein (Munich, 2004), pp. 578–94

Robert of Brunne, *Robert of Brunne's Handlyng synne . . .*, ed. F. J. Furnivall (2 vols, EETS, OS, 119, 123; 1901, 1903)

Robinson, J.A., 'Household roll of Bishop Ralph of Shrewsbury 1337–8', in *Collectanea I*, ed. T. F. Palmer (Somerset Record Society, 39; 1924), pp. 72–174

A roll of the household expenses of Richard de Swinfield, Bishop of Hereford, ed. J. Webb (2 vols, Camden Society, old series, 59, 62; 1854–5)

Rolle, Richard, *An edition of the Judica me Deus of Richard Rolle*, ed. J. P. Daly (Salzburg Studies in English Literature, 92: 14; 1984)

Rolls of the fifteenth of the ninth year of the reign of Henry III for Cambridgeshire, Lincolnshire and Wiltshire and rolls of the fortieth of the seventeenth year of the reign of Henry III for Kent, ed. F. A. Cazel, Jr., and A. P. Cazel (Pipe Roll Society, new series, 45; 1983)

Rolls of the justices in eyre, being the rolls of pleas and assizes for Lincolnshire, 1218–19, and Worcestershire, 1221, ed. D. M. Stenton (Selden Society, 53; 1934)

Ross, A. S. C., 'The Middle English poem on the names of a hare', *Proceedings of the Leeds Philosophical and Literary Society (Literary and Historical Section)* 3, part 6 (1935), pp. 347–77

Safford, E. W., 'An account of the expenses of Eleanor, sister of Edward III, on the occasion of her marriage to Reynald, Count of Guelders', *Archaeologia* 77 (1927), pp. 111–40

Sandred, K. I., *A Middle English version of the Gesta Romanorum, edited from Gloucester Cathedral MS 22* (Uppsala: Studia Anglistica Upsaliensis, 8; 1971)

Schöffler, H., 'Practica Phisicalia Magistri Johannis de Burgundia', *Beiträge zur mittelenglischen Medizinliteratur, Sächsische Forschungsinstitut in Leipzig, Forschungsinstitut für neuere Philologie. III. Anglistische Abteilung*, Heft I (1919)

Secular lyrics of the XIVth and XVth centuries, ed. R. H. Robbins (2nd edition, Oxford, 1955)

Select cases from the coroners' rolls A.D. 1265–1413 with a brief account of the history of the office of coroner, ed. C. Gross (Selden Society, 9; 1896)

Select cases from the ecclesiastical courts of the province of Canterbury c.1200–1301, ed. N. Adams and C. Donahue (Selden Society, 95; 1981)

Select documents of the English lands of the abbey of Bec, ed. M. Chibnall (Camden Society, 3rd series, 73; 1951)

The simonie: a parallel-text edition, ed. D. Embree and E. Urquhart (Heidelberg, 1991)

Sir Gawain and the Green Knight, ed. W. R. J. Barron (Manchester, 1974)

Smirke, E., 'Notice of the Custumal of Bleadon, Somerset and of the agricultural tenures of the thirteenth century', in *Memoirs illustrative of the history and antiquities of Wiltshire and the city of Salisbury, communicated to the annual meeting of the Archaeological Institute of Great Britain and Ireland, held at Salisbury, July, 1849* (1851), pp. 182–210

Southampton probate inventories, 1447–1575, ed. E. Roberts and K. Parker (2 vols, Southampton Records Series, 34–5; 1992)

The Southampton steward's book of 1492–93 and the terrier of 1495, ed. A. Thick (Southampton Records Series, 38; 1995)

Speculum sacerdotale, ed. E. H. Weatherly (EETS, OS, 200; 1936)

Statuta capitulorum generalium Ordinis Cisterciensis ab anno 1116 ad annum 1786 (8 vols, Louvain, 1933–41)

Statutes of the realm, ed. A. Luders, T. E. Tomlins, J. Raithby and others (11 vols, 1810–28)

Stengel, E., 'Die beiden Sammlungen altfranzösischer Sprichwörter in der Oxforder Handschrift Rawlinson C 641', *Zeitschrift für französische Sprache und Litteratur* 21 (1899), pp. 1–21

Stevens, D., 'A Somerset coroner's roll, 1315–1321', *Somerset and Dorset Notes and Queries* 31 (1985), pp. 451–72

The stewards' books of Southampton from 1428, vol. 2: *From 1434 to 1439*, ed. H. W. Gidden (Southampton Record Society, 1939)

The Stonor letters and papers, 1290–1483, ed. C. L. Kingsford (2 vols, Camden, 3rd series, 29–30; 1919)

Supplications from England and Wales in the registers of the Apostolic Penitentiary 1410–1503, vol. 2: *1464–1492*, ed. P. D. Clarke and P. N. R. Zutshi (Canterbury and York Society, 104; 2014)

A talkyng of þe loue of God, ed. M. S. Westra (The Hague, 1950)

Ten fifteenth-century comic poems, ed. M. M. Furrow (New York, 1985)

Testamenta Eboracensia, vols 1–4, ed. J. Raine (Surtees Society, 2, 30, 45, 53; 1836, 1855, 1865, 1869)

Testamentary records of the English and Welsh episcopate 1200–1413: wills, executors' accounts and inventories, and the probate process, ed. C. M. Woolgar (Canterbury and York Society, 102; 2011)

Three receptaria from medieval England: the languages of medicine in the fourteenth century, ed. T. Hunt (Medium Aevum Monographs, new series, 21, Oxford, 2001)

Tryon, R. W., 'Miracles of Our Lady in Middle English verse', *Proceedings of the Modern Language Association of America* 38 (1923), pp. 308–88

Two fifteenth-century cookery-books, ed. T. Austin (EETS, OS, 91; 1888)

Varnhagen, H., 'Zu mittelenglischen Gedichten: XI. Zu den Sprichwörtern Hending's', *Anglia* 4 (1881), pp. 182–200

Visitations of religious houses in the diocese of Lincoln: injunctions and other documents from the registers of Richard Flemyng and William Gray, Bishops of Lincoln, A.D. 1420 to A.D. 1436, ed. A. H. Thompson (Lincoln Record Society, 7; 1914)

Visitations of religious houses in the diocese of Lincoln: II. Records of visitations held by William Alnwick, Bishop of Lincoln, A.D. 1436 to A.D. 1449 (part I), ed. A. H. Thompson (Lincoln Record Society, 14; 1918)

Visitations of religious houses in the diocese of Lincoln: III. Records of visitations held by William Alnwick, Bishop of Lincoln, A.D. 1436 to A.D. 1449 (part II), ed. A. H. Thompson (Lincoln Record Society, 21; 1929)

Wace, *Le roman de Brut de Wace*, ed. I. Arnold (2 vols, Paris, 1938–40)

Wadington, W. de, *Le manuel des pechez*, in Robert of Brunne's *Handlyng synne*, ed. F. J. Furnivall (2 vols, EETS, OS, 119, 123; 1901–3)

Walter of Henley, *Walter of Henley and other treatises on estate management and accounting*, ed. D. Oschinsky (Oxford, 1971)

The wardrobe book of William de Norwell 12 July 1338 to 27 May 1340, ed. M. Lyon, B. Lyon, H. S. Lucas and J. de Sturler (Brussels, 1983)

Wellingborough manorial accounts A.D. 1258–1323 from the account rolls of Crowland Abbey, ed. F. M. Page (Northamptonshire Record Society, 8; 1935)

Whiting, B. J., and Whiting, H. W., *Proverbs, sentences, and proverbial phrases from English writings mainly before 1500* (Cambridge, MA, 1968)

Wilson, E., 'An unpublished alliterative poem on plant-names from Lincoln College, Oxford, MS Lat. 129(E)', *Notes and Queries* 224, new series, 26 (1979), pp. 504–8

Wilson, E., 'The Debate of the Carpenter's Tools', *Review of English Studies*, new series, 38, no. 152 (1987), pp. 445–70

The works of Sir Thomas Malory, ed. E. Vinaver, rev. P. J. C. Field (3 vols, 3rd edition, Oxford, 1990)

Wynnere and Wastoure, ed. S. Trigg (EETS, OS, 297; 1990)

Yorkshire writers: Richard Rolle of Hampole and his followers, ed. C. Horstmann (2 vols, 1895–6)

Secondary works

Albala, K., *Eating right in the Renaissance* (Berkeley, 2002)

Albarella, U., 'Pig husbandry and pork consumption in medieval England', in *FME*, pp. 72–87

Aungier, G. J., *History and antiquities of Syon* (1840)

Banegas López, R. A., *Europa carnívora. Comprar y comer carne en el mundo bajomedieval* (Gijón, 2012)

Barton, K. J., *Medieval Sussex pottery* (Chichester, 1979)

Bellis, J., 'The dregs of trembling, the draught of salvation: the dual symbolism of the cup in medieval literature', *Journal of Medieval History* 37 (2011), pp. 47–61

Bennett, J. M., *Ale, beer and brewsters in England: women's work in a changing world, 1300–1600* (Oxford, 1996)

Binski, P., 'Function, date, imagery, style and context of the Westminster Retable', in *The Westminster Retable: history, technique, conservation*, ed. P. Binski and A. Massing (2009), pp. 16–44

Binski, P., and Massing, A., ed., *The Westminster Retable: history, technique, conservation* (Cambridge, 2009)

Birrell, J., 'Deer and deer farming in medieval England', *Agricultural History Review* 40 (1992), pp. 112–26

Birrell, J., 'Procuring, preparing, and serving venison', in *FME*, pp. 176–88

Bond, C. J., and Weller, J. B., 'The Somerset barns of Glastonbury Abbey', in *The archaeology and history of Glastonbury Abbey: essays in honour of the ninetieth birthday of C. A. Ralegh Radford*, ed. L. Abrams and J. P. Carley (Woodbridge, 1991), pp. 57–87

Bonnassie, P., 'Consommation d'aliments immondes et cannibalisme de survie dans l'occident du haut moyen âge', *Annales: Économies, Sociétés, Civilisations* 44 (1989), pp. 1035–56

Bothwell, J. S., 'Making the Lancastrian capital at Leicester: the battle of Boroughbridge, civic diplomacy and seigneurial building projects in fourteenth-century England', *Journal of Medieval History* 38 (2012), pp. 335–57

Brears, P., *Cooking and dining in medieval England* (Blackawton, 2008)

Bridge, M., *Tree-ring analysis of timbers from the Abbey Barn, Glastonbury, Somerset* (English Heritage, Centre for Archaeology Report 39/2001)

Brisay, K. W. de, and Evans, K. A., ed., *Salt: the study of an ancient industry: report on the Salt Weekend held at the University of Essex, 20, 21, 22 September 1974* (Colchester, 1975)

British Beekeepers' Association, 'Honey', at http://www.bbka.org.uk/learn/general_information/honey

Brownsword, R., and Pitt, E. E. H., 'Some examples of medieval domestic pewter flatware', *Medieval Archaeology* 29 (1985), pp. 152–5

Camille, M., *Mirror in parchment: the Luttrell Psalter and the making of medieval England* (1998)

Campbell, M., 'Gold, silver and precious stones', in *English medieval industries: craftsmen, techniques, products*, ed. J. Blair and N. Ramsay (1991), pp. 107–66

Carlin, M., 'Putting dinner on the table in medieval London', in *London and the kingdom: essays in honour of Caroline M. Barron. Proceedings of the 2004 Harlaxton Symposium*, ed. M. Davies and A. Prescott (Donington, 2008), pp. 58–77

Carlin, M., 'Cheating the boss: Robert Carpenter's embezzlement instructions (1261×1268) and employee fraud in medieval England', in *Commercial activity, markets and entrepreneurs in the Middle Ages: essays in honour of Richard Britnell*, ed. B. Dodds and C. D. Liddy (Woodbridge, 2011), pp. 183–97

Carlin, M., 'Gaddesden, John (d.1348/9), physician', in *ODNB*, at http://www.oxforddnb.com/view/article/10267?docPos=1

Childs, W., 'Anglo-Portuguese trade in the fifteenth century', *Transactions of the Royal Historical Society*, 6th series, 11 (1992), pp. 195–219

Cholmeley, H. P., *John of Gaddesden and the Rosa medicinae* (Oxford, 1912)

Claridge, J., and Langdon, J., 'Storage in medieval England: the evidence from purveyance accounts, 1295–1349', *Economic History Review*, 2nd series, 64 (2011), pp. 1242–65

Clay, R. M., *The mediaeval hospitals of England* (1909)

Clifford, H. M., *A treasured inheritance: 600 years of Oxford college silver* (Oxford, 2004)

Colvin, H. M., ed., *The history of the king's works* (6 vols, 1963–82)

Cooper, L. M., 'Recipes for the realm: John Lydgate's "Soteltes" and the Debate of the horse, goose and sheep', in *Essays on aesthetics in medieval literature in honor of Howell Chickering*, ed. J. M. Hill, B. Wheeler and R. F. Yeager (Toronto, 2013), pp. 194–215

Corner, R., 'More fifteenth-century terms of association', *Review of English Studies*, new series, 13 (1962), pp. 229–44

Davis, J., 'Baking for the common good: a reassessment of the assize of bread in medieval England', *Economic History Review*, 2nd series, 57 (2004), pp. 465–502

Davis, J., *Medieval market morality: life, law and ethics in the English marketplace, 1200–1500* (Cambridge, 2012)

Davis, J. S., *A history of Southampton, partly from the MS of Dr Speed in the Southampton archives* (Southampton, 1883)

Dixon-Smith, S., 'The image and reality of alms-giving in the great halls of Henry III', *Journal of the British Archaeological Association* 152 (2000), pp. 79–96

Dunn, P., 'Trade', in *Medieval Norwich*, ed. C. Rawcliffe and R. Wilson (2004), pp. 213–34

Dyer, C., 'Changes in diet in the late Middle Ages: the case of harvest workers', *Agricultural History Review* 36 (1988), pp. 21–37

Dyer, C., 'Gardens and orchards in medieval England', in C. Dyer, *Everyday life in medieval England* (1994), pp. 113–31

Dyer, C., *Standards of living in the later Middle Ages* (2nd edition, Cambridge, 1998)

Dyer, C., 'Did the peasants really starve in medieval England?', in *Food and eating in medieval Europe*, ed. M. Carlin and J. T. Rosenthal (1998), pp. 53–71.

Dyer, C., 'Alternative agriculture: goats in medieval England', in *People, landscape and alternative agriculture: essays for Joan Thirsk*, ed. R. W. Hoyle (*Agricultural History Review*, supplement series 3; 2004), pp. 20–38

Dyer, C., 'Gardens and garden produce in the later Middle Ages', in *FME*, pp. 27–40

Dyer, J., 'Bede ale', *Notes and Queries*, 3rd series, 8 (1865), p. 436

Emery, A., *Greater medieval houses of England and Wales* (3 vols, Cambridge, 1996–2006)

Farmer, D. L., 'Marketing the produce of the countryside, 1200–1500', in *AHEW III*, pp. 324–525

Field, R. K., 'Worcestershire peasant buildings, household goods and farming equipment in the later Middle Ages', *Medieval Archaeology* 9 (1965), pp. 105–45

Flandrin, J. L., 'Le goût et la nécessité: sur l'usage des graisses dans les cuisines d'Europe occidentale (XIVe–XVIIIe siècle)', *Annales: Économies, Sociétés, Civilisations*, 38 (1983), pp. 369–401

Flandrin, J. L., 'Structure des menus français et anglais aux XIVe et XVe siècles', in *Du manuscrit à la table: essais sur la cuisine au moyen âge et répertoire des manuscrits médiévaux contenant des recettes culinaires*, ed. C. Lambert (Montreal, 1992), pp. 173–92

Flandrin, J. L., *Arranging the meal: a history of table service in France*, trans. J. E. Johnson, with S. Roder and A. Roder (Berkeley, 2007)

Flood, B. P., Jr., 'The medieval herbal tradition of Macer Floridus', *Pharmacy in History* 18, no. 2 (1976), pp. 62–6

Fransson, G., *Middle English surnames of occupation 1100–1350* (Lund Studies in English, 3; 1935)

Frantzen, A. J., *Food, eating and identity in early medieval England* (Woodbridge, 2014)

Freedman, P., ed., *Food: the history of taste* (2007)

Freedman, P., *Out of the East: spices and the medieval imagination* (New Haven, 2008)

Gardiner, J., with Allen, M. J., ed., *Before the mast: life and death aboard the Mary Rose* (2 vols, Portsmouth, 2005)

Gasper, G. E. M., and others, *Zinziber: sauces from Poitou. Twelfth-century culinary recipes from Sidney Sussex College, Cambridge, MS 51* (2015)

Gem, R., ed., *English Heritage book of St Augustine's Abbey, Canterbury* (1997)

Giles, K., and Clark, J., 'The archaeology of the guild buildings of Shakespeare's Stratford-upon-Avon', in *The guild and guild buildings of Shakespeare's Stratford: society, religion, school and stage*, ed. J. R. Mulryne (Farnham, 2012), pp. 135–69

Goldberg, P. J. P., 'The fashioning of bourgeois domesticity in later medieval England: a material culture perspective', in *Medieval domesticity: home, housing and household in medieval England*, ed. M. Kowaleski and P. J. P. Goldberg (Cambridge, 2008), pp. 124–44

Goody, J., *Cooking, cuisine and class: a study in comparative sociology* (Cambridge, 1982)

Gras, N. S. B., *The early English customs system* (Cambridge, MA, 1918)

Greatrex, J., *The English Benedictine cathedral priories: rule and practice, c.1270–c.1420* (Oxford, 2011)

Harvey, B. F., *Westminster Abbey and its estates in the Middle Ages* (Oxford, 1977)

Harvey, B. F., *Living and dying in England, 1100–1540: the monastic experience* (Oxford, 1993)

Harvey, B. F., 'Monastic pittances in the Middle Ages', in *FME*, pp. 215–27

Harvey, J. H., 'Vegetables in the Middle Ages', *Garden History* 12 (1984), pp. 89–99

Harvey, J. H., 'The first English garden book: Mayster John Gardener's treatise and its background', *Garden History* 13 (1985), pp. 83–101

Hatcher, J., and Barker, T. C., *A history of British pewter* (1974)

Henisch, B. A., *The medieval cook* (Woodbridge, 2009)

Hieatt, C. B., 'Medieval Britain', in *Regional cuisines of medieval Europe: a book of essays*, ed. M. Weiss Adamson (2002), pp. 19–45

Hieatt, C. B., *A gathering of medieval English recipes* (Turnhout, 2008)

Hieatt, C. B., Nutter, T., and Holloway, J. H., *Concordance of English recipes: thirteenth through fifteenth centuries* (Tempe, 2006)

Hinton, D. A., *Gold and gilt, pots and pins* (Oxford, 2005)

Hodgson, J. C., *A history of Northumberland*, vol. 7: *The parish of Edlingham, with the chapelry of Bolton . . .* (Newcastle-upon-Tyne, 1904)

Homans, G. C., *English villagers of the thirteenth century* (New York, 1970)

Homer, R. F., 'Tin, lead and pewter', in *English medieval industries: craftsmen, techniques, products*, ed. J. Blair and N. Ramsay (1991), pp. 57–80

Hope, W. J. St John, 'Of the English medieval drinking bowls called mazers', *Archaeologia* 50 (1887), pp. 176–81

Hunt, Tony, *Plant names of medieval England* (Cambridge, 1989)

Hussey, A., 'Calf's gadyr', *Notes and Queries*, 10th series, 2, no. 50 (1904), pp. 467–8

Jervis, B., *Pottery and social life in medieval England: towards a relational approach* (Oxford, 2014)

Jones, P. E., *The butchers of London: a history of the Worshipful Company of Butchers of the City of London* (1976)

Jordan, W. C., *The great famine: Northern Europe in the early fourteenth century* (Princeton, 1996)

Keen, L., 'Coastal salt production in Norman England', *Anglo-Norman Studies* 11 (1988), pp. 133–79

Keene, D., *Survey of medieval Winchester* (2 vols, Oxford, 1985)

Kirby, T. F., *Annals of Winchester College from its foundation in the year 1382 to the present time* (1892)

Lacy, N. J., 'Warmongering in verse: Les voeux du heron', in *Inscribing the Hundred Years' War in French and English cultures*, ed. D. N. Baker (Albany, New York, 2000), pp. 17–26

Lambert, H. C. M., *History of Banstead in Surrey* (Oxford, 1912)

Laughton, J., *Life in a late medieval city: Chester 1275–1520* (Oxford, 2008)

Laughton, J., and Dyer, C., 'Seasonal patterns of trade in the later Middle Ages: buying and selling at Melton Mowbray, Leicestershire, 1400–1520', *Nottingham Medieval Studies* 46 (2002), pp. 162–84

Laurioux, B., *Manger au moyen âge: pratiques et discours alimentaires en Europe aux XIVe et XVe siècles* (Paris, 2002)

Laurioux, B., *Gastronomie, humanisme et société à Rome au milieu du XVe siècle. Autour du De honesta voluptate de Platina* (Florence, 2006)

Lightbown, R. W., *Secular goldsmiths' work in medieval France: a history* (Reports of the Research Committee of the Society of Antiquaries of London, 36; 1978)

Macdonald, M., 'The guild of the Holy Cross and its buildings', in *The guild and guild buildings of Shakespeare's Stratford: society, religion, school and stage*, ed. J. R. Mulryne (Farnham, 2012), pp. 13–30

Maddicott, J. R., 'Follower, leader, pilgrim, saint: Robert de Vere, Earl of Oxford, at the shrine of Simon de Montfort, 1273', *EHR* 109 (1994), pp. 641–53

Marks, R., and Williamson, P., ed., *Gothic: art for England 1400–1547* (2003)

Marvin, J., 'Cannibalism as an aspect of famine in two English chronicles', in *Food and eating in medieval Europe*, ed. M. Carlin and J. T. Rosenthal (1998), pp. 73–86

Mate, M. E., *Women in medieval English society* (Cambridge, 1999)

Mazzoni, C., *The women in God's kitchen: cooking, eating and spiritual writing* (New York, 2005)

McCarthy, M. R., and Brooks, C. M., *Medieval pottery in Britain AD 900–1600* (Leicester, 1988)

Michael, M. A., 'The *Bible moralisée*, the *Golden Legend* and the *Salvator mundi*: observations on the iconography of the Westminster Retable', *Antiquaries Journal* 94 (2014), pp. 93–125

Michaelis, R. F., 'The pewter saucer', in *Excavations in medieval Southampton 1953–1969*, ed. C. Platt and R. Coleman-Smith (2 vols, Leicester, 1975), ii, p. 250

Miller, E., ed., *The agrarian history of England and Wales*, vol. 3: *1348–1500* (Cambridge, 1991)

Moorhouse, S., 'Documentary evidence for the uses of medieval pottery: an interim statement', *Medieval Ceramics* 2 (1978), pp. 3–21

Müller, M., 'Food, hierarchy, and class conflict', in *Survival and discord in medieval society: essays in honour of Christopher Dyer*, ed. R. Goddard, J. Langdon and M. Müller (Turnhout, 2010), pp. 231–48.

Muzzarelli, M. G., and Tarozzi, F., *Donne e cibo: una relazione nella storia* (n.p., 2003)

Nesbitt-Wood, G., 'Wall painting of a 16th-century great ship in St Dunstan's church, Snargate, Romney Marsh', *Archaeologia Cantiana* 87 (1972), pp. 208–9

Newhauser, R., 'John Gower's sweet tooth', *Review of English Studies*, new series, 64 (2013), pp. 752–69

Nicoud, M., *Les régimes de santé au moyen âge* (2 vols, Rome, 2007)

Nightingale, P., 'The London pepperers' guild and some twelfth-century English trading links with Spain', *Bulletin of the Institute of Historical Research* 58 (1985), pp. 123–32

Nightingale, P., *A medieval mercantile community: the Grocers' Company and the politics and trade of London 1000–1485* (New Haven, 1995)

Oliva, M., 'The French of England in female convents: the French kitcheners' accounts of Campsey Ash Priory', in *Language and culture in medieval Britain: the French of England c.1100–c.1500*, ed. J. Wogan-Browne (York, 2009), pp. 90–102

Ouerfelli, M., *Le sucre: production, commercialisation et usages dans la Méditerranée médiévale* (Leiden, 2008)

Owen, D., 'Bacon and eggs: Bishop Buckingham and superstition in Lincolnshire', in *Popular belief and practices*, ed. G. J. Cuming and D. Baker (Studies in Church History, 8; Cambridge, 1972), pp. 139–42

Owst, G. R., *Literature and pulpit in medieval England: a neglected chapter in the history of English letters and of the English people* (Cambridge, 1933)

Paravicini-Bagliani, A., *The pope's body*, trans. D. S. Peterson (Chicago, 2000)

Patrick, P., *The 'obese medieval monk': a multidisciplinary study of a stereotype* (Oxford, British Archaeological Reports, British series, 590; 2014)

Postles, D., 'The regular canons and the use of food, c.1200–1350', in *The regular canons in the medieval British Isles*, ed. J. Burton and K. Stober (Turnhout, 2011), pp. 233–49

Power, E., *Medieval English nunneries c.1275 to 1535* (Cambridge, 1922)

Rawcliffe, C., *Medicine and society in later medieval England* (Far Thrupp, 1995)

Rawcliffe, C., *Medicine for the soul: the life, death and resurrection of an English medieval hospital. St Giles's, Norwich, c.1249–1550* (Woodbridge, 1999)

Rawcliffe, C., *Leprosy in medieval England* (Woodbridge, 2006)

Rawcliffe, C., *Urban bodies: communal health in late medieval English towns and cities* (Woodbridge, 2013)

Richards, M. P., Mays, S., and Fuller, B., 'Stable carbon and nitrogen isotope values of bone and teeth reflect weaning age at the medieval Wharram Percy site, Yorkshire, U.K.', *American Journal of Physical Anthropology* 119, no. 3 (2002), pp. 205–10

Riley, H. T., *Memorials of London and London life, in the XIIIth, XIVth and XVth centuries . . .* (1868)

Rose, S., *The wine trade in medieval Europe 1000–1500* (2011)

Rosenthal, J. T., *Telling tales: sources and narration in late medieval England* (University Park, PA, 2003)

Rosser, G., 'Going to the fraternity feast: commensality and social relations in late medieval England', *Journal of British Studies* 33 (1994), pp. 430–46

Salzman, L. F., *Building in England down to 1540: a documentary history* (Oxford, 1952)

Saunders, H. W., *An introduction to the obedientiary and manor rolls of Norwich Cathedral Priory* (Norwich, 1930)

Savine, A., *English monasteries on the eve of the Dissolution* (Oxford, 1909)

Segalen, M., *Love and power in the peasant family: rural France in the nineteenth century*, trans. S. Matthews (Oxford, 1983)

Serjeantson, D., and Woolgar, C. M., 'Fish consumption in medieval England', in *FME*, pp. 102–30

Slavin, P., 'Goose management and rearing in late medieval eastern England, *c*.1250–1400', *Agricultural History Review* 58 (2010), pp. 1–29

Slavin, P., *Bread and ale for the brethren: the provisioning of Norwich Cathedral Priory 1260–1536* (Hertford, 2012)

Smith, K. A., *The Taymouth Hours: stories and the construction of the self in late medieval England* (2012)

Snape, M. G., 'Documentary evidence for the building of Durham Cathedral and its monastic buildings', in *Medieval art and architecture at Durham Cathedral*, ed. N. Coldstream (British Archaeological Association Conference Transactions, 3; 1980), pp. 20–36

Spufford, P., *Power and profit: the merchant in medieval Europe* (2004)

Stone, D. J., 'The consumption of field crops', in *FME*, pp. 15–26

Stone, D. J., 'The consumption and supply of birds in late medieval England', in *FME*, pp. 152–61

Swabey, F., 'The household of Alice de Bryene, 1412–13', in *Food and eating in medieval Europe*, ed. M. Carlin and J. T. Rosenthal (1998), pp. 133–44

Sweetinburgh, S., 'Remembering the dead at dinner-time', in *Everyday objects: medieval and early modern material culture and its meanings*, ed. T. Hamling and C. Richardson (Farnham, 2010), pp. 257–66

Sykes, N. J., 'The animal bones', in *A medieval royal complex at Guildford: excavations at the castle and palace*, ed. R. Poulton (Guildford, 2005), pp. 116–28

Sykes, N. J., 'From cu and sceap to beefe and mouton: the management, distribution, and consumption of cattle and sheep in medieval England', in *FME*, pp. 56–71

Sykes, N. J., 'The impact of the Normans on hunting practices in England', in *FME*, pp. 162–75

Tatton-Brown, T., 'The Abbey precinct, liberty and estate', in *English Heritage book of St Augustine's Abbey, Canterbury*, ed. R. Gem (1997), pp. 123–42

Tillotson, J. H., *Marrick Priory: a nunnery in late medieval Yorkshire* (York, Borthwick Papers, 75; 1989)

Trease, G. E., 'The spicers and apothecaries of the royal household in the reigns of Henry III, Edward I and Edward II', *Nottingham Medieval Studies* 3 (1959), pp. 19–52

Underhill, F. A., *For her good estate: the life of Elizabeth de Burgh* (New York, 1999)

Vale, M., *The princely court: medieval courts and culture in north-west Europe 1270–1380* (Oxford, 2001)

Walker Bynum, C., *Holy feast, holy fast: the religious significance of food to medieval women* (Berkeley, 1987)

Welch, C., *History of the Worshipful Company of Pewterers of the city of London* (2 vols, 1902)

Whiting, B. J., 'The Vows of the Heron', *Speculum* 20 (1945), pp. 261–78

Wilkinson, L. J., 'The *Rules* of Robert Grosseteste reconsidered: the lady as estate and household manager in thirteenth-century England', in *The medieval household in Christian Europe, c.850–c.1550*, ed. C. Beattie, A. Maslakovic and S. Rees Jones (Turnhout, 2003), pp. 293–306

Woolgar, C. M., *The great household in late medieval England* (New Haven, 1999)

Woolgar, C. M., 'Fast and feast: conspicuous consumption and the diet of the nobility in the fifteenth century', in *Revolution and consumption in late medieval England*, ed. M. Hicks (Woodbridge, 2001), pp. 7–25

Woolgar, C. M., ' "Take this penance now, and afterwards the fare will improve": seafood and late medieval diet', in *England's sea fisheries: the commercial sea fisheries of England and Wales since 1300*, ed. D. J. Starkey, C. Reid and N. Ashcroft (2003), pp. 36–44

Woolgar, C. M., *The senses in late medieval England* (New Haven, 2006)

Woolgar, C. M., 'Meat and dairy products in late medieval England', in *FME*, pp. 88–101

Woolgar, C. M., 'Group diets in late medieval England', in *FME*, pp. 191–200

Woolgar, C. M., 'Feasting and fasting: food and taste in Europe in the Middle Ages', in *Food: the history of taste*, ed. P. Freedman (2007), pp. 162–95

Woolgar, C. M., 'Food and the Middle Ages', *Journal of Medieval History* 36 (2010), pp. 1–19

Woolgar, C. M., 'Gifts of food in late medieval England', *Journal of Medieval History* 37 (2011), pp. 6–18

Woolgar, C. M., 'The cook', in *Historians on Chaucer: the 'General Prologue' to the Canterbury Tales*, ed. S. H. Rigby, with A. J. Minnis (Oxford, 2014), pp. 262–76

Woolgar, C. M., 'Queens and crowns: Philippa of Hainaut, possessions and the Queen's chamber in mid XIVth-century England', *Micrologus* 22 (2014), pp. 201–28

Woolgar, C. M., 'Treasure, material possessions and the bishops of late medieval England', in *The prelate in England and Europe, 1300–1560*, ed. M. Heale (York, 2014), pp. 173–190

Woolgar, C. M., 'The language of food and cooking', in *The language of the professions: proceedings of the 2013 Harlaxton Symposium*, ed. M. Carruthers (Donington, 2015), pp. 33–47

Woolgar, C. M., Serjeantson, D., and Waldron, T., ed., *Food in medieval England: diet and nutrition* (Oxford, 2006)

Yaxley, D., *The Prior's manor-houses: inventories of eleven of the manor-houses of the Prior of Norwich made in the year 1352 A.D.* (Dereham, 1988)

Online dictionaries

The Anglo-Norman Dictionary, ed. W. Rothwell and others (2nd edition, online at http://www.anglo-norman.net/)

Middle English Dictionary, ed. H. Kurath, S. M. Kuhn and others (Ann Arbor, 1956–2001; online edition at http://quod.lib.umich.edu/m/med/)

Oxford Dictionary of National Biography, ed. H. C. G. Matthew and B. Harrison (61 vols, Oxford, 2005; online edition at http://www.oxforddnb.com/)

Oxford English Dictionary, at www.oed.com/

INDEX

Places in the United Kingdom have been identified by their pre-1974 counties. Peers have been numbered according to the *Complete peerage of England, Scotland, Ireland, Great Britain and the United Kingdom...*, ed. G. E. Cokayne, rev. V. Gibbs and others (13 vols, 1910–59). Numbers in italic type refer to plates.